W9-ALM-391

Pacific Northwest
TRIPS

52 THEMED ITINERARIES **1009** LOCAL PLACES TO SEE

Danny Palmerlee,
Catherine Bodry, Mariella Krause, John Lee, Bradley Mayhew

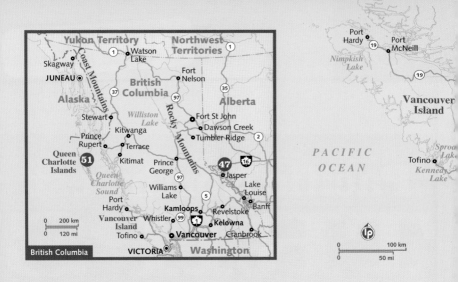

PACIFIC NORTHWEST TRIPS

Praise for *Mrs. Whaley and Her Charleston Garden*

"Delightful is the best word to describe this book."

—James Howard, *The Fresno Bee*
(one of the top ten recommended summer books)

"A delightful, rather breathless account . . . as she reveals how the gardening tradition fostered her own avid dedication, it is apparent how tending one's plants can enrich the spirit and forge admirable connections with friends and acquaintances."

—Alice Joyce, *Booklist*

"Utterly delightful, the perfect thing for the end of the day when you're done gardening and want to sit quietly and be reminded that all the work is worthwhile."

—Martha Smith, *Providence Journal-Bulletin*

"Charming."   —Michael Shnayerson, *Condé Nast Traveler*

"To read this book is to understand how to garden, entertain, and enjoy life—and not to worry too much about what other people think."   —Mae Woods Bell, *Rocky Mount Telegram*

"This is a fun book and the lady is a delight. Rarely does such a book furnish so many quotable quotes. . . . This is so much more than a book about gardening. It is a book about a remarkable woman and her way of life."

—Jerry Williams, *Richmond Times-Dispatch*

"An ageless and captivating visit with 85-year-old Emily Whaley. . . . Whaley's simple, direct language conveys not just her many frank opinions but her self-described joie de vivre and appreciation of the houses and gardens of her life."

—*Publishers Weekly*

"The book is small enough to fit in the pocket of a gardening smock and will charm and entertain the non-gardeners of the world as well as those with the greenest of thumbs."

—*Skirt!* (Charleston, SC)

"Her memoir . . . explores far more than horticulture. . . . Throughout the good times and bad, gardening has been her salvation, so she is as outspoken about it as she is life in general." —Danny Flanders, *Columbia State*

"A long time ago, I waltzed with Emily Whaley. I was ten years old when she taught me to relax and follow her lead around the dance floor. Now, after reading *Mrs. Whaley and Her Charleston Garden,* I find she has waltzed me again, this time through lovely and beguiling gardens of bloom and memory, with all the wit and grace and energy that have made her one of Charleston's favorites."

—Josephine Humphreys, author of *Rich in Love*

"Emily Whaley is wonderful, both in and out of her garden."

—Rosemary Verey, author of *The American Woman's Garden*

"I have a new gardening guru: octogenarian Emily Whaley. . . . I loved this book and plan to pass it around to all of my gardening friends."

—Nancy Wingate, *Wilmington News Journal*

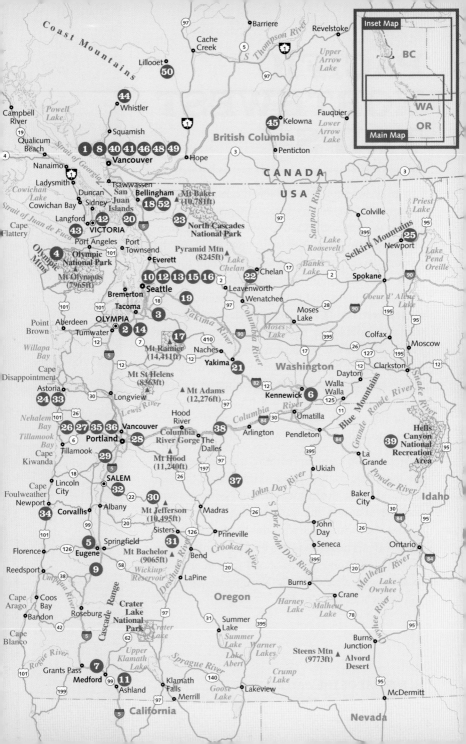

PACIFIC NORTHWEST TRIPS

Just when we thought we knew the Pacific Northwest, we discovered an entirely new world. It was a change in approach, based on one simple question: What *really* makes this place unique? We took the answers (volcanoes, fjords, temperate rain forests, chefs who champion local and sustainable products, totem poles, hot springs, beer, wine, cheese, apples, Lewis and Clark, killer whales) and created trips that would truly highlight the character of the Pacific Northwest. We'd seen Oregon's waterfalls, but we'd never hit 15 falls in four days. (Amazing.) A psychic helped us explore Washington's ghosts and legends. (Now *that* was a trip.) We'd soaked in the hot springs before, but stringing the best of them into a long weekend was utterly sublime.

In the end we came up with 52 trips that explore the most epic routes, the quirkiest places, the best food and drink, the history, the most gorgeous outdoor destinations, the most vibrant cities and, of course, the most iconic trips the Pacific Northwest has to offer. The result is this book, a compendium of short (and some not-so-short) trips guaranteed to show you a new Pacific Northwest – whether you know it already, or not.

THE WAY OF THE WATERFALL p219
Silver Falls State Park, Oregon

"We'd seen Oregon's waterfalls, but we'd never hit 15 falls in four days."

CASCADE GIANT

At 14,411ft, Washington's Mt Rainier is the highest peak in the Cascade Range. Like the other Cascade giants, the volcano dominates its surroundings for miles, luring hikers, climbers and glacier-lovers.

⊗ **WASHINGTON GHOSTS & LEGENDS** p123
Alexander's Castle, Fort Worden, Washington

⊕ **ICE & FIRE: VOLCANO TRAIL** p51
Mt Rainier, Washington

⊘ **WHISTLER ADRENALINE RUSH** p289
Skiers on Blackcomb Mountain, British Columbia

"From microbrewed beer to the Douglas fir, certain things are synonymous with the Pacific Northwest."

From microbrewed beer to the Douglas fir, certain things are synonymous with the Pacific Northwest. With these 11 trips, we hope to plunge you into the heart and soul of the region. Whether it's the three-week **Grand Tour** (p35), Amtrak's **Coast Starlight Train Journey** (p93) or our expert-guided tub-to-tub trip to the region's best **Hot Springs & Mineral Pools** (p57), these trips are all, in some way or another, iconic.

GOING COASTAL

From its northern terminus in Olympia, Highway 101 winds for 700 breathtaking miles down the Washington and Oregon coastline. Treats include tide pools, estuaries, marine geysers, forests and surf breaks galore.

NATIVE AMERICAN TRADITIONS TOUR p81
Totem pole in Stanley Park, Vancouver, British Columbia

ECCENTRIC PACIFIC NORTHWEST p75
Sea lions in Sea Lion Caves, Florence, Oregon

THE SIMPSONS TO THE SHINING p87
Timberline Lodge and Mt Hood, Oregon

Routes

Certain routes around the Pacific Northwest have an element of predictability: round another bend, more epic scenery. Although you can hardly pick an ugly road out here, a few classic routes really stand out, such as **Chuckanut Drive** (p139), one of the West Coast's most spectacular coastal back roads. When it comes to jaw-dropping coastal scenery, it's right up there with our **Southern Vancouver Island Tour** (p283). Head into thin air by exploring the **Scenic Byways of the Central Cascades** (p213), a volcano-riddled, lake-peppered trip through the Oregon Cascades. Or to really get away from it all, drive the **International Selkirk Loop** (p173), a three-day junket through Washington, Idaho and British Columbia. You can even ditch the car (and land) altogether with a trip **Up the Inside Passage** (p327).

SCENIC BYWAYS OF THE CENTRAL CASCADES p213
West Cascades Scenic Byway, Oregon

UP THE INSIDE PASSAGE p327
Alaska State Ferry vessel before Mendenhall Glacier, Juneau, Alaska

Food & Drink

From apples to onions, grapes to grass-fed beef, the Pacific Northwest is a gastronome's paradise. Leading the continent in the movement to use locally grown, sustainable and organic products, it's not only a land of plenty, it's a land of thoughtful preparation. We've concocted 10 trips to help you experience the best of it. On one, quaff some excellent microbrews by going **Beyond Beervana: A Brewery Jaunt** (p191) around Portland. Then taste your way through the most important wine regions by following the **Award-Wining Valley Wines Tour** (p153) in Washington, the **Okanagan Wine Tour** (p293) in British Columbia, and the **Willamette Valley Wine Tour** (p201) in Oregon. Definitely heed the advice of a cheese expert on our **Cheesemonger's Cheese Trip** (p239), and fill yourself up at our **Secret Seafood Spots** (p225). And remember, it's always **Teatime in Victoria** (p277).

BEERVANA

With 30 breweries and counting, Portland has more microbreweries than any other city on the planet. Most of them have brewpubs so you can sample the suds straight from the source.

CHEESEMONGER'S CHEESE TRIP p239
Wheels of goat cheese at Juniper Grove Farm, Redmond, Oregon

BEYOND BEERVANA: A BREWERY JAUNT p191
Jerry's Ice House, McMenamins Edgefield, Troutdale, Oregon

WILLAMETTE VALLEY WINE TOUR p201
Vineyards in the Willamette Valley, British Columbia

Outdoors

In so many ways, the outdoors are what the Pacific Northwest is all about, so excuse us while we gush: The remote and spectacular **Queen Charlotte Islands** (p323) never fail to blow us away. Neither does whale-watching, which is why we think **Islands & Orcas** (p147) is a trip of a lifetime. And, because there's nothing like hidden hot springs, we hope you'll try **Dippin' Down the Cascades** (p207). The more of these trips you take, the clearer it becomes just how diverse the region is. Compare the lush rain forests of the Olympic Peninsula on our **Olympic Odyssey** (p117) with the hot, rattlesnake-ridden Hells Canyon while traveling **From Heaven to Hells Canyon** (p255) in eastern Oregon. And then there are the tide pools, waterfalls, farmlands, gorges…

ISLANDS & ORCAS p147
Orcas breaching near the San Juan Islands, Washington

DIPPIN' DOWN THE CASCADES p207
Umpqua Hot Springs, Oregon

OLYMPIC ODYSSEY p117
Ruby Beach, Olympic National Park, Washington

History & Culture

Considering you're probably just as fond as we are of reading state park history signs in the glaring summer sun, we've created History & Culture tours with a bias – toward fun. Hence we give you our **Rock Pilgrimage** (p113) in the Seattle area, which will dose you with everything from Jimi Hendrix to – what's that grunge guy's name? But why not start from the beginning with our **Prehistoric Oregon Trip** (p245), where you'll see wild rock formations, multicolor hills and the remnants of a subtropical forest. Plunge into **BC's Pioneer Past** (p317) with visits to gold-rush towns, Chinese Rocks and…a camel barn? Even our **Northern BC Train Trek** (p301), which sends you into the Rocky Mountains by rail, is a trip back in time (not to mention fun).

MUSICAL NIRVANA

From Jimi Hendrix to The Decemberists, Soundgarden to Sir Mix-a-Lot, the Pacific Northwest has long been a hotbed of musical talent. Seattle's Experience Music Project is one of many places to pay tribute to the best.

ROCK PILGRIMAGE p113
Experience Music Project Museum, Seattle, Washington

BC'S PIONEER PAST p317
Interior of servants' quarters at Fort Langley National Historic Site, British Columbia

PREHISTORIC OREGON TRIP p245
Painted Hills Unit, John Day Fossil Beds National Monument, Oregon

② Offbeat

The Pacific Northwest isn't weird, it's just full of a lot of weird stuff. Like the Fremont Troll, the giant teapot near Zillah, and the full-scale replica of Stonehenge on the Columbia River. You'll see them all touring **Washington Roadside Curios** (p129). On the trip **Oddball Oregon** (p235), you'll experience the Oregon Vortex (note to self: I'm shorter than I am), witness the world's largest hairball, sleep in a tree house and, well, never mind about the doughnuts. We even consulted a psychic and ghost hunter to help craft a trip about **Washington Ghosts & Legends** (p123) – if you spook easily, skip it. Speaking of ghosts, there must be at least a few lurking along the **Graveyard of the Pacific Tour** (p169). And don't forget **Quirky BC** (p311)!

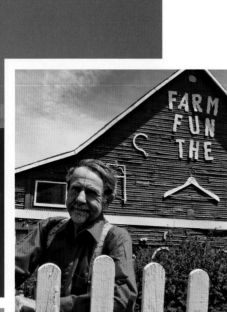

HONK IF YOU'RE WEIRD

For over 16 years, Gene
Carsey's Fun Farm has
taught travelers the
importance of stepping
back and having a good
laugh. And there are plenty
more to be had as you
explore the oddities of the
Pacific Northwest.

"Imagining we had just two days to show a friend around town, we packed everything we could into each trip…"

⊕ **48 HOURS IN VANCOUVER** p267
City skyline as seen from the Stanley Park Seawall

⊘ **48 HOURS IN PORTLAND** p185
Classical Chinese Gardens in Chinatown

⊕ **48 HOURS IN SEATTLE** p107
Seattle Art Museum in Downtown

Cities

From their brewpubs and coffee shops to their art galleries and restaurants, **Seattle** (p107), **Portland** (p185) and BC's **Vancouver** (p267) offer so much to do it's hard to know where to begin. Keeping this in mind, we've created three city trips with one common theme: 48 hours. Imagining we had just two days to show a friend around town, we packed everything we could into each trip, hoping to provide the best possible overview of each metropolis. In these City trips we start you out early, keep you busy all day and send you out for a drink before bed. And, of course, we give you our favorite places to sleep. Even if you're from the city in question, give the trip a read – it'll make the perfect checklist when your friends roll into town.

SEATTLE ART MUSEUM

BEST TRIPS

TEATIME IN VICTORIA p277
High tea at the Empress Hotel,
Victoria, British Columbia

**JOURNEY THROUGH
TIME SCENIC BYWAY** p249
Covered wagon on the historic
Oregon Trail, Baker City, Oregon

Contents

OREGON TRIPS 183

BRITISH COLUMBIA TRIPS 265

Trips by Theme

CITIES

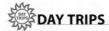

DAY TRIPS

Trips by Season

SPRING

SUMMER

AUTUMN

WINTER

YEAR-ROUND

Expert Recommended Trips

The Authors

DANNY PALMERLEE
Danny is a freelance writer and photographer based in Portland. He has written numerous Lonely Planet guidebooks, and his work has appeared in publications around the globe. While researching this book he fell in love with Cape Perpetua, had a fender-bender in Biggs and was blessed twice by a man at Terwilliger Hot Springs. His favorite trip was From Heaven to Hells Canyon.

CATHERINE BODRY
Catherine grew up in the Pacific Northwest, and attended college in Bellingham. There, she often watched the Alaska ferry depart, and it was partly the daydreams the ferry inspired that eventually led her to Alaska. She received an MA in English from the University of Alaska Anchorage, and now lives in Seward. Her favorite trip was Up the Inside Passage.

MARIELLA KRAUSE
Mariella has been smitten with the Pacific Northwest ever since her first trip to Seattle, where she dined on fresh wild salmon on a houseboat in Lake Union with otters paddling by. She lives in San Francisco, where she's happy to be just a few hours' drive from the Oregon border. Her favorite trip was Island & Orcas.

JOHN LEE
John moved from the UK to study at the University of Victoria in 1993, ultimately sticking around rather than returning to the land of Marmite and Yorkie bars. Now a Vancouver-based travel writer, his work appears in magazines and newspapers around the world and at www.johnleewriter.com. His favorite trip was the Queen Charlotte Islands.

LONELY PLANET AUTHORS
Why is our travel information the best in the world? It's simple: our authors are independent, dedicated travelers. They don't research using just the internet or phone, and they don't take freebies, so you can rely on their advice being well researched and impartial. They travel widely, to all the popular spots and off the beaten track. They personally visit thousands of hotels, restaurants, cafés, bars, galleries, palaces, museums and more – and they take pride in getting all the details right, and telling it how it is. Think you can do it? Find out how at lonelyplanet.com.

BRADLEY MAYHEW
Bradley has written over 25 titles for Lonely Planet, including *Tibet*, *Nepal*, *Central Asia* and *Bhutan*. An appreciation for mountains and wild spaces followed him on this trip around the Cascades, Olympic Peninsula and Mt Rainier. No stranger to American wilderness, Bradley currently lives in Montana. His favorite trip was Mt Rainier: Sunrise to Sunset.

CONTRIBUTING EXPERTS

Cole Danehower is editor in chief of *Northwest Palate Magazine*, a James Beard Award recipient and author of an upcoming book about wine regions of the Pacific Northwest. He helped craft the weekend wine trip, Willamette Valley Wine Tour.

Marjorie Gersh-Young is the author of *Hot Springs and Hot Pools of the Pacific Northwest*. She helped us get our feet wet in our trip Soak It Up! Hot Springs & Mineral Pools.

Bill Hanshumaker is the Marine Education Specialist at Newport's Hatfield Marine Science Center (www.hmsc.oregonstate.edu). He's been exploring Oregon's coast since 1977 and brought his knowledge to bear on the trip Life Aquatic: The Nature of the Coast.

Steve Jones is a cheesemonger and explorer. He owns Steve's Cheese (www.stevescheese.biz www.stevescheese.biz), a specialty cheese counter inside Northwest Portland's Square Deal Wine Shop. For the Cheesemonger's Cheese Trip he recommended his cheese producers, plus nearby hikes and breweries.

Bob Neroni co-owns Cannon Beach's EVOO Cannon Beach Cooking School (www.evoo.biz) with his wife, Lenore Emery. He lives in Cannon Beach, Oregon and recommended his favorite seafood haunts for Secret Seafood Spots.

Ben Schifrin is the co-author of *Pacific Crest Trail: Oregon and Washington* (Wilderness Press), as well as trail guides to California and the Emigrant Wilderness. Ben brought hundreds of

miles of trail experience to our trip Pacific Crest Trail: Alpine Lakes.

Nigel Springthorpe hails from Middlesborough in northern England. He became co-owner (with his wife) of Vancouver's Alibi Room bar in 2006. He brought his expert taste buds and insider bar knowledge to bear on Pub Crawl Vancouver.

Regan Vacknitz is a psychic, ghost-hunter, and cofounder of the Auburn Paranormal Activities Research Team. She shared some of her favorite haunts in the trip Washington Ghosts and Legends.

PACIFIC NORTHWEST ICONIC TRIPS

ICONIC TRIPS

Here you have them. Eleven trips around the northwestern seaboard that take you to the places and put you on paths that are somehow definitively Pacific Northwest. Microbreweries? Got 'em covered – only this time by train, from Eugene, OR, to Vancouver, BC. Hot Springs? You bet, thanks to an interview with a Pacific Northwest hot-springs specialist who shared her top soaks with us. Amtrak's *Coast Starlight* train trip? Of course. Native American traditions? Yep, on a trip that will have you marveling at totem poles, paddling a traditional dugout canoe and poking through the region's finest museums.

The trips in this chapter are the result of a bunch of us knocking heads, poring over maps and dreaming up journeys that really burrow into the culture, the art, the history and the exceptionally beautiful landscape of the Pacific Northwest. The result is a handful of trips which – despite the fact that we already know and love the place – truly blew us away, trips that really had us screaming, "This place is amazing!" We hope they have the same effect on you.

PLAYLIST ♫ Whenever you're in radio-wave distance of Seattle, tune into KEXP 90.3 FM, which cranks out some of the best indie, old-school country and modern world music in the Pacific Northwest. The rest of the time, just play the following songs over and over again.

- "Posse on Broadway," Sir Mix-a-Lot
- "Home," Joshua Morrison
- "Gone for Good," The Shins
- "Rose Parade," Elliott Smith
- "Keep Your Eyes Ahead," The Helio Sequence
- "Portland, Oregon," Loretta Lynn
- "Northwestern Girls," Say Hi
- "Mass Romantic," The New Pornographers
- "Heart Cooks Brain," Modest Mouse
- "Druganaut," Black Mountain

BEST ICONIC TRIPS

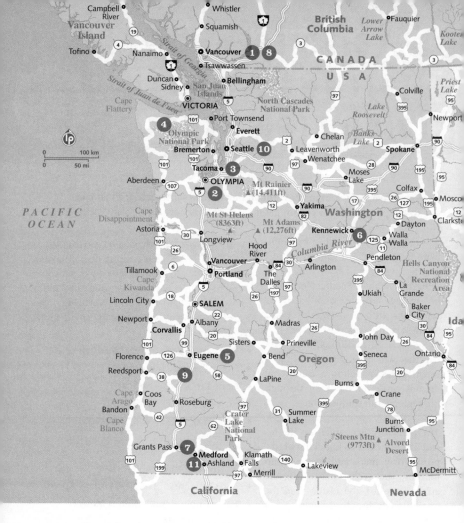

PACIFIC NORTHWEST ICONIC TRIPS

The Grand Tour

WHY GO The mother of all road trips, this meandering journey through the Pacific Northwest takes you from western Canada's largest city to the California border. En route, you'll cruise the San Juan Islands, traverse the mighty Cascades and explore the grooviest neighborhoods of the region's most exciting cities.

TIME
3 weeks

DISTANCE
1675 miles

BEST TIME TO GO
Jun – Sep

START
Vancouver, BC

END
Ashland, OR

ALSO GOOD FOR

OUTDOORS

There's simply no better place to kick off a trip down the northwestern seaboard than ❶ **Vancouver**. From the spectacular Stanley Park Seawall to the galleries and coffee shops of bohemian South Main, Vancouver offers fun aplenty – outside *and* in. Best of all, the city's top attractions are all accessible on foot. Historic Gastown is where the city started, so it makes perfect sense to begin here. Hit Chinatown (it's one of North America's largest) and wander west to Yaletown, the center of the city's gay community, chockablock with heritage homes, old-school apartment buildings, restaurants and shops. It's bordered by English Bay, whose narrow stretch of sandy beach and adjacent grass offers superb people-watching opportunities and panoramic views.

Needless to say, Vancouver has outstanding restaurants, but our favorite place to fill up is ❷ **Go Fish**, between Granville Island and Vanier Park. Little more than a waterfront shack, it serves up the city's best fish-and-chips, along with wild-salmon tacos and scallop burgers. And when sleep finally calls, slumber in style at the ❸ **Opus Hotel**, Vancouver's definitive boutique hotel.

After a stint in Vancouver, head 18.5 miles (30km) south to Tsawwassen, purchase a BC Ferries SailPass, ride the ferry across the Strait of Georgia and tool around the ❹ **Southern Gulf Islands** for a few days. This is where stressed-out Vancouverites go to chill out and – even though we know you're *already* chilled out – so should you. Trust us,

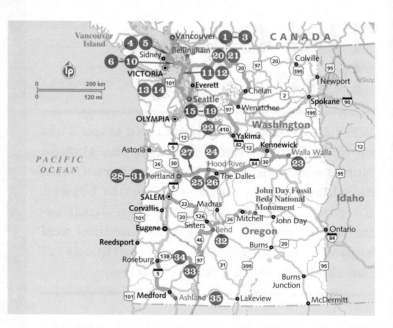

you'll love them. On Salt Spring Island, the so-called "island of the arts," don't miss the Saturday Market, where you can stock your cooler with ambrosial island-grown fruit and locally produced cheeses and fill your trunk with locally made arts and crafts. Salt Spring Island also happens to be home to the ❺ **Oceanside Cottages**, one of our favorite places to stay, if only because one of the three rustic cabins here is the shagadelic Love Shack! As for the other islands, they're all worth visiting, but Saturna Island, the closest of the islands to the US, is remote enough to discourage most casual visitors. Hence, it's a stunning nature-locked retreat offering the quintessential island escape from the busy mainland life.

From Salt Spring or North Pender Island, ferry to Swartz Bay, zip down to nearby Sydney and take a Washington State Ferries boat to the ❻ **San Juan Islands**, your red-carpet entry into the US. Blanketed in trees, this astoundingly scenic archipelago – where the Georgia Strait, Puget Sound and Strait of Juan de Fuca meet – is a definitive Pacific Northwest highlight. After landing at Friday Harbor's ferry terminal, on San Juan Island, and exploring Friday Harbor itself, travel up to ❼ **Lime Kiln Point State Park**. Clinging to the island's rocky west coast, this park overlooks the deep Haro Strait and is, reputedly, one of the best places in the world to view whales from the shoreline. Of San Juan Island's handful of accommodations, ❽ **Roche Harbor Resort** makes a superb getaway for all budgets. More than 100 years after its initiation as the company hotel of limestone king John McMillin,

the place is *still* taking guests. If you'd rather pitch a tent, head directly to
❾ **San Juan County Park Campground**, beautifully situated on the island's
scenic western shoreline.

During your San Juans adventure, see tranquil, quirky Shaw Island, then Lopez
Island (aka *Slow-pez*) and finally Orcas Island. Precipitous, unspoiled and rug-
gedly beautiful, Orcas is the San Juans' emerald jewel. This steeply, densely
wooded and sparsely populated outpost is home to a motley mix of folk, from
wealthy retirees and second-homers to traditional farmers, eccentrics, innkeep-
ers, back-to-the-landers, and plenty of other assorted dropouts from the big-
city rat race. Be sure to hit ❿ **Moran
State Park**, which is dominated by
2409ft Mt Constitution, the archipelago's highest peak. Hiking to the top
affords one of the Pacific Northwest's
most awe inspiring views.

From Orcas Island, ferry over to Anacortes and drive down scenic Hwy 20
to ⓫ **Whidbey Island**. This fiercely
independent 41-mile-long island is
endowed with six state parks, a unique
National Historical Reserve, a community of budding artists and writers, and a free – yes, free – island-wide

ASK A LOCAL

"**Deadman's Bay**, at low
tide, has great tide pools
and you can often see orcas going by. It's next
to Lime Kiln Point. Go to South Beach, on the
southern end of the island. You can see the Cascades to your left, Vancouver Island to the right
and the Olympic Peninsula in front of you. It's a
big wide beach with tons and tons of driftwood.
And at **America's Camp**, there are trails down to
the beach that no one ever goes on. "
*Captain Jim Maya, Maya's Westside Charters, Friday
Harbor, WA*

public bus service. It's also home to approximately 140 B&Bs! Our pick of the
lot is ⓬ **Captain Whidbey Inn** because, well, they just don't come any more
outlandish than this quaint and cozy 1907 inn built of rust-colored madrone
wood. So park your car, check in, jump on the bus and start exploring.

From Whidbey, continue south and swing west on mainland Highway 101
for a visit to Washington's ⓭ **Olympic National Park**. Spanning 1406 sq
miles, this astounding national park protects wildly diverse landscapes, from
glaciated mountain peaks to a 57-mile strip of coastal wilderness, to the lush
old-growth Hoh Rain Forest. To figure out exactly what you want to see, stop
into the ⓮ **Olympic National Park Visitor Center**, about 1 mile south of
Port Angeles. Be sure to drive to the top of 5200ft Hurricane Ridge, which
often puts you above the notorious cloud cover, and take a hike (whether it's
raining or not) in the Hoh Rain Forest.

After exploring the park, haul your wet, mud-covered, travel-weary body 58
miles east to ⓯ **Seattle**, check into the masterfully designed ⓰ **Ace Hotel**.
Inside, street style meets chic minimalism and decor can mean anything
from stark white walls to murals of Andre the Giant to refurbished, retro

furniture. After freshening up, head over to ⑰ **Brouwer's**, where you can nurse yourself back to life quaffing any of 60 beers on tap (not to mention 300 types in bottles) at this cathedral-sized beer emporium. Then take to the streets of the Emerald City. Hit the hip restaurants, boutique shops and cafés of the Ballard neighborhood by day and, come sundown, head to industrial Georgetown for bars and brews aplenty. ⑱ **Pike Place Market**? Yep, it's tourist flypaper, but don't miss it: The buzzing warren of fruits stands, cafés and wee shops makes for superb street theater. Just get there early and avoid weekends. When the midday hordes descend upon Pike Place, head instead to ⑲ **Gas Works Park**, Seattle's monument of urban reclamation, and take in the panoramic views of downtown. The park was converted from gas plant to public park in 1976 (20 years after the plant closed) and looks like the rusty remnant of a science-fiction novel. Of course, you can't miss stylish Capitol Hill, Seattle's primary gay and lesbian neighborhood either.

DETOUR

Instead of heading south from Anacortes, detour west on Hwy 20 to the mainland and drive up **Chuckanut Drive** (Rte 11). It's one of the West Coast's most spectacular coastal back roads and ends in the fabulous city of Bellingham. The 35 mile (one way) trip takes just over an hour, provided you don't stop for the views. And you could spend days exploring the secondhand bookstores, coffee bars and myriad restaurants of **Bellingham**.

With Seattle in your pocket (and a bag of fresh roasted coffee in your kit) head to ⑳ **North Cascades National Park**, where you'll plunge into the glacier-riddled wilderness of the northern Cascades. Stop at the visitors center for information and continue up Hwy 20 to ㉑ **Colonial Creek Campground** on Diablo Lake. Then hike the 3.5-mile trail to Cascade Pass: After ascending into this flower-carpeted glacier-flanked paradise, you can either turn back or stand around struggling for superlatives that will simply never measure up to the scenery.

Spend a few days hiking and relaxing before heading south to ㉒ **Mt Rainier National Park** where, if the clouds aren't covering it, you can marvel at the Cascades' highest peak, 14,411ft Mt Rainier. Set up camp at one of several campgrounds and take to the trails that wind through swathes of flower-blanketed meadows beneath the conical peak.

When you're peaked out, head southeast along Hwy 12, through the vineyards and apple orchards of the Yakima River Valley, to ㉓ **Walla Walla**, where you can shack up in a small inn and immediately start wine tasting. That's right – the old sweet-onion town is now the epicenter of a flourishing wine-growing region, arguably the most important in the Pacific Northwest. It's also home to a staggering number of historic houses which are mapped on free walking tour maps, available from a dispenser in Heritage Park on Main St.

ICONIC
TRIPS

From Walla Walla, follow the mighty Columbia River into Oregon and travel west along Hwy 84, into the Columbia River Gorge. Mt Hood, Oregon's highest peak, soon pops into view, and the landscape changes from dry to lushly forested. Stop in the town of **24** **Hood River** where you'll find loads of great restaurants, two breweries and some of the best windsurfing and kiteboarding conditions in the world. It's a great place to spend a few days taking windsurfing lessons, hiking and exploring Mt Hood, only 45 minutes away via Hwy 35. Be sure to eat at, sleep at or just plain walk around the historic **25** **Timberline Lodge** on the south side of the mountain. Built by Oregon's Works Progress Administration in 1936 and 1937, the 73,700-sq-ft log-and-stone lodge is a masterpiece of national-park architecture. Inside, the **26** **Cascade Dining Room** serves expertly prepared, gourmet meals with an emphasis on local cuisine. The all-you-can-eat buffet breakfasts are a great way to enjoy the dining room if you'd rather not shell out for dinner. Continue west from Hood River along Hwy 84 and be absolutely certain to stop at **27** **Multnomah Falls**. At 620ft, it's the second highest year-round waterfall in the country.

From the falls, it's less than 40 minutes to **28** **Portland**, where, once again, you can fill yourself up on the very best food, beer, wine, art and music that the Pacific Northwest has to offer. If you didn't book a room at **29** **Kennedy School**, you should at least pop into this elementary school-turned-brewpub, hotel and all around fun zone (have a drink in the detention room – it's now a bar!). Be sure to poke around the hip boutiques, cafés, bars, bike shops and bookstores along three eastside streets: N Mississippi Ave, NE Alberta St and SE Hawthorne Blvd. Then walk across the Willamette River on the Burnside Bridge (or, for that matter, one of five other pedestrian-friendly bridges that link the east side with downtown) and explore the art galleries and museums of downtown Portland and the Pearl District. Of course, no visit to Portland is complete without getting lost in **30** **Powell's City of Books**, likely the largest independent new-and-used bookstore on the planet. And if you're lucky enough to be in town on a weekend don't miss the craft and food frenzy of the **31** **Saturday Market** (held Sundays, too) beneath the west end of the Burnside Bridge.

SLEEPING GIANT

Mt Rainier is a marvel to look at and more fun to explore, but beneath its placid exterior, ominous forces brew. As an active stratovolcano, Rainier harnesses untold destructive powers which, if unleashed, could threaten Seattle with mudslides and cause tsunamis in Puget Sound. Not surprisingly, the mountain has long been mythical. Native Americans called it Tahoma or Tacoma, meaning the "mother of waters," George Vancouver named it Rainier after his colleague Rear Admiral Peter Rainier, while most Seattleites simply call it "the Mountain."

Whew. From Portland, journey south to Salem and head west along Hwy 22 to Hwy 126. Follow this up and over gorgeous Santiam Pass (4817ft) to the outdoorsy, high-desert town of Sisters and on to the adventure mecca of

32 Bend. Make your way through all the ugly housing developments (the result of an unfortunate media-driven population boom) and treat yourself to a cold pint at either of Bend's two microbreweries. With all its restaurants and lodging options, not to mention everything there is to do within an hour's drive of town, you could easily spend three days shacked up in Bend before returning to the road.

From Bend, wind your way south along the wildly scenic Cascade Lakes Hwy (Hwy 46), past Mt Bachelor, and camp beside whichever lake looks best. It's hard to go wrong, regardless of the lake you choose. Most of the campgrounds are first-come, first-served and if you roll in mid-week or early on a weekend morning, you should have no problem landing a campsite. From this lake-riddled national scenic byway, make your way south to the Cascade Range's crown jewel, **33 Crater Lake National Park.** You could spend days hiking the trails, motoring around the 33-mile Rim Drive and exploring The Pinnacles. Once you're acclimated to the thin air, hike the strenuous 2.5 miles (one way) to the top of 8929ft Mt Scott for the most epic views of all.

DETOUR

With an extra two days it's an easy detour northwest of Bend to the wildly eroded badlands of **John Day Fossil Beds National Monument** in eastern Oregon. Head west via Hwy 26 to the town of Mitchell, where you can bed down for the night at the old-fashioned, two story Oregon Hotel. See the multicolored hills of the Painted Hills Unit and, if there's time, drive to the Sheep Rock Unit, where you'll find the park's only visitor center.

Descend from on high via Hwy 138 west (toward Roseburg) and stop for a soak at the spectacular hike-in **34 Umpqua Hot Springs.** Trust us, this will be one of your most memorable stops on the trip. From there, continue west along the "Wild and Scenic" section of the North Umpqua River and make your way down I-5 to **35 Ashland,** home of the world famous Oregon Shakespeare Festival. Even if you didn't time it right for the Bill-fest, this well-heeled mountain town just over the border from California is home to so many B&Bs and groovy little restaurants that its worth a stop any time – especially at the end of a very long drive.

Danny Palmerlee

TRIP INFORMATION

GETTING THERE
Vancouver, BC lies 140 miles north of Seattle and 315 miles north of Portland; to get there, take I-5 and then Hwy 99.

DO

Crater Lake National Park
Information centers in Rim Village and Steel Visitors Center, both on south side of lake. Roads closed in winter. ☎ 541-594-2211; www.nps.gov/crla; admission per vehicle $10, free in winter; ☉ year-round; ♿ ☐

Lime Kiln Point State Park
This 36-acre day-use park lies 10 miles from Friday Harbor, San Juan Island, WA. Shuttles available in summer. **Admission free;** ☉ 8am-dusk; ♿ ☐

Moran State Park
Washington's fourth-largest state park, on Orcas Island, has enough attractions to consume a day, easily. ☎ 360-376-2326; San Juan Islands, WA; admission free; ☉ 6:30am-dusk Apr-Sep, 8am-dusk Oct-Mar; ♿ ☐

Mt Rainier National Park
Of four entrances, the most popular (and only year-round) is Nisqually entrance, Hwy 706, about 1½ hours southeast of Seattle, WA. **www.nps.gov/mora; admission per vehicle $15;** ☉ year-round; ♿ ☐

Olympic National Park
Fees collected year-round at Hoh and Heart o' the Hills entrances, and May to October at Elwha, Sol Duc and Staircase entrances. **www.nps.gov/olym; admission per vehicle $15;** ☉ year-round; ♿ ☐

Olympic National Park Visitor Center
The park's most comprehensive information center offers excellent free maps and leaflets, and has exhibits for children and a bookstore. ☎ 360-565-3130; www.nps.gov/olym; 3002 Mt Angeles Rd, Port Angeles, WA; ☉ 9am-4pm; ♿

Pike Place Market
Baked goods, fruits, veggies, meat and more. Don't miss the oddball shops on lower levels. ☎ 206-682-7453; www.pikeplacemarket.org; 1501 Pike Pl, Seattle, WA; ☉ stores 10am-6pm Mon-Sat, 11am-5pm Sun

Powell's City of Books
Portland's giant independent bookstore occupies an entire city block and deals in new and used titles. ☎ 503-228-4651; www.powells.com; 1005 W Burnside St, Portland, OR; ☉ 9am-11pm; ♿

Saturday Market
Fun outdoor crafts fair with street entertainers and food carts. ☎ 503-222-6072; www.portlandsaturdaymarket.com; 108 W Burnside St, Portland, OR; ☉ 10am-5pm Sat, 11am-4:30pm Sun, Mar-Dec; ♿

Umpqua Hot Springs
From Hwy 138, turn onto Rd 34 at Toketee Lake, OR. Drive 1 mile past campground; turn right on gravel road; continue 2 miles to parking area. **Northwest Foerst Pass $5;** ☉ 24 hrs

EAT & DRINK

Brouwer's
Outstanding international selection of craft brews, including many Belgian selections. ☎ 206-267-2437; 400 N 35th St, Seattle, WA; ☉ 11am-2am

Cascade Dining Room
Serves gourmet meals with an emphasis on Pacific Norwest cuisine; breakfast buffets also available. ☎ 503-622-0717; www.timberlinelodge.com; Timberline Lodge, OR; breakfast $13, mains $24-30; ☉ breakfast, lunch & dinner

Go Fish
Best fish-and-chips around. Not much seating, but take it to go to nearby Vanier Park. ☎ 604-730-5040; 1505 W 1st Ave, Vancouver, BC; mains $8-13; ☉ 11:30am-6:30pm Wed-Fri, noon-6:30pm Sat & Sun

SLEEP

Ace Hotel
The 28 unique rooms are so stylish you finally get something worthy of the rock star you are. ☎ 206-448-4721; www.acehotel.com; 2423 1st Ave, Seattle, WA; r $75-199

Captain Whidbey Inn
Captivating, surreal inn built in 1907, constructed entirely from rust-colored madrone. Rates include full breakfast. ☎ 360-678-4097; www.captainwhidbey.com; 2072 W Captain Whidbey Inn Rd, Whidbey Island, WA; r $95, cabins $175-$275

Colonial Creek Campground
Nearly 170 campsites skirt the Thunder Arm of Diablo Lake on either side of Hwy 20. Several walk-in campsites are also available. ☎ 206-386-4495; Hwy 20, milepost 130, WA; campsites $15; ☯ year-round

Kennedy School
Portland's most unusual hotel has several bars, a theater, restaurant, microbrewery and a soaking pool. ☎ 503-249-3983, 888-249-3983; www.mcmenamins.com; 5736 NE 33rd Ave, Portland, OR; r $99-130; ⚐

Oceanside Cottages
Three stunningly situated, fully equipped seafront cottages with ocean views, surrounded by greenery. ☎ 250-653-0007, 866-341-0007; www.oceansidecottages.com; 521 Isabella Rd, Salt Spring Island, BC; cottages $135

Opus Hotel
Vancouver's best boutique hotel combines designer esthetics with loungey West Coast comforts. ☎ 604-642-6787, 866-642-6787; www.opushotel.com; 322 Davie St, Vancouver, BC; r from $300

Roche Harbor Resort
Self-contained resort on historic country estate with waterfront restaurants and a delightfully old-fashioned hotel. Hotel bathrooms are shared. ☎ 800-451-8910; www.rocheharbor.com; Roche Harbor, San Juan Island; r $79-99

San Juan County Park Campground
Includes a beach, boat launch, 20 campsites and flush toilets. Summer reservations mandatory. ☎ 360-378-1842; 380 West Side Rd, San Juan Island, WA; campsites $20; ☯ year-round ⚐ ▢

Timberline Lodge
Landmark hotel on Mt Hood, OR, worth a visit even if you're not staying; options range from rustic bunks to luxury suites. ☎ 503-622-0717; www.timberlinelodge.com; r $105-290

USEFUL WEBSITES
www.bcferries.com
www.wsdot.wa.gov/ferries

LINK YOUR TRIP

www.lonelyplanet.com/trip-planner

Highway 101: Land's Edge Leg

WHY GO If one thing defines the Pacific Northwest, it's the region's perpetually dramatic coastline. And up here, the Pacific's definitive road is Highway 101. This trip takes you from its northern terminus in Olympia, Washington, around the Olympic Peninsula and down the entire storm-pounded, fog-shrouded, wildly spectacular Oregon coastline.

TIME
3 weeks

DISTANCE
700 miles

BEST TIME TO GO
July – Oct

START
Olympia, WA

END
Brookings, OR

ALSO GOOD FOR

ROUTE

In Oregon and Washington, Highway 101 traverses a shoreline beset by some notoriously fickle weather. Powerful storms ravage the coast in winter, and through much of the summer, thick fog and misty skies blanket the shoreline, sending many a sun-starved traveler home with a furrowed brow and goose bumps. But when that sun comes out (as it does quite often in September and October), you'll be treated to some spectacular sights, from picturesque seaside towns to wild, golden beaches backed by towering old-growth forests.

In Washington, Highway 101 starts (or ends, depending on your perspective) in ❶ Olympia. Although the plan is to hit the highway ASAP, you wouldn't be the first to get sidetracked by the state capital for a few days before heading out. It's an engaging place, with eye-catching architecture, a lively student population, a cluster of excellent brew pubs, independent coffee houses and a music scene that has helped define everything from grunge to riot grrrl feminism.

Once you've had your taste of Olympia, head north – *vzzzt*, record scratch, music stop… North? Yep, before heading south you have to loop up and around the spectacular Olympic Peninsula. Your first stop, ❷ Port Townsend, is only 105 miles away. After the urban sprawl of Puget Sound, this architectural gold mine is a sight for sore eyes. Check out the Victorian shop fronts on Water St, hit the art galleries (the visitors

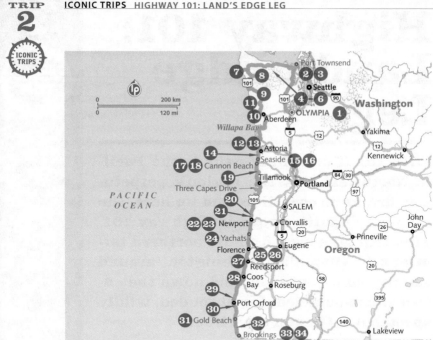

center has a map of the most prominent), treat yourself to a good meal and then shack up at the ③ **Palace Hotel**. Built in 1889, this beautiful Victorian building is a former brothel, once run by the locally notorious Madame Marie, who took care of business in the 2nd-floor corner suite. Each of the hotel's 15 rooms is named after the woman who once occupied it. Sweet dreams.

From Port Townsend, continue around the cape and into ④ **Olympic National Park**, a 1406-sq-mile expanse of rain-drenched magnificence. Take the road up to 5300ft ⑤ **Hurricane Ridge**, which often lifts you above the clouds and into the sun. Along with an excellent visitor center and fabulous views, Hurricane Ridge offers access to some fun short hikes which lead through meadows to vista points. You could also drive the white-knuckle 8-mile road to Obstruction Peak, which provides access to some outstanding hiking across alpine meadows and ridges, well above tree line.

From Hurricane Ridge continue west along Highway 101 past the road to the excellent ⑥ **Sol Duc Campground** (Hint: Camp here.) After bending south, Highway 101 hits the town of Forks, and from Forks, Rte 110 leads west to the remote town of La Push and the desolate, forest-backed ⑦ **Rialto Beach**. This 4-mile sandy wonderland is a must.

Further south (we're still in Olympic National Park), Hoh River Rd takes you the dense wonderland the ⑧ **Hoh Rain Forest**. Rainy it may be, but never mind that trivial fact. Rain is what this place is all about! This is the world's largest temperate rain forest and it wouldn't have such ethereal, Tolkienesque, utterly mind-bending arboreal scenery if it weren't for the 12 to 14ft (yes, feet!) of precipitation it receives each year. Bring a poncho, come in summer and hike the Hall of Moss Trail to experience the finest forest scenery the park has to offer. And when you're finished with the forest, treat yourself to a night at the ⑨ **Lake Quinault Lodge,** further south. It has everything you could want in a historic national park lodge: a huge, roaring fireplace, lake views, comfy leather sofas, a regal reception area and – arguably – the finest eating experience on the peninsula.

Back in the world of your automobile, leave the park and travel south to ⑩ **Grays Harbor,** an estuarine bay flanked by several rather unexceptional towns, including Kurt Cobain's birthplace, Aberdeen. It's worth poking around the bay for a few hours, but if you want the more desolate seascapes that makes this place worth stopping, drive up coastal Rte 109 to Sunset Beach and spend a night at the stellar ⑪ **Ocean Crest Resort,** which has ocean views, a heated indoor pool and private beach access.

WHALE WATCHING

Each year, gray whales undertake one of the longest migrations of any animal on earth, swimming from the Bering Strait and Chukchi Sea to Baja California – and back. In Oregon and Washington, they can be seen while migrating south (mid-December through mid-January) and migrating north (March through June). In Oregon, the town of Depoe Bay is known for its whale watching and is home to the interesting **Whale Watching Center** (www.whalespoken .org). Further south, in Newport, **Marine Discovery Tours** (www.marinediscovery.com) offers whale-watching cruises from the marina.

South of Grays Harbor, the even bigger Willapa Bay cuts into the coastline and is protected on its western side by the aptly named ⑫ **Long Beach Peninsula.** This narrow spit has an extraordinary 28 miles of uninterrupted sand which, unfortunately, is backed by 28 miles of uninterrupted development. But hey, you can drive out on the beach (Woohoo!) like the vacationers that swarm the place. Or, rather, you can hit the bay side of the peninsula, where you can explore the tiny old towns of Oysterville and Nahcotta and gorge yourself on the bay's famous oysters.

At the end of the day, head to Seaview and check into the ⑬ **Historic Sou'wester Lodge.** Built in 1892 by an Oregon senator, this three-story lodge – now owned by a well-traveled South African couple – has a self-amused air of eclecticism and humorous nonchalance. The proprietors insist that the establishment is a B&(MYOD)B – that is, "Bed and Make Your Own Damn Breakfast." In the original lodge, simple bedroom units share a kitchen, bathroom and living area, while apartment-style suites come fully equipped. Or you can sleep in a "TCH! TCH!" unit. The name (of course) refers to the Trailer Classics Hodgepodge, a collection of renovated 1950s house trailers.

After a stint in Long Beach, cross into Oregon, buzz through Astoria and stop in the tiny town of Gearhart where you can wade out at low tide and dig for razor clams. What, no shovel? Oh well, at least your heart was in the right place. Might as well head to **14** **Pacific Way Bakery & Cafe** and hope they're the night's special. Even if they're not, this charming little eatery serves some of the best haute cuisine on the coast, including dishes such as lavender-roasted duck and prosciutto-wrapped scallops. Soups and sandwiches make lunch far more casual.

From Gearhart, mosey on down the coast a further 3 miles to **15** **Seaside**, Oregon's biggest and busiest resort town. Seaside's 2-mile-long boardwalk – "The Prom" – is where you pull out your sense of humor and rent cruisers, eat candied apples, buy kitschy souvenirs, play video games and watch the hordes of out-of-towners wander up and down the Prom entertaining themselves. Rather than filling up on junk food, treat yourself to seafood at **16** **Bell Buoy**, on the south end of town. Best known as a seafood store, this down-to-earth, family-run establishment has an attached seafood restaurant serving outstanding fish-and-chips, chowder and more. And it's all fresh.

After dragging your travel-mate from Seaside's boardwalk, head south to the quieter town of **17** **Cannon Beach**. More upscale than Seaside, Cannon Beach has been a favorite getaway for generations of Portlanders who come out for quiet strolls on the beach and evening jaunts to the local candy shop. Cannon Beach is also home to Haystack Rock, the third-tallest sea stack in the world.

DETOUR South of the town of Tillamook, Highway 101 veers inland from the coast. An exhilarating alternative route is the slow, winding and sometimes bumpy **Three Capes Drive**, which hugs the shoreline for 30 miles. En route you'll traverse Cape Meares, Cape Lookout and Cape Kiwanda, three stunning headlands which you'd otherwise miss entirely. To do the Three Capes Drive, head due west on 3rd St out of Tillamook and bear right on Bayocean Rd. After encircling Cape Meares, the road heads down the coast.

For the area's best coastal hiking, head immediately north of town to **18** **Ecola State Park**, where you can hike to secluded beaches. At the end of the day, either hole up at one of the many hotels in town or, better yet, drive south to Nehalem and treat yourself to a night at the **19** **Old Wheeler Hotel**. The decor's a bit flowery, but it's a groovy old place, and the rooms have fabulous views of Nehalem Bay.

Wake up, drink your coffee and slowly poke your way 86 miles down the coast to **20** **Beverly Beach State Park**. With campsites, yurts and a long, wide beach lying just across the highway, this is the perfect place to base yourself for further marine exploration. Consult your tide book, don your marine-biologist cap and head 3 miles south to ㉑ **Yaquina Head Outstanding Natural Area**, a giant spit of land protruding nearly a mile into the ocean. This headland is home to some of the best touch pools on the Oregon coast and hitting them at low tide is key. When the tide is in, entertain yourself gazing at the coast's tallest still-functioning lighthouse.

Next stop is Newport, home to the ㉒ **Oregon Coast Aquarium**. Like wandering through a living kaleidoscope, a stroll through this place is an otherworldly experience. The seals and sea otters are cute as can be, and the jellyfish room is a near psychedelic experience. But what really knocks this place off the charts is the deep sea exhibit *through* which you walk, surrounded by a Plexiglas tunnel full of sharks, rays and other fish. In Newport, getting tanked is not just for the fish. After the aquarium, head to the ㉓ **Rogue Ales Public House**, where you can quaff Rogue Brewery's heavily hopped microbrews at outdoor tables or seated inside at the big wooden bar, closer to the 35 tap handles.

Spend a night in Newport before driving 23 miles south to the town of ㉔ **Yachats**. Located on the northern flanks Cape Perpetua, Yachats is a quiet, laidback getaway surrounded by hidden beaches, tide pools and coastal forest. Despite its wee size, it has several great eateries and loads of quaint B&Bs and guesthouses. If you're camping, head straight to the excellent ㉕ **Cape Perpetua Campground**, about 3 miles south of town. Wherever you stay, devote all non-eating, non-sleeping time to exploring ㉖ **Cape Perpetua Scenic Area**, where trails take you through moss-laden old growth forests to rocky beaches, tide pools and blasting marine geysers, and to a historic lookout with one of the most colossal views on the entire coast.

> **ASK A LOCAL** "Go check out the **Historic 804 Trail**. It starts in town and heads north up to the beach at Smelt Sands. It's part of the old 804 Hwy which ran along the beach [for 8 miles] to Alsea Bay. People traveled south on the beach until they hit Yachats, where the sand ends and they had the forest to deal with."
> *Dave Rieseck, Yachats, OR*

As you drive south from Yachats and Cape Perpetua, the forests get progressively drier and then, just south of the town of Florence, you start to notice something altogether different: sand. Lots of it. Florence marks the northern edge of the ㉗ **Oregon Dunes National Recreation Area**, the largest expanse of oceanfront sand dunes in the US. These mountains of sand, sometimes topping heights of 500ft and reaching inland up to 3 miles, undulate all the way to Coos Bay, 50 miles south. About 10 miles north of Reedsport, you'll pass the Oregon Dunes Overlook, the easiest place to get a look at the dunes. Several campgrounds lie just off Highway 101, and hotels are plentiful in Florence, Reedsport and Winchester Bay.

At Coos Bay, the Cape Arago Hwy leads 14 miles southwest of town to the day-use-only ㉘ **Cape Arago State Park**, which protects some of the best tide pools on the Oregon coast. It's well worth a detour out here before continuing 50 miles south to ㉙ **Cape Blanco State Park**, where you can camp out on the second most westerly point of the contiguous US. Allow yourself at least two days to explore the beaches and trails between Cape Blanco and ㉚ **Humbug Mountain State Park**, 10 miles south. At Humbug, a 3-mile trail leads through the coast's largest remaining groves of Port Orford cedar to the top of Humbug Mountain and dramatic views of Cape Sebastian and the Pacific.

Another 24 miles south of Humbug you'll pass through the summertime tourist hub of ㉛ **Gold Beach**, where you can take a jet boat excursion up the scenic Rogue River. But the real treat lies 13 miles south of town, when you enter the 12-mile stretch of coastal splendor known as the ㉜ **Samuel H Boardman State Scenic Corridor**. With giant stands of Sitka spruce, natural rock bridges, tide pools and loads of hiking trails, it's a vast coastal playground. At its southern end, ㉝ **Harris Beach State Park** offers the area's best (make that only) coastal camping. For the comfort of a room, head a mile south to ㉞ **Brookings**, the southernmost town on the Oregon Coast. From here, the quickest return north is via California's Hwy 199 to I-5 – unless of course, you want to take the scenic coastal route back.

Danny Palmerlee

TRIP INFORMATION

GETTING THERE
To reach Olympia from Portland, drive 115 miles north on I-5. From Seattle drive 60 miles south on I-5.

DO

Cape Blanco State Park
Beach access and great views, plus showers and flush toilets. Located on Hwy 101, 4 miles north of Brookings, OR.
☎ 541-332-6774, 800-452-5687; www.oregonstateparks.org; tents/RV sites/cabins $16/16/35; ⚿ □

Cape Perpetua Scenic Area
Rich tide-pool life, rock formations, trails, old-growth forest, views and more. Located 3 miles south of Yachats, OR, on Hwy 101. **Day-use sites $5;** ⚿

Ecola State Park
Stunning coastal day-use park with access to the Pacific Coast Trail, Indian Beach and Tillamook Head. ☎ 503-436-2844; www.oregonstateparks.org; Cannon Beach, OR; day-use $3; ⚿ □

Humbug Mountain State Park
Along with great hiking, there are campsites with showers and flush toilets. ☎ 541-332-6774, 800-452-5687; www.oregonstateparks.org; tents/RV sites $14/16; ⚿ □

Olympic National Park
For information and maps, stop into the excellent visitor center just off Hwy 101, on the road to Hurricane Ridge, WA. **Park admission per vehicle $15;** ⚿ □

Oregon Coast Aquarium
Exceptional aquarium with seals, sea otters, deep-sea exhibit, jellyfish room and more. ☎ 541-867-3474; www.aquarium.org; 2820 SE Ferry Slip Rd, Newport, OR; adult/3-13yr/senior $13/8/11; ⊙ 9am-6pm; ⚿

Oregon Dunes National Recreation Area
Largest expanse of oceanfront sand dunes in USA. **For information, contact Reedsport**

Chamber of Commerce ☎ 541-271-3495; 855 Highway Ave, Reedsport, OR; ⚿ □

Yaquina Head Outstanding Natural Area
Outstanding tide pools, views and visitor center, plus the coast's tallest functioning lighthouse. ☎ 541-574-3100; 750 Lighthouse Dr, Newport, OR; admission $5; ⊙ dawn-dusk; ⚿

EAT

Bell Buoy
Local fish market and family-style seafood restaurant. **Store** ☎ 503-738-2722, **restaurant** ☎ 503-738-6348; www.bellbuoyofseaside.com; 1800 S Roosevelt Dr, Seaside, OR; **mains $8-18; store** ⊙ 9:30am-6pm, **restaurant 11:30am-7:30pm, closed Tue & Wed in winter;** ⊙

Pacific Way Bakery & Cafe
Excellent sandwiches, soups for lunch and gourmet dinners. Great bakery next door. ☎ 503-738-0245; **601 Pacific Way, Gearhart, OR; mains $18-29;** ⊙ **11am-3:30pm, 5-9pm Thu-Mon, bakery from 7am**

Rogue Ales Public House
One of Oregon's longest-running breweries has an expansive food menu too. ☎ 541-265-3188; www.rogue.com; **748 SW Bay Blvd, Newport, OR; mains $8-22;** ⊙ **11am-1am Sun-Thu, to 2am Fri & Sat;** ⚿

SLEEP

Beverly Beach State Park
Large state campground with tents and heated yurts. Located 7 miles north of Newport. ☎ 877-444-6777; www.oregonstateparks.org; Hwy 101, OR; **tents $17-21, yurts $30;** ⊙ **year-round;** ⚿ □

Cape Perpetua Campground
Lovely, forested 38-site campground; no showers. Three miles south of Yachats ☎ 877-444-6777; Hwy 101, Cape Perpetua Scenic Area, OR; www.recreation.gov; **campsites $20;** ⊙ **mid-May–Sept;** ⚿ □

Harris Beach State Park
Camp beside the beach or sleep in a yurt. Showers, flush toilets and coin laundry available. Located 2 miles north of Brookings, OR. ☎ 541-469-2021, 800-452-5687; www.oregonstateparks.org; tents/yurts $17/29; 🚹 ☐

Historic Sou'wester Lodge
Historic lodge with simple rooms with shared baths, plus suites, refurbished trailers and tent sites. ☎ 360-642-2542; www.souwesterlodge.com; 38th Place, Seaview, OR; tents/RV sites $18/20, r $60-70, lodge ste $70-110, cabins $81

Lake Quinault Lodge
Historic 1926 lodge with wonderful rooms and warm, regal common areas. Reservations recommended for dinner. ☎ 360-288-2900; www.visitlakequinault.com; 345 S Shore Rd, Olympic National Park, WA; cabins $125-243, lodge r $135-170

Ocean Crest Resort
Stellar self-contained resort and hotel overlooking the Pacific with a good selection of room options and a decent, if exceedingly expensive, restaurant. ☎ 360-276-4465; www.oceancrestresort.com; Hwy 109, Sunset Beach, Moclips, WA; r $79-209; 🚹

Old Wheeler Hotel
Lovely historic hotel in Wheeler, 5 miles southeast of Manzanita. Continental breakfast included. ☎ 503-368-6000, 877-653-4683; www.oldwheelerhotel.com; 495 Hwy 101, Wheeler, OR; r $85-99

Palace Hotel
Attractive period hotel with antique furnishings, old-fashioned claw-foot baths, lovely rooms and a fascinating history. ☎ 360-385-0773; www.palacehotelpt.com; 1004 Water St, Port Townsend, WA; r $59-109

Sol Duc Campground
With tall fir and cedar trees and mossy undergrowth, Sol Duc offers its campers quintessential Olympic rain-forest experience. ☎ 360-327-3534; Olympic National Park, WA; sites $12; ⊙ year-round, barring heavy snow; 🚹 ☐

USEFUL WEBSITES
www.washingtoncoastchamber.org
www.visittheoregoncoast.com

LINK YOUR TRIP
www.lonelyplanet.com/trip-planner

Ice & Fire: Volcano Trail

WHY GO The volcanoes of the Pacific Northwest rank as the region's most iconic and breathtaking natural sights. Take the scenic route from Seattle to Portland and tiptoe around sleeping giants on this back roads trip down the exquisite volcanic spine of Mts Rainier, Adams, St Helens and Hood.

Kick off this trip by heading southeast from ❶ **Enumclaw** on the Chinook Scenic Byway and you quickly find yourself in the shadow of a volcano. Between Enumclaw and Greenwater you are effectively driving along the Osceola mudflow, a huge lahar (mud slide of water, rock and ash) created 5800 years ago when 2000ft of Mt Rainier collapsed, leaving Enumclaw 70ft deep in debris.

Twenty minutes down the road, the family-friendly trails through the magical old-growth forest of ❷ **Federation Forest State Park** are a good way to avoid the national park crowds. Kids in particular will love the 45-minute hike to the Hobbit House, where a tree stump has been converted into a residence worthy of Bilbo Baggins.

Hwy 410 continues up the White River Valley, past several national forest campgrounds and into ❸ **Mt Rainier National Park**. If the mountain is out (ie there's clear weather) the detour up the switchbacking road to ❹ **Sunrise**, the highest part of the park reachable by vehicle, is a must. A pause midway at Sunrise Point offers a unique view of five volcanoes, but it's the view from Sunrise and the trails beyond that reveals the true scale of Rainier, home to more snow and ice than all the other Cascade volcanoes combined.

With a giant the size of Rainier (14,411ft), sometimes you have to step back to get the best views. For one of the park's classic photo ops, and

TIME
4 days

DISTANCE
480 miles

BEST TIME TO GO
Jul – Sep

START
Enumclaw, WA

END
Portland, OR

ALSO GOOD FOR

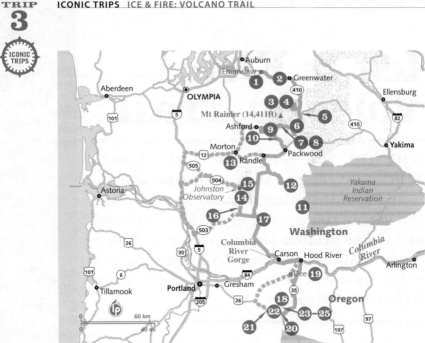

a fine picnic spot, detour east of the main road to Chinook Pass, where the mountain reflects perfectly in ⑤ Tipsoo Lake.

After the tundralike terrain above Sunrise, Hwy 123 drops quickly into the clear-running streams and old-growth forest of ⑥ Ohanapecosh, where the park-run campground offers a fine night's camping under a towering canopy of cedars and firs. Beat the crowds at dusk or early the next morning and hike the 1.3-mile Grove of the Patriarchs trail to a collection of 1000-year-old hemlocks and Douglas firs that occupy an island in the middle of the Ohanapecosh River.

⑦ Paradise is the busiest part of the park and a good place to avoid on summer weekends. Popular hikes here include the 1.2-mile Nisqually Vista loop (which offers views down onto the toe of Nisqually Glacier) and the Skyline Trail to Panorama Point (5 miles); but don't expect trails here to be snow free until the middle, or end, of July. Even Paradise needs a face-lift now and then and 2008 saw the opening of a new visitors center and the $22 million renovation of the flagship ⑧ Paradise Inn. Built in 1917, the historic hotel's barnlike interior boasts a good restaurant and live music each evening courtesy of the lobby's antique piano.

While the views around Rainier are spectacular, the food generally is not – one reason the ⑨ Copper Creek Inn is so outstanding. This former gas station just outside the park's Nisqually entrance has been knocking out killer pancake breakfasts for 50 years and the homemade blackberry pie is still worth driving across the state for.

There are two main routes to consider as you head south to Randle. The main Rte 706 passes the climbers' base camp at Ashford before swinging south to the logging town of Morton and then east to Randle. The shorter, and more adventurous, alternative (closed in winter) is ❿ **Skate Creek Road** (FR52), a rougher (though mostly paved) mountain road that short-cuts between Ashford and Packwood. Late September's blur of brilliant oranges and reds makes this one of the region's best fall drives.

Rainier is the region's big-name draw and summer weekends often translate into packed parking lots and full campgrounds. The antidote to this temporary park madness is ⓫ **Mt Adams**, an overlooked 12,276ft gem wrapped in 46,000 acres of wilderness. Nestled at the foot of the mountain, 34 miles southeast of Randle, ⓬ **Takhlakh Lake** offers perfect views of the peak from what is one of the nation's most scenic campgrounds. Watching the glacier-covered peak blush pink with twilight's alpenglow may just be the highlight of your trip. Getting to the lake involves navigating a series of forest roads (FR23 and FR2329), including 7 miles of dirt road, but it's worth it. Road conditions and campground opening dates change frequently here, so pop into the ⓭ **Cowlitz Valley Ranger Station** in Randle before setting off.

From Takhlakh Lake cut westward on FR76 and then FR25 to the ⓮ **Mt St Helens National Volcanic Monument**. Most people visit the west side of the mountain, which is fine as this leaves the remoter eastern side just for us. The east slope may lack facilities, but with its eerie views of the felled forest and lifeless Spirit Lake, it offers a far more palpable impression of the cataclysmic 1981 eruption.

"As you descend into the pitch-black lava tube it's hard not to feel like Jonah entering the belly of a whale."

Forestry Service road 99 winds into the blast zone, past the "miner's car," flipped and crushed by the eruption, and up to ⓯ **Windy Ridge**, where steps zigzag up the barren slopes for outstanding views of Spirit Lake. Once surrounded by lush forest, the lake's mat of decomposing logs is the result of the 850ft-high tsunami triggered by the eruption. Hikers can follow the 6-mile Truman Trail down onto the pumice plain for views of the partially collapsed crater, now bulging with a fresh lava dome. This is the perfect place to take in the eruption's mind-boggling statistics: a 600mph blast that sent 540 million tons of ash around the globe and melted 20 billion gallons of water off the peak in a single day. Yes, this is an awesome place.

The spectacular 1981 eruption was only the most recent of many volcanic events that have shaped the surrounding landscape. One place to get up close to (inside!) a 2000-year-old lava flow is **16 Ape Cave**, on the southern side of the mountain. As you descend into the pitch-black lava tube it's hard not to feel like Jonah entering the belly of a whale. In reality you are standing inside the cooled crust of an ancient lava flow; lava pulsed through the tube for months and you can still see the flow lines on the walls. This is no sanitized experience; there are no lights here, no trail, no guide. Turn off your flashlight deep inside the cave and you'll quickly feel the panic rise in your chest. It's a fantastic experience but come prepared with good shoes, a raincoat and two reliable flashlights.

From Ape Cave head back to the junction of FR90 and FR25 and take FR51 (Curly Creek Rd) and then FR30 south down the Wind River Hwy toward Carson. Thick forest blocks most of the views along this route, except at **17 McClellan Viewpoint** which offers superb views back toward the intact southern cone of Mt St Helens, superbly silhouetted at sunset.

DETOUR If late summer snow levels or storm damage have resulted in the closure of Rte 25 or the east side of Mt St Helens, you'll have to detour to I-5 and take the popular Spirit Lake Memorial Hwy (Hwy 504) up the west side of the mountain to the **Johnston Observatory**. As compensation for the crowds you'll find the mountain's best crater views. Back on I-5 you should then be able to cut round to the mountain's southern slopes on Hwy 503 to rejoin this trip near the Ape Cave.

As you head south from Hood River and the Columbia Gorge, snowcapped **18 Mt Hood** (11,239ft), Oregon's highest peak, rises into full, glorious view. If you have time, make the detour west on the Hood River Hwy (281) to **19 Dee** for lovely views of the mountain framed by rolling pear and apple orchards, as Mt Adams fills your rear-view mirror. Despite what the roadside "Nottingham" and "Sherwood" campgrounds would have you believe, Mt Hood is named not after Robin, but rather Samuel Hood, an 18th-century British admiral. Native Americans have long used their own name for the mountain (Wy'east), as they have for fellow volcanoes Rainier (Tacoma), Adams (Pahto) and Mt St Helens (Loowit, or "The Smoker").

The Mt Hood Scenic Byway hooks south and then east around the mountain, offering fabulous views at every turn, but there are a couple of classic detours to consider. Man-made **20 Trillium Lake** combines camping and kayaking with perfectly reflected views of the mountain. Further west, the mountain's most popular trail is the family-friendly 3-mile return hike to photogenic **21 Mirror Lake**; for even better views and fewer crowds continue up past huckleberry bushes to the top of Tom, Dick & Harry Peak for a moderate 6-mile return hike. Both lakes get very busy on summer weekends.

If you've dragged your teenagers around one too many dull mountain trails it may be time to reward them at the **22** **Mt Hood Skibowl**. The outdoor equivalent to an intravenous shot of Red Bull, the bowl's Adventure Park offers everything from a half-mile alpine slide to an 80ft reverse bungee jump (we feel sick just writing about it). Let the kids run wild, while you load your mountain bike onto the bowl's two lifts and freewheel back down miles of single track.

DETOUR If you've traveled the Mt Hood Scenic Byway before, consider taking the wilder **Lolo Pass Road** around the little-visited northwestern flanks of the mountain. The single-lane road is mostly paved (the section around the pass is gravel) but is still only motorable from late June to October. En route you'll pass several scenic viewpoints and the turnoff for the 7-mile return trail to feathery 120ft Ramona Falls, one of the mountain's best hikes.

There's really only one accommodations to consider in the Mt Hood area and that's the iconic **23** **Timberline Lodge**. Fans of *The Shining* will find it hard not to whisper "All work and no play makes Jack a dull boy" as they approach the lodge. The property allowed director Stanley Kubrick to film exterior shots here but requested he not use the book's original room number 217 (a real room in the lodge), fearing no-one would ever stay in it again. At least the hotel retains a sense of humor; look for the axe in the lobby with "Here's Johnny!" carved on it. For a classy meal you can't beat the lodge's superlative **24** **Cascade Dining Room**.

Several hiking trails tempt trekkers away from the lodge or you can join the summer skiers on the Magic Mile chairlift up to the meadows around the **25** **Silcox Hut**, a former warming hut converted into deliciously remote accommodations for groups of 12 or more. Watch the climbers set off from the hut on their ascent of the mountain, while the rest of us descend to the Timberline's cozy Ram's Head Bar to raise our own Ice Axe IPA in solidarity (albeit in pint form) and toast the end of this great mountain odyssey.
Bradley Mayhew

TRIP INFORMATION

GETTING THERE
From Seattle take I-5 and Hwy 167 south to Auburn and then Hwy 164 east to Enumclaw; a 41-mile drive.

DO
Ape Cave
Choose between the easier lower cave or the more strenuous upper route through this 2.25-mile lava tube. ☎ 360-449-7800; www.fs.fed.us/gpnf/mshnvm; Gifford Pinchot National Forest, WA; Northwest Forest Pass $5; ☽ Jun-Sep

Cowlitz Valley Ranger Station
Your best source of information on road, trail and campground conditions in the Gifford Pinchot National Forest. ☎ 360-497-1100; www.fs.fed.us/gpnf; Hwy 12, Randle, WA; ☽ 8am-noon & 1-4:30pm Mon-Sat

Federation Forest State Park
The 600 acres of old-growth forest here boast picnic sites, hiking trails and an interpretive center. ☎ 360-663-2207; www.parks.wa.gov; Hwy 410, WA; hdawn-dusk

Mt Hood Skibowl
Bungee jumps, zip lines and alpine slides make this adrenaline-junkie heaven. ☎ 503-222-2695; www.skibowl.com; Hwy 26, Mt Hood, OR; day pass $29-59, bike rental half/full day $25/32; ☽ 11am-6pm Mon-Fri, 10am-7pm Sat & Sun

Mt Rainier National Park
The Northwest's most popular park offers everything from rainforest to glaciers, along with four visitors centers and three campgrounds. ☎ 360-569-2211; www.nps.gov/mora; 7-day/annual pass $15/30

Mt St Helens National Volcanic Monument
Check the roads are open before setting off for the less-visited eastern side of the mountain. ☎ 360-449-7800; www.fs.fed.us/gpnf/mshnvm; Northwest Forest Pass $5; ☽ dawn-dusk Jun-Oct

EAT
Cascade Dining Room
World-class cuisine with a Northwest twist makes this the place for a special dinner. ☎ 503-622-0700; www.timberlinelodge.com; Timberline Lodge, Mt Hood; mains $26-40, 4-course set dinner $35; ☽ 5:30-8:30pm

Copper Creek Inn
Start the day with a fine breakfast or grab a house-roasted espresso and "copper topper" cinnamon roll at the counter. ☎ 360-569-2326; www.coppercreekinn.com; 35707 Rte 706E, Ashford, WA; mains $7-22; ☽ 7am-9pm

SLEEP
Paradise Inn
Not on a par with the Timberline, but still Rainier's best example of "parkitecture." The unbeatable location makes up for ho-hum rooms. ☎ 360-569-2275; http://rainier.guestservices.com; Mt Rainier National Park, WA; r $99-210, ste $228; ☽ mid-May–early Oct

Takhlakh Lake Campground
Reserve your site in advance at this breathtaking national forest campground and you'll have perfect lakeshore views of Mt Adams. ☎ 1-877-444-6777; www.recreation.gov; FR2329, WA; sites $15-17; ☽ Jul-Oct

Timberline Lodge
This gorgeous historic lodge on the flanks of Mt Hood boasts hand-crafted furniture, a three-story fireplace and rooms in all price ranges. ☎ 503-622-7979; www.timberlinelodge.com; d $105-290

USEFUL WEBSITES
www.mthood.info
www.visitrainier.com
www.lonelyplanet.com/trip-planner

LINK YOUR TRIP

Soak It Up!
Hot Springs &
Mineral Pools

WHY GO Curative powers? Who can say. But hot springs will certainly leave you feeling relaxed, and what could be more therapeutic than that? From remote hike-in springs to upscale resorts, Marjorie Gersh-Young acts as our dowsing rod to help us find the best places to soak in the Northwest.

TIME
7 – 9 days

DISTANCE
1172 miles

BEST TIME TO GO
Jun – Sep

START
**Port
Angeles, WA**

END
Ashland, OR

ALSO GOOD FOR

If anyone knows about hot springs, it's Marjorie Gersh-Young. Her book, *Hot Springs and Hot Pools of the Northwest*, offers all the details on just about every place to soak in the northwestern US, which means it's her duty to take long soaks in hot, relaxing mineral water. (No, she doesn't need an assistant.)

So, where in the Pacific Northwest would Marjorie send muscle-fatigued friends and dedicated tub-takers? Up in the northwest corner of Washington, tucked into the Olympic National Park, are scenic springs surrounded by evergreen forests. Start at the historic ❶ **Sol Duc Hot Springs Resort**, where you'll find cute-enough cabins and all the facilities you need to settle in, including a restaurant, a small store and, of course, pools and tubs filled with hot mineral water. (For more detailed directions for getting to the hot springs, refer to Trip Information.)

One of Sol Duc's best features, according to Gersh-Young, is its proximity to ❷ **Olympic Hot Springs**. "Olympic is the most gorgeous place to soak in all of Washington." Unfortunately, the primitive, volunteer-built pools also seem to be continually on the endangered list: "They've been trying to tear it down for years, so be sure to check before you go to make sure it's still there." The pools are all different sizes and all different temperatures, so it's easy to find one that's just right.

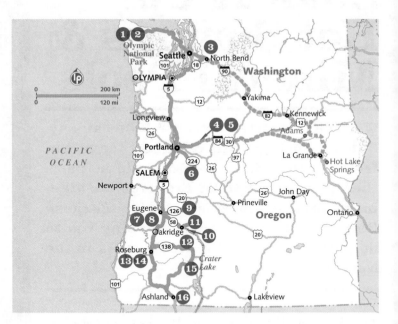

East of Seattle near the town of North Bend is the trickiest quarry of the hunt for hot springs. "You don't just get up in the morning and decide you're going to ❸ **Goldmyer Hot Springs**," says Gersh-Young. "It's on private land and you have to contact them ahead of time or you're just not getting in." They're trying hard to protect the scenic beauty and frail ecology of this remote springs, so it's never crowded, thanks to a limit of twenty visitors per day. It's 4.5 miles in to the springs, which you can reach by hiking, mountain biking or even cross-country skiing.

DETOUR Traveling with young'uns? It might be worth the four-hour drive from North Bend to **Bar M Ranch** (www.barmranch.com) in Adams, OR, offering all sorts of indoor and outdoor games and activities. Just an hour further south is the resort **Hot Lake Springs** (www.hotlakesprings.com), a former sanitarium to which visitors flocked in the early 1900s. One century and a massive restoration later, the site boasts a museum, restaurant, hotel and spa. Rejoin the road trip by taking Hwy 84 west to Bonneville.

From Goldmyer, head south on I-5. Your next stop is ❹ **Bonneville Hot Springs Resort**, near the Oregon border and just an hour east of Portland. A resort and day spa, this is no hippy-dippy sleepover. It's a luxurious shrine to mineral water, featuring an indoor lap pool, outdoor pool, indoor and outdoor hot soaking tubs, and even private tubs on the balcony of many of the rooms. Temperatures vary, but all are fed by the 97° springs. They even have two on-site restaurants, one serving Northwest cuisine and the other keeping it casual with burgers and beer.

If that all sounds a little too luxurious for you, ❺ **Carson Hot Springs Resort** lies just 11 miles away and is an affordable and considerably funkier option. With a little bit of an identity crisis, it's rustic in parts, but with motel-decor rooms and a randomly inserted golf course. But Gersh-Young says you can't deny its popularity: "There are people who have been going there for years and years and they love the fact that it's the old-fashioned way to soak, where you're in a bathtub in a little room, then they come and wrap you in towels and you lie on a bench."

When asked what her favorite hot spring in Oregon is, Gersh-Young doesn't hesitate: ❻ **Bagby Hot Springs**. "It's absolutely one of the best. The walk in is beautiful, truly one of these 'over the river and through the woods' kind of walks through a beautiful forest." Bagby's mineral water is piped in via a 150-foot log flume to appreciative and friendly soakers in cedar tubs. You have to work for it, though; Bagby is a couple of hours southeast of Portland off Hwy 224 and wonderfully located in the middle of nowhere. (You'll find more specific direction to this and other primitive hot springs in the trip information section.)

From Bagby, backtrack to I-5 and then head south an hour and a half to evergreen Eugene, which Gersh-Young recommends as a base for exploring several primitive springs in the area. This situates you perfectly for fueling up on beer and better-than-average pub food at ❼ **McMenamins North Bank**. Their lovely patio overlooking the Willamette River means you never have to be too far from water. Then, rest up for your next day's adventures at Eugene's ❽ **Phoenix Inn**. The building looks like a generic midrange hotel, and, well, that's technically what it is. But the modern rooms are comfy and smartly decorated, and they're a bargain for the money.

Head out Hwy 126 the next day about an hour east to ❾ **Terwilliger Hot Springs**, also known as Cougar Hot

DARE TO GO BARE?

Keep in mind the rules of etiquette before stripping down at a hot springs. At resorts, swimwear is expected. At primitive hot springs, there's a stronger tradition of nudity, but whoever arrives first usually sets the tone. If you want to get naked, ask if the other person minds; if they do, go for a hike till they're done. You can still be fined for nudity, but it's not likely unless someone complains.

Springs, in a picturesque canyon in the Willamette National Forest. "The water flows through a series of pools, getting cooler as it goes, so you can find the right temperature," says Gersh-Young. "It's one of the prettiest places you can soak in the Pacific Northwest."

Almost directly south (most easily accessed by backtracking to Eugene) are a pair of primitive springs you can hit in one trip. About 10 miles east of Oakridge, ❿ **McCredie Hot Springs** has a "strong skinny-dipping tradition," despite the fact it's right off the highway. Northeast of Oakridge, you'll find **⑪ Meditation Pool Warm Spring.** Gersh-Young says, "Meditation is absolutely charming. It's an easy walk in, it's not super hot, even in the summer, and it doesn't seem to be terribly over-populated."

If you like to combine hiking, soaking, and a little height-induced adrenaline rush, head south to Roseburg then east on Hwy 138 to the Umpqua National Forest, where, at the end of a beautiful tree-lined hike, you'll find **⑫ Umpqua Hot Springs.** According to Gersh-Young, "It's really lovely up there, on a rocky bluff overlooking the Umpqua River. It also gets really crowded on summer weekends, so bring a swimsuit and be prepared to wait your turn."

EXPLORING UMPQUA

Springs are known for soothing weary muscles, so earn your soak at Umpqua by starting with a hike – it is in a national forest, after all – where you'll be treated to lush, old-growth forest and waterfalls punctuating the landscape. Half a mile from the parking lot is the scenic **North Umpqua trail.** Also nearby is **Toketee Falls,** which drops off an 80ft cliff. And a couple of miles upstream is 272ft **Watson Falls,** accessible by a quarter-mile trail.

From Umpqua, you could spend the night in Roseburg at **⑬ Hokanson's Guest House,** a charming, Victorian inn filled with antiques, quilts, and claw-foot tubs. Then grab a bite at the **⑭ Roseburg Station Pub & Brewery,** a funky, colorful eatery located in the former train depot. Or, in keeping with the water theme, you could make your way down to stunning Crater Lake and spend the night at the rustic **⑮ Crater Lake Lodge.** The rooms are nothing fancy, but the stunning views from the lake-facing rooms are some of the prettiest in the state. keeping the water theme firmly in mind. Either route is almost the exact same distance to your next stop, Ashland.

Wrap up your trip with one final soak at the **⑯ Lithia Springs Inn.** Located right on a natural hot spring, this bed and breakfast pumps 100° mineral water right into tubs in your room. All of the water is spring-supplied, so be prepared if you're one of those people who thinks water should be flavorless and odorless. It's a relaxing end of a relaxing trip, and by now you should feel thoroughly floppy and well soaked.

Mariella Krause

TRIP INFORMATION

GETTING THERE
North of Seattle, take the ferry from Edmonds to Kingston, then drive about 100 miles further via Hwys 104 and 101 to Olympic National Park.

DO

Bagby Hot Springs
From Hwy 224, go south on Clackamas River Rd, right onto NF-63, right onto Bagby Rd (NF-70) and go another 7 miles. **Near Estacada, OR; Northwest Forest Pass required**

Goldmyer Hot Springs
They're protective of the directions, which you'll get when you make your reservations. ☎ 206-789-5631; www.goldmyer.org; **Near North Bend, WA; $15 per day (noon to noon)**

McCredie Hot Springs
A popular highway pit stop, this spring's is just off of Hwy 58; park on the right just past the 45-mile marker. **Near Oakridge, OR;** ☾ **dawn-dusk**

Meditation Pool Warm Spring
From Oakridge, go northeast 9 miles on Salmon Creek Rd to NF-1934. Look for sign marked "Warm Springs Trail No. 3582." **Near Oakridge, OR;** ☾ **dawn-dusk**

Olympic Hot Springs
From Hwy 101, go south on Olympic Hot Springs Rd till it ends, then park and follow the old road 2.2 miles. ☎ 360-565-3130; **Olympic National Park, WA; per vehicle $15**

Terwilliger Hot Springs
This wildly popular spring is on the west side of Cougar Reservoir; from Hwy 126, go south on NF-19. ☎ 541-822-2281; **Aufderheide Memorial Dr near Blue River, OR;** ☾ **dawn-dusk Fri-Wed; $5 per day**

Umpqua Hot Springs
From Hwy 138, turn north on FR-34, then right on Thorn Prairie Rd; parking is 2 miles further. **Umpqua National Forest, OR; Northwest Forest pass $5**

EAT

McMenamins North Bank
While you're not sitting in the water, you can still sit near it. ☎ 541-343-5622; **22 Club Rd, Eugene, OR; mains $7-17;** ☾ **11am-11pm Mon-Thu, to midnight Fri-Sat, noon-11pm Sun**

Roseburg Station Pub
All aboard for this brewpub located in the former train depot. ☎ 541-672-1934; **700 SE Sheridan St, Roseburg, WA; mains $7-11;** ☾ **11am-11pm Mon-Thu, to midnight Fri-Sat, to 10pm Sun**

SLEEP

Bonneville Hot Springs Resort
This beautiful resort is modern, luxurious, and even kind of romantic. ☎ 866-459-1678; www.bonnevilleresort.com; **1252 E Cascade Dr, Bonneville, WA; r $179-289**

Carson Hot Springs Resort
Rooms aren't perfect, but this historic resort offers bathers an old-fashioned soak. ☎ 509-427-8292; www.carsonhotsprings .com; **372 St Martins Rd, Carson, WA; r $75-85**

Crater Lake Lodge
The rooms aren't much to look at, but the crater sure is. ☎ 541-594-2255; www.crater lakelodges.com; **Crater Lake National Park, OR; r $148-278;** ☾ **late May–mid-Oct**

Lithia Springs Inn
Your room might have a mural or heart-shaped tub, but it will definitely have mineral water. ☎ 800-482-7128; www.ashlandinn .com; **2165 W Jackson Rd, Ashland, OR; r $149-249**

Phoenix Inn
Fresh and modern rooms and a generous breakfast make this minichain a great value option. ☎ 541-344-0001; www.phoenixinn

ICONIC
TRIPS

.com; 850 Franklin Rd, Eugene, OR;
r $119-269

Sol Duc Hot Springs Resort
A great base for soaking and exploring
Olympic National Park. ☎ 360-327-3583;
www.visitsolduc.com; 12076 Sol Duc Hot

Springs Rd, Port Angeles, WA; r $141-299,
RV sites $25

USEFUL WEBSITES
www.soakersforum.com
www.soakersbible.com

LINK YOUR TRIP

www.lonelyplanet.com/trip-planner

Whistle-Stop Brewery Tour

WHY GO Despite the coffee explosion and inroads made by the wine industry, beer – microbrewed beer – is still the Pacific Northwest's definitive beverage. It therefore follows that a brewery tour is the region's definitive trip. But rather than tearing across the region by car, travel by train. Best of all: no designated driver necessary.

TIME
10 days

DISTANCE
466 miles

BEST TIME TO GO
Apr – Oct

START
Eugene, OR

END
Vancouver, BC

ALSO GOOD FOR

FOOD &
DRINK

With more microbreweries than any region in the US, the Pacific Northwest is heaven on earth for beer drinkers. Name a town that's halfway worth visiting, and odds are it has a brewery. But that makes crafting a brewery tour an impossible task. So we wondered, what would really make a brewery tour great? Answering took all of thirty seconds: Not having to drive. Of course, riding the bus in the US is the traveler's equivalent of quaffing flat beer, which left one option: the train. So here you have it, the no-car-is-necessary, environmentally friendly, Pacific Northwest whistle-stop brewery tour.

Thanks to Amtrak's *Cascades* and *Coast Starlight* train routes, you can ride the rails all the way up the western flanks of the Pacific Northwest. For the sake of sampling beer, this tour begins in Eugene, OR (the southern terminus of the *Cascades* route) and ends in Vancouver, BC, the northern terminus of both routes. But first, a few logistics: Purchase your tickets by leg (ie Eugene to Portland, Portland to Centralia) ahead of time to save yourself money and guarantee you get a seat. You can change your ticket anytime (simply call up Amtrak), but you'll be charged additionally if the fare has gone up (fares get higher the closer you get to the day of travel).

Enough train talk. How about ❶ **Eugene**? With its vibrant mix of university students, track stars in training, and good ol', thirsty

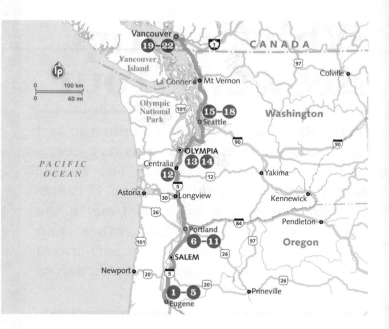

working-class folks, it's no wonder the town is home to several brewpubs. Make your way first to the ❷ **Eugene City Brewery**. Although it's owned by Rogue Ales (one of Oregon's largest breweries), Eugene City brews its own beers, too, and always has at least four of them available on tap. The other 31 taps (count 'em) are mostly Rogue Ales flavors with a few guest taps thrown in for fun. For happy hour, head to the ❸ **Starlight Lounge**, where you can quaff Ninkasi Brewing's Total Domination IPA and five other Ninkasi beers for a measly $2 a pint. (Ninkasi Brewing is production-only, and the Starlight pours the best selection of its beer). Save room for a pint at ❹ **Steelhead Brewing Co**, which brews much better beer than its run-of-the-mill dining room and bar area might suggest. At the end of the night, taxi on over to ❺ **C'est La Vie Inn**, a gorgeous B&B in a converted Victorian home.

From Eugene, ride up to the handsome Union Station in ❻ **Portland** and take a bus or taxi across the Willamette River to the ❼ **Bluebird Guesthouse**, in Southeast Portland. Situated on a happening stretch of SE Division St, the guesthouse offers modest but immaculate rooms (most with shared bathrooms) in a converted Arts and Crafts home. Visitors tend to gravitate toward downtown, but hunkering down in the southeast will allow you to hit some of Portland's best breweries without having to taxi all over the city. Plus, SE Hawthorne Blvd and SE Division St are packed with shops, cafés, restaurants and pubs.

First hit **8** **Hopworks Urban Brewery**, a new one on the Portland scene. Likely Bridgetown's most sustainable brewery, Hopworks composts all of its brewing waste, serves food made from organic, locally sourced products and, not surprisingly, pours organic beer. Long before Hopworks was even a notion, however, there was **9** **Roots Organic Brewery**. Opened in 2005, this was Oregon's first certified-organic brewery, and you should probably sidle in to pay your respects (sipping a pint of eXXXcalibur Imperial Stout is probably the best way to do so). Plus, its wooden surfboard tap handles are undoubtedly the coolest around.

Only four blocks away, in a refurbished warehouse, lies **10** **Lucky Labrador Brew Pub**. Around since 1994, Lucky Lab pours three to five of its own brews, plus a guest beer, and serves sandwiches salads and bento boxes. And if you want to taste a wide variety of beers in one great spot, head six blocks up to **11** **Green Dragon Bistro & Brewpub**. It's inside a converted warehouse, now filled with picnic tables and an expansive wooden bar. During summer, the big roll-down doors get rolled up, making sunny afternoons prime times to drop in for a pint.

SPIN CYCLE

Traveling by train means you're car-less once you get wherever you're going. Portland, Seattle and Vancouver all have great public bus systems, but why not rent a bike? In Southeast Portland, head to the cooperative **Citybikes Annex** (www.citybikes.coop) or, for something closer to Bluebird Guesthouse, **Veloce Bicycles** (www.velocebicycles.com). For something weirder try **Clevercycles** (http://clevercycles .com). In Seattle, try **Montlake Bicycle Shop** (www.montlakebike.com), about 2 miles north of the Gaslight Inn. In Vancouver, head to **Reckless** (www.rektek.com), which has shops on either side of Granville Island.

From Portland, it's two hours by train to Centralia, home of the McMenamin Brothers' **12** **Olympic Club Hotel**. One of Washington's funkiest and most innovative gathering spots, the legendary Olympic Club dates from 1908 when it was billed as a "gentlemen's resort" designed to satisfy the various needs of local miners and loggers. Now it's a boisterous brewpub, billiard hall, restaurant, hotel and movie theater all rolled into one. And it's a great reason to spend the night in little old Centralia.

The following day (or the same day, if you plan it right), make the 21-minute hop north to Olympia and hit the cozy **13** **Fish Tale BrewPub**, where you can drink the beers and ciders brewed by Washington's second-largest brewery, Fish Brewing Company. The brewpub pours the company's Fish Tale Ales, Leavenworth Beers and Spire Mountain Ciders. They're all organic. If you need to hole up in Olympia for the night, do so at the **14** **Olympia Inn**. The no-frills rooms have the usual mod cons, but the real advantage is you're situated just blocks from both the State Capitol complex and the downtown coffee bars, and only eight blocks from the brewpub.

From Olympia, it's a short train ride north to King Street Station, on the southern edge of downtown **⑮ Seattle**. Head first to the **⑯ Gaslight Inn**, about 2 miles away on Capitol Hill, and drop your bags. The Gaslight is a magnificently restored turn-of-the-20th-century home with touches including sleigh- and four-poster beds, plush chairs, and antique furniture. From there it's only five blocks to **⑰ Elysian Brewing Co**, to which you should walk immediately. Knock back a pint of crisp, cold Zephyrus Pilsner while feasting on a juicy hamburger, and then wander over toward the corner of Broadway and E John St for some of Seattle's funkiest shopping and best people-watching. Then tromp down to Pike Place Market and brave the tourists (it's worth it if you've never been there) before heading into **⑱ Pike Pub & Brewing**, where you can order a six-beer tasting flight, thus saving yourself the need to drink 96oz of beer.

DETOUR Detour back in time by getting off the train at Skagit Station in Mt Vernon (about 1½ hours north of Seattle), and taking bus No 615 west to the historic town of La Conner, on Skagit Bay. Undisturbed by modern development, La Conner itself is one of the Lower Skagit River Valley's oldest trading posts and still retains much of its 19th-century charm. When you arrive, head to **La Conner Brewing Co** (www.laconnerbrew .com), where you can enjoy your IPA with wood-fired pizza. Spend the night at the beautiful **Queen of the Valley Inn** (www.queenofthe valleyinn.com).

This is key, considering the only train to **⑲ Vancouver** departs at 7:40am. The good news is, four hours later you end up in a beautiful city with plenty to explore, including a half-dozen breweries. Of these, put **⑳ Granville Island Brewing** first on your list, if only to allow yourself one brewery tour on the trip. Three times a day, guides walk visitors through the brewery before depositing them in the taproom for samples of the beer, all of which are named after Vancouver neighborhoods. Since you're on the island, wander over to the Granville Island Hotel, which just happens to be home to the **㉑ Dockside Restaurant & Brewing Co**. The beer is undoubtedly delicious, but this place is really about the patio, which has stunning views of False Creek and downtown Vancouver.

Another Vancouver institution is **㉒ Steamworks Brewing Co**, in Gastown. In the cavernous downstairs section of this big converted brick warehouse, folks get noisy over pints of Lions Gate Lager, while, upstairs, they lounge in cushy leather seats and take in the views across to the North Shore. It's a spectacular spot, and well worth the train ride north.

Danny Palmerlee

TRIP INFORMATION

GETTING THERE
When traveling nonstop between Eugene and Vancouver, you must do the Seattle-Vancouver leg by bus, unless you spend a night in Seattle.

EATING & DRINKING

Dockside Restaurant & Brewing Co
Brewery restaurant with a fabulous patio; inside the outstanding Granville Island Hotel. ☎ 604-685-7070; www.docksidebrewing.com; 1253 Johnston St, Vancouver, BC; mains $14-30; ☻ 7am-10pm, lounge 5pm-midnight; ♿

Elysian Brewing Co
Offers 15 beers on tap, usually including a barley wine and a Hefeweizen. ☎ 206-860-1920; www.elysianbrewing.com; 1221 E Pike St, Seattle, WA; mains $9-12; ☻ 11:30am-2am Mon-Fri, noon-2am Sat & Sun

Eugene City Brewery
Inside a historic brewery building owned by Oregon's Rogue Ales; expansive menu. ☎ 541-345-4155; www.rogue.com; 844 Olive Street, Eugene, OR; mains $8-15; ☻ 11am-11pm Mon-Thu, 11am-midnight Fri & Sat; 11am-10pm Sun; ♿

Fish Tale BrewPub
Fourteen taps, plus a huge menu, including emu burgers, oyster burgers, beef burgers, salads and sandwiches. ☎ 360-943-3650; www.fishbrewing.com; 515 Jefferson St, Olympia, WA; mains $7-13; ☻ 11am-midnight Mon-Sat, noon-10pm Sun

Granville Island Brewing
Tours of this classic Vancouver brewery include four samples. Or just hit the taproom. ☎ 604-687-2739; www.gib.ca; 1441 Cartwright St, Vancouver, BC; tours $9.75; ☻ tours noon, 2pm & 4pm, taproom noon-8pm

Green Dragon Bistro & Brewpub
Excellent taproom and restaurant in a spacious converted warehouse. ☎ 503-517-0606; www.pdxgreendragon.com; 928 SE 9th St, Portland, OR; mains $6-10; ☻ 11am-11pm Sun-Wed, 11am-2am Thu-Sat; ♿

Hopworks Urban Brewery
Slick brewery with penchant for sustainability and great pizza. ☎ 503-232-4677; www.hopworksbeer.com; 2944 SE Powell Blvd, Portland, OR; pizzas $16-25; ☻ 11am-11pm Sun-Thu, 11am-midnight Fri & Sat; ♿

Lucky Labrador Brew Pub
Converted warehouse with brewery on site and a big dog-friendly back patio. Limited menu. Kids permitted till 9pm. ☎ 503-236-3555; www.luckylab.com; 915 SE Hawthorne, Portland, OR; ☻ 11am-midnight Mon-Sat, noon-10pm Sun; ♿ □

Pike Pub & Brewing
Serves great burgers, pizzas, brews in a funky neo-industrial space. ☎ 206-622-6044; www.pikebrewing.com; 1415 1st Ave, Seattle, WA; sandwiches $9-14, pizza from $14.95; ☻ 11am-11pm, 11am-midnight Fri & Sat; ♿

Roots Organic Brewery
Aim for $2.50 Tuesdays (when pints cost that all day): definitely *the* day to go. ☎ 503-235-7668; www.rootsorganicbrewing.com; 1520 7th Ave, Portland, OR; ☻ 3-11pm Mon, 11:30am-11pm Tue-Thu, 11:30am-midnight Fri, noon-1am Sat, noon-10pm Sun

Starlight Lounge
Eugene's Ninkasi Brewing is production only, but you'll find six of its beers on tap here. Happy hour runs 4 to 7pm. ☎ 541-343-3204; 830 Olive St, Eugene, OR; ☻ 4pm-2:30am

Steamworks Brewing Co
A giant Gastown microbrewery and a favorite place for the city's after-office crowd. Outstanding food. ☎ 604-689-2739; www.steamworks.com; 375 Water St, Vancouver, BC; mains $14-22; ☻ 11:30am-midnight Sun-Wed, 11:30am-1am Thu-Sat

Steelhead Brewing Co
Local fave with standard pub fare, plus a dozen homemade brews. ☎ 541-686-2739; www.steelheadbrewery.com; 199 E 5th Ave, Eugene, OR; mains $7-10; ☻ 11:30am-11:30pm Sun-Thu, to 1am Fri & Sat

SLEEPING

Bluebird Guesthouse
Seven comfy rooms, two with private bath; superb common areas, one fire place.

☎ 503-238-4333, 866-717-4333; www
.bluebirdguesthouse.com; 3517 SE Division,
Portland, OR; r $50-90

C'est La Vie Inn
Neighborhood show-stopper with antique
furniture, living room, dining room and four
tastefully appointed guest rooms. ☎ 541-
302-3014; www.cestlavieinn.com; 1006
Taylor St, Eugene, OR; r $125-250

Gaslight Inn
Offers 15 rooms in two neighboring homes.
In summer, it's refreshing to dive into the
outdoor pool or just hang out on the sun
deck. ☎ 206-325-3654; www.gaslight-inn
.com; 1727 15th Ave, Seattle, WA; r $88-158

Olympic Club Hotel
McMenamin Brothers masterpiece offering
groovy old rooms with shared bathrooms.
It's walking distance from the train station.
☎ 360-736-5164; www.mcmenamins.com;
112 N Tower Ave, Centralia, WA; r $40-80

Olympia Inn
This unpretentious downtown hotel is all
about location. Rooms are clean and have
fridge, microwave and cable TV. ☎ 360-352-
8533; 909 Capitol Way S, Olympia, WA; r $57

USEFUL WEBSITES
www.amtrakcascades.com
www.amtrak.com

LINK YOUR TRIP
www.lonelyplanet.com/trip-planner

On the Trail of Lewis & Clark

WHY GO Don your buckskins and pack your best whittling knife for this historic trip in the footsteps of America's greatest explorers. This snippet traverses enough territory to give you a taster of expedition life without its saddle sores. What the Corps took a month to cover you can now drive in four days.

TIME
3 – 4 days

DISTANCE
400 miles

BEST TIME TO GO
Year-round

START
Pasco, WA

END
Seaside, OR

ALSO GOOD FOR

HISTORY & CULTURE

It's a fairly arbitrary decision where to join the Lewis & Clark Trail but the ❶ **Sacajawea Interpretive Center**, at the confluence of the Snake and Columbia Rivers, just southeast of the Tri-Cities, is a logical choice. The arrival of the Corps of Discovery here on 16 October, 1805 marked a milestone achievement on its quest to map a river route to the Pacific. After a greeting by 200 Indians singing and drumming in a half circle, the band camped at this spot for two days, trading clothing for dried salmon.

As you continue south and west through dusty sagebrush country you'll pass a couple of minor sites – Wallua Gap, where the Corps first spotted Mt Hood (meaning they were finally back on the map) and the volcanic bluff of Hat Rock, first named by William Clark – before crossing the Columbia to reach the ❷ **Maryhill Museum of Art**, a delightful place with a small Lewis and Clark display. The peaceful gardens here are perfect for a classy picnic amid the exotic peacock cries. Interpretive signs point you to fine views down the Columbia Gorge to the riverside spot (now a state park) where Meriwether Lewis and Clark camped on 21 October, 1805. The park is just one of several along this trip where you can pitch a tent within a few hundred yards of the Corps' original camp.

A vivid imagination can be as important as sunscreen when following the "Trail." One example of this is the turnout 5 miles west of the museum that overlooks what was once the Indian salmon fishing center

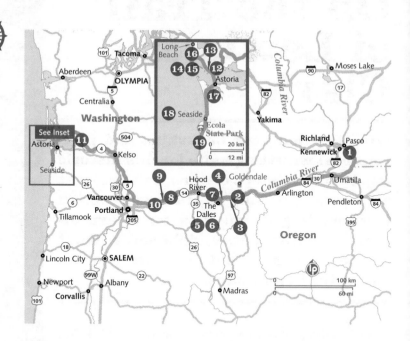

of **3** **Celilo Falls**. The explorers spent two days here in late October 1805, lowering their canoes down the crashing falls on elk-skin ropes. A century and a half later the rising waters of the dammed Columbia drowned the falls, rendering much of Clark's description of the region unrecognizable.

Indian tribes like the Nez Perce, Clatsop and Walla Walla were essential to the success of the Lewis and Clark expedition, supplying them not only with food but also horses and guides. One of the best places to view tangible traces of the region's rich Native American heritage is the Temani Pesh-wa (Written on Rocks) Trail at **4** **Horsethief Lake State Park**, which highlights the region's best petroglyphs. Reserve a spot in advance on the free guided tours on Friday and Saturday to view the famous but fragile pictograph of the god Tsagagalal (She Who Watches).

Of the several Lewis and Clark–related museums along this stretch of the Columbia, the best is probably the **5** **Columbia Gorge Discovery Center**, on the western edge of The Dalles. Its displays detail the 30 tons of equipment the Corps dragged across the continent and the animals they had to kill (including 190 dogs and a ferret). Kids will get a kick from dressing up in Lewis and Clark period costume. Back in town, you can keep the Wild West vibe going at historic **6** **Baldwin Saloon**, a onetime bar, brothel, steamboat office and coffin storage warehouse that's been going since 1876. Take a booth for dinner or saddle up to the mahogany bar to enjoy the live piano music weekends.

You can continue west from The Dalles on either side of the Columbia (the expedition traveled straight down the middle by canoe), though we suggest the slower but more scenic southern Oregon Rte 30 to Hood River via the Rowena Loops. En route look for the views down to macabre **7** **Memaloose Island**, once a burial site for Native Americans who left their dead here in canoes of cedar (Memaloose means "to die" in Chinook).

At this stage in their trip Lewis and Clark were flea-infested and half-starved from a diet of dog meat and starchy, potato-like wapto roots. If a mere 180 miles of driving has left you in a similar state, consider a stop at **8** **Bonneville Hot Springs Resort**, a luxurious hotel and mineral-fed pool complex situated just a mile or two east of Beacon Rock. We're pretty sure Lewis would have gone for the restorative eucalyptus wrap, had he the chance. This isn't quite as flippant as it sounds: Native Americans had already been using the therapeutic waters of the hot spring for centuries when the Corps unknowingly paddled past. Get here from Hood River by heading west for 32 miles along Rte 14, Washington's officially designated "Lewis & Clark Hwy."

On November 2, 1805, a day after passing modern Bonneville, Clark wrote about a remarkable 848ft-tall monolith he called Beaten Rock, changing the name on his return to **9** **Beacon Rock**. Just over a century later Henry Biddle bought the rock for the bargain price of $1 (!) and you can still hike his snaking 0.75-mile trail to the top of the former lava plug. As you enjoy the wonderful views, ponder the fact that you have effectively climbed up the *inside* of an ancient volcano. For the Corps the rock brought a momentous discovery, for it was here that the excited duo first noticed the tide, proving at last they were finally nearing their goal of crossing the American continent.

> **DETOUR** Just 10 miles north of Maryhill lies a nighttime treat in the shape of the **Goldendale Observatory State Park** (www.perr.com/gosp.html), the largest telescope dedicated solely to amateur astronomers. Come at dark (the site is open until midnight Wednesday to Sunday in summer) and state park ranger Steve Stout will take you on a guided tour of space, past moon craters to distant nebulas and quasars, quite possibly altering forever your perception of the universe. Not bad for a free evening's entertainment.

Your next stop along Rte 14 should be the fantastic views of the flood-carved gorge and its impressive cascades from the **10** **Cape Horn overview**. From here it's a straight shot on I-5 to Kelso and then over the Lewis & Clark Bridge to parallel the Columbia River westward on Hwy 4.

For most of their trip down the Columbia River, Lewis and Clark traveled not on foot but by canoe. There's nowhere better to paddle in the Corps' canoe wake than at the **11** **Skamokawa Center**, which offers one- or two-day kayak tours to Grays Bay or Pillar Rock, where Clark wrote "Great joy in camp we are in view of the Ocian, this great Pacific Octean which we been So long anxious to See" (November 7, 1805).

Just north of the Astoria Bridge a turnout marks **12** **Dismal Nitch**, where the drenched duo were stuck in a pounding weeklong storm that Clark described as "the most disagreeable time I have ever experienced." The Corps finally managed to make camp at **13** **Station Camp**, now an innocuous highway pullout, and stayed for 10 days while the two leaders, no doubt sick of each other by now, separately explored the headlands around Cape Disappointment. It was here that the Corps voted on where to spend the winter; the first time an Indian woman and black slave were known to cast a "vote."

> **DETOUR**
>
> If you're suffering from Lewis and Clark overload, make the 4-mile detour from Cape Disappointment to **Marsh's Free Museum** (www.marshs freemuseum.com) in Long Beach. The antique peep shows are entertaining enough, but dig through the shadows and you'll find darker treasures, from real shrunken heads and a rare Wyoming werewolf to Jake, the half-man, half-alligator who doubles as the store's horrifying mascot. It's worth coming here just to hear the sales assistant cry out "Doris, there's a gentleman here asking about the bowl made from human skin." Lewis and Clark would've loved it.

There's a tangible feeling of excitement as you pull into **14** **Cape Disappointment State Park**, make the short ascent of Mackenzie Hill in Clark's footprints and catch your first true sight of the Pacific. Time your visit here for the third weekend in July and you can go one better and watch Clark stroll out of the woods and set up his camp as part of the annual living history reenactment. (Don't bother asking him if you can take his photo though, as he won't know about anything that's happened since 1805!) Their arrival at the edge of the continent marked the achievement of the expedition's epic goal and you can almost hear the sighs of relief over two centuries later.

After a stroll on Waikiki Beach, head up to the fine museum at the **15** **Lewis & Clark Interpretive Center**, where you'll learn everything from how to use an octant to what kind of underpants Lewis wore (seriously). Kids will love the interactive exhibits, while adults can pore over the reproduction elk-hide diaries and the razor box hand-carved by Sacagawea. Brush up on your fire-making techniques at the park's nightly campfire talks before drifting to sleep in your campsite to the background roar of the Pacific. Alternatively, celebrate your Pacific arrival by retracing Clark's footsteps to the town of Seaview, where dinner and a microbrew awaits at the excellent **16** **Depot Restaurant**.

After 18 months and 4000 miles of travel, Lewis and Clark took a well-deserved rest over the winter of 1805–06 at **17** **Fort Clatsop**, the last major site on the Lewis & Clark Trail, 5 miles south of Astoria. Visitors can stroll down to the canoe landing and investigate the replica wooden fort where the Corps sheltered from 96 days of rain. Best of all are the buckskin-clad rangers who wander the camp between mid-June and Labor Day sewing moccasins (the Corps stockpiled an impressive 340 pairs for their return trip), tanning leather and firing their muskets.

Hardcore (hardcorps?) fans won't leave without ticking off the small monument, on the corner of Beach Dr and Lewis & Clark Way, in the town of ⑱ **Seaside** that marks the spot where the Corps spent weeks in early 1806 boiling seawater day and night to make salt for their return journey. (As one ranger told us "salt takes on an added significance when your diet consists largely of rotting elk meat.") News of a huge beached whale ("that monstrous fish") lured Lewis and Sacagawea, the expedition's Shoshone interpreter and only female, further south through what is now Ecola (Whale) State Park on January 6, 1806, and they returned with 300lb of blubber.

ASK A LOCAL

"Three Lewis and Clark–related 'Living History' events take place each year – the **Saltmakers' return at Seaside** (third weekend in August), **Clark's Camp** (third weekend in July), and between Christmas and New Year we recreate **Christmas at Fort Clatsop**. When people interact and experience a real conversation with historical figures like Lewis and Clark, they live for a moment in another time – it's one of the most powerful ways to experience history."

Aaron Webster, Washington State Parks Interpretive Specialist and member of the Pacific Northwest Living Historians

The stunning views of Ecola's ⑲ **Haystack Rock** mark a fitting end to this itinerary but the Corps still faced an arduous six-month return trip back across the continent. Here's an interesting postscript: Within three years of his return Lewis was dead, aged 35, most likely a suicide.
Bradley Mayhew

ICONIC TRIPS

TRIP INFORMATION

GETTING THERE
From Seattle take I-90 southeast and then follow I-82 and I-182 for 210 miles to Exit 102. Follow I-182 and Hwy 12 for 18 miles south of Pasco to the signed Sacajawea State Park.

DO
Columbia Gorge Discovery Center
This top-notch regional museum screens daily Lewis and Clark movies. ☎ 541-296-8600; www.gorgediscovery.org; 5000 Discovery Dr, The Dalles, OR; adult/child/senior $8/4/7; 9am-5pm;

Fort Clatsop
Worth half a day for its exhibits, hiking trails and reconstructed fort. Part of the Lewis & Clark National Historic Park. ☎ 503-861-2471; www.nps.gov/lewi; adult/child $5/2; 9am-6pm Jun-Aug, to 5pm Sep-May;

Horsethief Lake State Park
Riverside camping, picnic sites, a boat launch and local rock climbing. ☎ 509-767-1159; www.parks.wa.gov; Hwy 14, milepost 85, WA; pictograph tour 10am Fri & Sat Apr-Oct;

Lewis & Clark Interpretive Center
Excellent interactive displays and great views over the "graveyard of the Pacific." ☎ 360-642-3029; Camp Disappointment State Park, Hwy 100, WA; adult/youth $5/2.50; 10am-5pm;

Maryhill Museum of Art
An eclectic collection of Native American baskets, Russian icons and Rodin drawings fills this former mansion. ☎ 509-733-3733; www.maryhillmuseum.org; 35 Maryhill Museum Dr, Goldendale, WA; adult/child/senior $7/2/6; 9am-5pm Mar 15-Nov 15

Sacajawea Interpretive Center
Stroke an otter pelt and learn why the expedition needed 100 gallons of whiskey at this center celebrating the Corps' Shoshone interpreter. ☎ 509-545-2361; Sacajawea State Park, Pasco, WA; admission free; 10am-5pm late Mar-Nov 1;

Skamokawa Center
Kayak rental and tours that faithfully follow the Corps' river route past former Indian trading camps and nature reserves. ☎ 888-920-2777; www.skamokawakayak.com; 1391 Rte 4, Skamokawa, WA; 1-/2-day tour $90/195

EAT & DRINK
Baldwin Saloon
No longer spit and sawdust but still straightforward fare, plus decadent desserts. ☎ 541-296-5666; www.baldwinsaloon.com; 205 Court St, The Dalles, OR; lunch/dinner mains from $10/20; 11am-10pm, closed Sun

Depot Restaurant
Classy but casual dining with weekly gourmet burger nights. ☎ 360-642-7880; www.depot restaurantdining.com; 1208 38th Pl, Seaview, WA; mains $19-28; 5-11pm Wed-Mon

SLEEP
Bonneville Hot Springs Resort
Recover from the rigors of the trail at this plush hotel, pool and spa complex. Some rooms have private hot tubs. ☎ 866-459-1678; www.bon nevilleresort.com; 1252 E Cascade Dr, North Bonneville, WA; r $179-289

Cape Disappointment State Park
Camp like Clark at beachside sites, or splash out on one of three charming lighthouse keepers' residences. ☎ 360-642-3078; www .parks.wa.gov; Hwy 100, WA; tent sites $19-22, RV sites $25-31, yurts & cabins $45-50, lighthouse residences $133-377;

USEFUL WEBSITES
www.lewisandclarktrail.com

www.parks.wa.gov/lewisandclark

www.lonelyplanet.com/trip-planner

LINK YOUR TRIP

Eccentric Pacific Northwest

WHY GO With chain hotels and franchise restaurants homogenizing America, finding out what's unique about an area is what travel is all about. From sea lions to velvet paintings, esoteric museums to offbeat hotels, discover the quirky, interesting and downright odd places that give the Pacific Northwest its own special flavor.

Some attractions suck you in more than others, but the ❶ **Oregon Vortex** in Gold Hill has gravitational pull on its side, luring visitors with its unexplained phenomena: How did that broom stand up on its own? Why did that guy look shorter when he changed places with his girlfriend? What made that water run uphill? Detractors try to explain away the mysterious events that have drawn crowds since the 1930s, but it just sounds like, "Blah, blah, physics, blah." Isn't it more fun to just believe?

Once you've pulled yourself out of the Vortex's grasp, head north and follow Hwys 138 and 38 west to the coast, where you'll find an entirely different type of natural attraction: Florence's ❷ **Sea Lion Caves**. First, you get to pretend you're Batman and take an elevator 200 feet down into a cave. Then you get to watch the sea lions in their natural amphitheatre. These vociferous creatures put on a nonstop show, with their wild barking noise "Ort! Ort! Ort!" bouncing off the domed ceiling.

While perhaps not as exciting as playing the Caped Crusader, just half a mile further up the coast you can play lighthouse keeper for a night at the ❸ **Heceta Head Lighthouse B&B**. You don't actually stay in the lighthouse – it's way too bright to get any sleep – but you can stay in the keeper's cottage and pretend you're saving sailors from certain doom.

TIME
5 – 6 days

DISTANCE
692 miles

BEST TIME TO GO
Mar – Sep

START
Gold Hill, OR

END
Sequim, WA

ALSO GOOD FOR

OFFBEAT

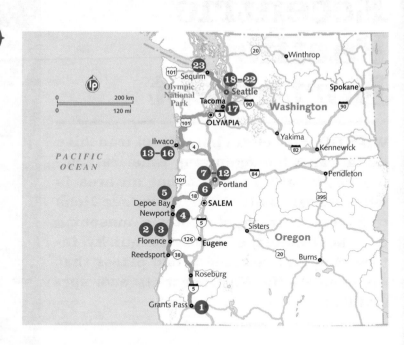

Just up the coast in Newport, you can also spend the night in a stern wheel riverboat – the only one in the US that you can sleep aboard, unless you count nodding off at a Missouri casino. The rooms are modest at the **4** **Newport Belle B&B**, but the exterior has a Mark Twain kind of charm that's straight out of the late 1800s.

"...no one can do eccentric quite like an obsessive-compulsive billionaire."

For dinner, head north to **5** **Gracie's Sea Hag Restaurant & Lounge** in Depoe Bay. Several times a night you'll hear a sound that rivals the sea lions coming from the lounge, as the barmaids use wooden sticks to play choreographed numbers on liquor bottles. It's good, noisy fun, kind of like a small-town version of Coyote Ugly.

Next, travel 60 miles inland for proof that no one can do eccentric quite like an obsessive-compulsive billionaire. The **6** **Evergreen Aviation & Space Museum** is the home of the *Spruce Goose*, a famous craft that was the dubious brainchild of Howard Hughes. He spent millions to build the world's largest flying boat – which would've been great, except it only flew once. For about a mile. Stand in awe and think of the dumbest thing you ever wasted money on, knowing there's no way it tops this extravagant mistake.

Next, head up to **7** **Portland** for one of the most fun places you'll ever spend the night, the **8** **Kennedy School**. Located in a former elementary school, this hotel has soaring ceilings, coatrooms for closets, and chalkboards in the guest rooms. Play hooky in the school halls and check out the cool art. Have dinner and drinks in the school cafeteria, now the lively **9 Courtyard Restaurant**. Or take your beer into the former gymnasium for nightly film screenings – none of which are hygiene films.

More subdued but no less unique is one of Portland's more contemplative attractions, **10 The Grotto**, a 62-acre sanctuary in the far northeast Portland, established by the Servite Friars in 1924. On the ground level, you'll find a massive shrine dedicated to Mary carved into a tall cliff wall. Take the elevator up to wander the rest of the grounds, where statues and shrines make flowers and trees do penance.

THE ORIGINAL FLYING SAUCER

In addition to hundreds of Bigfoot sightings, Mt Rainier can also claim credit for the first flying saucer sighting. Searching for a downed transport plane in the fall of 1947, Kenneth Arnold reported seeing nine discs flying in the sky. He described them as looking like a pie plate or a saucer, and the name "flying saucer" stuck as it was repeated over and over again in the press.

Also in the city's northeast, you can see Mary in a whole different light by heading to the **11 Velveteria**, a wildly impressive museum dedicated to the art of the velvet painting. Portraits of Mary and Jesus hang side by side with unicorns, sad clowns, and Elvis. The exuberant collection includes a black-light room and an ample collection of nudes.

There's plenty to see just cruising the streets of Portland, and while you're out exploring roadside attractions be sure to stop by **12 Roadside Attraction**, an eclectic bar in Southeast Portland with cheap drinks, a short menu, and kooky décor. The interior features tiki relics, an arch rescued from a Chinese restaurant, and other found objects that create a pleasingly kitschy atmosphere.

From Portland, cross into Washington and head out to the coast, where you'll find another pocket of eccentricity on the Long Beach Peninsula. Hole up at the **13 Historic Sou'wester Lodge**, a funky B&(MYOD)B – as in "Bed and Make Your Own Damn Breakfast." The lodge itself is eclectic, but it's the Trailer Classics Hodgepodge, a collection of 1950s Spartan trailers, that really sets this place apart. If you're not feeling quite that Bohemian, try the lovely **14 Inn at Harbor Village** in Ilwaco, housed in a 1928 Presbyterian church.

On the peninsula, visit **15 Marsh's Free Museum**, a quick pit stop that's half souvenir stand and half circus sideshow, starring conjoined calves and other taxidermied wonders, as well as Jake the Alligator Man, a mummified half man, half alligator tabloid star. For more lighthearted fun, drop by the **16 World Kite Museum**, one of those obscure odes to a niche interest.

From the Long Beach Peninsula, head up Highway 101 then take Hwy 5 into Tacoma, where you'll find the **⑰ Museum of Glass** in Tacoma. While it may not technically be eccentric, it's so uniquely Washington that it deserves a stop. Dale Chihuly's internationally renowned art-glass creations and his Pilchuck Glass School have made the Northwest famous for this fantastically colorful art form. Check out the Bridge of Glass outside of the museum, then venture inside to see glass doing all sorts of things you never knew it could.

From Tacoma, it's just a short hop to **⑱ Seattle**, where a whole crop of strange is just waiting to be picked. First stop is **⑲ Seattle Museum of the Mysteries**, which is light on museum and heavy on mysteries. A great place to discuss alien landings, plan your Big Foot hunt, or research what exactly happened to DB Cooper, there isn't a lot to look at it, but if you want to get to the bottom of something, this subterranean space is a good place to start.

If you want a more museum-like experience, head to the **⑳ Science Fiction Museum**. You don't have to be a fan of the genre to enjoy checking out the sheer breadth of movie costumes, television props, scale models and sci-fi weaponry, and, well, let's be honest: It attracts a crowd that's as interesting as the displays. You can pick up a sci-fi creature of your own at **㉑ Archie McPhee**, fine purveyors of novelties and accoutrements. They sell glow-in-the-dark extraterrestrials, punching nuns, and all manner of plastic spiders and sea creatures. Whether or not you actually need a yodeling pickle or a Big Foot action figure, it's fun just to wander the aisles.

ASK A LOCAL

"There's this funny little town called **Winthrop** out on Hwy 20. It was a Gold Rush town, and now it's kind of like a western theme town. There's a really old saloon there, and the buildings have an Old West feel to them, like there's about to be a shootout."

Rebecca & Donna, Kirkland, WA

So where does a hungry kitsch-hunter stop to eat? One of Seattle's quirkiest places to dine is **㉒ Bizarro Italian Cafe**, whose decor is *Alice in Wonderland* meets upside-down thrift shop. On the weekend, they pack patrons in for delicious, cheap pasta dishes served under bicycles, chandeliers, and upside-down tables hanging from the ceiling.

Finally, head toward the Olympic Peninsula on Highway 101 for an overnight stay at the quirky **㉓ Red Caboose Getaway** in Sequim. You'll get your choice of four cabooses, each with their own theme – Casey Jones, the Orient Express, the Circus, or the Western caboose – and breakfast is served in the Silver Eagle dining car.

And, really, what could be more fitting than ending with a caboose?

Mariella Krause

TRIP INFORMATION

GETTING THERE
From Portland, go south on I-5 and drive 260 miles to the town of Gold Hill.

DO
Archie McPhee
This store could easily call itself the Museum of Novelty Toys and charge admission. They're moving to the address provided mid-2009. ☎ 206-297-0240; ww.archiemcphee .com; 1300 N 45 St, Seattle, WA; ☼ 10am-7pm Mon-Sat, 11am-6pm Sun; ♿

Evergreen Aviation & Space Museum
Ironically (since it could barely fly) the Spruce Goose is the star attraction. ☎ 503-434-4180; www.sprucegoose.org; 500 NE Capt Michael King Smith Way, McMinnville, OR; adult/child $13/11; ☼ 9am-5pm

The Grotto
Less commonly (but more intimidatingly) known as the National Sanctuary of our Sorrowful Mother. ☎ 503-254-7371; www .thegrotto.org; cnr NE 85th St & Sandy Blvd, Portland, OR; lower level free, elevator $3; ☼ 9am-5pm

Marsh's Free Museum
It's free, but "museum" might be a stretch for this bizarre souvenir shop. ☎ 360-642-2188; www.marshsfreemuseum.com; 409 Pacific Ave S, Long Beach, WA; admission free; ☼ 9am-6pm; ♿

Museum of Glass
Not cups and bottles, but hand-blown art-glass creations in a kaleidoscope of colors. ☎ 253-284-4750; www.museumofglass .com; 1801 Dock St, Tacoma, WA; adult $10; ☼ 10am-5pm Mon-Sat, noon-5pm Sun

Oregon Vortex
Get sucked in by this perennial tourist attraction. ☎ 541-855-1543; www.theoregonvor tex.com; 4303 Sardine Creek L Fork Rd, Gold Hill, WA; adult/child/5 and under $9/7/free; ☼ 9am-4pm Mar-Oct (till 5pm Jun-Aug); ♿

Science Fiction Museum
Your admission also gets you into the Experience Music Project next door. ☎ 877-367-7361; www.empsfm.org; 325 N 5th Ave; adult/student/child $15/12/free; ☼ 10am-7pm

Sea Lion Caves
Noisy sea lions amuse and delight visitors to the world's largest sea cave. ☎ 541-547-3111; www.sealioncaves.com; 91560 N Hwy 101, Florence, OR; adult/child $10/$6; ☼ 9am-5:30pm with seasonal variations; ♿

Seattle Museum of the Mysteries
The truth is out there. Come to think of it, it's in here. ☎ 206-328-6499; www .seattlechatclub.org; 623 E Broadway, Seattle, WA; $2 suggested donation; ☼ call for hours

Velveteria
Sad clowns, blessed virgins and spangled pop stars hang side by side in this homage to kitsch culture. ☎ 503-233-5100; www.velveteria .com; 2448 E Burnside St, Portland, OR; admission $5; ☼ noon-5pm Thu-Sun

World Kite Museum
A breezy little niche museum that's extra kid-friendly. ☎ 360-642-4020; www.world kitemuseum.com; 303 Sid Snyder Dr, Long Beach, WA; adult/child $5/3; ☼ 11am-5pm daily May-Sep, Fri-Mon Oct-Apr; ♿

EAT & DRINK
Bizarro Italian Cafe
Their fun atmosphere and delish pasta will turn your world upside down. ☎ 206-632-7277; www.bizzarroitaliancafe.com; 1307 N 46th St, Seattle, WA; mains $16-22; ☼ 5pm-10pm

Courtyard Restaurant
The Kennedy School gets extra credit for this colorful brewpub in the former school cafeteria. ☎ 503-288-2192; www.mcmenamins .com; 5736 NE 33 Ave, Portland, OR; mains $6-19; ☼ 7am-1am

ICONIC
TRIPS

Gracie's Sea Hag Restaurant & Lounge
Seafood and bottle-playing barmaids are the specialties of the house. ☎ 541-765-2734; www.theseahag.com; 58 E Hwy 101, Depoe Bay, OR; mains $9-24; ☙ 7am-9:30pm

Roadside Attraction
This funky bar with a great patio turns found objects into art, with nary a beer sign in sight. ☎ 503-233-0743; 1000 SE 12th Ave, Portland, OR; ☙ 3pm-1am

SLEEP

Heceta Head Lighthouse B&B
You'll be glad to know the keeper's quarters comes with curtains. ☎ 866-547-3696; www.hecetalighthouse.com; 92072 Hwy 101 S, Yachats, OR; r $133-315

Historic Sou'wester Lodge
Irreverent, funky, and downright Bohemian – you'll never forget this place. ☎ 360-642-2542; www. souwesterlodge.com; 38th Pl, Seaview, WA; r $60-70, trailer $39-104

Inn at Harbor Village
This is the church, this is the steeple, open the doors, and see…your guest room.

☎ 360-642-0087; www.innatharborvillage .com; 120 NE Williams Ave, Ilwaco, WA; r $115-185

Kennedy School
Fall asleep in class at this former elementary school with an on-site theatre and brewpub. ☎ 503-249-3983; www.mcmenamins.com; 5736 NE 33rd Ave, Portland, OR; r $99-130

Newport Belle B&B
All aboard this classically styled riverboat; rooms are so-so, but the exterior's a winner. ☎ 541-867-6290; www.newportbelle .com; Dock H, South Beach Marina, Newport, OR; r $135-165

Red Caboose Getaway
Choo-choo-choose one of four themed cabooses, and take your breakfast in the old-fashioned dining car. ☎ 360-683-7350; www. redcaboosegetaway.com; 24 Old Coyote Way, Sequim, WA; r $135-205; ♿

USEFUL WEBSITES
www.roadsideamerica.com
www.roadtripamerica.com

LINK YOUR TRIP
www.lonelyplanet.com/trip-planner

Native American Traditions Tour

WHY GO Experiencing the Pacific Northwest's indigenous and First Nations traditions adds richness to any trip through the region. But don't limit yourself to museums. Follow this trip and you'll admire totem poles in tiny towns, paddle a Nuu-chah-nulth canoe across Clayoquot Sound and shack up in a teepee at a reservation resort.

① Vancouver, BC is a great place to kick off *any* trip, but, being home to the ② **UBC Museum of Anthropology** (MOA), it makes a particularly fine place to begin this one. MOA displays Canada's best collection of Northwest coast First Nations artifacts – over 5400 in total – from baskets and ceramics to traditional Haida houses. The totem poles alone, displayed against 45-foot walls of glass overlooking the ocean, are worth the admission. Later, head to ③ **Stanley Park** and check out the city's most photographed tourist attractions: the Nisga'a, Kwakwaka'wakw, Nuu-chah-nulth and Hesquiat totem poles near Brockton Point. In 2008, three welcome gateways were added to represent the Musqueam, Squamish and Tsleil-Waututh First Nations, Stanley Park's original inhabitants. Spend the night at the cheerful ④ **Buchan Hotel**, the closest good-value hotel to Stanley Park. The smiling front-desk staff are excellent and an all-around tidiness makes up for the dinged furnishing in the standard rooms; the suites are nicer.

From Vancouver, take the Horseshoe Bay Ferry to Nanaimo, on Vancouver Island, and head west along Hwy 4 to ⑤ **Tofino**. Nestled into the trees on Clayoquot Sound, Tofino is home to ⑥ **Tla-ook Cultural Adventures**, a First Nations–owned outfitter that offers guided paddles out to Meares Island in a traditional Nuu-chah-nulth dugout canoe. On the island you'll wander among old-growth trees, learning about Nuu-chah-nulth culture and the forest itself. At the end of the

TIME
3 weeks

DISTANCE
1255 miles

BEST TIME TO GO
Jun – Sep

START
Vancouver, BC

END
Warm
Springs, OR

ALSO GOOD FOR

HISTORY &
CULTURE

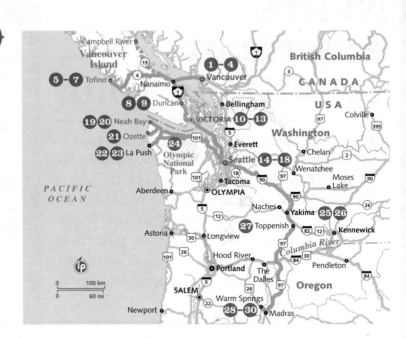

day, bed down at **7** **Gull Cottage**, a cozy, wood-scented haven set among old growth trees just a short trail walk from Chesterman Beach.

From Tofino, backtrack along Hwy 4 to and work your way down Hwy 1 to **8** **Duncan**. Wander around this former logging outpost and you'll quickly see why it's called the "City of Totems": Some 50 totem poles dot the town, including the thickest totem pole in the world, carved in the Kwakwaka'wakw style and measuring over 6ft thick. And don't miss the excellent **9** **Quw'utsun' Cultural & Conference Centre**, where you'll learn about pole carving, beading and traditions surrounding the local salmon runs.

From Duncan its 60km (37 miles) south to **10** **Victoria**, where you'll find the **11** **Royal BC Museum**, the province's best museum. There's loads to see (including dioramas and a recreated pioneer town), but make the 3rd-floor First Nations gallery a priority. Then head outside the museum to the adjacent **12** **Thunderbird Park**, where you'll find an outstanding collection of mostly Kwakwaka'wakw, Gitxsan and Haida totem poles. Spend a night or two in Victoria at the **13** **James Bay Inn**, where busy carpets and outdated furniture lend the otherwise unremarkable hotel and air of quirkiness. Then take the Victoria Clipper ferry service to **14** **Seattle**, WA.

Once in the Emerald City, hit the **15** **Seattle Art Museum** and find your way to the John H Hauberg Collection, an excellent display of masks, canoes, totems and other pieces from Northwest coastal Native American peoples. Across town, at the ⑯ **Burke Museum,** you'll find yet another excellent collection of Northwest coast Native American artifacts. Although the ⑰ **Daybreak Star Indian Cultural Center** has few facilities for outside visitors, it's worth a visit if only to hike the trails in surrounding Discovery Park. Peek into the center's small art gallery, and check out the view over Puget Sound out front.

Reserve one day in Seattle for the four hour trip with ⑱ **Tillicum Village Tours** to Blake Island, the birthplace of Seattle's namesake, Chief Seattle (or Sealth). It's a bit touristy, fair enough, but the trip includes a salmon bake, a native dance and a movie at an old Duwamish Native American village.

In all, it's a great way to learn more about local cultures outside the confines of museum walls. And, as far as we know, you won't find a traditional salmon bake in any restaurant.

From Seattle ferry over to the Olympic Peninsula, drive west along Highway 101 and onto the slow-going, incredibly scenic Hwy 112. Follow this along the Strait of Juan de Fuca all the way to ⑲ **Neah Bay.** Here, on the Makah Indian Reservation, among the weather-beaten boats and

DETOUR On your return from Tofino, instead of heading south along Hwy 19, detour 122km (76 miles; 1¼ hrs) up to Campbell River, where you can check out the **Museum at Campbell River** (www .crmuseum.ca). Along with exhibits on the logging industry, salmon fishing and pioneer life, it showcases an excellent collection of First Nations masks (the real reason to come), house posts, and coppers. Other exhibits detail the history and cultures of the region's First Nations peoples.

craning totem poles, you'll find the outstanding ⑳ **Makah Museum.** The museum displays artifacts from the 500-year-old Makah village of Ozette, which was destroyed in a mudslide in the early 18th century and lay covered until 1970, when it was exposed by tidal erosion. One of North America's most significant archeological discoveries, the village was a trove of native history, containing whaling weapons, canoes, spears, combs and more. From Neah Bay, backtrack slightly and then head down to ㉑ **Ozette** itself. Besides the original village site, you'll find one of the most accessible slices of isolated beach on the Olympic coastal strip.

Head back to Hwy 112 and bear south along Highway 101 to Hwy 110 west. Follow this out to spectacular Rialto Beach. When you're done exploring this desolate stretch of sand, check into the Quileute Indian Reservation-owned ㉒ **La Push Ocean Park Resort,** above the beach in La Push. Its sleeping options range from basic A-frame cabins with sleeping-bag lofts (no shower) to deluxe oceanfront cottages with stone fireplaces and whirlpool tubs. Or you can camp. La Push's only restaurant, ㉓ **River's Edge Restaurant** serves three or four freshly caught seafood dishes and, in summer, bakes salmon in the Quileute tradition. Return to Seattle the way you came, but take the faster

Highway 101 to the **㉔ Sol Duc Hot Springs Resort.** As Native American legend tells it, the geological phenomenon of the springs here is the legacy of a battle between two lightning fish. When neither fish won the contest, each crawled beneath the earth and shed bitter tears, forming the heated mineral springs that feed the three developed pools that are there today. Yes, the large, tiled pools are far cry from their original state, but the resort is well worth a stop for a night of hot-spring bliss.

Invigorated by mineral waters, head back to Seattle and rest up before the 325-mile journey southeast into Oregon. Start early, head east on I-90 and, after 145 miles, take a break in the town of Yakima. Stretch your legs with a walk through the **㉕ Yakima Valley Museum,** where you can study up on Yakama Native American heritage. If you'd rather break the trip here with a night's stay, you'll find several chain hotels and one hotel that breaks the mold: the **㉖ Birchfield Manor.** Set in parklike surroundings 2 miles east of town, this antique-packed B&B also has a renowned restaurant. From Yakima, continue 20 miles south to Toppenish, where you'll find the excellent **㉗ Yakama Nation Museum,** which exhibits costumes, baskets, beads and audio-visual displays. It also has a gift shop, a library *and* a restaurant. You owe it to yourself to stop in for a Pow Wow burger (made with buffalo meat, of course).

ECHO OF FALLING WATER

From Kettle Falls to the Pacific Ocean, the Columbia River was, for millennia, a major source of salmon for native peoples. One of the most important fishing areas on the entire river was **Celilo Falls**, between where Hwy 97 and The Dalles stand today. Native peoples from as far away as the Great Plains and Alaska gathered at Celilo Falls, which was known as Wyam, "the echo of falling water." In 1957, when the gates of the new Dalles Dam closed for the first time, it took only a few hours for Celilo Falls to be forever buried under water.

From Toppenish, it's another 160 miles south, across the Oregon boarder, to the **㉘ Warm Springs Indian Reservation.** Home to three groups – the Wasco, Warm Springs and Northern Paiute tribes – the reservation stretches from the peaks of the Cascades to the banks of the Deschutes River. The best reason to stop is the excellent **㉙ Warm Springs Museum,** a wonderful evocation of traditional Native American life and culture, with artifacts, audiovisual presentations and re-created villages. The other reason to come is the tribe-owned **㉚ Kah-Nee-Ta Resort,** home to a casino, a golf course, horseback riding, tennis, fishing and a spring-fed swimming pool. Shack up here for the night (in a teepee, no less), and try not to have *too* much fun!

Danny Palmerlee

TRIP INFORMATION

GETTING THERE
Vancouver, BC lies 140 miles north of Seattle and 315 miles north of Portland.

DO

Burke Museum
Superb collection of Northwest coast Native American artifacts housed on the University of Washington campus. ☎ 206-543-5590; www.washington.edu/burke museum; NE 45th St at 16th Ave, Seattle, WA; adult/student/senior $8/5/6.50; ◷ 10am-5pm; ⓺

Makah Museum
Reason enough to visit isolated Neah Bay. Displays findings from the 500-year-old Makah village of Ozette. ☎ 360-645-2711; www.makah.com/mcrchome.htm; 1880 Bayview Av, Neah Bay, WA; admission $5; ◷ 10am-5pm May-Sep; ⓺

Quw'utsun' Cultural & Conference Centre
Interpretive tours, art works, and a café serving traditional cuisine. ☎ 250-746-8119, 877-746-8119; www.quwutsun.ca; 200 Cowichan Way, Duncan, BC; adult/child/youth C$13/2/11; ◷ 10am-5pm Mon-Fri, 10am-4pm Sat & Sun mid-Apr–Sep; ⓺

Royal BC Museum
Vast museum with an entire floor dedicated to First Nations cultures. ☎ 250-356-7226, 888-447-7977; www.royalbcmuseum.bc.ca; 675 Belleville St, Victoria, BC; adult/child C$15/9; ◷ 9am-6pm Jul–mid-Oct, 9am-5pm mid-Oct–Jun; ⓺

Seattle Art Museum
Seattle's must-see art museum includes Native American art. ☎ 206-654-3100; www.seattleartmuseum.org; 1300 1st Ave, Seattle, WA; adult/child/student/senior $13/free/7/10; ◷ 10am-5pm Tue-Sun, to 9pm Thu & Fri; ⓺

Tla-ook Cultural Adventures
Learn about First Nations culture by paddling an authentic dugout canoe. Bear-watching tours also available. ☎ 250-725-2656, 877-942-2663; www.tlaook.com; Tofino, BC; tours 2/4/6hrs C$42/62/136; ⓺

UBC Museum of Anthropology
Outstanding museum with optional free guided tours. ☎ 604-822-3825; www.moa.ubc.ca; 6393 NW Marine Dr, Vancouver, BC; admission C$9, children under 6 free; ◷ 10am-5pm, until 9pm Tue, reduced winter hours; ⓺

Warm Springs Museum
This beautifully designed, reservation-owned museum houses fascinating exhibits on the indigenous Wasco, Warm Springs and Northern Paiute. ☎ 541-553-3331; www.warmsprings.com/museum; 2189 Hwy 26, Warm Springs, OR; adult/5-12yr/senior $7/3/5; ◷ 9am-5pm; ⓺

Yakama Nation Museum
Part of the larger Yaquima Nation cultural center, which has a restaurant serving good diner-style food. ☎ 509-865-2800; www.yakamamuseum.com; 280 Buster Rd, Toppenish, WA; adult/senior/child $5/3/1; ◷ 8am-5pm; ⓺

Yakima Valley Museum
Features a wide array of exhibits on regional history; includes an area specially for kids. ☎ 509-248-0747; www.yakimavalleymuseum.org; 2105 Tieton Dr, Yakima, WA; adult/senior $5/3; ◷ 10am-9pm, reduced winter hours; ⓺

EAT & SLEEP

Birchfield Manor
Renowned restaurant and wine cellar (stocked with Washington wines, of course); the inn has unusual antique-filled rooms and six guest cottages. ☎ 509-452-1960; www.birchfieldmanor.com; 2018 Birchfield Rd, Yakima, WA; manor r $119-159, cottage r $139-219

Buchan Hotel

Cheerful, tidy heritage hotel near Stanley Park with cheaper rooms with shared bathrooms and pricier suites. ☎ 604-685-5354, 800-668-6654; www.buchanhotel.com; 1906 Haro St, Vancouver, BC; r C$97-135

Gull Cottage

This coastal Victorian-style B&B is a cozy haven with three immaculate rooms, a book-filled TV room and a fabulous outdoor hot tub. ☎ 250-725-3177; www.gullcottage tofino.com; 1254 Lynn Rd, Tofino, BC; r C$132-161

James Bay Inn

A few minutes from the Inner Harbour, this quirky, well-maintained charmer has an old-school feel. Some rooms have kitchenettes. ☎ 250-384-7151, 800-836-2649; www .jamesbayinn.bc.ca; 270 Government St, Victoria, BC; r C$127-215

Kah-Nee-Ta Resort

Casino resort, popular with families, thanks to a giant swimming pool and waterslide. Hotel rooms, RV sites and deluxe teepees. ☎ 800-554-4786; www.kahneeta.com; Hwy 3, OR; teepee $72, r $146-260; 🏊 □

La Push Ocean Park Resort

A-frame cabins (no shower), deluxe cottages, standard motel rooms and campsites. ☎ 360-374-5267; www.quileutenation.org; 330 Ocean Park Dr, La Push, WA; motel r $55-78, cabins $80-160, townhouses $135-175

River's Edge Restaurant

In an old boathouse, this restaurant is famous for its free ornithological shows courtesy of resident eagles and pelicans. ☎ 360-374-5777; 41 Main St, La Push, WA; mains $8-25

Sol Duc Hot Springs Resort

Spa retreat with hot mineral pools, small store, restaurant and easy access to trails into the surrounding forest. ☎ 360-327-3583; www.visitsolduc.com; 12076 Sol Duc Hot Springs Rd, Port Angeles, WA; r $141-299, RV sites $25; 🕑 late Mar-Oct

Tillicum Village Tours

Offers a fun, four-hour educational tour to Blake Island, birthplace of Chief Sealth; tours depart from Pier 55. ☎ 206-933-8600, 800-426-1205; www.tillicumvillage.com; Pier 55, Seattle, WA; adult/child/senior $79/30/72; 🕑 Mar-Dec; 🏊

USEFUL WEBSITES

www.bcferries.com
www.clippervacations.com

LINK YOUR TRIP
www.lonelyplanet.com/trip-planner

The Simpsons to The Shining

WHY GO When Hollywood needs a film location, it heads up the coast to the Pacific Northwest. It's got waterfalls, army bases, creepy mountain lodges, and towns that are willing to dress up like Alaska. So turn off your TV and discover some of the famous sites you've already seen.

Cottage Grove is known for its covered bridges, but the most famous bridge here is an open-top railroad trestle that had a cameo in the movie *Stand By Me*. It's on screen for less than a minute, but the four pre-teen boys crossing over it as they set off on their journey into the woods has become one of the film's most iconic images. The rails have been paved over, and the **①** **Mosby Creek Trestle Bridge** is now part of the Row River Trail, easily accessible for hikers, bikers and film buffs.

Just north in Eugene, you'll find the ultimate party school: Faber College. It wasn't easy finding a campus that would agree to be in the movie *Animal House*, but the University of Oregon at Eugene had the good sense (of humor) to say yes. The president of the University, who was no Dean Wormer, even let them film scenes in his office in **②** **Johnson Hall**. You can't visit the Delta house anymore – it's been torn down – but you can still eat in the **③** **Erb Memorial Union Fishbowl**, famous for the food fight John Belushi's character started by spewing mashed potatoes at Kevin Bacon.

Just north in Salem, you'll find the hospital where they shot what many people consider to be one of the greatest American movies of all time: *One Flew Over the Cuckoo's Nest*, which swept the Oscars, taking Best Picture, Best Director, Best Actor, Best Actress, and Best Screenplay. The **④** **Oregon State Hospital** is still an operating facility, so don't expect a tour, but the beautiful old building surrounded by rhododendrons is still worth driving by for any Jack Nicholson fan.

TIME
5 – 6 days

DISTANCE
700 miles

BEST TIME TO GO
May – Sep

START
Cottage Grove, OR

END
Roslyn, WA

ALSO GOOD FOR

OFFBEAT

BEST TRIP

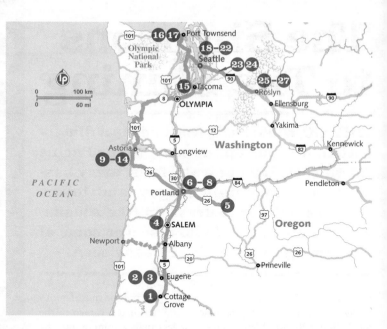

Continuing your Nicholson-goes-nuts tour, head north on I-5 and then east on Hwy 26 to **5** **Timberline Lodge**, which, if you've ever seen *The Shining*, will give you the creeps before you even get out of the car. It was used for exterior shots of the haunted Overlook Hotel, and, while you can't wander the hedge maze (that was just Hollywood magic) you can enjoy cocoa in front of the massive stone fireplace and be glad you're not trapped in for the winter with a crazed Jack Torrance.

"…be glad you're not trapped in for the winter with a crazed Jack Torrance."

In **6** **Portland**, it seems **7** **Jake's Famous Crawfish** is famous for more than just its crawfish. It's frequently used as a film location, including a scene in Gus Van Sant's *My Own Private Idaho*. Much of downtown was used in the dark indie flick, including the **8** **Thompson Elk Fountain** near City Hall, where the narcoleptic hustler played by River Phoenix lies passed out in Keanu Reeves' arms.

On a cheerier note, Portland is also the hometown of Matt Groening, and there are signs of *The Simpsons* all around town – literally. Several of the surnames used on the show are also downtown street names, including NW Quimby St, Lovejoy St, and NE Flanders St, which frequently gets the letter "D" spray painted in after the abbreviation for northeast.

Ready to roll credits on Portland? Head west to the coastal village of **9** **Astoria** , a virtual Hollywood by the Sea. Several movies have been filmed here, including *Short Circuit*, *Free Willy*, and *Kindergarten Cop*, but it's best known as the setting for the cult hit *The Goonies*. The opening scene with the Fratellis was shot in front of the ❿ **Clatsop County Jail**, and the most popular location in town is the ⓫ **Goonies House**. You can't actually go inside the house where Mikey and Brandon Walsh lived, but you can walk up the gravel driveway and do your own version of the Truffle Shuffle in front of the famous Victorian.

Just over the bridge, fans of the movie *Free Willy* can visit ⓬ **Hammond Mooring Basin**, site of the thrilling climax where Willy leaps through the air as he heads toward open waters. There are tons of other movie locations in Astoria, warranting at least an overnight stay to see them all. So

> **DETOUR** If **Yaquina Head Lighthouse** in Newport, Oregon, seems a little creepier than a lighthouse ought, that's because it was featured in the US version of the movie *The Ring*. Built in 1873, it was originally called Cape Foulweather Lighthouse, but in the movie it was known as the Moesko Island Lighthouse. (It was also in the 1977 TV masterpiece *Nancy Drew: The Mystery of Pirate's Cove*.) To get to Newport, turn off the I-5 between Eugene and Salem and drive 60 miles on Hwy 20.

where do filmmakers go when they're in town? ⓭ **Hotel Elliott** is a stylish boutique hotel that offers star-worthy accommodations in its deco-light rooms. And ⓮ **Baked Alaska** is a seafood-on-white-tablecloths kind of place, where cast and crew alike often dine after a day of shooting.

After you've had your fill of Astoria film locations, head north to Tacoma, a four-hour drive through farmlands and general greenery. Whether or not you're a fan of the movie *10 Things I Hate About You*, the school where it was shot is worth a stop. ⓯ **Stadium High School** was built in the late 1800s as a luxury hotel. Drive around back, where the castlelike structure – modeled after an actual château in France – looms over the sunken football field, where Heath Ledger's character pays the marching band to help him serenade Julia Stiles.

From Tacoma, head north for a meandering two-hour drive along two-lane highways to Port Townsend. This seaside town with a military base doubled as Pensacola in the filming of *An Officer and a Gentleman*. You might recognize some of the areas around ⓰ **Fort Worden State Park**, and you can reenact the love scenes in the exact same room at ⓱ **The Tides Inn** where Richard Gere and Debra Winger stayed the night. Although it doesn't have its original furnishings from the movie, the room is stuck somewhere back in the '80s, and there's a plaque outside the door and a movie poster over the bed, just to make sure you don't miss the point.

Head back down into ⓲ **Seattle**; it's only about fifty miles, but a ferry ride in the middle makes it a two-hour trip Seattle which has had many a star turn since it had its film debut in 1933's *Tugboat Annie*. Stay at the centrally located **⑲ Inn at the Market**, a small, elegant boutique hotel right perfectly located for exploring the city. It's right across the street from **⑳ Pike Place Market**, a perennial tourist attraction that is almost a mandatory location for any film set in Seattle. Rob Reiner and Tom Hanks wandered through this Seattle icon in *Sleepless in Seattle*, and Jeff Bridges filmed here for *The Fabulous Baker Boys*, among others.

ASK A LOCAL "Almost everyone who comes to visit wants to see the **Sleepless in Seattle houseboat**. You can't see it from the street, but there are a couple of boat tours that take you by – the Duck Ride and the Argosy tour. You could also try renting a kayak and paddling out to it. It's on the northwest side of Lake Union up by Gas Works Park, and Tom Hanks' houseboat is right at the end of the dock."

Rick Bartley, Seattle, WA

Seattle's **㉑ Gas Works Park** is a popular spot among both locals and filmmakers for its views of Lake Union and freaky industrial structures. It was the setting for a paintball fight in *10 Things I Hate About You*, as well as a heart-to-heart between Kyra Sedgwick and Campbell Scott in *Singles*.

In fact, the whole city features prominently in *Singles*, which was seen as practically a documentary of life and love in early 1990s Seattle. The unifying element was the **㉒ Coryell Court Apartments**, where the 20-something main characters lived. You won't find Matt Dillon hanging out in a flannel shirt in the courtyard, but driving by will bring back memories of the grunge-era film.

If you watched David Lynch's *Twin Peaks*, you'll instantly recognize the **㉓ Salish Lodge** from the opening credits. Half an hour east of Seattle, the lodge was used as the exterior for the Great Northern Hotel, and it sits right above Snoqualmie Falls, which was also featured on the show. Stop for Northwestern cuisine in one of their two restaurants, or just hike down to the falls for a fabulous photo op. And speaking of *Twin Peaks*, you can still get cherry pie at **㉔ Twede's Cafe** – also known as the "Double R" – where Kyle MacLachlan enjoyed a "Damn fine cup o' coffee."

Finally, head east for about 45 minutes to the little town of **㉕ Roslyn**, which doubled for Cicely, Alaska, in the show *Northern Exposure*. The main street looks just like it did in the show, and you can grab a beer at the **㉖ Brick Tavern** or have dinner at **㉗ Roslyn Cafe**, which still has the famous mural painted on its side, although the moose has since moved on.

Mariella Krause

TRIP INFORMATION

GETTING THERE
From Portland, Cottage Grove is130 miles south on I-5.

DO
Clatsop County Jail
This tiny building was the pokey from 1914 to 1976; now it's just a great photo op for *Goonies* fans. **732 Duane Street, Astoria, OR**

Coryell Court Apartments
The reddish-brown brick apartment building built around a courtyard will be recognizable to *Singles* fans. **1820 E Thomas St, Seattle, WA**

Fort Worden State Park
Do some pushups or run some laps at this film double for Pensacola's Naval Aviation Officer Candidate School. ☎ **360-344-4400; www.parks.wa.gov/fortworden; 200 Battery Way, Port Townsend, WA**

Gas Works Park
Even if you're unfamiliar with its film work, this cool park on Lake Union has great views of downtown. **Meridian Ave & N Northlake Way, Seattle, WA;** ⏱ **dawn-dusk**

Goonies House
Park at the bottom of the gravel driveway and walk up; feel free to snap a picture, but, remember, it's a private residence. **368 38th St, Astoria, OR**

Hammond Mooring Basin
If you're a fan of *Free Willy*, it's a must-see; if not, there's not much to look at. **1099 Iredale St, Hammond, OR**

Johnson Hall
This stately administration building is where Dean Wormer tried to shut down the Deltas, back in the day. **E 13 St btwn University & Kincaid Sts, Eugene, OR**

Mosby Creek Trestle Bridge
Part of the Row River Trail, this bridge is 3 miles southeast of town near the Mosby Creek Trailhead. **Cnr Mosby Creek Rd & Mosby Ranch Rd, Cottage Grove, OR;** ☐

Oregon State Hospital
Used as both exterior and interior for *One Flew Over the Cuckoo's Nest*, this facility is still operating as a state hospital. **2600 Center St NE, Salem, OR**

Pike Place Market
This crazily popular Seattle landmark has seen its share of celluloid. ☎ **206-682-7453; www.pikeplacemarket.org; 1501 Pike Pl;** ⏱ **stores 10am-6pm Mon-Sat, 11am-5pm Sun**

Stadium High School
Built as a luxury hotel, it was gutted by fire in 1898 and rebuilt to be an incredibly impressive high school. **111 N E St, Tacoma, WA**

Thompson Elk Fountain
This downtown elk statue is considered a traffic hazard – especially when it's got stars sleeping on it. **SW Main St between 3rd & 4th Aves, Portland, OR**

EAT
Baked Alaska
A favorite of film cast and crew when they're in town on a shoot, this local seafood place overlooks the Columbia Gorge. ☎ **503-325-7414; 1 12th St, Astoria, OR; mains $8-26;** ⏱ **11am-10pm**

Brick Tavern
Where the locals go to get a beer, whether they live in Roslyn, WA, or Cicely, AL. ☎ **509-649-2643; 1 Pennsylvania Ave, Roslyn, WA; mains $8-13;** ⏱ **11:30am-11pm Sun-Thu, 11am-2am Fri & Sat**

Erb Memorial Union Fishbowl
The cafeteria has been replaced with fast food chains, but you'll still recognize the dining area from *Animal House*. ☎ **541-346-3705; www.emu.uoregon.edu; 1222 E13 Ave, Eugene, OR;** ⏱ **7am-7pm Mon-Thu, 7am-5pm Fri**

Jake's Famous Crawfish
Killer crawfish, elegant digs, and over 100 years of history – no wonder they're famous. ☎ **503-226-1419; 401 SW 12th Ave, Portland, OR; mains $7-18;** ⏱ **11am-11pm Mon-Thu, to midnight Fri & Sat, 3pm-11pm Sun**

ICONIC TRIPS

Roslyn Cafe

Surprisingly cute, for a small-town café; be sure to get a picture of the mural. ☎ **509-649-2763; 201 W Pennsylvania Ave, Roslyn, WA; mains $9-25; 🕒 11am-9pm Mon-Sat, 9am-3pm Sun**

Salish Lodge

This hotel lacks the quirkiness of the Great Northern, but, then, no dead bodies, either. ☎ **425-888-2556; www.salishlodge.com; 6501 Railroad Ave SE, Snoqualmie, WA; Attic Bistro; mains $12-28; 🕒 11am-10pm**

Twede's Cafe

Cherry pie and coffee are still on the menu at the former Double R. ☎ **425-831-5511; www.twedescafe.com; 137 W North Bend Way, North Bend, WA; mains $5-15; 🕒 6:30am-8pm Mon-Thu, 6:30am-9pm Fri-Sat, 6:30am-7pm Sun**

SLEEP

Hotel Elliott

Plush, deco-style rooms make this boutique hotel Astoria's leading lady. ☎ **877-378-1924; www.hotelelliott.com; 357 12th St, Astoria, OR; r $109-395**

Inn at the Market

Elegant, modern, and located right above Pike's Place Market. ☎ **206-443-3600; www.innatthemarket.com; 86 Pine St, Seattle, WA; r $185-360**

The Tides Inn

The furniture is so dated, you might think it was left over from the film. But this ageing movie star is still a fun star sighting. ☎ **360-385-0595; www.tides-inn.com; 1807 Water St, Portt Townsend, WA; r $68-239**

Timberline Lodge

Built as a Works Project Administration project, this National Historic Landmark made of timber and stone has rustic, woodsy rooms. ☎ **503-231-5400; www.timberlinelodge.com; Timberline Lodge, OR; r $105-290**

USEFUL WEBSITES

www.ci.seattle.wa.us/filmoffice/filmmap.htm

LINK YOUR TRIP

www.lonelyplanet.com/trip-planner

TRIP
7 Eccentric Pacific Northwest p75
12 48 Hours in Seattle p107
26 48 hours in Portland p185

Coast Starlight Train Journey

WHY GO Harry Potter had the "Hogwarts Express." Lauren Bacall had the "Orient Express." And even Boxcar Willie snagged a ride now and again. Climb aboard for a leisurely, scenic journey and learn what they knew 100 years ago: That traveling by train is the only way to go.

Like the *Coast Starlight* itself, your journey begins in Seattle. If you don't live in Seattle, the **1** Arctic Club provides a fitting night-before-a-train-voyage atmosphere; 1920s decor in a historic Seattle building that was formerly a men's club.

The next morning, pack your hatboxes and steamer trunks and arrive at **2** King Street Station in time for your mid-morning departure. As you join your queue, take a moment to appreciate the ornate ceilings, marble walls, and inlaid-tile compass rose on the floor of the Compass Room, which rail travelers have been appreciating for over a hundred years.

Just like at the airport, traveling by train means waiting in a series of lines. One to get your ticket, one to get your boarding pass, and then, finally, the line where you get your seat assignment right before boarding the train. Don't be fooled by that "Reserved Coach" ticket. It sounds like you have a special seat picked out just for you, but really it just means that you get a seat. Arrive a little early to get that upper-deck window seat you want, and, if you can, nab a seat on the west side of the train for better views.

Sitting in the station, your view is nothing but gravel and pigeons. As you pull out from the station, there are lots of stops, giving your trip a staccato feel: slow, fast, slow, stop, slow, stop, slow. The view consists mainly of parking lots and back sides of buildings. You may

TIME
1 – 3 days

DISTANCE
452 miles

BEST TIME TO GO
Mar – Sep

START
Seattle, WA

END
Eugene, OR

ALSO GOOD FOR

be thinking, "Huh. This isn't what I expected." But all that will change. Patience, rail traveler. Your journey's just beginning.

The *Coast Starlight* cruises all the way down to Los Angeles from Seattle, then turns around and comes back, taking four days in all to make the round-trip. You'll soon discover, however, the name is a little misleading: The only time the *Coast Starlight* is on the coast is in southern California.

"Patience, rail traveler. Your journey's just beginning."

In other words, don't expect tracks that slice through the middle of the sand, scattering beach towels and sun bathers in its path.

Before you really get going in earnest, you'll stop in Tacoma. If you have a rail pass that allows you to get off and on the train along the way, it might be worth stopping overnight to see the spectacular ③ **Museum of Glass**, celebrating the art form for which the Pacific Northwest is famous. (Even if you don't stop, the train passes under the Chihuly Bridge of Glass, so don't forget to look up.)

Right past Tacoma is the ④ **Tacoma Narrows Bridge**. You could easily pass by and think nothing more of the pair of light green suspension bridges than, "Hmm, those are kind of pretty." But the bridge they replaced should be emblazoned on your memory if you've seen the grainy black and white footage of its collapse. In 1940, "Galloping Gertie" was caught on film violently wobbling and bucking before giving up completely. (Even though the new bridge doesn't flutter in the wind, you can't help but be glad you're on the train and not up there.)

Don't like your seatmate? Head to the lounge car, where you'll find unassigned swiveling seats that face out toward the huge windows that go from floor to ceiling. This car is made to optimize the views outside of the train, and would probably be packed except the regular seats are a little more comfortable for long-term sitting.

If you're lucky, you might catch a volunteer guide from the National Park Service Rails & Trails program. Based out of Klondike Gold Rush National Historical Park, they work the sightseer lounge from Memorial Day through Labor Day, explaining the oddities and points of interest along the way between Seattle and Portland. Then, they transfer to the Seattle-bound train and do it all over again in reverse.

Leaving Tacoma, you're treated to a half-hour view of Puget Sound out the west side of the train. According to our guide, you can sometimes actually see whales frolicking in the water from the train. Not often, granted, but, damn, that sure is a good excuse to stare out the window at the water.

Past Puget Sound, you start getting into some pretty countryside. A trestle bridge over a sparkling creek. Farmland. Old barns. The route is lined with fluffy ferns that look like green puffs of smoke, as well as Scotch Broom, the ubiquitous yellow flowers you see along roadsides. (Some call them "invasive weeds," but they're much prettier than that sounds.) You

ASK A LOCAL About ten minutes past Olympia, look for the **Mima Mounds**: hundreds of small mounds carpeting the land around the tracks. No one's sure how they came to be there. Many believed they were Native American burial grounds, but there was just one problem: no bodies or relics. There are dozens of theories, everything from giant gophers to aliens. I believe – and it's now a generally accepted explanation – they're the result of glacial ice melting, leaving deposits of rocks and dirt.
Harvey Bowen, Seattle, WA

see things you'd miss from the air, like a squirrel statue carved out of a tree stump, or a miniature herd of Shetland ponies with shaggy white manes. This is back roads travel at its best.

When you're driving, you have to pay attention, but on the train you're free to stare out the window and contemplate whatever. It's also a very ephemeral experience, the perfect Zen metaphor: You can't look back and see where you've been; you can't look forward to see where you're going. You can only watch the display shifting outside your window and practice living with impermanence.

Somewhere outside of Tacoma, you'll be given the opportunity to make reservations for lunch in the dining car. It's not the nicest restaurant you've ever eaten at, but you can't help feeling a little fancy sitting at a table on a train. You'll probably end up sharing a table, so there's a good chance you'll have a good story to tell later. It beats 90% of the restaurants you're whizzing by, as well as the downstairs snack bar.

Just over an hour past Tacoma, the train stops in the small town of Centralia, which has a cute downtown that's chock full of historic brick buildings and antique stores. Less than two blocks from the train station, you can bunk down at the McMenamins ⑤ Olympic Club. The former men's club has a colorful history of gamblers, bandits and generally dangerous types, but now it's a hotel and brewpub complete with dark woods, leaded glass and period details befitting a train trip.

Back on the train again, keep your eyes peeled as you whiz through Winlock. Look out the west side of the train and you should be able to glimpse the ⑥ World's Largest Egg passing by your window. You're in luck, because that's about the right amount of time to spend on this roadside attraction.

Heading into Portland, you'll cross the Willamette River, and west of the train is the gothic St. John's Bridge. If it looks familiar, that's because it was an engineering model for the Golden Gate bridge, made on a smaller scale to make sure it worked and wouldn't pull a Galloping Gertie.

NEXT STOP: WHEREVER YOU WANT

One advantage of rail travel is the flexibility to travel how you like. You can buy a single ticket and stay on the train. You can break the trip up with a stop or two by buying trip segments. Or you can keep things flexible with a rail pass that lets you hop off and on at your whim. (Try doing that with an airline!)

Next stop is Portland's ⑦ Union Station, which is just what you want your train station to be. Opened in 1896 and given a major renovation in time for its centennial, it has gleaming marble floors, long wooden benches, and a beautiful, high ceiling graced with beams and decorative medallions. It could instantly be used as a period-movie set, if you could just get everyone to change clothes.

If you're staying over, the ⑧ Heathman Hotel is a fitting choice for your trip. While not as much of a time capsule as the other hotels along the route, it is an elegant historic hotel from the 1920s with Deco-style common areas. Rooms are comfortable and elegant, and it's not all that far from the train station. Continuing with the historic theme, have dinner at ⑨ Jake's Famous Crawfish, an old-school seafood spot that's been drawing train passengers since it opened back in 1892.

Back on the train, take a moment to stroll through the cars and enjoy the multitude of ways people make their space their own. Teen girls with their feet up in their seat texting their friends (or maybe just each other). A toddler enraptured by a portable DVD player. A baby sleeping in his car seat on the floor between his parents' seat. It's kind of amazing, but not many people are talking on cells, even though the atmosphere is pretty casual. Everyone goes to great lengths to get comfortable and enjoy the ride.

Before heading east into the forests, the train stops in Eugene, a vibrant college town and very possibly your last stop, unless you're heading on to California. It's worth a stop just to stay at the ⑩ **C'est La Vie Inn**, a vibrant Queen Anne Victorian that's – not to gush – absolutely stunning. It's colorfully painted and beautifully landscaped, giving it an absurd amount of curb appeal. Eugene also has a surprisingly sophisticated dining scene for a college town, and one meal you shouldn't miss is ⑪ **Beppe & Gianni's Trattoria**. This local favorite has been making pastas by hand since 1998, and it's been voted the best Italian restaurant in Eugene most years since.

Not to spoil the ending if you're continuing on, but, after Eugene, the train turns slowly into the forest, shadowing the Willamette Hwy, traveling for a time along the south shore of Lookout Point Lake. The stops become fewer and farther between in this heavily forested area, as you enter what some people refer to as the "long green tunnel." From there, the *Coast Starlight* heads down to California, at last reaching the coast and fulfilling its ultimate destiny.

Mariella Krause

TRIP INFORMATION

GETTING THERE
To reach Seattle from Portland, drive 175 miles north on I-5. From Vancouver, drive 140 miles south on Hwy 99 and I-5.

DO

King Street Station
This grand old train station is where the *Coast Starlight* route begins or ends, depending on which direction you're heading. ☎ 206-382-4125; 303 S Jackson St, Seattle, WA; travel agents available 6:15am-8pm

Museum of Glass
The train goes right under the museum's Chihuly Bridge of Glass; stop sometime if you have the chance. ☎ 253-284-4750; www.museumofglass.com; 1801 Dock St, Tacoma, WA; adult $10; ◔ 10am-5pm Mon-Sat, noon-5pm Sun

Portland Union Station
A beautiful train station from 1896; check it out during your half-hour stop in Portland. ☎ 503-273-4866; 800 NW 6th Ave, Portland, OR; ◔ 7:15am-9:15pm

World's Largest Egg
See that white thing that's whizzing past the – oh, never mind. **Kerron St & Fir St, Winlock, WA**

EAT

Beppe & Gianni's Trattoria
Delicious, homemade pasta dishes served in an intimate, homey atmosphere. ☎ 541-683-6661; 1646 E 19 Ave, Eugene, OR; mains $12-20; ◔ 5pm-9pm Sun-Thu, to 10pm Fri-Sat

Jake's Famous Crawfish
A hundred years ago, you could have stepped off the train and eaten at this exact same restaurant. ☎ 503-226-1419; 401 SW 12th Ave, Portland, OR; mains $7-18; ◔ 11am-11pm Mon-Thu, to midnight Fri & Sat, 3pm-11pm Sun

SLEEP

Arctic Club
This plushly retro hotel sets the tone for your travels with its masculine, 1920s decor. ☎ 206-340-0340; www.arcticclubhotel.com; 700 3rd Ave, Seattle, WA; r $273-413

C'est La Vie Inn
This Queen Anne Victorian is a treat just to look at; imagine staying in it. ☎ 541-302-3014; www.cestlavieinn.com; 1006 Taylor St, Eugene, OR; r $125-250

Heathman Hotel
A boutique hotel in downtown Portland with plenty of dark woods and historic charm. ☎ 503-241-4100; www.heathmanhotel.com; 1001 SW Broadway, Portland, OR; r from $185

Olympic Club Hotel
Centralia closes down early; luckily, there's a pub and theatre on site. ☎ 360-736-5164; www.mcmenamins.com; 112 N Tower Ave, Centralia, WA; r $40-80

USEFUL WEBSITES
www.allaboardwashington.org
www.amtrak.com

LINK YOUR TRIP
www.lonelyplanet.com/trip-planner

Romance of the Pacific Northwest

WHY GO Call it a mystique. An allure. A je ne sais quoi. There's something about the Pacific Northwest that's always drawn people to it. It's hard not to be smitten with the dramatic coastline, the abundant nostalgia, and the grand gestures of a landscape that's never at rest.

Shakespeare knew a thing or two about romance. And for all the times he compared a woman's beauty to something from nature, we're sure he would have found ample inspiration in the Pacific Northwest. Shakespeare may never have road-tripped in Oregon, but, every summer, you can indulge in some of his most passionate works at the ❶ Oregon Shakespeare Festival.

With 11 productions ranging from Shakespeare to works by modern scribes, the festival runs February through October and is the main claim to fame of the Victorian-era town of Ashland. The town is also home to a slew of inns and B&Bs, and the ❷ Peerless Hotel has both the history and decor to make it a top pick. Built in 1900, its wrought-iron beds, antique woodworking, and Victorian details lend an easy elegance to its cozy guestrooms.

Just a few blocks away, the ❸ Dragonfly Cafe & Gardens is the perfect venue for hungry theatergoers. Tucked away on a side street, it has an outdoor patio lit by twinkle lights and candles, where inventive Latin-Asian fusion is served breakfast, lunch and dinner.

Had your fill of Shakespeare? For an entirely different kind of drama, up I-5 then take Hwy 38 west to the gorgeous Oregon coast. Many people are content to cruise up the highway and enjoy the view through bug-splattered windshields. But if you want to slow down and truly appreciate the experience, try riding along the beach on horseback.

TIME
6 – 7 days

DISTANCE
980 miles

BEST TIME TO GO
Apr – Oct

START
Ashland, OR

END
Lakewood, WA

ALSO GOOD FOR

HISTORY &
CULTURE

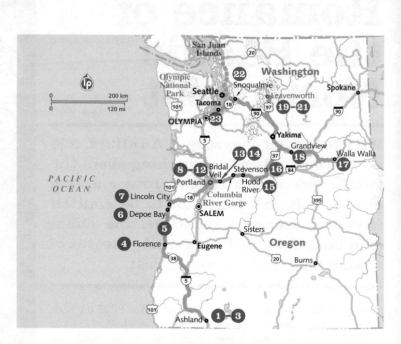

Saddle up with ④ **C&M Stables** in Florence; their sunset rides are one of the most magnificent ways to explore the coast.

As you wind north of Florence, the views get more and more dramatic until they reach a crescendo along the steep bluffs of ⑤ **Cape Perpetua**, the highest lookout point on the Oregon coast. If standing at the edge of the continent on a bluff 800 feet above sea level doesn't get your heart pounding, nothing will.

ASK A LOCAL

"I think one of the most romantic things you can do is go hide away in a ski lodge. In the winter, you can just hang out in front of the fire, and in the summer, there's almost no one else around. And when you go up on a ski lift, you've got each other all to yourself."

Terry Scoggins, Tacoma, WA

If you want to linger over the ocean views, indulge yourself at ⑥ **Channel House**, about half an hour north in Depoe Bay. The best rooms give you your own whirlpool located on a private deck overlooking the crashing waves. For dinner, head a little further north to ⑦ **Bay House**, where the massive wine list pairs perfectly with both the fresh cuisine and the panoramic vistas.

When you're ready to go back to the real world, rinse off the sand take the back roads two and a half hours northeast into ⑧ **Portland** on Hwy 18. ⑨ **Portland's White House B&B** is easily the most romantic lodging in town. This Greek Revival minimansion has big white columns (thus the name) and will make you feel like a lumber baron on holiday with its antique-filled rooms. Dining options abound in the city, but ❿ **El Gaucho** is a dark, sexy steakhouse with a Latin flair and old-school atmosphere.

Portland is called the City of Roses, so it's only fitting to take some time to stop and wander the fragrant paths of the ⓫ **International Rose Test Garden**, with thousands of varieties in every imaginable color. Right next door is the serene and manicured ⓬ **Portland Japanese Garden**, which stands in restrained contrast to all the untamed nature that lies to the east of the city.

Millions of years of geological events have dramatically shaped the landscape of the Pacific Northwest, sprinkling it liberally with volcanoes, hot springs, waterfalls, mountains—and one particularly lovely gorge. From Portland, head east along the dramatic Columbia River Gorge, a waterfall-lined river canyon that slices through the landscape.

"...hop on the Mt Hood Railroad for a nostalgic trip aboard a vintage train."

For prime waterfall spotting, take exit 22 and follow the signs to the Historic Columbia River Highway. This two-lane thoroughfare was built in the 1920s not just to get people where they were going, but to showcase the stunning natural surroundings. The highway takes you right over ⓭ **Bridal Veil Falls** and, a few miles later, delivers you to big, splashy ⓮ **Multnomah Falls**, where you can take the trail to the Benson Footbridge for prime viewing.

Twenty minutes further up the road, just past the Bridge of the Gods in Hood River, you can hop on the ⓯ **Mt Hood Railroad** for a nostalgic trip aboard a vintage train. For over a century, passengers have chugged along through orchards and beside rivers up to the base of Mt Hood. Climb aboard for a romantic dinner trip in the old-fashioned dining car, or a wintertime Christmas-tree trip where you can bring your greenery home on the train.

After your rigorous day of waterfalls and train rides, enjoy whatever pampering you require at the cushy ⓰ **Skamania Lodge**, back to the west and just over the Bridge of the Gods in Stevenson, WA. Dine in on Northwestern specialties, indulge in a couples' massage, or stay over in one of their comfortable rooms. The lobby is spectacular, with a massive stone fireplace and floor-to-ceiling windows overlooking the gorge.

The next day, head an hour east on I-84 and another hour northeast on Hwy 97 to get to Washington's wine country. What started as a smattering of wineries has blossomed into a respected region, with hundreds of vineyards blanketing the hills. Sample the region's lush reds and crisp whites while visiting the tasting chateaus, wine caves and grand estates where the vintners ply their craft.

For a super-secluded wine-country getaway, ensconce yourself in the countryside at the **17** **Inn at Abeja**, just east of Walla Walla. The owners have converted the centuries-old farm buildings into super-chic and oh-so-private lodgings, with a restrictive gate policy that would make even Brad and Angelina feel at home. Otherwise, the centrally located **18** **Cozy Rose Inn** in Grandview is an ubercozy spot for exploring the area. The suites are gorgeously decorated with big, enticing beds that you sink right into.

Just over two hours north of Grandview and through the leafy Wenatchee National Forest is **19** **Leavenworth**, a charming village straight out of a picture book. This Bavarian morsel of a town is particularly fetching in winter, and the best way to enjoy it is with a good old-fashioned sleigh ride. **20** **Icicle Outfitters** offers an idyllic afternoon on a horse-drawn sleigh, followed by hot cocoa in front of the fire. (In balmier weather, make it a trail ride.)

No matter what the season, bunk down for the night at Leavenworth's exquisite **21** **Run of the River**. This stylish sanctuary uses natural elements like log beams and river rocks to create a luxurious, woodsy retreat. The best way to enjoy it? Enjoying the view from a porch swing on your own private deck overlooking the Icicle River.

Leaving Leavenworth and heading west toward Seattle, be sure to stop at dramatic **22** **Salish Lodge**. Dangling off the top of the 268ft Snoqualmie Falls, this 1918 hotel has an elegant dining room specializing in Northwestern cuisine, and a bistro for more casual appetites. While you're there, stroll down to the viewing platform for the best views of the falls and the lodge.

DETOUR Completely removed from the everyday world, the San Juan Islands are a romantic getaway all on their own. But the experience can be downright magical with a moonlight kayak tour from **Shearwater Adventures** (www.shearwaterkayaks.com). Offered only a few days a month – right around the time of the full moon – these moonlight paddles around Orcas Island are a memorable way to experience the San Juans.

Finally, we end our trip with the perfect blend of history and elegance. Nothing says romance like having a fifteenth-century castle moved from England and reconstructed for your beloved, and one man's romantic gesture is yours to enjoy just south of Tacoma. **23** **Thornewood Castle** is a truly spectacular Tudor-Gothic manor that was a gift from Chester Thorne to his wife Anna. Hidden behind gates and surrounded by bushes, it's a very private getaway to share with someone special.

Mariella Krause

TRIP INFORMATION

GETTING THERE
From Portland, drive 285 miles south on I-5 to Ashland.

DO

C&M Stables
Horseback-riding down the beach at sunset is an ideal way to slow down and enjoy the coast. ☎ 541-997-7540; www.oregonhorse backriding.com; 90241 Hwy 101, Heceta Head, OR; rides $45-65; ⏱ 10am-dusk

Icicle Outfitters
Horse-drawn sleigh rides through the snow prove that winter has a romantic side.
☎ 509-669-1518; www.icicleoutfitters.com; 7935 East Leavenworth Rd, Leavenworth, WA; sleigh rides adult/youth $18/9; ⏱ 9am-5pm

International Rose Test Garden
It might sound like a laboratory, but it's actually quite lovely. ☎ 503-823-3636; www .portlandparks.com; 400 SW Kingston Ave, Washington Park, Portland, OR; admission free; ⏱ dawn-dusk

Mt Hood Railroad
Embrace the nostalgia of a good old-fashioned train ride. ☎ 541-386-3556; www.mthoodrr.com; 110 Railroad Ave, Hood River, OR; excursions $30, dinner $80; ⏱ 10am-8:30pm Apr-Dec

Oregon Shakespeare Festival
It's now almost a year-round event, with three stages, 11 plays, and excellent production values. ☎ 541-482-0940; www.or shakes.org; 15 S Pioneer St, Ashland, OR; tickets $20-81; ⏱ 10am-10pm Feb-Nov

Portland Japanese Garden
Five acres of formal gardens include koi ponds and cherry blossoms. ☎ 503-223-1321; www.japanesegarden.com; 611 SW Kingston Ave, Washington Park, Portland, OR; ⏱ 10am-7pm Tue-Sun, noon-7pm Mon, to 4pm Oct-Mar; $8

EAT

Bay House
Ocean views are just part of what makes this one of the premier restaurants on the Oregon coast. ☎ 541-996-3222; www.thebayhouse .org; 5911 SW Hwy 101, Lincoln City, OR; mains $37-45; ⏱ 11:30am-2pm; 5:30pm-10pm

Dragonfly Cafe & Gardens
This sweet café serves beautifully presented dishes all day long. ☎ 541-488-4855; www .dragonflyashland.com; 241 Hargadine St, Ashland, OR; mains $12-19; ⏱ 8am-3pm, dinner from 5pm

El Gaucho
Dark timbers, intimate lighting and Latin guitar music make this steakhouse a romantic dinner out. ☎ 503-227-8794; www .elgaucho.com; 319 SW Broadway, Portland, OR; mains $28-117; ⏱ 4:30pm-1am Mon-Sat, 4pm-11pm Sun

Salish Lodge
Hike down to the bottom of Snoqualmie Falls after dining right above them. ☎ 425-888-2556; www.salishlodge.com; 6501 Railroad Ave SE, Snoqualmie, WA; Attic Bistro mains $12-28; ⏱ 11am-10pm

Skamania Lodge
This traditional Northwestern-style lodge and restaurant surrounded by mountains and forests has everything to offer. ☎ 509-427-7700; www.skamania.com; 1131 SW Skamania Lodge Way, Stevenson, WA; mains $8-24; ⏱ 8am-9pm

SLEEP

Channel House
Oceanfront suites put surf, sand and sunsets right at the foot of your bed. ☎ 541-765-2140; www.channelhouse.com; 35 Ellingson St, Depoe Bay, OR; r $100-330

Cozy Rose Inn
This wine country inn has plush, romantic rooms where every last detail has been carefully thought out. ☎ 509-882-4669; www .cozyroseinn.com; 1220 Forsell Rd, Grand-view, WA; r $149-225

Inn at Abeja
Remote, private and serene, this inn and winery is a getaway in itself. ☎ 509-522-1234; www.abeja.net; 2014 Mill Creek Rd, Walla Walla, WA; r $215-285

Peerless Hotel
Antique furnishings and Victorian touches make the perfect denouement to your evening of Shakespeare. ☎ 541-488-1082; www.peerlesshotel.com; 234 4th Street, Ashland, OR; r $82-264

Portland's White House B&B
Claw-foot tubs and huge antique beds make this inviting inn as warm as it is elegant. ☎ 503-287-7131; www.portlandswhite house.com; 1914 NE 22 Ave, Portland, OR; r $125-225

Run of the River
The rooms feel like Ralph Lauren designed a cabin in the woods just for you. ☎ 509-548-7171; www.runoftheriver.com; 9308 E Leavenworth Rd, Leavenworth, WA; r $220-255

Thornewood Castle
A reconstructed fifteenth-century English castle that's quite literally a little slice of Europe. ☎ 253-584-4393; www.thornewoodcastle .com; 8601 Thorne Lane, Lakewood, WA; r $270-525

LINK YOUR TRIP
www.lonelyplanet.com/trip-planner

WASHINGTON TRIPS

There's some irony in the fact that Washington is known for both its persistent rainfall *and* a population that loves to be outdoors. But it's not surprising – not with an outdoors that looks like this. Besides, Washington offers way too much to do to let a few clouds slow anyone down.

On a clear day, you can see Mt Rainier or Mt St Helens from miles away, but you can't truly appreciate them until you've seen them up close. Water lovers have miles of coastline to explore, as well as a mystical sprinkling of islands that came dangerously close to being snapped up by Canada. East of the Cascades, you can leave the rain behind and enjoy fresh produce by the bushel and an impressive wine country that rivals Napa Valley.

But the state has more to offer than just its outdoorsy endeavors. You can immerse yourself in cowboy culture, take a rock pilgrimage or explore the shipwrecks of the nautical Northwest. And while you're at it, you'll find quirky roadside attractions and maybe even a ghost or two along the way.

PLAYLIST ♫ Hit the road with a whole MP3 player's worth of Washington artists. Seattle was the birthplace not only of Jimi Hendrix, but of an entire musical genre, so there's plenty of local music to be found (even if it is a little Seattle-centric).

- "The Wind Cries Mary," Jimi Hendrix
- "Come As You Are," Nirvana
- "Float On," Modest Mouse
- "Doll Parts," Hole
- "Everlong," Foo Fighters
- "You're No Rock 'n' Roll Fun," Sleater-Kinney
- "Fell on Black Days," Soundgarden
- "I Will Follow You Into the Dark," Death Cab for Cutie
- "Even Flow," Pearl Jam

⭐ WASHINGTON'S BEST TRIPS

WASHINGTON TRIPS

48 Hours in Seattle

WHY GO A little rain never hurt anybody. All the more reason to stroll through a museum or linger over coffee. The second the sun comes out, you'll relish your time outdoors all the more, and the nonstop spectacle of rhododendron and evergreens will make the rain all seem worthwhile.

The heavily caffeinated Seattle coffee drinker isn't just a stereotype: they drink it all day long and lots of it so they can power through weather-induced energy lags. So start this trip the way Seattleites start their every day: with a latte. You'll find chain coffee shops on every corner, but ❶ **Zeitgeist Coffee**, located in a converted warehouse space in Downtown, is a great place to hang out and get caffeinated.

If you need something a little more solid to sustain you, head straight to ❷ **Salumi**. Known for their cured meats and cheeses, this deli owned by Mario Batali's dad serves downright addictive sandwiches that have people lining up out the door. They close at four and are only open Tuesday through Friday, so depending on your timing, this might be your only chance to indulge.

Ready for a little culture? The ❸ **Seattle Art Museum** is the place to get it. The collections span multiple genres, from modern to tribal to classic. Whether it's Warhol's version of a gun-slinging Elvis, Northwestern totem poles, or flowery stained glass, everyone will find something they wish they owned.

When you're done, pop around the corner and check out the ❹ **Seattle Public Library**, one of the most dazzling modern structures in the city. The building is made almost entirely of diamond-shaped panes of glass, and, on certain days, it manages to feel sunnier indoors than out. Be sure to check out the wow-inducing, 12,000-sq-ft reading room with 40ft glass ceilings.

TIME
2 days

BEST TIME TO GO
Apr – Aug

START
Downtown

END
Downtown

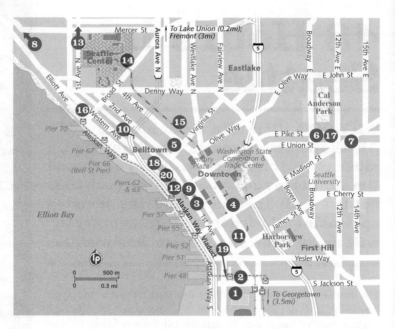

For dinner, make reservations for **5** **Dahlia Lounge**. It's an institution, and one of those rare places that locals and tourists seem to agree on. With crimson walls, fabulous desserts, and celebrity chef Tom Douglas, it's an easy choice for dinner, but, if nothing else, stop by and get something sweet to go from the Dahlia Bakery next door.

FUNKY FREMONT

If you have a few extra hours, head north to the neighborhood of Fremont – although let's be clear: it seceded in 1994 and now the preferred title is "Republic of Fremont, Center of the Known Universe." Its most famous denizen is the **Fremont Troll**, a concrete sculpture that lurks under the Aurora Bridge, but it's also known for an art-filled Saturday Market and the Fremont Fair, a colorful street party held each year during the summer solstice.

If there's anything else besides coffee that Seattle is known for, it's – well, you already know, it's live music. Check out the local listings to see what's playing. If you're not sure where to start, try **6** **Neumo's** for indie rock, **7** **Tractor Tavern** for rockabilly, alt country and acoustic, or **8** **Chop Suey** for an eclectic lineup that includes both live music and local DJs.

By now, you're surely ready for bed. Many travelers on a budget have found the **9** **Green Tortoise Hostel** – located mere steps from Pike's Market – to be a cheap, pleasant and convenient place to bunk down for the night. Belltown's **10** **Ace Hotel** is artsy in a hip, minimalist kind of way, although it's more fit for heavy drinkers than light sleepers, since the downstairs bar is always hopping.

A fairly recent addition to your sleeping options is the elegant ⓫ **Arctic Club**, opened in 2008. This historic building – known for decades as the "walrus building" for the plaster walrus medallions adorning the exterior – was established in 1908 as a men's club for Klondike explorers. Now it's a lavish hotel, where you can slumber in rooms that look like they could have been teleported from the 1920s.

The next morning, hit ⓬ **Pike Place Market** early so you can spend more time dodging flying fish and less time dodging hordes of people. Locals love it because you can buy fresh flowers, produce, and seafood. Out-of-towners love it because of its buzzing energy, and its big neon sign is a quintessential Seattle photo op.

> **ASK A LOCAL**
>
> "One of my favorite things to do in Seattle is rent a kayak and go out on **Lake Union**, especially when the weather's nice. You get great views of Downtown and the Space Needle, and you can row right by Gas Works Park, which has the neat old towers and generators from when it was a power plant."
>
> *Tameika Taylor, Seattle, WA*

Afterwards fuel up for a full day with breakfast at ⓭ **5 Spot** in Queen Anne. The five spots in question refers to the five US regions from which the eatery takes inspiration, with a changing decor to match the mood. For a gastronomic homage to Seattle grunge scene, try the Red Flannel Hash.

You may have noticed that huge, crazily colorful building at the foot of the Space Needle that looks like a huge blob of children's toys melted under a heat lamp. That would be the ⓮ **Experience Music Project & Science Fiction Museum**. Say what you will about Frank Gehry's design (many already have), this pair of genre museums is a fun place to immerse yourself in rock and roll and/or sci-fi for one admission price.

The music side, while a little Seattle-centric, does have some significant memorabilia, as well as crazy stage costumes that include touches such as fur leg warmers or spiked codpieces. The sci-fi side has beamed up a multidimensional collection ranging from Klingons to *The War of the Worlds* to *The Jetsons*. (Geek out if you must.)

More caffeine? Coming right up. Head downtown to ⓯ **Top Pot Doughnuts** for some brew and something to dunk in it. Floor-to-ceiling windows and a mezzanine level make it an ideal place to people watch while you refuel.

If the weather is cooperating, head toward the water and check out the new ⓰ **Olympic Sculpture Park**, where the artwork and the view compete for your attention. This 9-acre strip of park gives you the chance to wander among major works of art in front of a backdrop of Puget Sound and the Olympic Mountains.

"At the Olympic Sculpture Park, the artwork and the view compete for your attention."

You've had your nice dinner out; now it's time for some casual dining that's uniquely Seattle: ⓱ **Bimbo's Cantina**. They serve killer quesadillas and fab burritos in a funky, colorful room decorated in the wrestling theme of *lucha libre*. The music is always way too loud SO YOU'LL HAVE TO TALK LIKE THIS, but there will be plenty of time to chat later and the carbs will come in handy as you end your evening with a good, old-fashioned pub crawl.

A delicious, next-morning follow-up to what we hope was a satisfying evening is brunch at ⓲ **Etta's Seafood**. Their Bloody Mary's have a huge following among the late-night crowd, and their eggs benedict with fresh Dungeness crab make everything all feel better.

DETOUR

Ballard is known for its nightlife, but if you've been there, done that, head south to **Georgetown** and a row of worthwhile watering holes that are ideal for pub-hopping. **Georgetown Liquor Company** (www.georgetownliquorcompany.com) offers industrial-chic design, retro video games and a hipster scene. **Jules Maes Saloon** is an old-fashioned saloon stocked with punk rockers and tattoos. And **Smartypants** (www.smartypantsseattle.com) has a thriving sports-bike scene. Mix them together and you've got **Nine Pound Hammer** (www.ninepoundhammer.com), a reassuring blend of hipster, punk, biker and you.

Book lovers shouldn't miss ⓳ **Elliott Bay Bookstore**. Taking up an entire block near Pioneer Square, it's one of those great independent bookstores with warmth, character, author events, and displays that help you find something even if you don't know what you're looking for. (There's also a café in the basement, so you really can kill a whole afternoon if you want.)

Finally, we end our trip where it began: with coffee. And, believe it or not, we're actually going to suggest a ⓴ **Starbucks**. The first-ever store is located downtown right near Pike's Market. It's small, and it's usually packed, but remember: before it became the megachain that it is, it was once part of what was unique about Seattle.

Mariella Krause

TRIP INFORMATION

GETTING THERE
To get to Seattle from Portland, drive 175 miles north on I-5. From Vancouver, drive 140 miles south on Hwy 99 and I-5.

DO
Chop Suey
The intimate setting with kitschy Asian touches makes this a great place for catching up-and-coming indie artists. ☎ 206-860-5155; 1325 E Madison St; admission $5-15; ☻ 9pm-2am

Elliott Bay Bookstore
This huge independent bookstore is ideal for browsing on a rainy afternoon. ☎ 206-624-6600; www.elliottbaybook.com; 101 S Main St; ☻ 9:30am-10pm Mon-Sat, 11am-7pm Sun

Experience Music Project & Science Fiction Museum
One admission gets you into both, and there's plenty of memorabilia to keep you amused. ☎ 877-367-7361; www.empsfm.org; 325 5th Ave N; adult/student/child $15/12/free; ☻ 10am-7pm

Neumo's
It gets hot and crowded, sure, but their lineup keeps people coming back. ☎ 206-709-9467; www.neumos.com; 925 E Pike St; ☻ schedule varies

Olympic Sculpture Park
When the sun comes out, you don't want to be inside an art museum. ☎ 206-654-3100; 2901 Western Ave; admission free; ☻ 6am-9pm May-Sep, 7am-6pm Oct-Apr

Pike Place Market
Come watch the fishmongers tossing huge king salmon, and soak in the Seattle atmosphere. ☎ 206-682-7453; www.pikeplacemarket.org; 1501 Pike Pl; admission free; ☻ stores 10am-6pm Mon-Sat, 11am-5pm Sun

Seattle Art Museum
This excellent museum, which doubled in size in 2007, packs in everything from tribal masks to tea cups. ☎ 206-654-3100; www.seattleartmuseum.org; 1300 1st Ave; adult/child/student/senior $13/free/7/10; ☻ 10am-5pm Tue-Sun, to 9pm Thu & Fri

Seattle Public Library
When everyone says you have to go to the library, you know it must be good. ☎ 206-386-4636; 1000 4th Ave; ☻ 10am-8pm Mon-Wed, 10am-6pm Thu-Sat, 1-5pm Sun

Tractor Tavern
Check out live rockabilly, alt country and acoustic sets (but be prepared to stand). ☎ 206-789-3599; www.tractortavern.com; 5213 Ballard Ave NW; admission $8-15; ☻ 8pm-2am

EAT
5 Spot
Huge portions and a cute neon sign make this neighborhood spot a favorite. ☎ 206-285-7768; 1502 Queen Anne Ave N; mains $8-14; ☻ breakfast, lunch & dinner

Bimbo's Cantina
Killer burritos in a fun, loud atmosphere that's decorated in a *lucha libre* style. ☎ 206-322-9950; 1013 E Pike St; mains $6-10; ☻ 11am-2am

Dahlia Lounge
Chef Tom Douglas is Seattle's favorite foodie; at least come for dessert. ☎ 206-682-4142; 2001 4th Ave; mains $22-36; ☻ 11am-2:30pm & 5-10pm Mon-Thu, 5-11pm Fri & Sat, 5-10pm Sun

Etta's Seafood
Make reservations for this popular seafood spot near Pike's Place Market. ☎ 206-443-6000; 2020 Western Ave; mains $12-25; ☻ lunch & dinner daily, brunch 9am-3pm Sat & Sun

Salumi
Hope for a table in this tiny deli, but be prepared to take your sandwiches to go.

☎ 206-621-8772; 309 3rd Ave S; mains $7-4; ☯ 11am-4pm Tue-Fri

Top Pot Doughnuts

Whether or not this place serves the finest coffee in town, it's definitely got the best doughnuts. ☎ 206-728-1966; 2124 5th Ave; ☯ 6am-7pm Mon-Fri, 7am-7pm Sat & Sun

DRINK

Starbucks

Pretend it's just a little independent coffee shop; there was a time it was. ☎ 206-448-8762; 1912 Pike Pl; ☯ 6am-7:30pm

Zeitgeist Coffee

Need a latte? This place will keep you from having to go someplace you have back home. ☎ 206-583-0497; www.zeitgeistcoffee .com; 171 S Jackson St; ☯ 6am-7pm Mon-Fri, 8am-7pm Sat & Sun

SLEEP

Ace Hotel

Stylish and modern, this place has the feel of a converted loft that your artist friend owns. ☎ 206-448-4721; www.acehotel.com; 2423 1st Ave; r $75-199

Arctic Club

Nostalgia is just one of the amenities of this plush, retro hotel; don't miss the Dome Room's leaded-glass ceiling. ☎ 206-340-0340; www.arcticclubhotel.com; 700 3rd Ave; r $273-413

Green Tortoise Hostel

Located just steps from Pike's Place Market, it's got the best location and the lowest prices in town. ☎ 206-340-1222; www.greentortoise .net; 105 Pike St; d $24-29, r $77-80

USEFUL WEBSITES

www.thestranger.com
www.visitseattle.org

LINK YOUR TRIP

www.lonelyplanet.com/trip-planner

Rock Pilgrimage

WHY GO From Cobain to Hendrix, Grohl to Hole, Sub Pop to hip-hop, music is one of the first things people think of when they think of Seattle. For a quick introduction to Rock and Roll 101, take this tour of music landmarks around the Seattle area.

While the average out-of-towner wants to see the *Sleepless in Seattle* houseboat, the typical music fan wants to see the house Kurt Cobain lived in with Courtney Love. Yes, *that* house. **1 Kurt Cobain's House** sits on quiet Lake Washington Blvd, a ritzy street lined with ridiculously optimistic rhododendron bushes in every imaginable color. There's no parking, lots of bikers, and an unspoken disapproval of what you're there to do.

The house is, understandably, fenced and gated, and there's not even a good place to pull over. But wedged between Kurt's house and the next house over is tiny **2 Viretta Park**. Not only does it give you a place to stop and ponder the house's roofline (that's about all you can see), but it's also become an unofficial shrine. A towering pine tree sports a spray-painted "RIP" tattoo, and the benches are covered in hundreds of graffiti eulogies.

Of course, while you're in Seattle, you have to take advantage of its still-thriving music scene. For some history and a show, all rolled into one, see who's playing at **3 El Corazon**. This venue has had many incarnations; in fact, it might be called something else entirely by the time you visit. But when it was the Off Ramp, it was where Pearl Jam first played back in 1990 when they were still called "Mookie Blaylock."

One of *the* places to see live music at the height of the grunge era was Moe's Mo'Roc'N Café, and you can still rock out at its successor, **4 Neumo's**. Some people grumble about the restrictive door policy,

TIME
3 days

DISTANCE
130 miles

BEST TIME TO GO
Apr – Sep

START
Seattle

END
Aberdeen

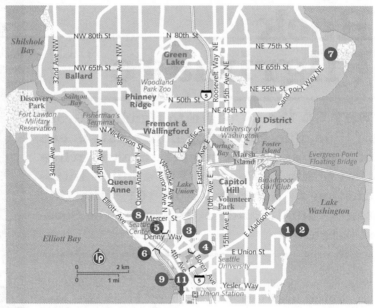

but the place is an institution. To find out who else is playing around town, check the local weekly *The Stranger*.

Moe's may be gone, but the cool wooden entrance through which thousands of grunge fans dutifully filed is now on display at the **5 Experience Music Project**. This rock-and-roll museum housed in a brightly colored lump of a building has lots of cool music memorabilia, including stage costumes, a tower of electric guitars, and old concert posters chronicling the local scene. Some argue that the museum is too commercial, so if you're worried about damaging your street cred, you might rather go to a coffee shop and talk about who's a sellout and who's not.

ASK A LOCAL

"If you're really into live music, you have to come during **Bumbershoot**. It started out as an arts festival, but, Seattle being what it is, it's now a major music festival, too. They have several stages at the Seattle Center every year on Labor Day weekend, kind of the last hurrah of summer."

Dan Richards, Seattle, WA

So where do tuckered-out megafans hang their guitar straps for the night? The **6 Edgewater Hotel** has a history of catering to touring rockers, going back at least to the Beatles' tour in 1964 when they were photographed fishing out a window. They've hosted Elvis, Led Zeppelin and a whole Lollapalooza's worth of more obscure artists. But the Edgewater is no rocker dive: The luxurious rooms are like a high-end mountain lodge with supermodern amenities.

You might not get to hear Soundgarden play while you're in town, but that doesn't mean you can't visit the **7** **Sound Garden** – a local sculpture installation from which the band took its name. A series of pipes mounted on tall metal towers catch the wind and create a creaky, haunting soundtrack that's somewhere between a didgeridoo and a vociferous whale. The only problem is getting in: It's located on the grounds of the National Oceanic and Atmospheric Administration, open only during the week. Security restrictions mandate that you show an ID at the gate, and no cars are allowed in.

"They've hosted Elvis, Led Zeppelin and a whole Lollapalooza's worth of more obscure artists."

One place any music fan can get into is **8** **Easy Street Records**. The place is enormous, and they have a huge selection of both CDs and vinyl. They also host lots of in-store events, so you might be able to catch a cool, never-heard-of-'em band while you're there.

But not every stop on this rock-and-roll road trip is in Seattle. Just ten miles south of Seattle in Renton is **9** **Greenwood Memorial Park**, where you can pay your respects to Seattle native Jimi Hendrix. Standing in front of the main building, you can see his gray granite memorial looming just across the lawn. Fans bring boom boxes, practice chords and leave guitar picks under the shelter of its 30ft-tall dome.

For a finale, fans of Kurt Cobain can travel the 100 miles southwest to **10** **Aberdeen** to see the coastal town he grew up in. Aberdeen embraces its role in Cobain's life, with signs at the city limits reading "Welcome to Aberdeen. Come as you are." At the **11** **Aberdeen Museum of History**, you can pick up a Kurt Cobain walking tour map, including the store where Kurt's uncle bought him his first guitar, and a couple of sad-looking former homes.

Take a moment while you're there to stop by the Wishkah River. Kurt sometimes slept under a bridge there

BLACK HOLE SUN

We're not saying Soundgarden took the name of their biggest hit from a sculpture – mostly because they're not saying it – but there happens to be a black granite sculpture on display in Seattle's Volunteer Park called **Black Sun**, by Isamu Noguchi. It's shaped roughly like a doughnut, with what some might call a *hole* through the middle of it. Coincidence?

after dropping out of high school, and it was there that Courtney scattered some of his ashes. Then, get back in your car, crank up your stereo, and ponder the nature of fame.

Mariella Krause

TRIP INFORMATION

GETTING THERE

From Portland, Seattle is an easy 175-mile drive north on I-5. From Vancouver, head south for 140 miles on Hwy 99 and I-5.

DO

Aberdeen Museum of History

The museum's Kurt Cobain walking tour can also be found online. ☎ 360-533-1976; www.aberdeen-museum.org; 111 E 3rd St, Aberdeen; suggested donation $2; ⌚ 10am-5pm Tue-Sat, noon-4pm Sun

Easy Street Records

In-store appearances and tons of vinyl make this one of Seattle's favorite record stores. ☎ 206-691-3279; www.easystreetonline.com; 20 Mercer St, Seattle; ⌚ 9am-10pm Sun-Thu, 9am-11pm Fri & Sat

Experience Music Project

If you care to mix genres, your admission also gets you into the Science Fiction Museum next door. ☎ 877-367-7361; www.empsfm.org; 325 5th Ave N; adult/student/child $15/12/free; ⌚ 10am-7pm

Greenwood Memorial Park

Pay your last respects to Jimi Hendrix in this cemetery south of Seattle. ☎ 425-255-1511; 350 Monroe Ave NE, Renton; ⌚ dawn-dusk

Kurt Cobain's House

Don't bother looking for the guesthouse over the garage; it's long since been torn down. 171 Lake Washington Blvd E, Seattle; private residence

Sound Garden

An interesting sculpture park, even if you aren't a fan of the band. ☎ 206-526-6163; www.seattle.gov/parks/magnuson/art.htm; 7400 Sand Point Way NE, Seattle; ⌚ 9am-5pm Mon-Fri

Viretta Park

Parking is tricky at this informal Cobain memorial; drive around back to 39 Ave & John St. ☎ 206-684-4075; 151 Lake Washington Blvd E, Seattle; ⌚ 4am-11:30pm

DRINK

El Corazon

Formerly the Off Ramp and then Graceland; no matter what it is, it rocks. ☎ 206-381-3094; www.elcorazonseattle.com; 109 Eastlake Ave E, Seattle; ⌚ schedule varies

Neumo's

This midsized club books some of the best rock shows in town. ☎ 206-709-9467; www.neumos.com; 925 E Pike St, Seattle; ⌚ schedule varies

SLEEP

Edgewater Hotel

The Beatles wouldn't recognize this supermodern hotel where they once fished out the window. ☎ 800-624-0670; www.edgewaterhotel.com; 2411 Alaskan Way, Pier 67, Seattle; r $299-439

USEFUL WEBSITES

www.seattle.gov/music/map

www.thestranger.com

LINK YOUR TRIP

TRIP 12 48 Hours in Seattle p107

www.lonelyplanet.com/trip-planner

Olympic Odyssey

WHY GO Forget "four seasons in one day" – on the Olympic Peninsula you get four landscapes in one afternoon. Stroll wild Pacific beaches, view snow-capped peaks, hike rain-forest trails and adjust your eyes to more shades of green than you even thought possible on this outdoorsy four-day loop around Mt Olympus.

TIME
4 days

DISTANCE
450 miles

BEST TIME TO GO
Jun – Sep

START
Olympia

END
Port Townsend

The cultured capital of **❶ Olympia** is the logical starting point for an Olympic odyssey, but this trip is all about the great outdoors, so head swiftly along Highway 101 and Hwy 12 past Aberdeen to Lake Quinault.

The river valleys that tumble off the sides of Mt Olympus (7965ft) shelter America's finest temperate rain forest and the trees surrounding **❷ Lake Quinault** rank as some of the world's oldest and biggest. As you crane your neck up toward these giants, ponder the fact some of the trees here were already 200 years old before Columbus arrived on the continent. With an incredible average annual rainfall of 16ft the western Olympic peninsula is also one of the wettest corners of the nation, so you definitely want to pack an umbrella and some Gore-Tex for this trip. It's not called rain forest for nothing.

ALSO GOOD FOR

Several fine forest trails line Lake Quinault, but one you shouldn't miss is the **❸ Maple Glade Trail**, which meanders past inky black streams and primeval-looking giant ferns into the green gloom of the moss-drenched forest. Keep an eye open underfoot for foot-long banana slugs, local monsters that sport a rasping tongue covered in thousands of tiny teeth. Just a mile or two away, the nearby July Creek picnic area offers a peaceful spot to take in views of the lake over a packed lunch.

After a walk through the rainforest, retire to Lake Quinault and the classic **❹ Lake Quinault Lodge**, built in 1926 on the southern shores.

BEST TRIP

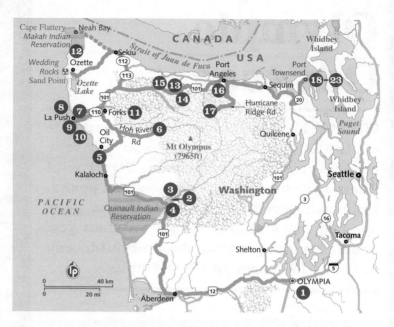

Order a pint of organic amber and relax on the cricket-pitch-quality lawn or lose yourself in one of the overstuffed leather chairs beside the crackling fireplace. The restaurant here is considered one of the best on the peninsula and with advance reservations you can dine at the very same corner table occupied by President Roosevelt during his 1937 stay at the lodge. Hiking trails start from the lodge's front door and staff lead free guided walks here weekends (nonguests are welcome). Also worth a visit is the world's biggest Sitka spruce, just a mile east of the lodge.

West from Quinault Lake, Highway 101 continues through the Quinault Indian Reservation before entering a thin strip of national park territory that protects the beaches around Kalaloch. Much of the peninsula is parceled up like this into a complex jigsaw of national park, national forest, wilderness and tribal territories. ⑤ **Ruby Beach** is the prettiest of the beaches here but you'll find wilder and more scenic beaches further north.

The most popular detour off Highway 101 is the 19-mile paved road to the Hoh Valley, where the short but fascinating ⑥ **Hall of Moss Trail** offers an easy 0.75-mile loop through the kind of weird, ethereal scenery that even a tripping Tolkien couldn't have invented. Old-man's beard drips from branches above you like corduroy fringe, while trailside licorice ferns and lettuce lichens overwhelm the massive fallen trunks of maple and Sitka spruce. Rangers lead interesting free guided walks here twice a day during summer and can help you spot some of the park's 5000-strong herd of Roosevelt elk.

Further north along Highway 101, the main reason to stop in the logging center of Forks is because the town has the only traffic lights for 160 miles. Turn west for the coast on Hwy 110. If you're camping, reserve your spot at deep forested **7** **Mora Campground** and drive the extra 2 miles for a sunset stroll along the crashing surf of **8** **Rialto Beach**. You can hike for 1.5 miles to the Hole-in-the-Wall, an eroded sea stack, or simply savor the changing hues over a bottle of wine, before heading back to make camp among the dripping ferns and campfire crackles of Mora.

The coastline just south of Mora at La Push hides some of the prettiest wilderness beaches on the peninsula. If you're here between October and May you might just spot migrating whales. The toss of a coin is the only way to decide between the trails to secluded **9** **Second Beach** (0.8 miles) or **10** **Third Beach** (1.4 miles) – both are superb. After an early morning's beachcombing, head back to Forks and slide into local diner **11** **The In Place** for a reviving slice of bumbleberry pie, a luscious blend of blackberries, blueberries, rhubarb and apple.

BACKPACKING OLYMPIA

If you're up for a multiday hiking challenge, Hoh is the trailhead for the peninsula's classic backpacking trip; a 35-mile return four-day trek through old-growth forest up into alpine meadows and face-to-face with the glacial moraines of Olympus' northern flank. For something completely different, consider the three- or four-day beach treks from Rialto to Ozette (24 miles) or from Third Beach to Oil City (17 miles), both of which take you past scenic sea stacks and the region's most achingly remote coastline.

Heading north from Forks, our bet for the peninsula's best coastal day hike is the **12** **Cape Alava Beach hike**, a satisfying half-day walk (9.2 miles) that starts on a gingerbread boardwalk through dense forest to the Pacific tide pools of Sand Point and then swings north along the windswept beach to Cape Alava. Keep your eyes peeled en route for rock carvings (notably a whale and a human face) on the southern side of the "Wedding Rocks," a spot considered sacred by the local Makah Indians (the tribe actually calls itself the Kwihdichchuhahtx but has long given up on anyone being able to pronounce that). This section of the hike is really only feasible at low tide so pop into a ranger station beforehand to consult a tide table. The hike starts in Ozette; get there via Hwys 113 and 112 and the settlement of Sekiu.

"…the tribe actually calls itself the Kwihdichchuhahtx but has long given up on anyone being able to pronounce that."

Olympic's national park campgrounds are excellent but nothing beats a night wilderness camping on one of the park's deserted Pacific beaches.

Come prepared with camping equipment, a wilderness permit and a bear-canister (to stop the pesky raccoons from stealing your dinner) and you'll get to live out all your Robinson Crusoe fantasies as you stoke your driftwood campfire and fall asleep to the crashing Pacific surf. Wilderness sites at Second or Third Beaches are perfect for first-time campers, or reserve one of the limited sites at Sand Point or Cape Alava to turn the Cape Alava hike into an overnight adventure.

DETOUR If you've made it all the way to Sekiu it's worth continuing the 19 miles to Neah Bay and the Makah Indian Reservation. The **Makah Museum** (www .makah.com) boasts a replica tribal longhouse, archaeological artifacts from nearby Ozette and four cedar whaling canoes (the Makah resumed whaling in 1999). From here you can continue to the northwesternmost edge of the contiguous US, at Cape Flattery, to spot puffins and sea otters at the Tatoosh Island lookout. Sail west from here and the next landfall is Japan.

Back on Highway 101, before you've even had time to brush the Pacific sand from between your toes, the scenery shifts again as the road winds along the glittering pine-scented shores of glacial-carved **13 Lake Crescent**. The lake looks best from water level, on a rental kayak, or from high above at the lake's eastern edge on the Storm King Mountain hiking trail (named after the peak's wrathful spirit).

Whatever your interests, make sure you make it to **14 Lake Crescent Lodge** in enough time to grab a seat, a pint of Singer Tavern Ale (brewed exclusively for the lodge) and the views as the sun sets over the lake. The lodge started life in 1915 as a fishing resort and retains a marvelously relaxed vibe, with lakeside deck chairs and a sunroom angled to catch superb views of the lake. Accommodations at the lodge are excellent, or head back to **15 Fairholme Campground** for campfire marshmallows.

Time to review. Rain forest: check. Pacific beaches: done. Alpine lake: seen it. OK, so it must be time for the park's best high-altitude views, and for those you'll have to drive south from Port Angeles, past the **16 Olympic National Park Visitor Center** and along the narrow winding mountain road that snakes up to **17 Hurricane Ridge**. A short stroll across fragile meadows reveals huge views north over the Strait of San Juan de Fuca to Vancouver Island and Victoria beyond, while Mt Olympus is just in view to the southwest. For even better views hike the 3.2-mile return trail west to Hurricane Hill to gain an extra 700ft.

Leaving the park behind it's time to ease back into civilization with the cultured Victorian comforts of **18 Port Townsend**, whose period charm dates from the railroad boom of the 1890s, when the town was earmarked to become the "New York of the West." That never happened but you can pick up a historic walking tour map from the **19 Port Townsend visitors center** and wander the waterfront's collection of specialist shops, galleries and antique malls. Don't miss the old-time Belmont Saloon on Water St, the ㉓ **Rose Theatre**, a gorgeously renovated theater that's been showing movies since 1908, and the fine Victorian mansions on the bluff above town, where several of the most charming residences have been turned into period B&Bs.

A colorful overnight alternative to the B&Bs is the ㉑ **Palace Hotel**. Built in 1889, this charismatic brick building is the former brothel of locally notorious Madame Marie, who ran her business out of the 2nd-floor corner suite. Nonguests are welcome to peruse any of the unoccupied 15 rooms, each named after the working girl who once occupied it.

After several days of canned backcountry food you might find yourself wandering up to the town's excellent eateries and just staring open-mouthed through the windows. The delicious rosemary roast lamb sandwich on fig bread at the excellent ㉒ **Bread & Roses Eatery** is an unbeatable lunch, then for dinner join the locals queuing for a table at the ㉓ **Fountain Café**, a warm and casual place with a global music, well-prepared Northwest cuisine and impeccable service.

Round off your trip with the 30-minute ferry ride across Puget Sound to Whidbey Island, the perfect way to leave the former port.
Bradley Mayhew

VICTORIAN DAYS

If you're headed to Port Townsend in late March be sure to pack your best handlebar moustache for the town's **Victorian Days** (www.victorian festival.org), which offers a three-day array of exhibits, walking tours and crafts workshops. Horses and carriages are dusted off, manners are polished and half the town dons asphyxiating corsets or buttoned-down waistcoats to celebrate the days when lamb-chop whiskers were the very definition of cool.

TRIP INFORMATION

GETTING THERE
From Seattle take I-5 south for 60 miles to Olympia and then head west on Hwy 101. Note that you can also do this trip in reverse.

DO
Olympic National Park Visitor Center
The park's nerve center offers information, a movie, wilderness permits and a few displays. ☎ 360-565-3130; www.nps.gov/olym; 3002 Mt Angeles Rd, Port Angeles; park admission $15; ⬩

Port Townsend Visitor Center
Helpful advice and armfuls of brochures at the eastern entrance to town. ☎ 360-385-2722; www.enjoypt.com; 2437 E Sims Way, Port Townsend; ⬩ 9am-5pm Mon-Fri, 10am-4pm Sat, 11am-4pm Sun

Rose Theatre
If only all movie houses were like this one; restored to glory with plush velvet curtains and hosted movie introductions. ☎ 360-385-1089; www.rosetheatre.com; 235 Taylor St, Port Townsend

EAT
Bread & Roses Eatery
Deli salads, homemade cakes, organic coffee, outdoor seating, live weekend music and art exhibits: perfect. ☎ 360-379-3355; www.breadandrosespt.com; 230 Quincy St, Port Townsend; lunch $7-10; ⬩ 7am-7pm Wed-Mon, to 9pm Fri & Sat

Fountain Café
This local favorite sources local ingredients to create Northwest staples, great seafood specials and fine desserts. No reservations. ☎ 360-385-1364; www.thefountaincafept

.com; 920 Washington St, Port Townsend; mains $16-22; ⬩ 11:30am-3pm & 5-9:30pm

The In Place
This unpretentious local diner serves the peninsula's best pie. ☎ 360-372-6258; 320 S Forks Ave, Forks; mains $7-17; ⬩

SLEEP
Fairholme Campground
National park campground on the western shore of Lake Crescent featuring 88 sites, a general store and boat rentals. ☎ 360-928-3380; sites $12; ⬩ year-round; ⬩

Lake Crescent Lodge
All the rooms at this superbly relaxing lodge boast lake views. Book a year in advance for the Roosevelt cottages. ☎ 360-928-3211; www.lakecrescentlodge.com; 416 Lake Crescent Rd, Port Angeles; r $68-211; ⬩ May-Oct

Lake Quinault Lodge
Everything you could want in a historic national park lodge. Reservations are essential. ☎ 360-288-2900; www.visitlakequinault.com; 345 S Shore Rd, Lake Quinault; cabins $125-243, lodge r $134-167

Mora Campground
Offers 95 sites set in deep forest on the Quillayute River, with guided nature walks in summer. ☎ 360-374-5460; sites $12; ⬩ year-round; ⬩

Palace Hotel
Period boudoir charm and a quirky sprinkling of mod cons make this former brothel a memorable stay. ☎ 360-385-0773; www.palacehotelpt.com; 1004 Water St, Port Townsend; r $59-109

USEFUL WEBSITES
www.nps.gov/olym
www.olympicpeninsula.org

LINK YOUR TRIP
www.lonelyplanet.com/trip-planner

Washington Ghosts & Legends

WHY GO If you love a good ghost story, Washington is full of them. But why just talk about ghosts? Psychic and ghost hunter Regan Vacknitz – cofounder of the Auburn Paranormal Activities Research Team – has more than a few suggestions on where to go to meet some of Washington's oldest inhabitants.

It's hard to believe a tourist attraction like ❶ **Pike Place Market** could possibly be haunted by anything more than the ghosts of the king salmon whizzing past your head. But it's not just the living who are drawn there. It's said to be almost as crowded with ghosts as it is with people, including Chief Seattle's oldest daughter, Princess Angeline. Despite the 1855 Treaty of Point Elliott, she declined to leave the city named after her father, and some would say she's never left.

Although Vacknitz has yet to see Princess Angeline herself, she doesn't doubt the market is haunted. "Even as a kid, I thought the whole back area seemed kind of off, and I didn't feel right there." After hours, mischievous ghost children are said to play unsupervised, keeping the market bustling with activity even after everyone's gone home.

One place that's easy to believe is haunted is ❷ **Kells Irish Pub**, on Post Alley, where you can enjoy Irish ale and kidney pie in the basement of the former Butterworth Mortuary. For decades, the mortuary housed the remains of 1500 children who died in the flu pandemic of 1918. Which is why we believe Vacknitz when she says, "Don't be surprised if you find yourself in the presence of a girl around eight or ten years old."

Also near Pike Place is the multi-spirited ❸ **Alibi Room**. This busy bar and restaurant can be crowded and loud, but during quiet moments, you never know who you might bump into. "Upstairs, there's a neat and tidy

TIME
5 – 6 days

DISTANCE
420 miles

BEST TIME TO GO
Year-round

START
Seattle

END
Issaquah

ALSO GOOD FOR

HISTORY & CULTURE

spirit who will clean up and rearrange things. In the kitchen, there's a young foreign girl who haunts her former quarters." And then there's Frank, who, ever the gentleman, will politely introduce himself if you meet on the stairs.

Just east, in the neighborhood of First Hill, you'll find the ④ **Richard Hugo House**, a Victorian home that's now a writing center and performance space. When Vacknitz investigated the house, she knew nothing about its history. "When I went in the basement," she said, "I could see dead bodies everywhere, literally stacked on top of each other. Later I found out it was the Bonney-Watson Funeral Home, and they kept bodies in the cellar all winter waiting for the ground to thaw in spring."

While you're exploring Seattle's many haunted locales, you can actually stay in a couple of them, too. "⑤ **Hotel Andra** was built in the Roaring Twenties, and some of the party guests never left. You can still sometimes hear voices, clinking glasses and disembodied music." You could also end up with an unexpected roommate at the historic ⑥ **Sorrento Hotel**. "Ask for room 408," says Vacknitz. "There've been many reports of strange encounters, moving objects, and a female spirit wandering one of the upper floors."

So what's the most haunted place in Washington? Vacknitz's vote would be ⑦ **Harvard Exit Theatre**, where she once got trapped in a bathroom by a playful spirit. "The place began as the Women's Century Club, and you can still see women in period clothing from the 1920s wandering the aisles of the movie theatre." It's also watched over by the most prominent spirit of Capitol Hill, Bertha Knight-Landes. "She was Seattle's first female mayor and founder of the Women's Century Club, and she's been seen sitting by the fireplace and watching the lobby as if times had never changed."

Adjoining the theatre is **8** **Seattle Museum of the Mysteries.** You can find out about everything from ghosts to Big Foot to alien landings, and get a haunted tour of Capitol Hill. "It's definitely the place to visit to learn all the strange lore of Washington state," says Vacknitz.

Seattle's not the only place for ghost seekers to give themselves goose bumps. Head just an hour north to the little town of Snohomish and visit the **9** **Oxford Saloon.** "The saloon has a history," says Vacknitz. It also has an appropriately creepy atmosphere, and it's easy to imagine reports of spooky goings-on. Disembodied voices? Movement out of the corner of your eye? That's probably just Henry, the policeman who was fatally stabbed on the back stairs, still keeping an eye on things.

> **DETOUR** The lost city of **Wellington** is a ghost town in every sense of the word. In 1910, an avalanche swept a Great Northern Railway passenger train from the depot down into the river, and 96 people lost their lives. The town was abandoned and all the buildings are gone, but you can still feel the spirits lingering. And it's not just your imagination: You know it's serious when the park rangers won't even stay past dusk. To get here, drive 50 miles east from Snohomish on Hwy 2; the site is at Steven's Pass on the Iron Goat Trail, about 10 miles after the town of Skykomish.

From Snohomish, head west and take the Edmonds–Kingston ferry, then continue on the scenic route to Port Townsend, a little over a two-hour trip, depending on how you time the ferry. Seaside Port Townsend has two eerie stops for the wandering ghost-hunter. Built in 1893, **10** **Manresa Castle** is a hotel with lots of period details and a decidedly haunted feel. During an investigation, Vacknitz and her team stayed in room 302. "Whenever anyone needed to go back to the room, we'd feel uneasy going in, like we should knock first." Awakening in the middle of the night with an eerie feeling, she grabbed her camera and snapped some shots. "There were so many orbs it looked like fog."

Just ten minutes' drive away is **11** **Fort Worden State Park.** Once home to military personnel, this former Army base is now home to several spirits. Visitors have reported ghostly encounters at the Lighthouse, the guard house, and **12** **Alexander's Castle,** a tiny tower that can be rented overnight – all the better for exploring the grounds in the dark.

For the next stop on your haunted hit parade, head 120 miles south to Aberdeen, where you'll find **13** **Billy's Bar & Grill.** A former brothel, it was also home to a notorious local legend, Billy Ghol, in the early 1900s. When Billy was around, people had a way of disappearing and buildings burned down a little more often than they should. Many say "Billy the Ghoul" still hangs around. "The bar shakes, bottles vibrate, and people feel watched. It's even said that some of the ladies of the house still inhabit the upstairs."

Just an hour's drive around the coast leads to Tokeland and the ⑭ **Tokeland Hotel**. Let's hope you have a better stay than Charley, a Chinese immigrant who died while hiding out there in the 1930s, and who still has yet to check out. Charley's not alone, though, as there are also reports of a ghost cat roaming the premises.

Break the long drive back to Seattle with a stop at ⑮ **Fort Lewis Military Museum**, where the restless spirits of military personnel have been known to stay on active duty. The museum held an exorcism in 2004, and they say there hasn't been any paranormal activity since. However, says Vacknitz, "A friend of ours lives on the base and still says you can hear troops marching where there are no troops, and people still report sightings to this day."

> "…people had a way of disappearing, and buildings burned down more often than they should."

Nearby, you'll find that not all haunted mansions are creaky and cobwebby. ⑯ **Thornewood Castle** is a gorgeous, 500-year-old estate shipped from England and reassembled south of Tacoma. that operates as a romantic B&B. During an investigation, Vacknitz awoke to find herself face to face with a well-dressed man who emerged suddenly in a pool of moonlight, then disappeared a moment later. For a ghost hunter, that's quite some room service.

Not as resplendent, but no less haunted, is Puyallup's ⑰ **Meeker Mansion**, a 17-room Victorian that was completed in 1890. In the master bedroom, the bedspread always needs to be re-smoothed. "Mrs Meeker is still there, sitting on the corner of the bed waiting for her husband to come home," says Vacknitz. There was also the matter of the teacup, which the late Mrs Meeker persists in turning on its side. "The historical society finally took it out of the room because they got tired of fixing it."

The final resting place on our haunted tour is ⑱ **Issaquah Depot**. "Walking through the old train depot, you feel like you're walking through the early 1900s," says Vacknitz. "The energy of all the passengers still hovers around." If you notice a little boy playing hide-and-seek, don't bother reporting it to the historical society. He's been there for many decades. And he's not going anywhere.

Mwa-ha-ha-ha.
Mariella Krause

TRIP INFORMATION

GETTING THERE
To reach Seattle from Portland, drive
175 miles north on I-5. From Vancouver,
drive140 miles south on Hwy 99 and I-5.

DO
Fort Lewis Military Museum
If you see someone there in a WWII uniform,
he's probably not a reenactor. ☎ 253-967-
4523; www.fortlewismuseum.com; Fort
Lewis Army Base, Fort Lewis; admission free;
🕒 noon-4pm Wed-Sun

Fort Worden State Park
This former Army base is well maintained,
but its tidy appearance doesn't scare off the
ghosts. ☎ 360-344-4400; www.parks
.wa.gov/fortworden; 200 Battery Way, Port
Townsend

Harvard Exit Theatre
You might get to see more than just a movie
in this famously haunted theatre. ☎ 206-781-
5755; 807 E Roy, Seattle; 🕒 show times vary

Issaquah Depot
Trains went in, trains went out, but some of
the spirits stuck around. ☎ 425-392-3500;
www.issaquahhistory.org; 50 Rainier Blvd
N, Issaquah; adult/child $2/1; 🕒 11am-3pm
Fri-Sun, plus 11am-8pm Thu Jun-Aug

Meeker Mansion
Mrs Meeker is sitting on her bed, waiting for
you to come visit. ☎ 253-848-1770; www
.meekermansion.com; 312 Spring St,
Puyallup; adult/child $4/2; 🕒 noon-4pm
Mar–mid-Dec

Pike Place Market
It's a whole different place after the tourists
have gone home. ☎ 206-682-7453; www
.pikeplacemarket.org; 1501 Pike Pl, Seattle;
admission free; 🕒 stores 10am-6pm Mon-
Sat, 11am-5pm Sun

Richard Hugo House
This vibrant center for the literary arts has
secrets in the basement. ☎ 206-322-7030;
www.hugohouse.org; 1634 11th Ave,
Seattle; 🕒 noon-9pm Mon-Fri, noon-5pm
Sat, plus performances

Seattle Museum of the Mysteries
Learn about all sorts of weird stuff, and
ask about their haunted lock-ins. ☎ 206-
328-6499; www.seattlechatclub.org; 623
Broadway E, Seattle; suggested donation $2;
🕒 call for hours

EAT & DRINK
Alibi Room
Different ghosts haunt the different levels of
this bar and restaurant in downtown Seattle.
☎ 206-623-3180; www,seattlealibi.com;
85 Pike St #410, Seattle; mains $8-13;
🕒 4pm-2am

Billy's Bar & Grill
Come for burgers and beer, stay for Billy the
Ghoul. ☎ 360-533-7144; 322 E Heron St,
Aberdeen; mains $8-18; 🕒 8am-11pm Mon-
Sat, 8am-9pm Sun

Kells Irish Pub
A pub in the basement of a former mortuary?
Even if weren't haunted, it'd still be creepy.
☎ 206-728-1916; 1916 Post Alley, Seattle;
mains $6-13; 🕒 11:30am-2am

Oxford Saloon
If you're nice to the bartenders, they might
show you some really creepy ghost pictures.
☎ 360-568-3845; 912 First St, Snohomish;
🕒 10am-midnight Sun-Thu, to 2am Sat
& Sun

SLEEP
Alexander's Castle
This funny little place in Port Townsend
looks like they plopped down a turret and
forgot the rest of the castle. ☎ 360-344-
4434; www.parks.wa.gov/fortworden
/accommodations; 200 Battery Way, Port
Townsend; r $185-200

Hotel Andra
Flapper ghosts still haunt this Roaring
Twenties–era hotel. ☎ 206-448-8600;

TRIP
15

②
OFFBEAT

www.hotelandra.com; 2000 4th Ave, Seattle; r from $219

Manresa Castle

Dark woods and spooky hallways give this place an appropriately haunted feel. ☎ 360-385-5750; www.manresacastle.com; 7th & Sheridan, Port Townsend; r $109-229

Sorrento Hotel

This elegant downtown hotel caters to rich and famous ghosts. ☎ 206-622-6400; www.hotelsorrento.com; 900 Madison St, Seattle; r from $339

Thornewood Castle

Not for looky-loos; if you don't have a reservation, don't bother trying to get past the gate. ☎ 253-584-4393; www.thornewoodcastle.com; 8601 N Thorne Lane SW, Lakewood; r $270-525

Tokeland Hotel

This place is cozy and informal, and there's no extra charge for the ghost cat. ☎ 360-267-7006; www.tokelandhotel.com; 100 Hotel Rd, Tokeland; r $43-65

USEFUL WEBSITES

www.apartofwa.com

LINK YOUR TRIP
www.lonelyplanet.com/trip-planner

Washington Roadside Curios

WHY GO What's a road trip without roadside attractions? From funny-shaped buildings to World's Largest Something-or-Other, these short stop-offs make great photo ops. With no admission and no real time commitment, they're a good excuse to pull over, stretch your legs, snap some photos, and be on your way.

If all the roadside attractions in the state of Washington got together to elect a mascot, a likely candidate would be the ❶ **Fremont Troll**. Long used as an example of the quirkiness of Seattle's Fremont neighborhood, the 18ft-tall concrete troll lurks fittingly beneath Fremont's Aurora Bridge, clutching an actual Volkswagen Beetle in the long, spindly fingers of his left hand.

Get a picture with the troll, then head east and across the Cascade Range on the two-hour trip to Ellensburg. ❷ **Dick & Jane's Spot** is the residential equivalent of an art car, with bottle caps and reflectors bedazzling every available surface, including several colorful sculptures. It's a private home, so you can't wander through their yard, but you're more than welcome to gawk at their creative assemblage from the curb.

Some 55 miles south of Ellensburg, sitting forlornly on the side of the road outside of Zillah, is the abandoned former gas station known as ❸ **Teapot Dome**, a perfect specimen of the roadside phenomenon known as "Buildings Shaped Like Other Things." The "Teapot" part of the name is obvious, since the building has both handle and spout. The "Dome" was added as an obscure reference to the Teapot Dome scandal under the Harding administration, which, to be fair, *was* petroleum-related. Plans are underway to restore the teapot and move it, so if it's missing, ask around. Also in Zillah is ❹ **Cherry Wood B&B**, with quirky lodging that makes it the perfect complement to your trip.

TIME
3 days

DISTANCE
690 miles

BEST TIME TO GO
Year-round

START
Seattle

END
Tacoma

Rest up in their well-appointed teepees or themed Airstream trailers before getting back on the road and continuing south on Hwy 97.

Behind every Stonehenge replica, there's an eccentric visionary, and the one behind Washington's ❺ **Stonehenge** was named Sam Hill, as in "What in the…?" Down near the Columbia River Gorge, it was meant more as a WWI protest than a roadside attraction, but, come on, Stonehenges are just fun. Pack a druid picnic and enjoy Sam's lasting contribution to Washington's roadside fun.

> **DETOUR** In the farming town of Colfax, three hours east of Ellensburg, stands the famous **Codger Pole**. This looming chainsaw sculpture made of five cedar logs was carved totem-pole style to commemorate the players in the 1988 Codger Bowl, a grudge football match between the Colfax Bulldogs and the rivals who had beaten them, St John High. Neither team let the fact that the original match had been 50 years earlier slow them down. The old-timers faced off once again and this time the Bulldogs won.

For your next stop, drive three and a half hours west toward the coast. There's a dearth of quirk along the way, but it's a pretty drive and a good chunk of it is along the scenic Columbia River Gorge.

Packed with roadside goodness, wee Long Beach has two great roadside stops. ❻ **Marsh's Free Museum** dates back to the 1930s and isn't a museum so much as an opportunity to peddle tchotchkes to tourists. Souvenirs and sea shells intermingle with sideshow-worthy attractions and oddities, such as a stuffed two-headed calf, a skeleton found in an attic, and an authentic shrunken head. The real star of the show is Jake the Alligator Man. Half-alligator, half-man, he was found in the Florida Everglades (as diligently chronicled in the *Weekly World News*), and his suspiciously plasterlike remains hold packs of 'tweens in his thrall. Across the street from Marsh's is the **7** **World's Largest Frying Pan**, measuring over 18ft tall. It's not just for show; it's actually made of cast iron and was used to cook up the world's largest fritter during the 1941 Razor Clam Festival. Occupying the same lot is the World's Largest Squirting Clam. It's not quite the photographer's darling the super-sized skillet is, but since you're standing right there, you might as well take a look, right?

> **ASK A LOCAL**
>
> "If you have kids, take them to the **Dinosaur Park** in Granger. They have a whole bunch of dinosaurs, like twenty of them, and they're pretty big, too. My two boys love to play in the sandboxes there, and you can take lots of really fun pictures with the dinosaurs."
>
> *Amelia Thompson, Seattle, WA*

Follow the winding back roads a couple hours inland into Centralia, where you'll find the whacked-out **8** **RichArt's Art Yard**. While his neighbors may not have the taste or culture to appreciate RichArt's elaborate, ongoing art project, which he's been adding to nonstop since the early Eighties, passers-through delight in the junk-art creations made from packing materials and found objects.

Perhaps a good match for the World's Largest Frying Pan is the **9** **World's Largest Egg**; too bad it's 100 miles away in Winlock. You don't need to plan your day around this stop; it's not as if the egg hatches into the world's largest chicken before your very eyes. But, since it's just a few miles out of your way, it's worth visiting if only to crack a few omelette jokes.

Not all roadside attractions have to have an element of kitsch. If you want to class up your road trip a bit, stop by **10** **Ex Nihilo Sculpture Park** near the entrance to Mt Rainier National Park on Hwy 706. Ex Nihilo means "something out of nothing" in Latin. Metal artist Daniel Klennert creates something, well, if not quite out of nothing, then out of scrap metal. Creations include horses, dinosaurs, sea creatures and more, with a skeleton on a motorcycle called "The Angel from Hell" and a risqué, R-rated section to keep things from getting too staid.

A 50-mile drive north leads to Tacoma and the last stop on your tour. With a name like **11** **Bob's Java Jive** and a location inside a giant coffee pot, it would be easy to assume that early hours and hot coffee are the specialty of the house. In reality, Bob's is a bar, and a dive bar at that, with a dark, crazy decor. Bob's started in 1927 as the Coffee Pot Restaurant, and is one of only a few surviving Buildings Shaped Like Other Things in the state; apparently being shaped like a vessel that holds a liquid drink is essential to long-term survival.

Mariella Krause

TRIP INFORMATION

GETTING THERE
To reach Seattle from Portland, head north for 175 miles on I-5. From Vancouver, head south 140 miles on Hwy 99 and I-5. Fremont is 6 miles northwest of downtown Seattle.

DO

Dick & Jane's Spot
A colorful whirligig of a home; good thing they don't have to answer to any homeowners' association. **www.reflectorart.com; 101 N Pearl St, Ellensburg**

Ex Nihilo Sculpture Park
Scrap metal comes to life in this unique sculpture garden. ☎ **360-569-2280; www .danielklennert.com; 22410 SR-706, Ashford; dawn-dusk**

Fremont Troll
He lurks beneath the Aurora bridge, Beetle in hand, just waiting for you to take his picture. **N 36th St & Troll Ave N, Seattle**

Marsh's Free Museum
Buy a souvenir so Jake the Alligator Man doesn't have to go get a real job. ☎ **360-642-2188; 409 Pacific Ave S, Long Beach; admission free; 9am-6pm**

RichArt's Art Yard
If you're lucky, you'll catch RichArt in his yard; even if he's gone in for the day, there's plenty to admire from the street. ☎ **360-736-7990; 203 M St, Centralia; hours vary**

Stonehenge
Celebrate the solstice at America's first Stonehenge replica, built in 1918 overlooking the Columbia River Gorge. **Just south of OR-14 on Stonehenge Dr, Maryhill; admission free; dawn-dusk**

Teapot Dome
A cute little piece of roadside Americana that's, sadly, out of gas – but there's talk of turning it into a visitors center. **14691 Yakima Valley Hwy, Zillah**

World's Largest Egg
Large, ovoid…odds are, you'll know it when you see it: It should be the only one on a pole. **Kerron St & Fir St, Winlock**

World's Largest Frying Pan
If only it were closer to the World's Largest Egg. It does make a good photo op, though. **Pacific Ave & 4th St, Long Beach; dawn-dusk**

EAT & SLEEP

Bob's Java Jive
Okay, so you can't get coffee, but you can have a beer in this roadside classic. ☎ **253-475-9843; 2102 S Tacoma Way, Tacoma; 9pm-2am**

Cherry Wood B&B
Sleep in a teepee or a vintage trailer – or a comfy room in the farmhouse if you must. ☎ **509-829-3500; www.cherrywoodbbandb .com; 3271 Roza Dr, Zillah; r $145-165**

USEFUL WEBSITES
www.roadsideamerica.com

LINK YOUR TRIP
www.lonelyplanet.com/trip-planner

Mt Rainier: Sunrise to Sunset

WHY GO Rainier is without doubt the single most awesome natural site in the Pacific Northwest. At every turn this flirtatious peak flaunts its curves, dominating the horizon. From steam trains to sledding in Paradise, discover new ways to experience "the mountain" in your own personal quest for the perfect Rainier view.

TIME
2 – 3 days

BEST TIME TO GO
Jul – Sep

START
Sunrise

END
Crystal Mountain

With close to 2.5 million visitors a year, most of them arriving between July and September, it's important to time your Rainier trip well. Repeat this mantra after us: "I will reserve park accommodations well in advance, aim to visit midweek (or mid-September) and hit the trails early in the day." Follow these rules and you'll thank us.

With that pep talk over, let's start at our favorite corner of ❶ Mt Rainier National Park. ❷ Sunrise offers the park's highest and most spectacular roadside views, and from this angle Mt Rainier looks like a giant bowl of whipped cream. If the weather is clear there's hardly a hike in the state that can touch the 6-mile scenic loop from the Sunrise parking lot up past huge views of Emmons Glacier (Rainier's largest), to up close views of Rainier from the arcticlike tundra of ❸ Burroughs Ridge. Tag on the 2-mile return side trip from Frozen Lake to the ❹ Fremont Lookout Tower (71781ft) and on a clear day you'll get awesome views north as far as Mt Baker and the northern Cascades. This is as good a place as any to remind yourself that you are indeed looking at a giant volcano, albeit one slumbering under 20ft of snow.

If the thought of hauling yourself up the side of these volcanic glaciers leaves you flushed with excitement rather than the dry heaves, then consider signing up for a guided summit climb. There's no doubt the climb is a physical challenge (only about half the 9000 climbers who attempt it

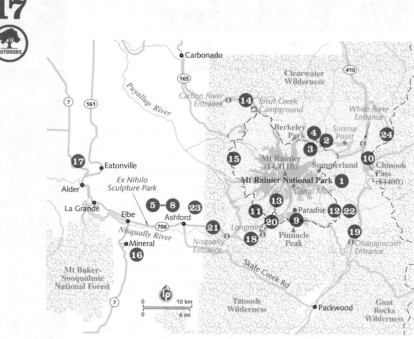

each year reach the summit), but it's still an achievable goal for fit nonmountaineers under trained supervision. The peak was first climbed in 1870 by tweed-clad Hazard Stevens and PB Van Trump, who ended up spending a night in a steam cave inside the crater. **5 Rainier Mountaineering**, in Ashford, is one of several companies licensed to lead clients up (and, more importantly, back down) Mt Rainier. You'll learn how to use an ice axe and crampons before hiking up from Paradise to overnight at Camp Muir at about 10,000ft. The final climb (likened to "climbing a mile-high ladder") kicks off at 2am, getting you to the 14,411ft summit around dawn for incredible views and an intense natural high.

Rainier's unofficial "Base Camp" and hub of the local climbing scene is **6 Ashford**, 6 miles west of the park. The region's densest concentration of crampons congregates at **7 Whittaker's Bunkhouse**, a former loggers' bunkhouse established by one of Rainier's most experienced mountain guides. The simple dorms and private rooms are perfect for spreading out all your gear and there's a good grab-and-run espresso stand here. Just across the green is **8 Whittaker Mountaineering**, a one-stop shop for visitor information, gear rental and the widget that fell off your stove five minutes outside Seattle. It's a great place to gem up on the latest park conditions while the kids practice their moves on the free climbing wall.

You may not have your eyes on the summit but you still want to track down the park's perfect view, so where to go? The sunrise view of the mountain from ❾ **Reflection Lakes**, south of Paradise, gets many people's vote, especially if you tack on the grandstand views from the Tatoosh Range on the nearby Pinnacle Peak hike. The sunset silhouette of the peak mirrored in ❿ **Tipsoo Lake** just below Chinook Pass is another stop-you-in-your-tracks view, again especially if you add on the 4.5-mile clockwise loop hike to Naches Peak and Dewey Lake.

Toughest but least crowded of the classic three viewpoints is the full-day 14-mile return hike (gaining 2100ft) to the alpine meadows and glaciers of ⑪ **Indian Henry's Hunting Ground**, where the picture-perfect view from nearby Mirror Lake is so good they made a postage stamp of it in 1934.

One of the great joys of summer hiking in Rainier is the annual explosion of wildflowers that carpets the mountain's freshly melted meadows. From late July to early August the busy trails around ⑫ **Paradise** frame the mountain in a Jackson Pollock canvas of lupine, paintbrush, monkey flower and lilies. For the best blooms take the classic Skyline Trail via Glacier Vista up to Panorama Point (5 miles) or consider the longer hike further west from Christine Falls up to ⑬ **Van Trump Park** (6 miles) via 320ft-long Comet Falls. Rainier's summertime spectacular is a short-lived sweetness; within a month of the bloom, fall colors are already starting to creep in.

> **DETOUR**
>
> If you're headed to Rainier in September be sure to catch Ashford's **Rainier Mountain Festival** (www.rainiermountainfest.com), a celebration of the wild outdoors that brings together films, backcountry workshops, slide shows and lectures from world-class climbers like Ed Viesturs and Dave Hahn. Gear freaks can pick up discounted and raffled gear from Patagonia, Mountain Hardwear and others or join one of the demos to learn some backcountry skills.

August may bring the wildflowers but it also brings the crowds. One way to avoid an ugly fistfight over the park's last parking spot is to focus on one of the less-visited areas of the park, such as the northwest corner. The 2006 storms that left the ⑭ **Carbon River Road** unmotorable were bad news for RVers but great news for hikers and mountain bikers, who can now lose the road warriors on a traffic-free ride to Ipsut Creek Campground, from where trails continue into the rain forests around Carbon Glacier, the longest, lowest and thickest icefall on the mountain.

No discussion of hiking in Rainier is complete without mention of the ⑮ **Wonderland Trail**, a rugged 93-mile loop of the mountain that ranks as the Northwest's classic hike. Set up in 1915 as a ranger's patrol trail, the hike takes you past dripping rain-forest subalpine meadows and two-dozen glaciers, grinding up a total of 20,000 vertical feet in 10 to 12 days. It's the mother of all Rainier hikes and the goal of every serious hiker in the region. Campsites line the trail every few miles so even if you don't have time for the whole loop, you could consider a section of the trail like the Summerland or Berkeley Park loop. Amazingly, the park at one point considered turning the trail into a paved ring road.

Thankfully, not everything on Mt Rainier revolves around blisters and trail mix. In the western foothills of the mountain, near the settlement of Elbe, the **16 Mt Rainier Scenic Railroad** offers weekend rides on its vintage steam locomotive ("the ultimate time machine"). There's something delicious about the clickety-clack of the wooden trestles and the wheezing bursts of steam, as you take in the Rainier views at an old-school pace. Enthusiasts can check out the cabooses and railroad dining car converted into a hotel and restaurant in nearby Elbe.

Families can get a different blast from the past at the **17 Pioneer Farm Museum**, which faithfully recreates life on a 1887 pioneer homestead. Put on your best bonnet and learn to churn butter or dress up in native Salish clothes and help chip out a canoe in the recreated Native American camp of Ohop (watch the crestfallen faces of the kids as they realize they aren't here for a pancake breakfast). You'll probably have to sign some kind of release form before you let your pride and joy loose pounding horseshoes in the forge.

DETOUR For a quick shot of weird, drive east from Elbe along Hwy 706 and pull over when you see a metal giraffe leaning over the fence, fresh grass dripping from his mouth. The **Ex Nihilo Sculpture Park** (www.danielklennert.com) features the art of Dan Klennert who recycles shapes out of anything from driftwood to metal screws (*ex nihilo* means "something from nothing" in Latin). I personally thought the horse made of horseshoes was cool but my wife was less impressed. "It's scrap," she sighed enigmatically, and she's right, but it's still worth a stop.

History lovers may also want to visit the **18 Longmire** section of the park, home to an early hot springs resort set up by James Longmire in 1883. One evening each August park rangers stage their living history tour here, guiding guests at dusk along the Trail of Shadows as costumed historical characters like Longmire and John Muir emerge from the forest shadows by lamp light to recreate the park's early history. Check the park newspaper for exact details of this and other ranger activities such as the guided walks at Paradise and Sunrise.

As with most national parks, Rainier's accommodations options are somewhat limited. The excellent national park campgrounds at **19 Ohanapecosh** and **20 Cougar Rock** offer the essential mix of ranger talks, crackling campfires and toasted marshmallows. For the best formal accommodations head a couple of miles outside the park to the cozy cabins and excellent roadside restaurant of **21 Copper Creek Inn**. Best bets here are the Dreamweaver cabin (perfect for romantic couples) or the "Art Studio," which boasts its own picture-perfect private hot tub on the banks of Copper Creek.

Rainier's fun and games are not limited to the brief summer months. Between mid-December and April bring your inner tube or plastic sled to the **22 Paradise snow play area** for great family sledding, or join a ranger on a two-hour guided snowshoe walk (departures twice daily mid-December to January and on weekends the rest of winter). Snowshoes are available for rent in exchange for a small donation.

Most remarkable of all is the nonprofit **23 Mt Tahoma Trails Association**, North America's largest free hut-to-hut trail system, located on the mountain's southwestern flanks. Where else could you hike or ski past frozen ghost trees and sweeping views of Rainier to overnight in your own private furnished hut or Mongolian-style yurt, for the grand fee of $10 per person? Huts come with kitchens, propane fires and sleeping mats; all you need is a sleeping bag, food and water purification for a luxury winter adventure on the cheap.

ASK A LOCAL

"Volunteering is a great way to experience a different side of Mt Rainier National Park. Contact the park's **Volunteer Coordinator** (www.nps.gov/mora/supportyourpark/volunteer.htm) or the **Washington Trails Association** (www.wta.org) for details. Projects range from trail reconstruction (half the trail repairs following the 2006 floods were done by volunteers) to amphibian surveys, and at the end of a day's work you'll have that warm glow of knowing you've helped preserve the park you love."

Kevin Bacher, Mt Rainier Volunteer Program Manager

So what's Rainier's best view? For that we turn to the **24 Summit House**, atop the Crystal Mountain ski resort, outside the park's northeastern entrance. The price might be almost as steep as the chairlift but it's worth it, as you savor the Rainier sunset over an Emmental-Brie fondue or pistachio-crusted rack of lamb. And that's our perfect Rainier trip; Sunrise to sunset.

Bradley Mayhew

TRIP INFORMATION

GETTING THERE
From Seattle take Hwy 167 to Auburn and then either Hwys 161 and 7 to Elbe (70 miles) or Hwys 164 and 410 to the park's northeast entrance via Enumclaw (108 miles).

DO
Mt Rainier National Park
The region's star attraction since 1899. Check the website for road closures, trail reports and trip planning advice. ☎ 360-569-2211; www.nps.gov/mora; 7-day/annual pass $15/30; ♿

Mt Rainier Scenic Railroad
Trainiacs can take a two-hour ride on a former logging train and then tour the restoration workshop in Mineral. ☎ 360-492-5528; www.mrsr.com; 349 Mineral Creek Rd, Mineral; 2-hour ride $20; ⊙ Sat & Sun Memorial Day-late Sep

Mt Tahoma Trails Association
Fifty miles of trails plus two huts and one yurt makes Mt Rainier one winter paradise. ☎ 360-569-2451; www.skimtta.org; c/o Whittaker Mountaineering, Ashford; accommodations permit fee per person, per night $10

Pioneer Farm Museum
Learn about life as an 1890s pioneer at this engaging living history lesson. ☎ 360-832-6300; www.pioneerfarmmuseum.org; 7716 Ohop Valley Rd, Eatonville; adult/child $7.50/6.50; ⊙ 11am-4pm daily mid-Jun–Labor Day, Sat & Sun only mid-Mar–mid-Jun & Sep-Nov; ♿

Rainier Mountaineering
Three-day summit climbs from $900 from Paradise, with trickier alternative routes possible via Emmons Glacier. ☎ 888-892-5462; www.rmiguides.com; Hwy 706, Ashford

Whittaker Mountaineering
Outdoor gear store and information center for anyone hell-bent on a Rainier adventure. ☎ 360-569-2982; www.whittakermountaineering.com, www.rainierbasecamp.com; 30027 Hwy 706E, Ashford; ⊙ 7am-8pm

EAT
Summit House
Savor sunset views over Mt Rainier from Washington's highest restaurant. ☎ 360-663-3098; www.skicrystal.com; Crystal Mountain Ski Resort; meal & chairlift ticket adult/child $79/39; ⊙ seatings 5:30pm & 8:30pm Fri & Sat mid-Jun–mid-Sep

SLEEP
Copper Creek Inn
Cabins to suit anyone from romantic couples to group reunions, most with private hot tubs. ☎ 360-569-2926; www.coppercreekinn.com; 35707 Hwy 706E, Ashford; r from $79, cabins $175-195; ♿

Ohanapecosh & Cougar Rock Campgrounds
Huge national park service campgrounds with sites reservable from July to Labor Day. ☎ reservations 800-365-2267; www.recreation.gov; sites $12-15; ⊙ Jun–mid-Oct; ♿

Whittaker's Bunkhouse
Unpretentious climbers' hostel offering good breakfasts and internet access. ☎ 360-569-2439; www.whittakersbunkhouse.com; Hwy 706, Ashford; dm $35, r $85-115

USEFUL WEBSITES
www.nps.gov/mora
www.visitrainier.com

LINK YOUR TRIP

www.lonelyplanet.com/trip-planner

TRIP
3 Ice & Fire: Volcano Trail p51

Chuckanut Drive

WHY GO There are few sweeter moments than watching the sun dip behind the San Juans over a plate of Samish Bay oysters, so fresh that they were asleep in the bay below you a few hours ago. Add secluded coves and the boutique delights of historic Fairhaven and here's a lazy weekend that's hard to beat.

Short and sweet, the ribbonlike Chuckanut Drive (Hwy 11) winds for 21 brief miles between the emerald ridges of the Chuckanut Mountains and the silvery waters of Bellingham and Samish Bays. A stone's throw from parallel I-5, this country drive couldn't feel further removed. One thing to remember: sunsets here provide such a spectacular backdrop that it's worth arranging your entire itinerary around them.

The starting (or end) point for the Chuckanut Drive is wonderful **①** **Bellingham**, a relaxed outdoorsy town that shares many of the cool credentials of Portland while avoiding its grit. You could easily spend a few hours exploring the exposed brick buildings of the historic downtown, stopping at everything from kooky stores such as Merchbot ("we sell stupid stuff") to the tottering piles of books that line the educated aisles of Henderson's bookstore.

Bellingham's grandest building is the former city hall, now home to the elegant **②** **Whatcom Museum of History & Art** and well worth an hour for its range of contemporary art and regional history. Pick up a walking tour map of the historic district and en route check out what's playing at the Moorish-styled Mt Baker Theater.

If you're here on the weekend a browse of Bellingham's scrumptious Saturday farmers market on Railroad Ave is a must, after which you should check out the amazing homemade ice cream at nearby

TIME
1 – 2 days

DISTANCE
21 miles

BEST TIME TO GO
May – Oct

START
Bellingham

END
Burlington

ALSO GOOD FOR

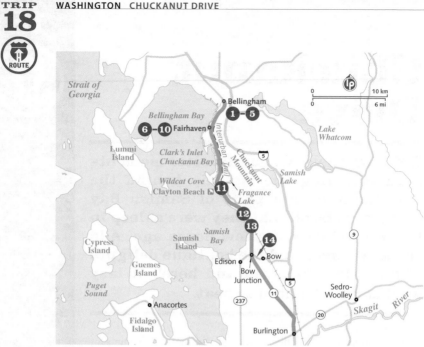

3 **Mallard's**, a Bellingham institution. "Taste Mallard's chili ice cream" should be on everyone's list of things to do before they die.

You don't have to go further than a block to kick-start the evening at the award-winning **4** **Boundary Bay Brewery & Bistro**, one of the Northwest's premier microbrewers. Order the six-brew sampler to find your perfect shade between blonde and oatmeal stout.

ASK A LOCAL

"While summer weekends can certainly be busy, they do offer the best farmers markets and evening entertainment. Bear in mind also that many businesses along the Chuckanut Drive are closed early in the week."
Steve Wilson, Bellingham, WA

Bellingham wears its independent spirit on its sleeve but does so with an admirable sense of humor. Aside from its own screenings, every Thursday at the Boundary Bay Brewery the **5** **Pickford Cinema** shows cult movies, which the locals often attend in full costume; think a bathrobe and a bowling ball for *The Big Lebowski*. In Bellingham the Dude abideth.

Nearby **6** **Fairhaven** is another left-field gem, offering similarly fine shopping and dining but on a more intimate scale. With the excellent **7** **Colophon Café & Deli** on one side of the village green, the comfortable **8** **Fairhaven Village Inn** on the other and a great Wednesday afternoon farmers market in between, Fairhaven is our choice for an overnight stop. It's also the kick-off point for tomorrow's drive proper.

One alternative way to savor the Chuckanut is not on the road itself but by bike along the 6-mile **9** **Interurban Trail**, a deliciously flat former electric trolley bed that parallels the tarmac past deep forest and lovely views of Chuckanut Bay. The good folks at **10** **Fairhaven Bike & Ski** will rent you a bike for the easy two-hour ride.

At the southern end of the Interurban Trail, just 6 miles south of Fairhaven, is **11** **Larrabee State Park**, a square chunk of emerald green forest that spills into the bay at popular Clayton Beach and Wildcat Cove. Poking around in the tide pools or hiking up to Fragrance Lake trail (5.1 miles return) are the most popular activities, though the trails can be crowded at weekends.

As you continue the drive south several pullouts lure you with fine views over Samish Bay as they explain the history of the road and its oyster industry. Oysters just adore the brackish waters of the bay and nearby **12** **Taylor Shellfish Farms** has been hand harvesting and shucking 1800 acres of seabed here since the 1880s. Staff can lead you through oyster etiquette as you learn to differentiate between a buttery Shigoku or a creamy Kumamoto.

PADDLING CHUCKANUT BAY

Easily the best way to appreciate crystal-clear Chuckanut Bay is by kayak. Tiny Clark's Inlet hides some fossilized palm trees, while paddling to protected Chuckanut Island offers a fun landing and the chance to spot guillemots, harbor seals and the occasional nude sunbather on secluded Teddy Bear Cove. Launch your own boat at the marsh flats of the northern bay (high tide only) or rent kayaks from Fairhaven's **Bellingham Bay Community Boating Center** (www.sailpaddlerow.org) and paddle down from Bellingham Bay in an hour.

Both Taylor's and nearby Blau, across the bay on Samish Island, deliver their freshest catch to a pair of Chuckanut Drive restaurants that between them boast the region's most hypnotic views. Of the two, foodies crow loudest over the wine menu of the Oyster House, though we prefer the more relaxed sunset deck of nearby **13** **Chuckanut Manor**, whose Friday blowout "seafood smorgasbord" pulls in punters from a 100-mile radius.

South of Blanchard Mountain the lower Skagit Valley flattens to checkerboard farmland. The views are gone but the Bow junction holds a few surprises, from the exotic roadside herds of bison and alpaca to the gourmet cumin organic Goudas of **14** **Samish Bay Cheese**, just up the road.

The Chuckanut Drive ends all too soon at bland Burlington, famed for its outlet malls and little else. For something altogether more charming we suggest continuing on to nearby La Conner or the San Juan Islands; the latter via ferry service from Anacortes or Bellingham.

Bradley Mayhew

TRIP INFORMATION

GETTING THERE
From Seattle drive 80 miles north on I-5 to Bellingham Exit 251.

DO

Fairhaven Bike & Ski
Offers local trail information and bike rental at $20 to $40 a day. ☎ 360-733-3344; www.fairhavenbike.com; 1103 11th St, Fairhaven; ◷ 9:30am-7pm Mon-Thu, 9:30am-8pm Fri, 10am-6pm Sat, 11am-5pm Sun

Larrabee State Park
Washington's first state park boasts 12 miles of hiking and biking trails, plus a 5-mile gravel road that winds up the hillside to fine views. ☎ 360-676-2093; www.parks.wa.gov; Chuckanut Dr; ◷ dawn-dusk; 🚻 ♿

Pickford Cinema
Art-house and foreign films at Bellingham's premier independent theater. ☎ 360-738-0735; www.pickfordcinema.org; 1318 Bay St, Bellingham

Samish Bay Cheese
Wander the family-run organic cheese factory then pick up a variety pack of flavored Gouda, Italian-style Montasio and Mont Blanchard cheddar. ☎ 360-766-6707; www.samishbaycheese.com; 15115 Bow Hill Rd, Bow; ◷ 10am-5pm Mon-Fri, noon-5pm Sat & Sun

Taylor Shellfish Farms
Stuff your cooler with the bay's freshest geo-duck oysters, Manila clams and Dungeness crab. ☎ 360-766-6002; www.taylorshellfish.com; 2182 Chuckanut Dr, Bow; ◷ 9am-6pm

Whatcom Museum of History & Art
Revolving exhibitions and local history in Bellingham's most eye-catching building. ☎ 360-676-6981; www.whatcommuseum.org; 121 Prospect St, Bellingham; admission by donation; ◷ noon-5pm Tue-Sun

LINK YOUR TRIP

EAT & DRINK

Boundary Bay Brewery & Bistro
Perennially popular place with a wooden warehouse interior and family-friendly beer garden, plus lots of specials. ☎ 360-647-5593; www.bbaybrewery.com; 1107 Railroad Ave, Bellingham; mains $8-19; ◷ 11am-late; 🚻

Chuckanut Manor
A winning combination of fresh Totten Inlet mussels, cold microbrews and mesmerizing sunset deck views. ☎ 360-766-6191; www.chuckanutmanor.com; 3056 Chuckanut Dr; mains $16-28, seafood smorgasbord $32; ◷ 11:30am-10pm, closed Mon

Colophon Café & Deli
A renowned African peanut soup and the attached Village Books make this a meeting place for the literati. ☎ 360-647-0092; www.colophoncafe.com; 1208 11th St, Fairhaven; mains $7-10; ◷ 9am-10pm Mon-Sat; 🚻 ♿

Mallard's
Don't embarrass everyone by ordering a scoop of vanilla, go wild over eyebrow-arching flavors like chai tea or ginger lemon. ☎ 360-734-3884; 1323 Railroad Ave, Bellingham; ◷ 8:30am-10pm Mon-Wed, 8:30am-11pm Thu & Fri, 11am-11pm Sat, 11am-10pm Sun; 🚻

SLEEP

Fairhaven Village Inn
Super-convenient location and an intimate vibe here (though some train noise), offering 22 rooms with fireplace and balcony. ☎ 360-733-1311; www.fairhavenvillageinn.com; 1200 10th St, Fairhaven; r with bay/park view $179/219

USEFUL WEBSITES
www.chuckanutdrive.com
www.fairhaven.com
www.lonelyplanet.com/trip-planner

Pacific Crest Trail: Alpine Lakes

OUTDOORS

WHY GO If you're feeling pain at the pump this summer, dust off your hiking boots, leave your car keys behind and add "hike a section of America's most incredible trail" to your to-do list. We persuaded Wilderness Press author Ben Schifrin to act as your personal guide for this trek along the Pacific Crest Trail.

The Pacific Crest Trail (PCT) is not just a hiking route, it's *the* hiking route, the trail that makes ever other trail in the nation bow down and cry out "we're not worthy!" Ben Schifrin walked over 500 miles of the trail for Wilderness Press' *Pacific Crest Trail: Oregon and Washington* guide and he shared his top tips with us.

Weighing in at 2650 miles, the PCT is a walk that's measured not in hours, nor even days, but months. The Washington section alone crosses four national forests and nine wilderness areas. Schifrin ranks the Goat Rocks and Pasayten wildernesses among the state's most scenic sections of trail, though his personal favorite is Glacier Peak: "I'm a people-hater when I hike, and this is the most-remote, most-strenuous, and least-populated portion, with the best views to boot."

While hard-core through-hikers aim to complete the route in one giant bite, most sane people tick off the trail in chunks, taking years to complete the route. For a superb first-time taste of the trail, Schifrin suggests the spectacular ❶ **Alpine Lakes Wilderness** between Snoqualmie Pass and Stevens Pass. "Of all PCT sections in Washington, the Alpine Lakes is the most logical single stretch to do," he says, "with easy access and shuttling from the Seattle area."

At 75 miles long, this is still a tough trip; a rugged, challenging rollercoaster that alternates between high, rocky vista-packed ridges and

---

TIME
7 days

DISTANCE
75 miles

BEST TIME TO GO
Aug – Sep

START
Snoqualmie Pass

END
Leavenworth

ALSO GOOD FOR

ROUTE

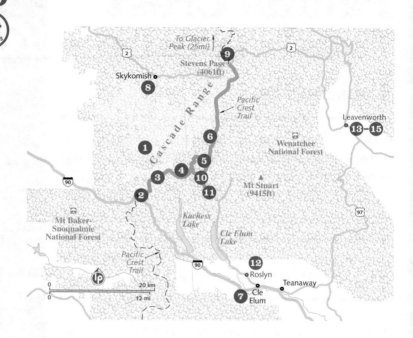

deep, lake-encrusted valleys. "Well-conditioned through-hikers often cruise its length in two or three days," says Schifrin, "most others will take a week." Your rewards? Dozens of jewel-like lakes, rugged Cascade panoramas, stunning wilderness campgrounds and pristine wildflower-filled meadows.

From ❷ **Snoqualmie Pass**, the trail leads north into perhaps the most spectacular part of the trail, climbing the Commonwealth Basin to stunning views from Kendall Ridge and the ❸ **Kendall Katwalk**, an exposed ledge blasted out of the cliffs. The scenery only gets better from here. According to Schifrin, "Every step from Chikamin Pass to Kendall Katwalk encompasses terrific, wide-ranging panoramas, often from Mt Rainier to Glacier Peak." Indeed, many hikers focus all their efforts on this section, making a four-day return trip to the Parks Lake Basin and Spectacle Lake overlook.

It's a scary fact that over half of Washington's population lives within an hour's drive of Alpine Lakes, so if you want to shake the crowds you need to continue into the remoter central section of the wilderness. Schifrin's favorite spot here is ❹ **Spectacle Lake**: "True to its name, it is in a spectacular location, nestled in a pocket of forest below the looming cliffs of Chikamin Ridge and Lemah Mountain." Another highlight is ❺ **Waptus Lake**, the largest of the region's 700 lakes and a popular place to camp off the main trail. The northern section of the trail features larger, forested valley lakes such as the northern string of Josephine Lake, Surprise Lake and ❻ **Deep Lake**. For overnight camps on the three-day stretch from Waptus Lake to Stevens Pass, Schifrin recommends Mig Lake, Trap Lake, Glacier Lake, Deception Lakes or Deep Lake.

It's possible to hike this section of the PCT in either direction. Heading north follows the direction of the through-hikers and ends with a night on the town in Leavenworth, but Schifrin recommends heading in the other direction: "This is the one stretch where I'd violate my walk-south-to-north rule. Start at Stevens, do the easier, lower terrain first, then finish spectacularly via the Kendall Katwalk before dropping down to Snoqualmie Pass." Either way, trail and weather conditions change frequently, so check with the **7 Wenatchee National Forest office** in Cle Elum or the **8 Mt Baker-Snoqualmie National Forest office** in Skykomish before heading off.

THROUGH-HIKERS

Every spring around 300 die-hard through-hikers don their ultra-light packs, post their freeze-dried food caches and set off from the Mexican border, hoping to reach Canada before the winter storms set in. Only around 60% of them will actually make it. The hardest thing about tackling the trail? Schifrin smiles when paraphrasing Babe Ruth: "Ninety per cent of doing the PCT is mental, and the other half is physical."

Transportation is the main logistical puzzle to solve. **9 Northwest Trailways** runs a bus service between Seattle and Stevens Pass but to get to/from Snoqualmie Pass you'll need a buddy with a car. One way to avoid transportation hassles is to make a loop hike from the east, via **10 Pete Lake**, joining the PCT for its central stretch to Waptus Lake. Base camp for this loop is **11 Owhi Campground** on the shores of Cooper Lake, deep in the Wenatchee National Forest. Access from I-90 is via the small community of **12 Roslyn**, which trivia fans will know as the location for the TV series *Northern Exposure*.

Even to half-starved through-hikers, food and accommodations options around the Snoqualmie Pass and Stevens Pass trailheads are pretty dire. To end your trek in style, swap your Gore-Tex for a fresh pair of lederhosen and head east from Stevens Pass to the kitschy Bavarian-theme town of **13 Leavenworth**. Schifrin's favorite German restaurant here is **14 Café Christa**, where you can wash down a plate of Wiener schnitzel and spätzle with a stein of Hofbräuhaus Munich lager. For your first bed in a week you can't do much better than the **15 Enzian Inn**, where owner Bob Johnson will serenade you with a morning blast on his famous alpenhorn. And here's a final tip from Schifrin: pick up some of the town's fabulous pastries for the drive home. Don't worry about the calories, after this spectacular weeklong backpacking trip, you totally deserve it.

Bradley Mayhew

TRIP INFORMATION

GETTING THERE
From Seattle drive east on I-90 for 50 miles to Snoqualmie Pass and park at the Pacific Crest Trail trailhead. To hike in the reverse direction take the bus or drive east on Hwy 2 for 80 miles to Stevens Pass.

DO
Mt Baker-Snoqualmie National Forest Office
Responsible for the Alpine Lakes section of the PCT north of Deception Pass. It's 1 mile east of Skykomish. ☎ 360-677-2414; www .fs.fed.us/r6/mbs; 74920 NE Stevens Pass Hwy; h8am-4:30pm Mon-Sat
Northwest Trailways
Two buses a day run between Seattle and Stevens Pass and vice versa; one in the morning the other in the afternoon. ☎ 800-366-3830; http://66.193.141.11; 1-way fare $24
Wenatchee National Forest Office
Call for trail conditions and information on the southeastern section of the Alpine Lakes Wilderness. ☎ 509-852-1100; www.fs.fed .us/r6/wenatchee; 803 W 2nd St, Cle Elum; ☾ 7:45am-4:30pm Mon-Fri

EAT & SLEEP
Café Christa
Quaint European decor, old-world German cooking and great sausage and potato pancakes. Lecker! ☎ 509-548-5074; www .cafechrista.com; 801 Front St, Leavenworth; lunch $9-14, dinner $16-23
Enzian Inn
Recover from the rigors of the trail in the indoor pool and hot tubs of this Bavarian-style inn. ☎ 509-548-5269; www.enzianinn.com; 590 Hwy 2, Leavenworth; r $115-245
Owhi Campground
This fine national forest campground offers 22 walk-in, first-come first-served sites beside Cooper Lake. ☎ 509-852-1100; www .fs.fed.us/r6/wenatchee; FR4616; sites $11; ☾ Jun–mid-Oct; ♿

TREK NOTES
- Between June 15 and October 15 you need a self-issued trail permit, available free from trailheads.
- To park a car at the trailheads, buy in advance and display a Northwest Forest Pass (www.naturenw.org; $5 per day or $30 annual pass).
- Note that campfires are not allowed above 5000ft (4000ft in some areas) or at many popular lakes.
- Schifrin recommends the USFS Alpine Lakes Wilderness map as sufficiently detailed and up-to-date, or invest in maps from Green Trails (www.greenttrails.com): Nos 207 (Snoqualmie Pass), 176 (Stevens Pass) and part of 208 (Kachess Lake) cover this trip.

SUGGESTED READS
- Backpacking Washington's Alpine Lakes Wilderness: The Longer Trails, Jeffrey L Smoot (Falcon)
- Pacific Crest Trail: Oregon And Washington, Ben Schifrin, Andy Selters and Jeffrey Schaffer (Wilderness Press)

USEFUL WEBSITES
www.leavenotrace.org

www.pcta.org

LINK YOUR TRIP
www.lonelyplanet.com/trip-planner

Islands & Orcas

WHY GO **Whale-watching, kayaking, biking, and generally leaving the world behind are among the many reasons to visit the magical San Juan Islands. Sprinkled liberally between the Washington mainland and Canadian border, these tiny islands number in the hundreds – and a few of them are even big enough to welcome visitors.**

The San Juans are a surprising addition to the land mass of the United States. Reachable only by ferry or private craft, they have a serene, otherworldly quality about them. They're tall, rocky, and heavily forested, with a vertical feel that says, "There will be no beach volleyball here, friend."

Start your trip at ❶ **Anacortes Ferry Terminal**, where you'll board the ferry for Friday Harbor. If you're bringing your car, you could end up waiting for hours in the busy summer months. Plan on spending the night in Anacortes and getting to the ferry early, or parking at the terminal and making the trip on foot or by bike.

After an hour-long ferry ride, you'll land at ❷ **Friday Harbor**, a welcoming little hillside town and the only one on San Juan Island. If you want to stay right in the middle of things, try ❸ **Friday Harbor House**, where you'll rewarded with a short trip from the ferry landing as well as smartly appointed, contemporary rooms.

Friday Harbor is where you'll find all the food, drink, and shopping, not to mention one of the best-smelling places on the island: the ❹ **Pelindaba Lavender Store & Cafe**. Unless you're one of those rare lavender haters, just walking in the door makes you feel aromatherapeutically enhanced. Snack on lavender-chocolate cookies, drink lavender tea, or buy some lavender-scented linen spray.

TIME
4 days

DISTANCE
100 miles

BEST TIME TO GO
May – Sep

START
Anacortes

END
Anacortes

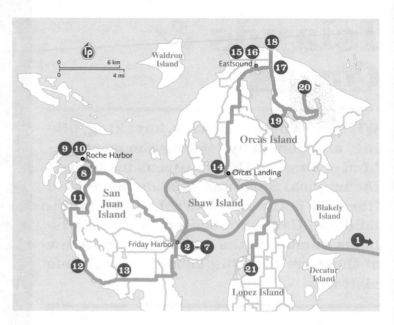

During the week, you can grab some lunch or stock up on gourmet picnic supplies at **5** **Market Chef** before heading out for the day. Their small café has a deli case full of specialty sandwiches and salads that they'll pack up nicely for whatever your excursion.

San Juan Island has the good fortune to be right in the migration path of three pods of orcas (aka killer whales), unimaginatively named the J, K and L pods. (Pod members' names aren't much better: "K-17, meet L-9.") To learn more about the island's unofficial mascot, stop by the **6** **Whale Museum**. It can be a little more scientific than some might like (there are things in jars) but you can learn a lot about orcas and find out which pods are in town.

> **ASK A LOCAL** "If you're here on a Sunday morning, go to **Downriggers** right by the ferry landing for brunch. They have an incredible crab Benedict that's to die for. It's a lot of food, so you could split it with someone, but it's totally worth the calories."
> *Elizabeth Clark, Friday Harbor, WA*

Ready for your whale close-up? Right near the ferry landing is **7** **San Juan Excursions**, who will take you out to watch the local orca pods frolicking in the straights. No whales that day? Never fear, your trip is guaranteed and they'll take you out again for free.

About 9 miles north of Friday Harbor lies the rurally inclined Roche Harbor, home of **8** **Westcott Bay Sculpture Park**. Here, you can wander among more than 100 sculptures scattered over 19 acres. Half the fun is the sheer variety; each was made by a different artist, and materials range from aluminum to granite to recovered redwood.

If Friday Harbor's population of around 2000 is about 1920 too many, consider holing up at this end of the island at **9** **Roche Harbor Resort**. They have a range of lodging options, from charmingly old-fashioned rooms in the historic hotel to plush, modern suites in freshly built buildings. If nothing else, stop in at the **10** **Lime Kiln Cafe** for a San Juan scramble or some fish-and-chips and gawk at the multi-million-dollar yachts moored at Roche Harbor's marina.

"...you have a decent chance to spot orcas right from the shoreline..."

Just down the road is the **11** **Krystal Acres Alpaca Farm**. The 80-acre farm is picturesque verging on idyllic, with green lawns, white fences, and fuzzy alpacas that look more like plush toys than natural-fiber producers. If you think they look cozy, stop by the farm's Country Store for an alpaca hat or sweater.

Next stop is **12** **Lime Kiln Point State Park**, where you have a decent chance to spot orcas right from the rocky shoreline – the most ecofriendly option of all. Bring your binoculars, but, if the orcas don't show, you can at least enjoy the views and the short, easy hike to the lighthouse.

On your way back to Friday Harbor, stop in at **13** **Pelindaba Lavender Farm**, where they grow the lavender that supplies the store in town. When the lavender is in bloom, mid-June through mid-September, the fields are right out of a postcard of Provence and the air smells heavenly. You can wander the fields anytime, and picnic tables have been thoughtfully provided to help you prolong the experience.

You might feel like you want to stay on the island forever, but remember: you still have a whole other island to experience, so park your car in the ferry line and take a final stroll around downtown before hopping over to Orcas Island.

On Orcas, you'll find a wilder, less manicured landscape than on San Juan Island, with the residents tucked away down long gravel drives. There's not a lot to see or do around the ferry landing, but if you want to drop your stuff (which you'll appreciate if you're on a bike), **14** **Orcas Hotel** is steps away, offering almost instant gratification. Their rooms are quaint and homey, kind of like staying in grandma's guest bedroom, with oodles of quilts and pillow shams.

The island itself is shaped like a pair of saddlebags, with the main town, **15** **Eastsound**, diplomatically in the middle. From the ferry landing, it's just over 8 miles through hilly farmland to get there, and that's where you'll find most of the dining. The town does shut down early, though, so don't wait till you're hungry to plan dinner.

Open later than most is ⑯ **Bilbo's Festivo**, a funky little Mexican joint with a homey atmosphere and an outdoor patio that's perfect for sipping margaritas on warm evenings. ⑰ **Café Olga** is another local favorite, which shares a space with a local art gallery and gift store. It's cute and casual, with a totally decadent-but-worth-it selection of baked goods.

Paddling around the island gives you an entirely different view of things, and ⑱ **Osprey Tours** offers guided excursions from the north side of the island. Take anything from a quick, one-hour splashabout to an all-day outing in their hand-crafted, Aleut-style kayaks.

Five miles south of Eastsound is ⑲ **Rosario Resort**, the onetime estate of Seattle's first mayor, Robert Moran. The historic home houses the front desk, day spa, restaurants and swimming pool, as well as a 2nd-floor museum and music room. Guests stay in more modern rooms scattered about the grounds, and, although they lack the ambience of the historical home, the waterfront location is stellar.

CATCHING THE FERRY

Ferry schedules are divided into westbound sailings (the ones going to the islands) and eastbound sailings (coming back to Anacortes). You only pay going out; return trips are included. So if you're driving, pay for the farthest island you want to visit – probably Friday Harbor. Then, you can visit Orcas, Lopez, and Shaw on the way back for no extra charge. If you're on foot or bike, you can pay to get out there, then hop around via inter-island ferry for free.

The resort also leaves you perfectly situated to explore Moran's gift to the island ⑳ **Moran State Park**, where over 5000 acres of forest lie draped over two mountains. On a clear day, the view from Mt Constitution is stunning; you can see mountains, islands, even Vancouver. Sadly, on a foggy day, you can only see the person standing next to you. Thirty miles of trails give you ample opportunity to explore on foot, but there's also a road straight to the top if you have a ferry to catch.

The first two islands are more than relaxing enough, but, if you have a little extra time, visit Lopez Island, especially if you enjoy pedaling slowly through your vacation. The island is super bike-friendly, with flat roads and few cars, and ㉑ **Lopez Bicycle Works** can set you up with a rental.

The ferry also stops at Shaw Island, but, with no lodging, restaurants, or stores, there's not much more to do than bike, look at more pretty trees, and check your watch to see when the ferry's coming back for you. Which, if you're not quite ready to re-enter society, might just be a welcome distraction.

Mariella Krause

TRIP INFORMATION

GETTING THERE

To get to Anacortes from Seattle, drive 80 miles north via I-5 and Hwy 20. From Vancouver, drive 150km (92 miles) south on Hwy 99, I-5 and Hwy 20.

DO

Anacortes Ferry Terminal

Call ahead for help planning your trip; ticket agents are too busy to answer questions patiently. ☎ 206-464-6400; www.wsdot .wa.gov/ferries; 2100 Ferry Terminal Rd, Anacortes; ☾ 7am-9pm

Krystal Acres Alpaca Farm

Come find out just how much cuter than llamas they really are. ☎ 360-378-6125; www .krystalacres.com; 152 Blazing Tree Rd, Friday Harbor, San Juan Island; ☾ 10am-5pm Apr-Dec, 11am-5pm Fri-Mon Jan-Mar; ☝

Lime Kiln Point State Park

Be patient and you might spot a whale; copious picnic tables make it easy to wait. ☎ 802-434-3387; 6158 Lighthouse Rd, Friday Harbor, San Juan Island; ☾ 8am-dusk

Lopez Bicycle Works

Don't even bother getting off the ferry if you're not prepared to pedal. ☎ 360-468-2847; www.lopezbicycleworks.com; 2847 Fisherman Bay Rd, Lopez Island; hr/day $5/$25; ☾ 10am-5pm, to 6pm Jun-Aug

Moran State Park

Hike to the top of Mt Constitution and wave at Canada. ☎ 360-376-2326; Mountain Rd & Olga Rd, Orcas Island; ☾ 6:30am-dusk Apr-Sep, from 8am Oct-Mar

Osprey Tours

Cool, Aleut-style kayaks are handcrafted right here on the island and offer a uniquely local experience. ☎ 360-376-3677; www.osprey tours.com; 178 Fossil Bay Dr, Eastsound, Orcas Island; $70/half-day tour; ☾ schedule varies

Pelindaba Lavender Farm

If only all farms smelled this good; close your eyes and you're in the south of France. ☎ 360-378-4248; www.pelindabalavender .com; 33 Hawthorne Lane, Friday Harbor, San Juan Island; ☾ store 10am-5pm, May-Sep

San Juan Excursions

Four-hour whale-watching excursions on the ecofriendly *Odyssey* depart from right next to the ferry landing. ☎ 800-809-4253; www.watchwhales.com; Friday Harbor, San Juan Island; adult/child $69/49; ☾ schedule varies

Westcott Bay Sculpture Park

Sculptures grow like wildflowers in this open-air art museum. ☎ 360-370-5050; www.wbay.org/sculpture.html; Westcott Dr & Roche Harbor Rd, Friday Harbor, San Juan Island; ☾ dawn-dusk

Whale Museum

Learn all about the orcas, including their whereabouts, at this informative museum. ☎ 360-378-4710; www.whale-museum.org; 62 First St N, Friday Harbor, San Juan Island; adult/child $6/3; ☾ 9am-6pm

EAT

Bilbo's Festivo

Guacamole, enchiladas, and margaritas add some unexpected spice to your island visit. ☎ 360-376-4728; 310 A St, Eastsound, Orcas Island; mains $9-11; ☾ 5-9:30pm year-round, 11:30am-3pm Jun-Sep

Café Olga

Fuel up for your outdoor adventures at this popular local spot inside Orcas Island Artworks. ☎ 360-376-5098; 103 Olga Rd, Eastsound, Orcas Island; mains $9-26; ☾ 8am-7pm, with seasonal variations Mar-Dec

Lime Kiln Cafe

Get a gander at historical Roche Harbor and its many yachts at this waterfront café. ☎ 360-378-1065; 248 Reuben Memorial Dr, Friday Harbor, San Juan Island; mains $5-11; ☾ 8am-2pm with seasonal variations

Market Chef

Boxed lunches, deli salads, and picnic supplies will get you on your way. ☎ 360-378-4546; 225 A St, Friday Harbor, San Juan Island; mains $8-15; ◷ 10am-6pm Mon-Fri

Pelindaba Lavender Store & Cafe

Free wi-fi makes this delicious smelling café a great place to wait for the ferry. ☎ 360-378-6900; 150 First St, Friday Harbor, San Juan Island; ◷ 9am-5pm

Rose's Bakery & Cafe

This sunny lunch spot also has wine and deli supplies to go. ☎ 360-376-4292; 382 Prune Alley, Eastsound, Orcas Island; ◷ 10am-4pm Mon-Sat, plus 6-9pm Wed-Fri Feb-Dec

SLEEP

Friday Harbor House

Soothing earth tones and floor-to-ceiling windows put this contemporary hotel in harmony with its surroundings. ☎ 360-378-8455; www.fridayharborhouse.com; 130 West St, Friday Harbor, San Juan Island; r $150-360

Orcas Hotel

A homey, B&B ambience just up the hill from the ferry landing. ☎ 360-376-4300; www.orcashotel.com; Orcas Ferry Landing, Orcas Island; r $89-208

Roche Harbor Resort

The suites are fancy, but the budget options are absolutely charming. ☎ 360-378-1065; www.rocheharbor.com; 248 Reuben Memorial Dr, Friday Harbor, San Juan Island; r $79-99, ste $200-400

Rosario Resort

Too bad the rooms aren't as charming as the original home, but there's tons to do at this tucked-away resort. ☎ 800-562-8820; www.rosarioresort.com; 1400 Rosario Rd, Eastsound, Orcas Island; r $188-400

USEFUL WEBSITES

www.guidetosanjuans.com
www.wsdot.wa.gov/ferries

LINK YOUR TRIP

www.lonelyplanet.com/trip-planner

Award-Winning Valley Wines Tour

WHY GO Napa? Too crowded. France? Too far away. The Columbia Valley's laid-back wine country is emerging as a major wine-making destination. Come learn about terroir, mesoclimates and viticulture, or just dedicate yourself to sampling lush reds and crisp whites in your search for your new favorite appellation.

TIME
3 days

DISTANCE
150 miles

BEST TIME TO GO
May – Oct

START
Yakima

END
Walla Walla

Southeastern Washington isn't just a wine-country wannabe. Turns out, the climate, soil and geography – collectively known as the "terroir" – are ideal for growing grapes. It's on the same latitude as the premier wine-producing regions of France, and, in the summer, gets two more hours of sunshine a day than Napa Valley.

Because of this fortuitous convergence of elements, there are now hundreds of wineries in the fertile Columbia Valley. If you really want to understand the enormity of your options, stop by the ❶ **Yakima Valley Visitor Information Center**, where you'll find lots of maps and brochures of the region.

Yakima's sleeping options are limited, so if you want to arrive the night before and get an early start, kick off your trip at ❷ **Birchfield Manor**. This cozy, antique-filled inn that was formerly part of a sheep ranch is a good alternative to the chain hotels that seem to spring up here as readily as the grapes.

The wine country offers all kinds of tasting experiences, from charming tasting rooms to elegant chateaus to industrial complexes. Start at ❸ **Bonair Winery** in Zillah, where you're heartily encouraged to picnic. Spread out on the lawn overlooking the pond, or grab a table in front of their buttery yellow chateau. Then, break open a Cabernet or Riesling and drink a toast to both your trip and their tasty tapas menu.

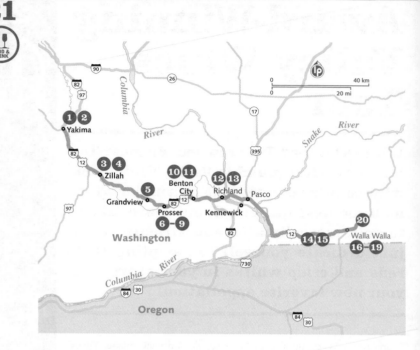

Just north of Bonair, ❹ **Silver Lake Winery** sits at the top of a hill overlooking the whole valley, making it a prime location for weddings and fancyschmancy events. Silver Lake is a collective with over 1200 owners, so if your trip inspires you to want to buy a winery, this is an easy way to do it without all the hard work.

Twenty miles farther down the road is the town of Grandview, which contains a great base of operations for exploring the central valley: the ❺ **Cozy Rose Inn**. From the outside, it looks like a cute farmhouse surrounded by rose bushes. But the rooms are plushly decorated in a style befitting a wine country getaway, and the Jacuzzi tubs make the perfect end to your day.

Just east in the tiny town of Prosser is ❻ **Snoqualmie Vineyards**, a winery that's pure Washington. Although it's located in a former grape-juice plant, the tasting room pulls off a rustic-but-modern timber-lodge feel. Stop by for some of their excellent, food-friendly Cabernets and Syrahs.

On the eastern edge of town, Lee Rd has a cluster of tasting rooms for easy, one-stop shopping. Sure, the outside is about as charming as a strip mall, but you can hit four places that are just steps apart. ❼ **Alexandria Nicole Cellars** encourages you to linger with tapas served in front of a fireplace and a cozy ambience that will make you forget your surroundings. (Or was it the merlot?)

If all the loveliness and sophistication of the wine country is getting too much and you need a little down-and-dirty hamburger action, ⑧ **Bern's Tavern** is a great place to decompress. Grab some beer at the antique wooden bar and kick back with the locals for satisfying pub food. But if you had something a little more wine-countryesque in mind, you'll find it just down the street at ⑨ **Picazo 7 Seventeen**. The local wine crowd loves this restaurant's tapas, seafood, and paella (the specialty of the house), served in a chic setting with bright orange walls and local art.

> **ASK A LOCAL**
>
> "When you get to Prosser, be sure to stop at the **Chukar Cherries store**. They have all these amazing chocolate covered cherries – not like those gooey ones you get in a box at Christmas; these are really great. Some of them even have wine flavors, like Cabernet chocolate cherries. My favorite is the Black Forest."
>
> *Wendy Beck, Yakima, WA*

Back on the road, another 17 miles of highway brings you to Benton City and the sprawling, Tuscan-style villa at ⑩ **Chandler Reach Vineyards**. It sticks out here in humble Washington, and whether your find it impressive or ostentatious depends on your style. But it's the kind of estate Napa visitors flock to, so if you want a little grandeur with your wine, this is the place to get it.

The wineries might start to blend together after a while, but one you won't forget is ⑪ **Blackwood Canyon**. This is no superficial swish-and-spit. There's no glossy tasting chateau, just a jumble of buildings at the end of a long gravel road. And don't expect chit chat. You'd better be serious about the wine, or at least prepared to spend some serious time learning about it. That is not to say that the winemaker is some snooty oenophile. Look for a guy in a grape-stained sweatshirt who makes wine the old-fashioned way, eschewing (and potentially ranting about) the modern techniques used by many of the Valley's newcomers and hobbyists. If that doesn't scare you off, you'll taste some amazing wine and leave feeling educated, if a bit confused by where your afternoon went.

Next stop? The Tri-Cities: Richland, Kennewick, and Pasco. Nicknamed the Tri-Windies for the insanely pushy gusts of winds that scoot you into the tasting rooms, the trio of towns is home to another strong batch of worthwhile wineries, among them, ⑫ **Barnard Griffin** in Richland. You don't have to ask if they've won any awards; the medals are practically used as decor, with bottles decorated like Olympians lining the walls.

"…the medals are practically used as decor, with bottles decorated like Olympians lining the walls."

It's a lot easier to find a great bottle of wine than a sophisticated restaurant in Washington's wine country – a fact that's sure to change as more and more tourists demand fine dining. But just next door at Tagaris Winery, ⑬ **Taverna** offers a sophisticated option that's wine-country worthy. Their seasonal menu includes beautifully plated seafood and wood-fired pizzas, served in a dramatic dining room with red walls and high ceilings.

For the last leg of your wine journey, continue about an hour east. About 11 miles before you get to Walla Walla you'll find the charming ⑭ **Woodward Canyon** winery. Their tasting room is located in an 1870s farmhouse with a creaky wooden porch and huge peony bushes. With such a homey setting, it's no surprise that this winery is family-owned. Just next door you'll notice a picturesque old schoolhouse built in the early 1900s. In the room where first graders once learned their ABCs, visitors can now learn about the wines produced by ⑮ **L'Ecole No 41.** The building alone is worth a visit, but their Syrah and Bordeaux earn an easy "A" among wine lovers.

WINE TASTING 101

Don't feel like you have to buy any wine. It's perfectly acceptable to say thank you and be on your way. Do buy some if you love it, especially if it's a limited production. Be careful with your wine consumption, and don't drive drunk. Either designate a driver or hire one. And feel free to spit out the wine into a spit bucket. It may feel rude, but it will allow you to control your consumption.

Just a little farther east is ⑯ **Walla Walla,** a thriving town with a sophisticated palate. You can find whatever meal you're craving at ⑰ **Luscious by Nature,** a spunky little eatery located in a former gas station. The interior is contemporary and colorful, and you can start your day with coffee and pastries, grab a quick salad or sandwich for lunch, or enjoy a nice dinner with a selection from a great list of local wines.

For fine dining, make a reservation at ⑱ **Whitehouse-Crawford Restaurant.** The setting inside a renovated woodworking mill is spectacular, with soaring ceilings and dramatic lighting, and the menu changes in response to what's fresh and available. Their wine list reads like a book, and you might just discover some great local wineries you want to hit the next day.

The most elegant sleeping option in town is the historic ⑲ **Marcus Whitman Hotel,** with its stately exterior and richly decorated interior. But if you really want to indulge in some wine country luxury, head east to ⑳ **Inn at Abeja.** Located on a picturesque farm in the rolling foothills of the Blue Mountains, the inn is remote and private, with gorgeously appointed suites located in century-old buildings. The last wine tasting on your trip? Head toward the barn: Abeja is also a winery.

Mariella Krause

TRIP INFORMATION

GETTING THERE
To reach Yakima from Seattle, travel 110 miles southeast on I-90 and then 33 miles south on I-82.

DO

Alexandria Nicole Cellars
Don't let the building scare you off; the interior is warm and inviting and the wine is excellent. ☎ 509-786-3497; www.alexandrianicolecellars.com; 2880 Lee Rd, Suite C, Prosser; ⏱ 11am-5pm

Barnard Griffin
The tasting room is nothing special, but their wines have sure racked up a lot of medals. ☎ 509-627-0266; www.barnardgriffin.com; 878 Tulip Lane, Richland; ⏱ 10am-6pm

Blackwood Canyon
Not for the casual visitor; come prepared to stay a while and learn about the excellent wines. ☎ 509-588-7124; www.blackwoodwine.com; 53258 N Sunset Rd, Benton City; ⏱ 10am-5pm

Bonair Winery
They're a little hard to find, but the lovely picnic grounds and tapas make it a worthwhile stop. ☎ 509-829-6027; www.bonairwine.com; 500 S Bonair Rd, Zillah; ⏱ 10am-5pm

Chandler Reach Vineyards
The Tuscan-style chateau sits grandly on the side of the highway, as if to say, "Take that, Napa!" ☎ 509-588-8800; www.chandlerreach.com; 9506 West Chandler Rd, Benton City; ⏱ 10am-5pm

L'Ecole No 41
This 1915 schoolhouse is as charming as can be, and drinking in a class won't even get you detention. ☎ 509-525-0940; www.lecole.com; 41 Lowden School Rd, Lowden; ⏱ 10am-5pm

Silver Lake Winery
Perched on a hilltop, this winery gets a commanding view of just about everything. ☎ 509-829-6235; www.silverlakewinery.com; 1500 Vintage Road, Zillah; ⏱ 10am-5pm Apr-Nov, 11am-4pm Thu-Mon Dec-Mar

Snoqualmie Vineyards
Don't let the exterior scare you off; the tasting room is charming and chock full of delicious reds. ☎ 509-786-5558; www.snoqualmie.com; 660 Frontier Rd, Prosser; ⏱ 10am-5pm

Woodward Canyon
Servers in the cute tasting room of this family-owned winery will make you feel right at home. ☎ 509-525-4129; www.woodwardcanyon.com; 11920 W Hwy 12, Lowden; ⏱ 10am-5pm

Yakima Valley Visitor Information Center
If you're not easily overwhelmed, there are hundreds of other wineries you could visit. ☎ 800-221-0751; www.visityakima.com; 101 Fair Ave, Yakima; ⏱ 9am-5pm Mon-Sat, 10am-4pm Sun

EAT

Bern's Tavern
An antique wooden bar, friendly service and great burgers are among this place's many virtues. ☎ 509-786-1422; 618 6th St, Prosser; mains $8-10; ⏱ 9am-10pm Sun-Thu, to 2am Fri & Sat

Luscious By Nature
Fresh, local ingredients rule, and they'll get you from your morning coffee to your evening nightcap. ☎ 509-522-0424; 33 S Colville St, Walla Walla; mains $9-14; ⏱ 9am-9pm Wed-Mon

Picazo 7 Seventeen
Share some paella or munch on tapas in this sophisticated Spanish wine bar. ☎ 509-786-1116; 717 6th St, Prosser; mains $19-24; ⏱ 4pm-9pm Tue-Thu, 11am-10pm Fri & Sat

Taverna
The dining room is impressive, but on a pretty day, the patio rules. ☎ 509-628-0020; Tagaris Winery, 844 Tulip Lane, Richland; mains $9-28; ⏱ noon-4pm daily, 5-10pm Mon-Sat

Whitehouse-Crawford Restaurant

Located in a former woodworking mill, the space has been smartly converted and the food is fabulous. ☎ 509-525-2222; 55 W Cherry St, Walla Walla; mains $15-39; ⏰ 4-10pm Wed-Mon

SLEEP

Birchfield Manor

Locals love the on-site restaurant; travelers love that it's not another chain. ☎ 509-452-1960; www.birchfieldmanor.com; 2018 Birchfield Rd, Yakima; r $119-159

Cozy Rose Inn

Cozy is exactly what you'll feel in these elegant rooms that are made for comfort.
☎ 509-882-4668; www.cozyroseinn.com; 1220 Forsell Rd, Grandview; r $149-225

Inn at Abeja

Wine tastings are by appointment only, so unless you're a guest, call before you come.
☎ 509-522-1234; www.abeja.net; 2014 Mill Creek Rd, Walla Walla; r $215-285

Marcus Whitman Hotel

Recent renovations have made this historic hotel a dignified lodging option. ☎ 866-826-9422; www.marcuswhitmanhotel.com; 6 W Rose, Walla Walla; r $124-219

USEFUL WEBSITES

www.washingtonwine.org
www.winetrailsnw.com

LINK YOUR TRIP

www.lonelyplanet.com/trip-planner

TRIP
28 Columbia River Gorge p195

Bounty of the Apple Valley Picnic Trip

WHY GO In Wenatchee Valley, the climate is just right for spreading out a picnic under the awning of a clear, blue sky. In summer, you can load up on cherries, peaches, and plums along the roadsides – and sample a dizzying array of crisp, Washington apples.

Cloudy skies and grocery-store produce just don't compare to munching on tree-ripened fruit on a warm, sunny day. If you're lucky enough to be in driving distance of the so-called "Apple Valley," you can gorge yourself on just-picked fruit that has never seen the back of a semi. The downside is, you might never hold a your everyday apples in as high regard again.

Start your trip about 11 miles north of Orondo with a visit to the ❶ **Orondo Cider Works**. This big red barn on Hwy 97 (not to be confused with parallel doppelganger Hwy 97A) is known for fresh-pressed cider, and on Saturdays you can watch cider-pressing demonstrations and tour the orchards. If it's warm out, they'll even whip up fresh fruit ice cream right in front of you.

Once you've drunk your fill and stocked your coolers, head south toward ❷ **Wenatchee**, the self-proclaimed – and who's arguing? – Apple Capital of the World. (It is perhaps worth mentioning that it's also called the "Buckle of the Powerbelt of the Great Northwest," which is nowhere near as catchy.)

You'll pass several fruit stands and crop stalls along the way, and, as summer wears on, the road starts looking more and more like a gypsy camp as people set up shop in the back of their trucks. One permanent fixture that's worth a stop is ❸ **Feil Pioneer Fruit Stand**, whose operators truly were pioneers when they opened this stand more than 80 years ago. You can sample an unfathomable variety of tree-ripened apples here – more

TIME
2 days

DISTANCE
45 miles

BEST TIME TO GO
Jul – Oct

START
Orondo

END
Leavenworth

than a hundred – with names like Idared, Northern Spy and the mysterious-sounding Transparent.

Just an apple-core toss down the road is the **4** **B&B Fruit Stand**, a small, family-owned stand that's been selling fresh fruit straight from their orchard to hungry passers-by since 1962. They have apples, too, but their specialty is soft fruits – think anything with a pit – such as cherries, peaches and apricots.

To bone up on the relative merits of a Gala versus a Honeycrisp, stop by the **5** **Washington Apple Commission Visitors Center** on the way into Wenatchee. There, you can learn all about different apple varieties and pick up plenty of local information while you're at it.

If it happens to be a Saturday or Wednesday, you can overwhelm yourself with the bounty of nature and support local family-owned farms at the **6** **Wenatchee Valley Farmers Market**. Stand after stand displays fruits and vegetables and flowers, plucked from the source just days (or hours) before.

Twenty minutes west in Peshastin, **7** **Smallwood's Harvest** is a kiddy picnic paradise. This family-friendly fruit stand has fresh produce and a shop for extras such as jams, condiments and wine. But the real attraction is the inviting grounds strewn with picnic tables and diversions for the apple-weary child, including a petting zoo, a train painted like a cow, and a late-autumn pumpkin patch.

If down-home toddler fun is too much to bear on an empty stomach, roll on down the road to ⑧ **Prey's Fruit Barn**, one of the largest fruit stands in the state (hold the scarecrows and baby ducks) where you can buy fresh fruits and vegetables, including over forty different kinds of apples and pears. While you're there, duck in to the bakery next door for a couple loaves of bread to fortify your picnic basket.

By now, you should have a car brimming with produce, but you'll likely need more than crisp apple slices to keep you sated. Continue west another 2 miles to ⑨ **Leavenworth**, a Bavarian theme village and excellent source of protein. The ⑩ **Cheesemonger's Shop** has, first and foremost, cheese: Bricks, slices, wedges, wheels, and cubes of Goudas, Havartis, Cheddars, and Gruyeres from around the world. The Irish Porter cheese is particularly impressive, both in flavor and appearance. They also have a small selection of meats, as well as wine and any picnic implements you might find yourself in need of, such as bottle openers and those ridiculously small knives.

> **ASK A LOCAL**
>
> "One of my favorite places in Wenatchee is **Ohme Gardens**. You can't take food in there, unfortunately, but they planted all this beautiful, lush stuff on the side of this big, ugly mountain. There are all these pretty, stone paths, and the view from up there is awesome."
>
> *Dana Sandoval, Leavenworth, WA*

What The Cheesemonger's Shop is to cheese, ⑪ **Munchen Haus** is to German sausages. Get some links to go, or enjoy them in the lively outdoor biergarten, complete with hanging flower baskets and a live accordion music.

Whether you're exhausted from the full day of foraging or just storing up some strength for a next-day picnic, the ⑫ **Bavarian Lodge** is cute and tidy, not to mention a great bargain when you take into account the gut-busting breakfast that's included in the price. (And this trip *is* all about eating, right?)

As for where to stop and enjoy your feast? With the Wenatchee Forest and Icicle Creek Canyon nearby, scenic options abound for places not only

THE TIME IS RIPE

Plan your trip according to what's in season, and remember that most fruits aren't ripe until late summer or early fall. If you're coming for the apples, harvest is August to October. For cherries, mid-June through mid-August is the time to go, and for peaches and nectarines, try August to September.

to spread out al fresco, but to hike away the calories until they've become a distant, fond memory. You can stop by the ⑬ **Wenatchee National Forest Park Station** in downtown Wenatchee for maps and recommendations, but pulling up a large flat rock overlooking the rushing Wenatchee River can't be beat.

Mariella Krause

TRIP INFORMATION

GETTING THERE
From Seattle, head 85 miles east on I-90, then take Hwy 97 north for 75 miles through the Wenatchee National Forest up to Orondo.

DO

B&B Fruit Stand
Stock up on stone fruits – cherries, apricots, peaches and nectarines – at this family-owned roadside stand. ☎ 509-884-2522; 13041 Hwy 2, East Wenatchee; ☺ 8:30am-6pm Jun-Oct

Feil Pioneer Fruit Stand
With over 100 different varieties, it's easy to compare apples to apples. ☎ 509-679-3378; www.wenatcheefruit.com; 13041 Hwy 2, East Wenatchee; ☺ 8:30am-6pm Jun-Oct

Prey's Fruit Barn
Over 130 acres' worth of produce – mostly apples, but also some veggies – fills this barn every summer. ☎ 509-548-5771; www.preysfruitbarn.com; 11007 Hwy 2, Leavenworth; ☺ 8:30am-6pm; late May-Oct

Washington Apple Commission Visitors Center
Get the crunchy facts about apples and local agri-tourism. ☎ 509-663-9600; www.bestapples.com; 2900 Euclid Ave, Wenatchee; ☺ 8am-5pm Mon-Fri year-round, plus 9am-5pm Sat & 10am-4pm Sun May-Dec

Wenatchee Valley Farmers Market
Join the locals in living off the land. ☎ 509-668-0497; www.wenatcheefarmersmarket.com; Columbia St & Palouse St, Wenatchee; ☺ 8am-1pm, Wed & Sat, May-Oct, 9am-1pm Sun, July-Oct; ☖

EAT

Cheesemonger's Shop
Every kind of cheese you can think of, plus some you didn't know existed. ☎ 877-888-7389; www.cheesemongersshop.com; 819 Front St, Leavenworth; ☺ 10am-6pm with seasonal variations

Munchen Haus
Balance out all of that wholesome produce with some tasty German sausage at this colorful little biergarten. ☎ 509-548-1158; www.muchenhaus.com; 709 Front St, Leavenworth; ☺ 11am-8pm May-Oct

Orondo Cider Works
Fresh apple cider and homemade ice cream are just two delicious incentives to visit. ☎ 509-784-1029; www.orondociderworks.com; 1 Edgewater Dr, Orondo; ☺ 7am-6pm, to 9pm in summer; ☖

Smallwood's Harvest
Enjoy petting zoos, picnic tables, and wholesome fun at this farm brimming with produce and children. ☎ 509-548-4196; www.smallwoodsharvest.com; 10461 Stemm Rd, Peshastin; ☺ 8am-7pm Jun-Oct, 9am-4pm Nov-May; ☖

SLEEP

Bavarian Lodge
A friendly, cheerful base for all your picnic adventures, this alpine-themed lodge includes a bountiful breakfast. ☎ 509-548-7878; www.bavarianlodge.com; 810 Hwy 2, Leavenworth; r $109-195; ☖

USEFUL WEBSITES
www.pickyourown.org
www.wenatcheevalley.org

LINK YOUR TRIP

www.lonelyplanet.com/trip-planner

TRIP
21 Award-Winning Valley Wines Tour p153

Cowboys & Kerouac: The North Cascades

WHY GO Put simply, Washington's North Cascades Scenic Highway is one of the nation's premier mountain drives. Join Kerouac's "rucksack revolution" on a pilgrimage to Desolation Peak, paddle the sparkling turquoise waters of Diablo Lake or simply take in the outstanding roadside views on this alpine itinerary through the heart of the wild Cascades.

TIME
3 – 4 days

DISTANCE
140 miles

BEST TIME TO GO
Jun – Sep

START
Burlington

END
Winthrop

ALSO GOOD FOR

ROUTE

The drive starts unpromisingly, passing the logging town of Sedro-Woolley and the gray cement silos that mark the town of Concrete (whose tourist slogan should read "not as interesting as it sounds"). Around 4 miles past Rockport the miragelike appearance of an Indonesian-style Batak hut marks the ❶ **Cascadian Home Farm**, worth a stop for its organic strawberries, delicious fruit shakes and life-saving espresso, which you can slurp down on a short self-guided tour of the farm.

Blink and you'll miss the town of Marblemount but consider a pit stop here, mainly because it's the last place for 70 miles where you can fill up on gas and a good meal. The popular ❷ **Buffalo Run Restaurant** offers a gamey selection of elk and venison alongside that perennial tourist favorite, "Cascade Mountain oysters" (deep-fried buffalo testicles). Don't panic, there are also vegetarian options.

By the time you get to ❸ **Newhalem Campground** the mountains have closed in and you start to see why it took until 1972 to complete Hwy 20. The surrounding peaks and glaciers are some of the wildest territory in the Lower 48 and the names alone of such surrounding peaks as Mt Terror, Mt Despair and "The Chopping Board" are enough to give a city slicker the willies. Even today the road is blocked by snow from mid-November to mid-April.

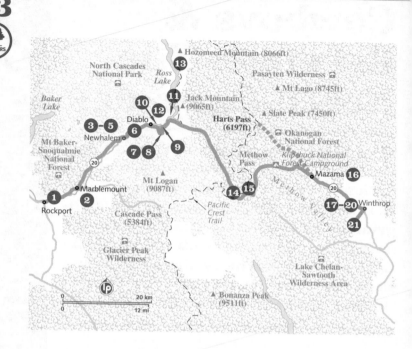

The campground's **4 North Cascades National Park Visitor Center** is the route's first mandatory stop and the essential orientation point for first-time visitors. The visitor displays are well worth some time, if only to horrify your kids with the 18-times life-size model of a crab spider (and then take them camping...). A short trail behind the center offers a fine spot from which to contemplate the wild peaks of the Picket Range.

The odd thing about much of the landscape on this trip is that it's unnatural, born from the construction of three huge dams that still supply Seattle with much of its electricity. The orderly company town of **5 Newhalem** is home to many of the dam's employees and is worth a stop to pick up some fudge at the general store and invest an hour in two short walks. The delightful Trail of the Cedars (1 mile) meanders through towering old-growth cedars and Douglas firs, while the Ladder Falls Trail winds behind the power station to a charming 1930s-era garden and dramatic views of the sinuous falls. At night the brooding power station lights up like Frankenstein's laboratory.

From Newhalem the highway passes the dramatic **6 Gorge Falls** pullout and soon reveals the first views of turquoise **7 Diablo Lake**. Diablo is understandably the most popular part of the park, offering beaches, gorgeous lake views and a boat launch at **8 Colonial Creek campground**, with fine nearby hikes to Thunder Knob (3.6 miles return) and Thunder Creek. The drive's classic (and unmissable) photo op comes courtesy of the breathtaking **⑨ Diablo Lake overlook**.

One of the overlooked gems of the Cascades is the well-respected **⑩ North Cascades Institute**, which offers an extensive series of residential programs at its environmental learning center on the northern shore of Diablo Lake. Courses run the gamut from outdoor photography to hardcore backpacking trips, though our favorite is the "Diablo Downtime," a relaxing, kids-free weekend of paddling, hiking, yoga and slow food. On Saturdays in Summer the institute also offers free canoe paddles and forest hikes; you need to sign up by 8:30am to secure a spot.

Accommodations options in the park are limited. Colonial Creek and Newhalem are excellent park-run campgrounds that offer shady sites set deep in old-growth forest. The only formal accommodations are at **⑪ Ross Lake Resort**, a collection of 12 floating lakeshore cabins that date from the 1930s. There are no phones, no TVs, no restaurant; in fact there's not even a road here. Access is only possible via ferry and resort truck from Diablo Lake or by a 1-mile walk and short boat ride from Hwy 20. It's the perfect launch pad for a boat trip around Lake Ross.

RED TAPE

Travel in the North Cascade wilderness involves more red tape than you'd imagine. For a trip to Desolation Peak or any other backcountry campsite you need to get a free backcountry permit, available within 24 hours of your departure from Marblemount ranger station, Colonial Creek Campground or Newhalem Visitor Center. Furthermore, most day-hike trailheads require a **Northwest Forest Permit** (www.naturenw.org), available from the same locations and several private stores.

There's something in the feral nature of the Cascades that has long attracted poets and writers. Zen-influenced Beat poet (and inspiration for the character Japhy Rider in Jack Kerouac's *Dharma Bums*) Gary Snyder spent two summers manning the park's fire lookouts, including a season atop **⑫ Sourdough Mountain** in 1953. A well-maintained trail still climbs to the lookout (11.4 miles return), but the monster 5500ft height gain makes the hike best suited to an overnight or three-day trip.

A turnout at milepost 135 celebrates the Cascades' other literary star with the drive's only roadside views of **⑬ Desolation Peak**. The peak's lookout tower was famously home to Kerouac in 1953 when he spent 63 days in splendid isolation here, honing his evolving Buddhist philosophy, raging at "The Void" of nearby Hozomeen Mountain (also visible from the turnout) and penning drafts of *Desolation Angels*. It was the last time Kerouac would enjoy such anonymity; the following year saw the publication of *On the Road*, and his propulsion to the status of literary icon.

To make a literary pilgrimage to the lookout, you need to first hike the long 16 miles up the east side of Ross Lake to Lightning Creek or assemble some friends to share the $80 one-way boat charter from Ross Lake Resort. From here it's a hot, steep and dry 6.8-mile one-way haul to the summit, gaining 4400ft, though with a backcountry permit you could camp at Desolation Camp, a mile below the 6102ft peak, and hike up the next morning to enjoy the dawn views (the fire tower itself is closed to the public). This is one walk where it would be remiss not to pack a well-thumbed copy of *Desolation Angels* or *The Dharma Bums,* both of which chronicle Kerouac's time on the mountain.

> **DETOUR**

Mazama is also the jumping-off point for the adventurous detour to **Hart's Pass**, a 24-mile white-knuckle drive past scary unguarded drop-offs to unrivalled 360-degree Cascade views. From the 6197ft pass die-hards can continue a further 3 miles along Washington's highest road to the base of Slate Peak (7450ft), where a short hike leads up to an abandoned fire lookout. Be warned: the one-lane gravel road requires a cool head and lots of patience. This is not a road to tackle in an RV, a rental car or your brother's new Prius.

By the time the highway reaches ⑭ **Rainy Pass**, the air has chilled and you're well into the high country, a hop and a skip from the drive's highest hiking trails. The 6.2-mile Maple Pass loop trail is one of our favorite hikes in this region, climbing 2150ft to aerial views over jewel-like Lake Ann. The epic Pacific Crest Trail also crosses Hwy 20 nearby, so keep an eye open for wide-eyed and bushy-bearded through-hikers popping out of the undergrowth. Perhaps the best choice to shake the crowds is the excellent climb up to Easy Pass (7.4 miles return). It's hardly "easy" (the trail climbs 2900ft) but the pass rewards the hiker with spectacular views of Mt Logan and the Fisher Basin below. Expect all these trails to be snowbound until July.

Luckily, buns of steel are not an essential requirement to score alpine Cascade views. Venture less than 100yd from your car at the ⑮ **Washington Pass overlook** (5477ft) and you'll be rewarded with fine views of the towering Liberty Bell and its Early Winter Spires, while the highway drops below you in ribbonlike loops.

From Washington Pass it's all downhill, past Lone Fir and Klipchuck National Forest Campgrounds, into the cross-country ski and biking mecca of Methow Valley. Stop and get your bearings (and a brownie) at the ⑯ **Mazama Store**, aka "The Goat," whose espresso bar is a hub for outdoorsy locals and a great place to pick up trail tips.

The first real town after the pass is a weird one. When the Cascade Hwy reached town in 1972 the hitherto quite ordinary former mining community of ⑰ **Winthrop** decided to tart itself up like a set from *High Noon*, except with mountain bikes tied to the hitching posts instead of horses. The result is the kind of place John Wayne would have felt right at home in, had he drank microbrews and enjoyed a fetish for tight-fitting Lycra.

The facades of downtown Winthrop are actually so authentic that it's easy to miss the collection of homesteader cabins that make up the nearby ⑱ **Shafer Museum**. Pass by and you'll miss the corkscrew-shaped 19th-century tooth extractor, horse-hide coat and antique bear trap that, jammed alongside hundreds of other fascinating pieces, give a wonderful taste of frontier life a century ago.

"...like a set from High Noon, *except with mountain bikes tied to the hitching posts instead of horses."*

If energy levels flag, pop into the ⑲ **Winthrop Brewing Company**, an unusual pub – even by Winthrop standards – that occupies a little red schoolhouse on the main street and knocks out an impressive range of hand-crafted ales. For something sweeter lift yourself into one of the horse-saddle seats at ⑳ **Sheri's** and dive into one of its excellent homemade ice creams or fresh cinnamon rolls.

Mountain bikers, hikers and anyone who enjoys cold beer and fine food (ie anyone with a pulse) should set aside the final half-day of their Cascade itinerary for some quality downtime at tiny ㉑ **Sun Mountain Lodge**, 6 miles southeast of Winthrop. If you're going to treat yourself anywhere on this trip, Sun Mountain, with its fine dining, spa treatments and relaxed vibe, is the place to do it. You can even try out that Stetson you bought in Winthrop on the lodge's horse trips and cowboy cookouts. Nonguests are equally welcome to bike the lodge's extensive trail network (rentals are available), before retiring to the bar

ASK A LOCAL

"If you only have time for one hike at Sun Mountain Lodge, I'd suggest **Patterson Hill**, a 4-mile loop that climbs up to great 360-degree views of the Methow Valley and the Cascades beyond. The **View Ridge Trail** is perfect for a family bike ride, while intermediate riders can head up **Thompson Ridge Rd** and then descend via Patterson Lake for a great half-day workout."
Grace Shaddox, Activities Desk, Sun Mountain Lodge, WA

balcony to contemplate the fine views back toward the Cascade range you just traversed.
Bradley Mayhew

TRIP INFORMATION

GETTING THERE
From Seattle drive 65 miles north on I-5 and turn onto Hwy 20 at junction 230, direction Sedro-Woolley.

DO

Cascadian Home Farm
Load up on organic homemade blueberry ice cream, jams, shakes and muffins. ☎ 360-853-8173; milepost 100, Hwy 20; ⊙ May-Oct; ⚑

Mazama Store
Organic local foods, fine pastries, espresso and the first gas for 70 miles at this very cool local store. ☎ 509-996-2855; 50 Lost River Rd, Mazama; ⊙ 7am-6pm, to 7pm Fri & Sat

North Cascades Institute
Courses with an environmental and artistic twist, plus the occasional Kerouac-related program, at this respected learning center on the north shore of Diablo Lake. ☎ 360-856-5700; www.ncascades.org; Hwy 20, milepost 127

North Cascades National Park Visitor Center
An essential first stop for visitors, offering exhibits, movies, 3D maps and park permits. ☎ 206-386-4495; Newhalem Campground; ⊙ 9am-6pm May-Aug; ⚑

Shafer Museum
Jam-packed with everything from a stage coach to a penny-farthing bike, based around the original cabin of the town's founding father. ☎ 509-996-2712; 285 Castle Ave, Winthrop; admission by donation; ⊙ 10am-5pm Memorial Day-Labor Day

EAT & DRINK

Buffalo Run Restaurant
The exotic ostrich and elk burgers make for a good lunch; dinner is heavier fare like buffalo T-bone. ☎ 360-873-2461; www.buffalorun inn.com; 60084 Hwy 20, Marblemount; lunch $7-9, dinner mains $15-20; ⊙ 11am-9pm

Sheri's
Delightful outdoor espresso bar and ice-cream parlor full of tempting homemade treats. ☎ 509-996-3834; 201 Riverside Ave, Winthrop; ⚑ ☃

Winthrop Brewing Company
Opt for the light-bodied Black Canyon Porter or the heavier Grampa Clem's Brown Ale at this riverside brewpub. ☎ 509-996-3183; 155 Riverside Ave, Winthrop; mains $7-13

SLEEP

Newhalem & Colonial Creek Campgrounds
Fire rings and campfire talks make these the classic park experience. A third of the Newhalem sites are reservable for a premium. ☎ reservations 877-444-6777; www.recreation.gov; campsites $12; ⊙ May-Sep; ⚑ ☃

Ross Lake Resort
Secluded lakeshore cabins just north of Ross Dam. Bring your own food. ☎ 206-386-4437; www.rosslakeresort.com; cabins $122-261, kayak rental per day $29-39; ⊙ mid-Jun–Oct

Sun Mountain Lodge
One of the state's classiest lodges, offering fine dining, spa treatments and activities galore, 6 miles from Winthrop. ☎ 509-996-2211; www.sunmountainlodge.com; r $160-375, lakeshore cabins $250-410; ⚑

USEFUL WEBSITES
www.cascadeloop.com

www.nps.gov/noca

SUGGESTED READING
- *Desolation Angels*, Jack Kerouac
- *The Dharma Bums*, Jack Kerouac
- *Poets on the Peaks: Gary Snyder, Philip Whalen, and Jack Kerouac in the North Cascades*, John Suiter

www.lonelyplanet.com/trip-planner

LINK YOUR TRIP

Graveyard of the Pacific Tour

WHY GO Named for its relatively calm waters, the Pacific Ocean has a fiendish side, especially where tide meets current at the mouth of the Columbia River. Explore shipwrecks, lighthouses and maritime museums – and find out if you're seaworthy in this landlubber's tour of the nautical Northwest.

TIME
2 days

DISTANCE
110 miles

BEST TIME TO GO
Apr – Sep

START
Hammond, OR

END
Westport

ALSO GOOD FOR

They call it the Graveyard of the Pacific. The area from northern Oregon to Vancouver Island is known for its unpredictable weather, unforgiving coastline, and bad habit of gobbling up ships. Thousands of vessels have been lost, from war ships to barges to freighters, and those are just the ones on record. There are likely countless smaller craft littering the ocean floor.

A few are still visible occasionally at low tide, but the easiest one to spot is the ❶ **Peter Iredale**, resting peacefully at Hammond, in northern Oregon. The ship was driven onto the shore by rough seas on October 25, 1906, and the wreckage has sat embedded in the sand for over a century. Toddlers climb over the rusted skeleton, and you can picnic right in its shadow. (No lives were lost, if that helps you enjoy your potato salad.)

Just inland in Astoria, you can explore both flotsam and jetsam at ❷ **Columbia River Maritime Museum**. It sits right on the edge of the Columbia River, offering a look at everything from old boats to maritime mementos that have washed up in the area. A Coast Guard exhibit – featuring a rescue boat tilted at a 45 degree angle on dramatic, fake waves – makes you really appreciate the danger of their job.

The river might look placid, but where river and ocean collide, the waters are especially treacherous. According to local writer Russell Sadler,

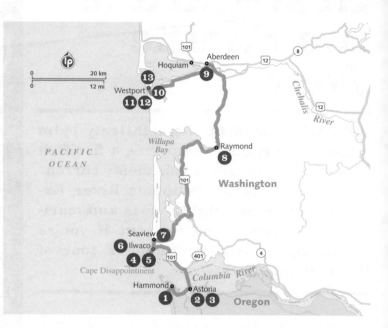

the Columbia River Bar can be "as calm as a teacup. Then the tide changes. Millions of gallons of river water trying to get out suddenly meet millions of gallons of ocean trying to get in," adding that it can turn into a "swirling white maelstrom in a matter of minutes."

WHAT'S IN A NAME?

Despair, gloom, general gruesomeness — that's what you'd expect from the Pacific Northwest coast if you were going by geographical names alone. The Graveyard of the Pacific sounds daunting, as does Cape Disappointment and Dead Man's Cove. And just north are the none-too-cheery sounding Deception Pass, Destruction Island, and Point No Point. But don't despair: while the early travelers who named these places clearly encountered some troubles, nowadays all of these destinations are surprisingly doom-free.

If all this leaves you overcome by a romantic notion to gaze out to sea and watch for boats, there's no better roost than ❸ **Cannery Pier Hotel**. Its historic, waterfront location on the site of a former cannery makes it ideally situated, with luxurious, modern rooms and enormous windows looking out onto the Columbia River.

Just over the Astoria Bridge Washington, two lighthouses have been warning sailors away from the shore for over 100 years. Cape Disappointment Lighthouse is part of ❹ **Cape Disappointment State Park** and, if you aren't up for the hike, you might find the lighthouse lives up to its name – it's not open to the public and it's at the end of a hilly, muddy, nearly mile-long path. Passing by Dead Man's Cove makes it worthwhile, as long as you're not disappointed there aren't any dead men there.

If that sounds like too much work, drive five minutes north to the easy-access ⑤ **North Head Lighthouse**. It welcomes visitors with a flat, quarter-mile hike, public tours, a gift shop, and even overnight accommodations in the keepers' residences. For dinner, go into ⑥ **Ilwaco**, a cute seaside village decorated with driftwood, glass floats, and fishermen's nets, where you can find lots of casual seafood eateries. Or head up the peninsula to Seaview, where you'll find oyster and crab specialties at local favorite ⑦ **42nd Street Cafe**.

About an hour up Highway 101 is Raymond, home of the ⑧ **Willapa Seaport Museum**. Small and cluttered, the exhibits sometimes seem more like a fisherman's garage sale than a formal museum, but that's part of its charm, and it's a good leg-stretch on your way to your next stop: Aberdeen.

Aberdeen's Gray's Harbor is the home port of ⑨ **Lady Washington**, the Official Ship of the State of Washington. This impressive reproduction of a 1788 tall ship – featured in *Pirates of the Caribbean* if that helps give you a visual – is available for dockside tours and adventure sails all along the state's coast. Check the online schedule to find out where along the way you might catch her.

WHICH WAY TO THE PETER IREDALE?

It's not like a shipwreck has a street address. And asking the locals for directions can be more confusing than helpful. So: Go over the bridge from Astoria to Hammond and turn right on East Harbor Dr, which becomes Pacific Dr. Take a left at Lake Dr (referred to locally as "that four-way stop…honey, what's that street called?"). Take a right at the KOA campground and go straight until you see the signs.

Heading west out of Aberdeen toward Westport, stop for an aphrodisiacal sailor-style snack at ⑩ **Brady's Oysters**. This family-owned oyster shop has been harvesting and selling clean-water oysters since the early '70s. It's nothing fancy, but, seriously, you won't care.

Your final stop on your grand tour is ⑪ **Westport**, a seaside town with two worthwhile stops. First, head to the superlative ⑫ **Grays Harbor Lighthouse**, the tallest lighthouse in Washington. It's always available for photo ops, and tours up the 135-step circular staircase (pant, wheeze) are available seasonally.

Next, head over to the ⑬ **Westport Maritime Museum**, a noteworthy Cape Cod-style building at the northern tip of town. It offers your typical array of nautical knick-knacks, but most impressive is the authentic Fresnel lighthouse lens. It's a first-order lens, which is really impressive if you know about lens rankings; loosely translated, that means it's big enough to need its own separate building. Made in 1889 to go on Destruction Island, it's the only Fresnel operating outside of a lighthouse, giving you a rare opportunity to almost literally blind yourself with its beauty.

Mariella Krause

OFFBEAT

TRIP INFORMATION

GETTING THERE

From Seattle, go 130 miles south on I-5, cross over into Oregon, and go west 60 miles to reach the coast.

DO

Cape Disappointment State Park
This dramatic, cliff-side state park contains two lighthouses and does absolutely nothing to live up to its name. **☎ 360-642-3078; 244 Robert Gray Dr, Ilwaco; dawn-dusk**

Columbia River Maritime Museum
Find out what's on the ocean floor at this maritime-history buff's dream destination. **☎ 503-325-2323; www.crmm.org; 1792 Marine Dr, Astoria, OR; adult/child 6-17yr/senior $8/4/7; 9:30am-5pm**

Grays Harbor Lighthouse
Built in 1898, this well-maintained, 107-foot-tall lighthouse looms as the tallest in Washington. **☎ 360-268-6214; 1020 W Ocean Ave, Westport; tours $3; 10am-4pm Apr-Sep, noon-4pm Fri-Mon Oct-Nov & Feb-Mar**

Lady Washington
Take to the seas on this tall ship that was featured in *Pirates of the Caribbean*. **☎ 800-200-5239; www.ladywashington.org; 712 Hagara St, Aberdeen; sailings $35-60, tours by donation**

Westport Maritime Museum
The best (but not only) reason to visit is the enormous Fresnel lens. **☎ 360-268-0078; www.westportwa.com/museum; 2201 Westhaven Dr, Westport; adult/child $4/2; 10am-4pm Apr-Sep, noon-4pm Fri-Mon Oct-Mar**

Willapa Seaport Museum
When it's open, this quirky little place is worth a stop. **☎ 360 942-4149; www.willapaseaport.org; 310 Alder St, Raymond; by donation; noon-4pm Wed-Sat or by appointment**

SLEEP & EAT

42nd Street Cafe
An extensive wine list and cozy atmosphere complement the seafood specialties. **☎ 360.642.2323; 4201 Pacific Way, Seaview; mains $7-25; 8am-2pm & 4:30pm-close**

Brady's Oysters
Stock your coolers with some delicious bivalve mollusks at this family-owned institution. **☎ 800-572-3252; www.bradysoysters.com; 3714 Oyster Place E, Aberdeen; 9am-6pm**

Cannery Pier Hotel
Each room has a window seat facing the Columbia River so you can watch the boats floating by. **☎ 503-325-4996; www.canner ypierhotel.com; 10 Basin St, Astoria, OR; r $179-299**

North Head Lighthouse
Play lighthouse keeper in one of three comfortably furnished keepers' residences; each sleeps up to six people. **☎ 800-360-4240; Cape Disappointment State Park, Ilwaco; $133-377**

USEFUL WEBSITES

www.maritimeheritage.net

LINK YOUR TRIP

www.lonelyplanet.com/trip-planner

TRIP 2 Highway 101: Land's Edge Leg p43

International Selkirk Loop

WHY GO It's an understatement to say this Selkirk scenic drive is somewhat off the beaten track; "crowded" here means the occasional moose blocking your views of stunning Kootenay Lake. Pack your passport and shake the crowds on this uncommonly scenic binational loop through the forgotten corners of Washington, Idaho and British Columbia.

Within 45 minutes' of leaving Washington at Newport you hit one of the Northwest's undiscovered gems at **1 Sandpoint**, Idaho. Squeezed between the downhill runs of Schweitzer Mountain and the glittering waters of Lake Pend Oreille, Sandpoint is the kind of town that you want to tell your friends about, but only once you're sure no-one else is listening (*Outside* magazine has voted it one of America's "Top Ten Towns"). Budget a couple of hours to stroll the bars, restaurants and shops of First Ave, including the flagship store of local hero Coldwater Creek. The nearby **2 Pend D'Oreille Winery** offers tastings and a tour of the French-influenced production process. Try the huckleberry blush.

As the summer temperatures rise, Sandpoint residents shift their focus two minutes' walk east to the City Beach, where the white sand and jet skis provide the closest the Idaho Panhandle ever gets to a Caribbean vibe. **3 Lake Pend Oreille** screams out summer fun and feels like it could have provided the perfect lake backdrop for a dozen teen slasher movies (though the only monsters here are some oversized trout). Pend Oreille ("hanging from the ears," pronounced "Ponderay") gets its unusual French name from the earrings of the local Kalispel tribe and is one of the deepest lakes in the nation, still used by the US Navy for sonar research. You'll soon realize that water is a major theme on this trip (you'll follow lakes and rivers for over three-quarters of the drive) so bring a swimsuit and preferably some kind of boat.

TIME
3 Days

DISTANCE
280 miles

BEST TIME TO GO
May – Oct

START
Newport

END
Newport

ALSO GOOD FOR

OUTDOORS

173

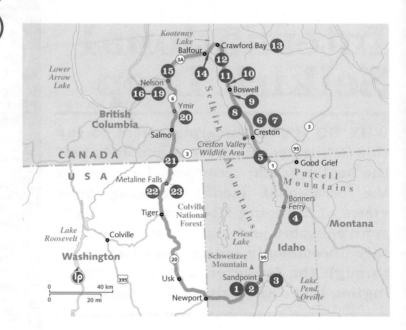

Hwy 15 heads to ④ **Bonner's Ferry**, originally built on stilts at the site of a gold rush river crossing, and continues north past ranches, Christmas tree farms and the world's largest hop farm at Elk Mountain (supplier to brewing giants Anheuser-Busch). It's tempting to continue to Good Grief, if only to take your photo next to the road sign, but turn instead onto Hwy 1 for the ⑤ **Porthill–Rykerts border crossing**. Apart from the change to Canadian dollars, kilometers and noticeably slower driving speeds, you shouldn't notice too many cultural differences, eh? Remember to bring your passport or enhanced driving license when new border regulations are enforced in 2009.

As you pull into Creston, don't freak out if you spot a 7ft Sasquatch carrying a six-pack. The mascot marks the entrance to ⑥ **Columbia Brewery**, home to the Kokanee and Kootenay brands, where you can take a tour and visit the sample room. They may not be the most interesting brews in the region but, hey, free beer, dude!

For a different taste of Creston head east out of town to the fruit stands that line Hwy 3 and pop into the ⑦ **Chocolate Orchard**, where a European chocolatier concocts chocolate-covered cherries, pinot noir truffles and caramel dips with the attention of a Canadian Willy Wonka. This is one shop that may just leave you drooling in the aisles. Load up on red and juicy Lapin cherries and strawberries for the drive ahead, but remember you can't take fruit back with you into the US.

The jewellike fjord of **8** **Kootenay Lake** bursts into view a few miles outside Creston, a 145km-long (90 mile) slice of turquoise framed by the peaks of the Selkirk and Purcell ranges and so clear that its waters are pure enough to drink. This section is the most scenic of the entire drive and is a favorite of motorcyclists who get off on a speed of 270 curves per hour.

The wackiest sight on the eastern shore is without doubt **9** **The Glass House**. With a mortuarist's sense of humor, funeral director David H Brown decided to build his dream retirement home out of used embalming fluid bottles, half a million of them in total (and more incredibly then persuaded his wife this was a good idea). The result is a whimsy of

DETOUR ▶ Nature lovers and birders should detour 6 miles west of Creston to the **Creston Valley Wildlife Area** (www.crestonwildlife.ca), part of the region's most important wildlife corridor. Walk the boardwalks and spot osprey, tundra swans, pelicans or great blue herons from the two birding towers, or sign up for an hour-long guided canoe paddle through the wetlands. Dawn and dusk are the best times to spot wildlife, including the occasional moose chomping in the shadows. Don't miss the very sweet "turtle crossing" road sign.

turrets, towers, bridges and even a garden shed, all made from recycled bottles. Brown then topped this off with an interior decorated with fearless 1970s panache (imagine your color-blind grandma choosing fabric on LSD) and a small army of garden gnomes. No, it ain't pretty, but it is weird.

With so much lakeshore property available it's tempting to put down roots on Kootenay Lake, but if you're just here for the night it's hard to beat the waterfront cottages of **10** **Destiny Bay Resort**. The giant garden chess set and the goats grazing on the sod roofs of the half-dozen cottages add an Alice-in-Wonderland feel but it's the fairy-tale private beach, with lakeside sauna, fire pit and kayak that provide the real magic.

Several spots north of Destiny Bay offer the best public access to the lake. **11** **Lockhart Beach** offers picnic tables on the fine pebble beach but the more clandestine option is the lovely, secluded cove 5 miles further at **12** **Burden's Cut**. Should you choose to find the spot, park opposite the interpretive sign and follow the trail down to what will probably be your own private shoreline. Tell anyone else about this secret spot, though, and we'll be forced to kill you.

"...don't freak out if you spot a 7ft Sasquatch carrying a six-pack."

Fans of Harry Potter and the Amish will want to stop at nearby Crawford Bay to visit **13** **North Woven Broom**, maker of traditional brooms since 1975. The workshop's feathery golden hues and musky broomcorn fragrance are surprisingly beguiling, almost sensual, and there's something comforting about the workshop's almost total lack of modernity.

Anyone who understands the word "Quidditch" will want to check out the replica Nimbus 2000 (Harry Potter's broomstick), 50 copies of which the owners created for a Vancouver book launch (the broom makers also supplied the props for the film *Bewitched*). While you're here check out the glass blowers, blacksmith's forge and weavers' studio across the road.

Just 3 miles north of Crawford Bay, it's time for another freebie, the world's longest free ferry ride, courtesy of the Canadian government and the ⑭ **Kootenay Lake Ferry**. The scenic crossing departs every hour or so and offers 40 minutes of superb lake views before docking at Balfour, some 20 miles northeast of Nelson. Nelson's quirkiness precedes it and even before you reach town you'll get a hint of the residents' lateral thinking as you pass the antique paddle steamer ⑮ **SS Nasookin**, moored in someone's garden and converted into a wacky private residence.

You could easily spend a full day soaking up the Victorian charms of ⑯ **Nelson**. Outdoorsy, alternative and organic, the historic former mining town has a Victorian charm that makes it one of the most interesting towns east of Vancouver. Pick up a free architectural walking tour pamphlet to track down the most interesting of the town's 360 heritage buildings, or stroll the waterfront pathway 1.2 miles to the beaches of Lakeside Park, returning on the restored century-old "Streetcar No 23." If you find yourself on Vernon St, head to the school of Chinese medicine and look for the mural of Steve Martin dressed as a Nelson volunteer firefighter in a scene from *Roxanne* (filmed in town).

ASK A LOCAL

"There's no better place to understand the local community than the **Kootenay Co-op** on Baker St, where you can find out about upcoming Tibetan Buddhist lectures while shopping for organic, locally sourced cheeses. For a caffeine fix try the excellent **Oso Negro**, on the corner of Victoria and Ward Sts, which in true Nelson style roasts its own organic fair-trade coffee. "
Chris Drysdale, Nelson, BC

Fight your way past Baker St's sitar music and "positive energy generators" and you'll find the town's most interesting shopping, with local fashions running the gamut from hemp to Gore-Tex. For liquid refreshment head for the historic 1898 Hume Hotel, pull up a pew at the ⑰ **Library Lounge** and order a pint of organic Liplock or Wild Honey ale, brewed right in town at the Nelson Brewery. If you discover your new favorite brew, pick up a six-pack in the attached liquor store.

The most widely lauded of Nelson's fine restaurants is ⑱ **All Seasons Café**, whose romantic patio also offers one of the town's nicest hideaways. The seasonally changing menu pairs locally sourced produce and global influences to create "Left Coast Inland Cuisine" – think artisanal BC cheeses with Armenian flatbread and fig chutney. Just a stumble away is the contemporary

⑲ Cloudside Inn, a good choice if you prefer your Victorian-era B&Bs fresh rather than frilly. Global travelers will find a kindred spirit in the peripatetic British owners, whose continent-spanning travel photos line the hallways.

Leaving Nelson, the final day's drive takes you south along the Pend Oreille Scenic Byway, past remote, forested (and slightly odd) communities like historic **⑳ Ymir** (pronounced "Why-mur," though grinning locals may well try to persuade you the name stands for "Why Am I Here?"). Connoisseurs of the unusual should pop in to the Ymir Hotel, a 1916 flophouse that stands frozen in time. Try to imagine a Western saloon-style boarding house run by Bela Lugosi and you'll get an idea of the vibe here (and one reason why the rooms cost under $30).

After completing your US border formalities at the sleepy **㉑ Nelway–Metaline border crossing**, continue straight down Washington Hwy 31 to the town of **㉒ Metaline Falls**, backdrop to the dreadful Kevin Costner film *The Postman* (the residents ask you not to hold it against them). Campers should detour to picturesque **㉓ Sullivan Lake**, where twin national forest campgrounds offer lakeshore sites, a swimming beach and the occasional bear visitor. Back on the highway it's a straight shot along the languid banks of the dammed Pend Oreille River, through the tiny settlements of Tiger (with its restored 1914 general store) and Usk and past the bison herds and log mills of the Kalispell Indian Reservation back to Newport.

Bradley Mayhew

> **DETOUR**
>
> If you have some time to kill before the next ferry departure, drive south from the ferry terminal for 3 miles (partially on a gravel road) to a turnout that marks a section of Pilot Bay Provincial Park. A short trail leads through forest to the charming white clapboard 1907 **Pilot Bay lighthouse**, where you can clamber to the upper story for fine views over Pilot Bay and Kootenay Lake. An overlook and bench offer a stellar spot for a picnic.

TRIP INFORMATION

GETTING THERE

From Seattle, drive 280 miles east on I-90 to Spokane, then north on Hwy 2 for 47 miles to Newport.

DO

Columbia Brewery

Tour the brewing process before sampling the finished product. ☎ 250-428-9344; 1220 Erikson St, Creston, BC; ☼ tours every 30 min 9:30am-4:30pm Mon-Fri mid-May–mid-Oct

Glass House

Admission to BC's ground zero of kitsch includes a tour of the residence and the small gardens. ☎ 250-223-8372; Hwy 3A, Boswell, BC; admission C$8; ☼ 8am-8pm Jul & Aug, 9am-5pm May-Jun & Sep-Oct

North Woven Broom

One of half a dozen studios and artist workshops that line crafty Crawford Bay. ☎ 250-227-9245; www.northwovenbroom.com; Hwy 3A, Crawford Bay, BC; ☼ 9am-5pm Mar–mid-Oct

Pend D'Oreille Winery

Award-wining wine bar and retail store, with live music Friday and Saturday evenings. ☎ 208-265-8545; www.powine .com; 220 Cedar St, Sandpoint; ☼ 10am-6pm Mon-Thu, 10am-7pm Fri & Sat, noon-5pm Sun

EAT & DRINK

All Seasons Café

Elegant and eclectic bistro hidden down a side alley. ☎ 250-352-0101; www.allseasonscafe .com; 620 Herridge Lane, Nelson, BC; mains C$17-30

Chocolate Orchard

Gourmet housemade toffees, caramels, truffles and dried fruit at this sweet treat. ☎ 250-428-7067; 2931 Hwy 3, Creston, BC; ☼ 8am-8pm; ☗

Library Lounge

Wood paneling, period detail and prime outdoor seating make this the most charming of the Hume Hotel's three bars. ☎ 250-352-5331; www.humehotel.com; 422 Vernon St, Nelson, BC; ☼ 11am-midnight

SLEEP

Cloudside Inn

Formerly Inn the Garden, this contemporary-styled B&B boasts bright rooms, a sun deck and a top-floor family suite. ☎ 250-352-3226; www.cloudside.ca; 408 Victoria St, Nelson, BC; r C$99-135, ste C$239

Destiny Bay Resort

Rates at this superbly romantic lakeshore hideaway include a four-course dinner and breakfast. ☎ 250-223-8234; www.destiny bay.com; 11935 Hwy 3A, Boswell, BC; r C$215-235; ☼ May-Oct

Sullivan Lake

The two national forest campgrounds here offer 48 reservable campsites, plus great boating and swimming. ☎ reservations 877-444-6777; www.reserveusa.com, www .fs.fed.us/r6/colville; Colville National Forest; sites $12

USEFUL WEBSITES

www.discovernelson.com
www.selkirkloop.org

LINK YOUR TRIP
www.lonelyplanet.com/trip-planner

TRIP
50 BC's Pioneer Past p317

Day Trips Around Seattle

Seattle is surrounded by easy opportunities to get out of town, even if you only have a couple of hours. And the city's close proximity to Canada means you can visit a whole other country and come back the same night.

WOODINVILLE

A wine-country getaway may seem out of reach, but just twenty miles north of Seattle is a little taste of life on the vineyards. Much of Woodinville is ridiculously suburban, filled with strip malls and generic homes. But it's also home to nearly fifty wineries, providing ample tasting opportunities for the dedicated oenophile. Come early and have breakfast at the excellent Woodinville Cafe, then pick up a wine map from the Chamber of Commerce. Chateau St Michelle (www.ste-michelle.com) is the best-known winery, with gorgeous grounds that are ideal for picnicking. In the summer, it hosts live concerts, drawing artists such as James Taylor, Lyle Lovett and Smokey Robinson. **Take I-5 and exit 168B toward Bellevue. After crossing the Evergreen Point Bridge, merge onto Hwy 405 N. After 9 miles, take exit 23 onto Hwy 522, then exit immediately at Hwy-202.**

SNOQUALMIE

David Lynch made this town famous back in the '90s when he used it as the setting for his show *Twin Peaks*. On TV, it looked like it was absolutely out in the middle of god-knows-where, but in reality, it's just a quick half hour outside of Seattle. The lodge that doubled as the Great Northern Hotel actually exists, sitting atop Snoqualmie Falls and going by its real name: Salish Lodge. It's easy to see why this location was a no-brainer, and a short hike down a winding trail gives you the dramatic view from the opening credits. The town of Snoqualmie itself has antique stores, shops and restaurants, plus a number of roadside stands where you can grab supplies for a picnic. **Go east on I-90 for 25 miles. After taking exit 25, turn left onto Snoqualmie Parkway, which will end at Railroad Ave SE. Turn left to get to the falls, or right for the rest of the town.**

See also **TRIPS 9 & 11**

BAINBRIDGE ISLAND

For locals and tourists alike, one of the quickest and easiest ways to get out of Seattle is a visit to Bainbridge Island. Leave the car behind and you can hop right on the ferry. The ride over is half the fun, with half an hour each way to enjoy views of the Olympic mountains and Seattle's skyline. The island has a small-town feel accentuated by a charming main street full of shops and cafés, just a few minutes' walk from the ferry landing. Bring your bike and you can pedal the four miles out to the Bainbridge Island Vineyard & Winery (www.bainbridgevineyards.com). A more ambitious bike ride (or an easy cab ride) is the Bloedel Reserve (www.bloedelreserve.org), a 150-acre nature reserve with a Japanese garden, rhododendron glade, and bird refuge. **Catch the ferry in downtown Seattle at Pier 52; when you disembark, walk up the hill to Winslow Way.**

TACOMA

Yes, Tacoma. Long mocked by Seattleites for, well, lots of things, it's getting the last laugh with an enviable cultural district that makes it easily worth the half-hour drive. The best reason to visit? The Museum of Glass. This is an absolute must-see for anyone who's even vaguely appreciative of the Pacific Northwest's art glass movement led by Dale Chihuly and the Pilchuck Glass School. Cross the Bridge of Glass and check out the copper-domed Beaux Arts Union Station building. It's now a federal courthouse, which means you have to go through security to get in, but you're rewarded with soaring windows full of orange, jellyfish-shaped Chihuly creations. Next door is the Washington State History Museum, and just north is the impressive and twice-as-big-as-before Tacoma Art Museum. **Drive south on I-5. Take exit 133, turn right onto Hwy 705 toward the city center.**

See also **TRIPS 7 & 10**

SNOHOMISH

Looking for an antique chifforobe? Victorian gewgaws? Funky vintage clothing? Or a life-sized Plexiglas horse that sat outside a feed store for 40 years? Get up to Snohomish, the Antique Capital of the Northwest. More than 400 antique stores – most of them centered around First St – make it a scavenger's paradise, but don't come expecting anything but old-fashioned charm. You won't be able to enjoy a thriving nightlife or attend cultural events, but you can always stop for a beer at the Oxford, a haunted, century-old saloon. If you really want to get crazy, you can take a walking tour of the town's many historic homes. **Head north on I-5 for 20 miles and take exit 186, turning right onto Hwy-96. Turn left at Seattle Hill Rd, left at Marsh Rd, and left again on Hwy 9. After 1 mile, take the exit toward Snohomish and turn right onto 2nd St.**

See also **TRIP 15**

WHIDBEY ISLAND

Somehow they managed to fit six state parks, a writers' and artists' community, a dramatic bridge over rushing rapids, and one of the oldest towns in Washington, all on one long, skinny island. Outdoorsy types won't want to miss Deception Pass and its famous bridge, which was considered a feat of engineering when it was built in the 1930s and is still really impressive even today. Beside the views, there's scuba diving, boating, hiking, kayaking, and just about anything else you'd want in a park. Artsy types should head straight to Coupeville, Washington's third-oldest town, for art galleries, antique stores, historical museums and a walking tour of vintage homes. **Head north on I-5 about 50 miles. Take exit 230 and drive west on Hwy 20, then follow the signs for the bridge to Whidbey Island. Or take the ferry: head north on I-5 to exit 189, then follow signs to the Mukilteo–Clinton ferry for a 20-minute ride.**

BELLINGHAM

What once was a blue-collar lumber town is now an up-and-comer in the race to the top of those Most Livable Cities lists. With coffee shops, ethnic restaurants, secondhand bookstores and farmers markets, the city center feels like a laid-back college town – perhaps because it is, with students and professors of Western Washington University making up a large part of the population. But it's a college town in love with the great outdoors, with plenty of skiing, cycling and kayaking. **Take I-5 89 miles north to exit 253. Holly St is a major downtown artery.**

LA CONNER

Coming up with the tagline for La Conner must have been easy. Just about everything you read about this historic waterfront village refers to it as "The Historic Waterfront Village" because, well, it's a gorgeous Victorian-era waterfront village. An easy hour or so from Seattle, the town – sorry, village – comes by the "historic" part honestly, as it was established in 1867 and pretty much froze itself in time around 1890. The village really comes alive in April with the Skagit Valley Tulip Festival, which, you can probably guess, given their penchant for straightforward nomenclature, is a month-long celebration of everything tulip. With a parade, a street fair, art shows, barbecues, and even bike rides along the tulip fields, there's really no better time to visit. **Head north on I-5 about 50 miles. Take exit 230 and drive west on Hwy 20, then south on La Conner-Whitney Rd. Follow road traffic to the traffic circle, then bear right onto Morris St.**

PORT TOWNSEND

Perched right on the ocean, Port Townsend is the kind of town people visit and immediately start wondering what it would be like if they moved there. It has a historic, 19th-century charm and has retained much of its Victorian architecture, but it also stays current with art galleries and cafés. During Victorian Days in March it feels like you're in a time warp, with ladies in corsets and gentlemen in waistcoats rushing to catch horses and carriages. Or take a tour of Fort Worden State Park (www.parks.wa.gov/fortworden), built in 1896 and still featuring Victorian officers' houses. Then, to ease your transition back to modern times, head out to eat at one of the many fashionable restaurants, where the ahi tuna on arugula or organic coffees will ease you back to the 21st century. **Go north on I-5. Exit 177 and head west on Hwy 104, following signs for the Edmonds–Kingston Ferry. Take the ferry to Kingston, and continue on Hwy 104 across the Hood Canal Bridge. Turn right onto Hwy 19, which will merge into northbound Hwy 20, which will lead you into town.**

See also **TRIPS 9 & 15**

LEAVENWORTH

Is it possible for a town to be too cute? Well, perhaps. But if your threshold for storybook charm is high, head to this Bavarian theme village that could be straight out of Disney's EPCOT. The Bavarian schtick was agreed upon back in the 1960s as a way to lure visitors, and it worked. Now the tiny town is filled with enough roadside Bavarian bric-a-brac to decorate an infinite supply of cuckoo clocks. Every summer, Leavenworth's hills are alive with *The Sound of Music*, as they perform the musical in an outdoor amphitheatre in front a mountainous, movie-set-worthy backdrop. And where else can you find a Nutcracker Museum, endless amounts of brats and schnitzel, and make frequent lederhosen sightings, all set to an oompah band soundtrack? **Head east on I-90. Just past Cle Elum, exit onto Hwy 970 North toward Wenatchee, then after 10 miles, turn left onto Hwy 97. After driving through the Wenatchee National Forest, turn left onto US-2, which brings you right into town.**

See also **TRIP 22**

VICTORIA, BC

It's almost unfathomable that you can take a day trip to a whole different country, but Victoria, BC, is close enough to pull it off. Hop on an early morning ferry in Seattle and you can be in Victoria well before lunchtime, spend six or seven hours, and be home in time to sleep in your own bed. This comely city has a distinctly British feel, and the streets are lined with English-style lamp posts and hanging baskets full of colorful flowers. Partake in high tea at the Fairmont Empress, check out the gorgeously domed Parliament Buildings, and go bloom crazy at the internationally-known Butchart Gardens. **Catch the Victoria Clipper service in Seattle at Pier 69.**

See also **TRIP 42**

OREGON TRIPS

Volcanoes have a way of wreaking havoc upon the landscape, but give them an eon or two to settle down and you get some gorgeous results. Take a few trips around Oregon and you'll see what we mean. On our hot springs tour you'll benefit immensely from Oregon's volcanic past. Snowcapped volcanoes will keep you constant company as you travel the scenic byways of the Central Cascades. And thanks to all that volcanic basalt, Oregon is home to a plethora of giant waterfalls – you'll see the best of them on our waterfall trip.

For your inner epicurean, we've consulted an Oregonian cheese-monger about his ultimate cheese tour, a Cannon Beach chef about his favorite seafood haunts and a respected local wine editor about Willamette Valley wineries. When you want to get away from it all take a trip to eastern Oregon, where you'll find North America's deepest river gorge, ghost towns and gold rush towns and, at the John Day Fossil Beds, some *very* surreal landscapes. And then there's the weird stuff... all in Oregon.

PLAYLIST Trips require the proper soundtrack, so roll down the windows and turn up the volume on these Oregon tunes. When you're in reach of Portland's radio waves, tune to commercial-free KBOO (90.7) or the new KZME (91.1 FM).

- "Chinese Translation," M Ward
- "Taking Too Long," The Wipers
- "Roll on Columbia," Woody Guthrie
- "Have Love, Will Travel," Paul Revere & the Raiders
- "Doesn't Matter," Josh Hodges
- "So Says I," The Shins
- "Swing Low," The Gossip
- "Portland Life II," Cool Nutz
- "The Soldiering Life", The Decemberists
- "Find Me in the Air", The Builders & the Butchers

OREGON'S BEST TRIPS

OREGON

48 Hours in Portland

WHY GO We'll start with the obvious: handcrafted beer, green spaces galore, the world's largest independent bookstore, art, a vibrant food culture and a livability rating that's off the charts. The rest is a matter of exploration, which, in Portland, is as easy by bus or bike as it is by car.

TIME
2 days

BEST TIME TO GO
Jun – Sep

START
Downtown

END
Downtown

ALSO GOOD FOR

FOOD & DRINK

Two days is hardly enough time to scratch the surface of any city. But with proper planning (leave it to us), it's downright amazing how much you can see. The best thing about visiting Portland during summer is that the days are long: the sun's well up by 6am and it stays light until nearly 9:30pm. Of course, that leaves several hours *after* dark for the really fun stuff.

There's no better way to kick off a long day in Portland than with coffee at ❶ **Stumptown Coffee**. Roasting its own coffee (and nearly everyone else's in town) since 1999, Stumptown is the city's definitive coffee shop. Once you're awake, head up 4th Ave through Portland's small Chinatown district to the ❷ **Classical Chinese Gardens**. This one-block haven of tranquility was built by 65 craftsmen from Suzhou, China, Portland's sister city. Walls around traditional Chinese gardens *lack* windows, but Portland's building code requires that all walls have them – hence, a fine example of East-meets-West architecture.

If you're in town on a weekend, walk to the west side of the Burnside Bridge and wander around the ❸ **Saturday Market** (held on Sundays, too). Although it has its share of tourists, cheap hats and incense booths, there's enough fine jewelry, art, crafts and other goodies to make it well worth a visit. The food court is fabulous, and the combination of buskers and old brick buildings gives the whole scene a distinctly European flare.

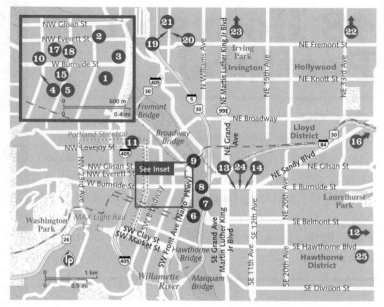

Now that it's hotel check-in time, head to the ultra-hip **4 Ace Hotel**, kick your feet up for a bit (hopefully you booked a room with a turntable), and head downstairs for a bite to eat next door at **5 Kenny & Zukes**. Probably Portland's most hoppin' deli, Kenny & Zukes is known for its insanely delicious house-cured pastrami. When packed between two butter-laden slices of toast and accompanied by a whopping portion of crispy fries, it's utter lunchtime nirvana.

Now it's time to get nerdy. Portland wouldn't be Portland without bridges. Know them – their names, their history, the views from their spans – and you know what makes the city tick. Eight bridges link to downtown: moving north to south they are Fremont Bridge, Broadway Bridge, Steel Bridge, Burnside, Morrison, Hawthorne, Marquam and Ross Island Bridge. Of these, Broadway, Steel, Burnside, Morrison and Hawthorne are movable. When author and bridge historian Sharon Wood Wortman (aka the Portland Bridge Lady) takes people on bridge walks, she leads them onto **6 Morrison Bridge**, from which you can see the seven other bridges. Check out the view and continue over the bridge to **7 East Bank Esplanade**, and follow the waterfront north past **8 Burnside Bridge** to **9 Steel Bridge**. Then take the walkway/bikeway along Steel Bridge's bottom deck back across the Willamette River. If you're itching to learn more about Portland's bridges,

"Since walking makes you thirsty and you're in Beervana, it's high time for a pint."

pick up a copy of Wood Wortman's *Portland Bridge Book* over at ⑩ **Powell's City of Books**, which, until someone proves otherwise, is the world's largest independent bookstore.

Since walking makes you thirsty and you're in Beervana (there's actually a group lobbying to make this Portland's official name), it's high time for a pint. Portland has more breweries (30) than any other city on planet earth. Bridgeport Brewery is the city's oldest, and you can imbibe its tasty ales at ⑪ **Bridgeport Brewpub & Bakery**. Of the 29 others, it's hard to go wrong. But the best place to sample a *variety* of local and regional brews is Southeast Portland's celebrated ⑫ **Horse Brass Pub**, half a mile southeast of Laurelhurst Park.

Like all pubs in Portland, the Horse Brass serves food, but save yourself. Head instead to East Burnside's ⑬ **Le Pigeon**, where you'll be treated to an ever-changing menu of sublimely prepared meat. And we're not just talking steaks. This is sweetbread, foie gras and beef cheeks territory, where you'll eat what you're not used to eating – *and you'll love it*. Of course, you could always order the burger.

Considering Portland is known for its strip clubs (it has the nation's highest number of strip clubs per capita), you probably owe it to yourself to pop into ⑭ **Union Jacks**, which is (what a coincidence!) just up the street from Le Pigeon. It's practically a hipster

UNDERGROUND PORTLAND

Some of Portland's darkest history lies underground. Running beneath the streets of Old Town and Chinatown are the so-called **Shanghai Tunnels**, a series of underground passages dug in the late 1800s to link the basements of businesses with the waterfront. Unscrupulous traders would kidnap or "shanghai" men, drug them and then drag them through the tunnels to the Willamette River. There they would sell them to sea captains looking for indentured workers. To see the tunnels, contact Portland Walking Tours (www.portlandwalkingtours.com).

hangout, with plenty of couples staring at the stage or chilling at the bar, so you won't be out of place strolling in on a date. (We tried it.) If you'd rather justify your trip to a strip club with history, head downtown to ⑮ **Mary's Club**. It's been around for over 50 years. But it's also pretty raunchy.

On day two (hiccup), have no regrets about the night before, because you'll eventually repent yourself of all sins at ⑯ **The Grotto**, a Catholic shrine built into a dripping cave beneath a massive cliff face in northeast Portland, about 5 miles from downtown. With views of Mt Hood, ponds and lazy pathways meandering through a verdant urban forest, the Grotto is not just a peaceful sanctuary, it's a Portland highlight. But before you make your way across the Willamette, head over to the ⑰ **North Park Blocks** and pop into downtown's outstanding ⑱ **Museum of Contemporary Craft**. Not only is it free, it hosts some of the best exhibits you'll find anywhere in Portland, generally featuring fine crafts from artists throughout the Pacific Northwest. Several other top-notch galleries can be found on this block (including one of Portland's best photography galleries, around the corner on NW 8th Ave), so there's plenty of exploring to do. And if you're toting children, turn them loose at the North Park Blocks playground across the street.

Since brunch (and waiting in line for it) is as quintessentially Portland as brews and tattoos, cross the Willamette River and head to ⑲ **Gravy**, on hip N Mississippi Ave. Invariably packed anytime after 9am, this hoppin' North Portland breakfast joint puts a down-home gourmet spin on all the usual plates: rib eye in the steak-and-eggs, triple-glazed ham, thick bacon – you get the point. Afterwards, poke around the many shops along Mississippi Ave.

Be certain to hit ⑳ **Flutter**, an eclectic hodgepodge of altered antiques, redesigned dresses, local crafts and bizarre finds. It's just south of another Mississippi Ave must: ㉑ **Mississippi Records**, where vinyl freaks can flip through all the records that really count. *Then* visit the Grotto.

LOCAL PRODUCE

For many Portlanders, the perfect Saturday means nothing more than a morning at the **Portland Farmers Market** (www.portland farmersmarket.org), held April through December at Portland State University. Vendors sell everything from artisan cheeses, local fish and grass-fed beef to mushrooms, jams and handmade soaps. Not in town on market day? Worry not. PFM holds additional markets on Wednesday (same location) and Thursday (Eastbank Esplanade).

After restoring your inner calm, take body, mind and soul over to the ㉒ **Kennedy School** – inside a former elementary school a mile north of NE Freemont St, this is Portland's zaniest hotel and brewpub – and plop into the 102°F soaking pool. You will then be revived enough to take a late-afternoon stroll along nearby NE Alberta St, the lifeline of the so-called Alberta Arts District. (From the Kennedy School, simply walk south on 33rd Ave and hang a right on Alberta.) Since you've been stuffing yourself silly, cruise down to 10th and Alberta for a light meal and a drink at the ㉓ **Bye & Bye**, a clean, stylish, bicycle-friendly bar with a vegan-only menu. We figure you just won't find a place like this outside Portland.

Resist all temptation to retire early and drag yourself over to the ㉔ **Doug Fir** for a last hurrah. Boasting what's possibly the best sound system in town, this midsize live music venue is one of the top places to catch a band. If you'd prefer something mellower, head to SE Hawthorne Blvd and catch a flick at the historic ㉕ **Bagdad Theater**, where you can watch reruns and art flicks with a pint of beer in hand. And if that isn't Portland, we don't know what is.
Danny Palmerlee

TRIP INFORMATION

GETTING THERE

To get to Portland from Seattle, drive 175 miles south on I-5. From Vancouver, drive 315 miles south on Hwy 99 and I-5.

DO

Bagdad Theater

This reclaimed theater is another unforgettable McMenamins venue with bargain flicks, pints of beer and food. ☎ 503-236-9234; www.mcmenamins.com; 3702 SE Hawthorne Blvd; admission $3

Classical Chinese Gardens

These gardens are modeled after a Ming dynasty scholar's garden. Free tours available with admission. ☎ 503-228-8131; www.portland chinesegarden.org; cnr NW 3rd Ave & Everett St; adult/senior $7/6; ☽ 10am-5pm; ♿

Doug Fir

Paul Bunyan meets the Jetsons at this ultra-trendy venue featuring an edgy and diverse array of talent. ☎ 503-231-9663; www.dougfirlounge.com; 830 E Burnside St; admission from $5

Flutter

Eclectic shop specializing in refurbished antiques and home decor and new apothecary, books and other oddities. ☎ 503-288-1649; www.flutterclutter.com; 3948 N Mississippi Ave; ☽ 11am-6pm Mon-Wed, 11am-8pm Thu-Sat, 11am-5pm Sun

The Grotto

Beautiful 62-acre shrine-and-garden complex complete with pietà replica in a carved-out basalt cave. ☎ 503-254-7371; www.the grotto.org; NE 85th at Sandy Blvd; admission free, elevator $3; ☽ 9am-5pm; ♿

Kennedy School

Former elementary school, now home to a hotel, restaurant, bars, movie theater and soaking pool. ☎ 503-249-3983, 888-249-3983; www.mcmenamins.com; 5736 NE 33rd Ave; soaking pool $5; r $99-130; ♿

Mary's Club

Portland's oldest strip club is a bit rough around the edges but still a favorite for some. Topless since 1965. ☎ 503-227-3023; www.marysclub.com; 129 SW Broadway; admission $2; ☽ 11am-2:30am

Mississippi Records

Small but excellent record store dealing exclusively in collectible vinyl. It doesn't get much better than this. ☎ 503-282-2990; 4007 N Mississippi Ave; ☽ 10am-8pm Wed-Mon

Museum of Contemporary Craft

Excellent collection of regionally made crafts, plus notable temporary exhibits. ☎ 503-223-2654; www.museumofcontemporarycraft.org; 724 NW Davis St; admission free; ☽ 11am-6pm Tue-Sun, to 8pm Thu; ♿

Powell's City of Books

Portland's giant independent bookstore occupies an entire city block and deals in new and used titles. ☎ 503-228-4651; www.powells.com; 1005 W Burnside St; ☽ 9am-11pm; ♿

Saturday Market

Fun outdoor crafts fair with street entertainers and food carts. ☎ 503-222-6072; www.portlandsaturdaymarket.com; 108 W Burnside St; ☽ 10am-5pm Sat, 11am-4:30pm Sun Mar-Dec; ♿

Union Jacks

One of Portland's hippest strip clubs with a neon-lit loungelike atmosphere; known for its music, tattooed dancers and impressive pole acrobatics. ☎ 503-236-1125; www.unionjacksclub.com; 938 E Burnside St; admission $3; ☽ 2:30pm-2:30am

DRINK

Bridgeport Brewpub & Bakery

Portland's oldest brewpub has an espresso bar, bakery, atrium and rooftop bar. ☎ 503-241-3612; www.bridgeportbrew.com; 1313 NW Marshall St; ☽ 7am-midnight Mon-Thu, 7am-1am Fri & Sat, 7am-10pm Sun

Horse Brass Pub

With well over 20 beers on tap, many of them local, this is the place to sample Oregon's brews. Breakfast served weekends. ☎ 503-232-2202; www.horsebrass.com; 4534 SE Belmont St; ⏱ 11:30am-2:30am Mon-Fri, 9am-2:30am Sat & Sun

Stumptown Coffee

Portland's best coffee. The crema's always spot-on, the caps piping hot and the coffee perfectly strong. ☎ 503-295-6144; 128 SW 3rd Ave; ⏱ 6am-9pm Mon-Fri, 7am-9pm Sat, 7am-8pm Sun

EAT & SLEEP

Ace Hotel

Retro meets modern with stunning results at Portland's hippest hotel. Cheapest rooms share bathrooms; suites have turntables. ☎ 503-228-2277; www.acehotel.com; 1022 SW Stark St; r $95-140, ste $175-250

Bye & Bye

Open-front bar with a friendly crowd, good art, outdoor seating and an all-vegan menu of bar food. ☎ 503-281-0537; 1011 NE Alberta St; mains $6-9; ⏱ to 2:30am

Gravy

Hip joint serving up huge portions for breakfast and brunch. Expect to wait on weekends. ☎ 503-287-8800; 3957 N Mississippi Ave; mains $6-10; ⏱ Tue-Sun

Kenny & Zukes

Jewish delicatessen with superb house-cured pastrami, plus sandwiches, meatloaf, knishes and huge breakfasts. ☎ 503-222-3354; www.kennyandzukes.com; 1038 SW Stark St; mains $7-14; ⏱ 7am-8pm, to 9pm Fri & Sat; ♿

Le Pigeon

Intimate but casual award-winning restaurant that remains unpretentious and friendly; the menu is heavy on meat. ☎ 503-546-8796; www.lepigeon.com; 738 E Burnside St; burgers $11, mains $20-28; ⏱ 5-10pm Mon-Sat, 5-9pm Sun

USEFUL WEBSITES

www.travelportland.com
www.wweek.com

LINK YOUR TRIP

www.lonelyplanet.com/trip-planner

TRIP
27 Beyond Beervana: A Brewery Jaunt p191

Beyond Beervana: A Brewery Jaunt

WHY GO Forget the weekend traffic through wine country, it's beer-tasting time! Nine breweries, two pubs and one designated driver make for the perfect two-day brewery loop, from Portland to Hood River and back. Best of all? You'll never hear the term "fruit-forward" – and no one expects you to spit!

With 30 breweries and counting, ❶ Portland is, without a doubt, beer heaven. But sometimes you just need to get out of town. For those who cannot bear the thought of leaving the taps behind, we've concocted a trip to the best small-town breweries within an hour of Portland proper.

First, round up three friends and convince one of them to be the designated driver. (The trip was your idea, after all.) Then make your way east of Portland to Troutdale and kick things off at ❷ McMenamins Edgefield. Fair enough, McMenamins are everywhere. But the Edgefield is special (c'mon, it has a golf course!), and has hotel rooms for those who aren't lucky enough to have a bed in Portland.

From Troutdale, head east along Hwy 84. Since you have four more breweries to hit before the day is through, limit your Columbia River Gorge sightseeing to something quick and easy, like the 1-mile hike up Tanner Creek to ❸ Wahclella Falls. To get there from Hwy 84, take the Bonneville Dam exit (Exit 40) and turn right to the trailhead.

After hiking, proceed east to ❹ Hood River and head directly to the ❺ Full Sail Tasting Room & Pub. Although Full Sail beers are as ubiquitous in Oregon as Douglas firs, drinking them straight from the source while taking in the views of the Columbia River is a must. From there head to Hood River's excellent ❻ Big Horse Brewpub, where

TIME
2 days

DISTANCE
170 miles

BEST TIME TO GO
May – Oct

START
Portland

END
Portland

ALSO GOOD FOR

OUTDOORS

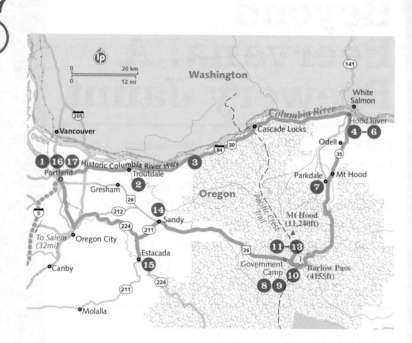

you can – and should – eat a very big lunch. It's worth hitting Big Horse for the building alone, which has giant windows overlooking the gorge and a supremely inviting interior. (At this point, shower words of encouragement upon your designated driver for their noble and unwavering altruism.)

Next, make your way up the Hood River Valley through the orchards and past the fruit stands to the little town of Parkdale. Here, direct your driver toward the ⑦ **Elliot Glacier Public House**. Setting, views, food and darn good beer make this one of our favorites. Plus, it serves one of the best named beers in Oregon: Crevasse-Yer-Ass Winter Ale. How can you go wrong with a pint of that?

"At this point, shower words of encouragement upon your designated driver..."

From Parkdale, return to Hwy 35 and follow it south around Mt Hood to Hwy 26 and ⑧ **Government Camp**. Hit the ⑨ **Ice Axe Grill & Mt Hood Brewing Co**, where you can choose from between six to eight ales, including a cask-conditioned ale and the brewery's flagship beer, Ice Axe IPA. Dinner's on order, too, with imaginative sandwiches, pizzas, salads, fish-and-chips, and grilled salmon and steak all on the menu.

At this point you should be dead tired and have no trouble sleeping through the night at nearby ⑩ **Trillium Lake Campground**. It's a busy spot, but considering you're spending most of your daylight hours in the pub rather than at the campground, it's a solid choice. If you'd rather sleep in style, head up to Mt Hood's historic ⓫ **Timberline Lodge**. The centerpiece of this National Historic Landmark, which was completed in 1937, is a 92ft-tall stone fireplace and chimney that rises through three floors of open lobby space.

Begin day two with a whopping buffet breakfast at the Timberline Lodge's ⓬ **Cascade Dining Room**. Besides the fact that it will likely be one of your most memorable meals in Oregon, it makes for extremely convenient access to the ⓭ **Pacific Crest Trail (PCT)**, your post-breakfast destination. Whether you hike 2 miles or 12 miles along the PCT, the views of Mt Hood are incredible. The trail is easy to find – follow the signs to the right of the lodge.

After working off your breakfast and sweating out what you consumed the day before, swap drivers and head west along Hwy 26 to the town of Sandy. Make sure it's late enough in the day, and stop into ⓮ **Karlsson Brewing Company** at the west end of town. Not only is this the one brewery on the loop that makes a lager, it's probably the only place in Oregon where you can knock one back with a Scotch egg (basically, a hard-boiled egg wrapped in sausage).

> **DETOUR**
>
> We said "breweries" but we never said "beer." A 45-mile (one-way) detour from Portland will put you in Salem, where you can taste the scrumptious cider at **Wandering Aengus Ciderworks** (www.wanderingaengus.com). You'll have to make an appointment to get through the otherwise closed tasting room doors. Named after a WB Yeats poem, Wandering Aengus makes its cider entirely from organic cider apples. If you can pin down an appointment, it's well worth a visit.

From Sandy, head southeast along Hwy 211 to Estacada and down a pint and a batch of onion rings at ⓯ **Fearless Brewing Company**. The rings should be fuel enough to get you back to Portland where you can wrap up your trip at one of two outstanding pubs. The first – a no-brainer, really – is the ⓰ **Horse Brass Pub**, where you'll find a mind-boggling selection of Pacific Northwest brews on tap. For something under-the-radar, hit ⓱ **Concordia Ale House**. Inside and outside it has the atmosphere of a strip-mall pizzeria, but one look at the beer list quickly reveals this place as anything but ordinary. Order a pint and a plate of fries (they're excellent) and raise your glass to your driver – then talk them into the soda so you can have another round!

Danny Palmerlee

TRIP INFORMATION

GETTING THERE
From Portland, take Hwy 84 16 miles east to Exit 16. Follow 238th Dr to Halsey; go left to McMenamins Edgefield.

EAT & DRINK

Big Horse Brewpub
Brewery with a full menu including baby back ribs, smoked salmon linguini, pulled pork sandwiches and great burgers. ☎ 541-386-4411; 115 State St, Hood River; mains $6-15; ☻ 11:30am-about 10pm

Cascade Dining Room
At Timberline Lodge. Superb food, and the buffet breakfasts are great value. ☎ 503-622-0717; www.timberlinelodge.com; breakfast $12.95, mains $24-30; ☻ breakfast, lunch & dinner

Concordia Ale House
Atmosphere? Zilch. Beer list? Arguably the best in Portland. ☎ 503-287-3929; 3276 NE Killingsworth St, Portland; mains $6.50-12; ☻ 11am-2:30am Mon-Fri, 9am-2:30am Sat, 9am-midnight Sun

Elliot Glacier Public House
Great beer, atmosphere and outdoor seating. Monday and Tuesday taco nights get packed. ☎ 541-352-1022; www.elliotglacierpublichouse.com, 4945 Baseline Dr, Parkdale; mains $6-10; ☻ 11:30am-9pm Thu-Sun, 5-9pm Mon & Tue

Fearless Brewing Company
Chili, sandwiches and burgers, Norse iconography and microbrewed beer. ☎ 503-630-2337; www.fearless1.com; 326 S Broadway, Estacada; mains $5-10; ☻ 4-10pm Mon-Thu, noon-11pm Fri & Sat, noon-10pm Sun

Full Sail Tasting Room & Pub
Offers limited food selections, but plenty of beer. Outdoor patio, too. ☎ 541-386-2247; 506 Columbia St, Hood River; mains $8-14; ☻ 11:30am-9:30pm Sun-Thu, to 10:30pm Fri & Sat

Horse Brass Pub
With well over 20 beers on tap, many of them local, this is the place to sample Oregon's brews. ☎ 503-232-2202; www.horsebrass.com; 4534 SE Belmont, Portland; ☻ 11:30am-2:30am Mon-Fri, 9am-2:30am Sat & Sun

Ice Axe Grill & Mt Hood Brewing Co
The brews here go down like a dream, and the pub-style food is delicious. ☎ 503-272-3172; www.iceaxegrill.com; 87304 E Government Camp Loop, Government Camp; mains $11-15; ☻ 11:30am-9pm Sun-Thu, to 10pm Fri & Sat

Karlsson Brewing Company
Chicken pot pie, taquitos and jalapeño peppers complement the beer splendidly. ☎ 503-826-8770; www.karlssonbrewing.com; 35900 SE Industrial Way, Sandy; mains $6-12; ☻ 4-10pm Mon-Thu, to midnight Fri & Sat

SLEEP

McMenamins Edgefield
Not just a great hotel: also a golf course, brewery, movie theater, live music and gardens. ☎ 503-492-3086; www.mcmenamins.com; 2126 SW Halsey St, Troutdale; dm $35, r $58-120; ☻

Timberline Lodge
Landmark hotel on Mt Hood. Good rooms, luxurious common spaces. ☎ 503-622-0717; www.timberlinelodge.com; r $115-270

Trillium Lake Campground
Popular 57-site campground on Trillium Lake, southeast of Government Camp; good trail access and fishing. ☎ 877-444-6777; www.recreation.gov; E Trillium Lakes Rd; campsites $16-32; ☻ ☻

USEFUL WEBSITES
www.mthood.info
www.oregonbeer.org
www.lonelyplanet.com/trip-planner

LINK YOUR TRIP

Columbia River Gorge

WHY GO Towering waterfalls, excellent hiking, cold swimming holes, world-class windsurfing, soothing hot springs, U-pick fruit farms – what else could you want from a long weekend? For good measure, Mother Nature threw in a backdrop of forested cliffs and the snowcapped volcanic cone of Mt Hood, just to make sure you're satisfied.

TIME
3 days

DISTANCE
110 miles

BEST TIME TO GO
Jun – Aug

START
Troutdale

END
The Dalles

ALSO GOOD FOR

Few places symbolize the grandeur of the Pacific Northwest like the Columbia River Gorge. This massive cleft in the Cascade Range measures 80 miles long and up to 4000ft deep. At the bottom lies the mighty Columbia River, flanked on the Oregon side by dense forests of giant conifers and big leaf maples that cling to the gorge's precipitous cliffs. Rivers and creeks flow from the snowy Cascades, plunge from cliff tops and wind through fern-laden slot canyons to join the Columbia below. In all, 77 waterfalls grace the gorge, one of the highest concentrations in the world. Let's just say, it's a sight to see.

If you're not holed up in Portland, spend your first night in Troutdale at ❶ **McMenamins Edgefield**. How can you go wrong with a refurbished, early-20th-century manor on 38 acres of farmland at the mouth of the Columbia River Gorge? In the morning, head east into the gorge along the winding Historic Columbia River Highway (not the newer Hwy 84/US 30). Soon you'll pass the ❷ **Portland Women's Forum State Scenic Viewpoint**, which offers one of the most photographed vistas into the gorge. Looking east from here, you can see the octagonal ❸ **Vista House** in the distance. That's your next stop. Built between 1916 and 1918, the roadside rotunda sits atop Crown Point, 733ft above the Columbia River. It houses an information center and offers another classic gorge panorama.

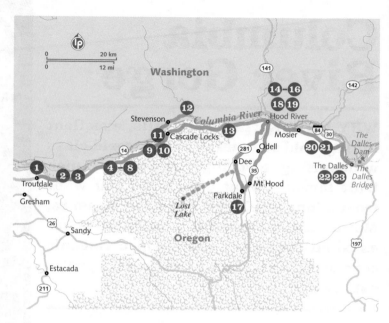

After taking in the views, wind your way east to the gorge's most famous sight, 620ft ❹ **Multnomah Falls**. Of course, you won't be the only one stopping at Multnomah to ogle the country's second-highest year-round waterfall – *au contraire,* this is camera country. And should you brave the one-hour grunt to the top of the falls, rest assured – you'll find plenty of camaraderie in the noisy families slogging their merry way to the top along with you. Despite the crowds, it's undoubtedly worth it. At the base of the falls stands the historic ❺ **Multnomah Falls Lodge & Visitor Center**, which offers nary a bed, but does provide excellent information (including maps).

"walk, scramble and hop your way to the back of the canyon to 65ft-high Oneonta Falls."

The hike to the top of Multnomah Falls and beyond is undoubtedly one of the gorge's finest walks, but (and we say this cautiously) leave it for later. Instead, hike up ❻ **Oneonta Gorge**. Thanks to all the weird plants that dangle from Oneonta's vertical walls, this incredibly deep, claustrophobically narrow slot canyon is a specially designated "botanical area," and is one hell of a sight. Hiking into it alongside (and often inside) Oneonta Creek is a must. When the water is low enough, you can wade, walk, scramble and hop your way to the back of the canyon to 65ft-high Oneonta Falls. Oneonta is accessible from two parking areas on either side of the highway bridge that crosses Oneonta Creek, east of Multnomah Falls.

If you'd rather not wet your feet, drive further east to ❼ **Horsetail Falls**. This is another of the gorge's water-meets-gravity marvels, but following the trail above it leads to an even better one: ❽ **Ponytail Falls** (also known as Upper Horsetail Falls). OK, so it's shorter than Horsetail Falls, but you can actually walk *behind* this falls into the rock grotto. If you follow the trail behind the falls and continue westward and around the cliffs, you'll soon come to a network of trails that lead to dizzying viewpoints over the gorge. These flat spots make *the* perfect spot for a picnic lunch (trust us, nab the spot before someone else does). If you keep walking west, you'll soon cross a footbridge over Oneonta Gorge, which you can see from above rather than below. The trail then zigzags down to another parking lot, so either return to your car by looping back along the road or turn back at the gorge and return by trail.

Back in the car, continue east and the Historic Columbia River Highway will soon spit you out onto the larger Hwy 84/US 30 eastbound. After 3 miles on Hwy 84, take exit 40 to ❾ **Bonneville Dam**. Upon its completion in 1938, Bonneville became the first dam on the Columbia River, permanently altering one of the continent's mightiest rivers, as well as one of the world's most important salmon runs. It's worth stopping here to check out the underwater viewing room into the fish ladder, as well as the ❿ **Bonneville Fish Hatchery**. The latter is home to a gargantuan 10ft-long sturgeon named Herman (don't tap *his* tank!).

About 3.5 miles upstream from the Bonneville Dam, hit your turn signal at Exit 44 and cross the ⓫ **Bridge of the Gods** into Washington. Head east on Hwy 14, turn left on Wind River Rd, right on Hot Springs Ave and, *voila!*, you're at ⓬ **Carson Hot Springs Resort**. Carson is hardly fancy, but its modesty is its finest feature. And your weary body will thank you as you dip into a claw-foot tub filled with hot mineral water and then wrap yourself in towels for a serious sweat, before staying the night. If you'd rather camp, you can do so at ⓭ **Viento State Park**, just west of Hood River. This is a small park, with 57 campsites, picnic areas, a few short trails and excellent access to the Columbia River. It's also close to the train tracks, so expect a little noise!

ASK A LOCAL "As a member of the team that designed and built the gorge, I am proud of the product. However, I thought that we missed a great naming opportunity, such as the "Tostitos Gorge" or the "UPS Canyon." Going along with just using the river name was far too traditional. A missed opportunity up there with "Grand Canyon" (ie "Big Canyon"). I think Dasani or Aquafina would have gotten into a bidding war. Too late now."
Chris Shine, Portland, OR

Day two takes you into the windy riverside town of ⓮ **Hood River**, one of the world's top windsurfing and kiteboarding destinations. It's also one very attractive town, thanks to its old homes and a stunning setting on the

Columbia River. Oh, and Mt Hood, with its hiking trails and ski runs, is only a stone's throw away. It should come as no surprise that Hood River has a youthful, adrenaline-hungry population and a main drag packed with good restaurants, boutique shops and adventure sports stores. Of course, it wasn't always so hopping. Before the windsurfers blew in, this was just a sleepy town in the heart of orchard country. The good news? It's still orchard country.

Before you run off to the fruit trees, however, treat yourself to a fabulous lunch at **⑮ Celilo**. Not only is the food fantastic and the atmosphere sublime, but nearly everything on the menu is locally produced. And you simply can't visit Hood River without having a pint at the **⑯ Full Sail Tasting Room & Pub**. The beer is good, and the views over the river superb.

One of the highlights of the Hood River area is the so called Fruit Loop, a 35-mile round-trip drive into the fruit-laden hills that lie between Hood River and Mt Hood. The road (Hwy 35) winds south of town, past U-pick orchards and berry farms, lavender fields, family fruit stands, alpaca farms and a smattering of wine tasting rooms and eventually returns to Hood River by way of Hwy 281. Should you find yourself feeling the need for nourishment halfway through, stop at **⑰ Elliot Glacier Public House**, in Parkdale, and sip a handcrafted beer with an afternoon snack while taking in the views of Mt Hood.

DETOUR

For a classic Mt Hood photo op, detour 25 miles south of Hood River to spectacular **Lost Lake**. Flanked by forest, this stunning blue body of mountain water frames the white cone of Mt Hood like a perfect postcard. Along with fabulous views, the detour offers respite from the heat when the gorge gets too hot. To get there from Hood River, take Hwy 281 to Dee and follow the signs. Allow at least half a day for the excursion.

After returning to Hood River, check into your hotel. Hood River has several excellent B&Bs and a couple of exquisite hotels, but we always end up staying at the reliable, easygoing **⑱ Vagabond Lodge**. It's perfectly comfortable, the landscaping is pleasant, the location is good, and you don't have to shield your eyes against too much frilly B&B decor. Once you're settled, head to **⑲ Stonehedge Gardens & Bistro** for dinner. At the end of a short gravel road on a hill west of downtown, Stonehedge is an upscale restaurant in a restored 1898 house. Sitting on the huge Italian stone patio and feasting on dishes like coconut-crusted chicken or flame-broiled pork loin is a rather transcendental experience on a warm summer evening.

On day three drive about 6 miles east of Hood River to the town of Mosier (get off at Exit 69) and take the Historic Columbia River Highway (it reappears here) east to the top of **⑳ Rowena Crest**. Here, you'll encounter some of the most spectacular views of the gorge anywhere. You can see both the moist, heavily forested western gorge to your left and the basaltic cliffs and bunchgrasses of the drier eastern gorge to the right. Because Rowena Crest lies within the transition zone between these two areas, it's also home to an astounding number of wildflowers. The abundance of plants on the plateau (over 200 species can be found, including four that are endemic to the gorge) spurred the Nature Conservancy to purchase 271 acres of it and establish ㉑ **Tom McCall Preserve**. From the Rowena Crest parking lot, you can hike one of two short trails in the preserve – but watch out for rattlesnakes and poison oak and check yourself for ticks.

From Rowena Crest make your way back to Hwy 84, and continue east to ㉒ **The Dalles**, where you can wrap up your jaunt at the fascinating ㉓ **Columbia Gorge Discovery Center**. This informative place covers the history of the gorge from its creation by cataclysmic floods, through its Native American inhabitants, to the early pioneers, settlers and eventual damming of the river. Whether you're a gorge fanatic or a first-time visitor, the center will undoubtedly increase your appreciation for one of the Pacific Northwest's most amazing natural landscapes.

Danny Palmerlee

TRIP INFORMATION

GETTING THERE
From Portland, take Hwy 84 east to Exit 16/238th Dr. Follow 238th Dr to Halsey; go left to McMenamins Edgefield.

DO
Bonneville Dam
The visitors center has exhibits on Native American culture along with tributes to hydroelectric power. Salmon run May to September. ☎ 541-374-8820; Hwy 84, Cascade Locks; admission free; ⊙ 9am-5pm; ♿

Columbia Gorge Discovery Center
This museum lies 3 miles west of The Dalles; it has a good café with outdoor seating. ☎ 541-296-8600; 5000 Discovery Dr, The Dalles; adult/child 6-16yr/senior $8/4/7; ⊙ 9am-5pm; ♿

Multnomah Falls Lodge & Visitor Center
This historic lodge serves breakfast, lunch and dinner, and houses a visitors center and gift shop. ☎ 503-695-2376, 503-695-2372; www.multnomahfallslodge.com; ⊙ visitors center 9am-5pm, lodge 8am-9pm; ♿

DRINK
Elliot Glacier Public House
Great setting with views, food an an array of fine beers on offer. Gets very busy on Monday and Tuesday taco nights ☎ 541-352-1022; 4945 Baseline Dr, Parkdale; mains $6-10; ⊙ 11:30am-9pm Thu-Sun, 5-9pm Mon & Tue

Full Sail Tasting Room & Pub
Offers limited food selections, but plenty of beer. Outdoor patio, too. ☎ 541-386-2247; 506 Columbia St, Hood River; mains $8-14; ⊙ 11:30am-9:30pm Sun-Thu, to 10:30pm Fri & Sat

LINK YOUR TRIP

EAT
Celilo
Upscale organic dining at its Oregonian best; the walls open to the sidewalk on warm afternoons. ☎ 541-386-5710; 16 Oak St, Hood River; mains $15-25; ⊙ 11:30am-3pm & 5-9:30pm

Stonehedge Gardens & Bistro
Treat yourself to a romantic setting in the trees above town; reserve early for summer weekends. ☎ 541-386-3940; 3405 Cascade Ave, Hood River; mains $22-27; ⊙ 5-9pm

SLEEP
Carson Hot Springs Resort
Locally loved resort with claw-foot tubs ($20) and wraps with massage ($60). ☎ 509-427-8292, 800-607-3678; www.carsonhotspringresort.com; 372 St Martin Rd, Carson; r $75-85; ⊙ spa 8am-7pm

McMenamins Edgefield
A superb place to take anyone from out of town, the hotel offers golf, microbrews, movies and live music. ☎ 503-492-3086; www.mcmenamins.com; 2126 SW Halsey St, Troutdale; dm $35, r $58-120; ♿

Vagabond Lodge
Reliable hotel 3 miles west of town off the highway; near woodsy areas and gardens. Suites have kitchens. ☎ 541-386-2992; www.vagabondlodge.com; 4070 Westcliff Dr, Hood River; r $69-111; ♿ 🐾

Viento State Park
Campground 8 miles west of Hood River with river access and walking trails; expect highway and train noise. ☎ 541-374-8811; www.oregonstateparks.org; Hwy 84, Exit 56; tents/hookups $14/16; ⊙ Mar-Oct; ♿ 🐾

USEFUL WEBSITES
www.fs.fed.us/r6/columbia
www.hoodriverfruitloop.com
www.lonelyplanet.com/trip-planner

Willamette Valley Wine Tour

WHY GO Who better to guide you through Oregon's premier wine region than Cole Danehower, editor in chief of Northwest Palate Magazine and author of an upcoming book on wine regions of the Pacific Northwest? After visiting the wineries, B&Bs and restaurants he recommends, you'll likely answer as we did: no one.

Oregon's Willamette Valley is big. It stretches over 100 miles from Eugene to Portland, and more than 200 wineries lie within its six subappellations. Most Willamette Valley wineries are approachable, family-run operations dedicated to producing small quantities of high-quality wine. And most of them do so according to organic, sustainable and sometimes even biodynamic practices.

Dundee is the urban hub of the Dundee Hills, the Willamette Valley's preeminent subappellation. The region's cool climate and fertile soils attracted wine pioneer David Lett, aka "Papa Pinot," to the Willamette Valley in 1965, and his 1975 South Block Reserve put the Willamette Valley on the international wine map. Carlton lies about 8 miles west (as the crow flies) and is surrounded by the Yamhill-Carlton District subappellation. Its first winery opened in 1974, and today the region is home to 20 wineries and 60 vineyards.

Most of the wineries in the Willamette Valley charge a tasting fee of about $10 per person, which is usually – though not always – refunded after purchasing a few bottles of wine. Some words of advice from Danehower: "Learn to spit. Don't be self-conscious about it. Spitting will actually mark you as a pro rather than an amateur."

When you roll into ❶ **Dundee** on Friday evening, head straight for the sumptuous ❷ **Black Walnut Inn & Vineyard**. Described by

TIME
2 days

DISTANCE
33 miles

BEST TIME TO GO
Apr – Aug

START
Dundee

END
Carlton

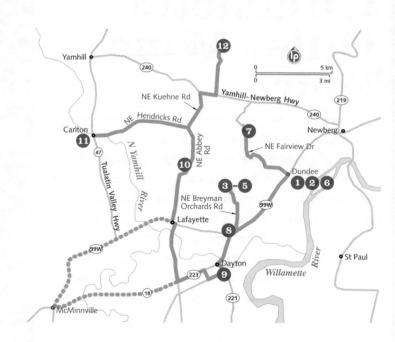

Danehower as "luxurious and intimate," it's a modern rendition of the classic Tuscan villa, with nine exquisite rooms and a prime location in the Dundee Hills. The rooms are enormous, and the furniture – which can be anything from plush leather chairs to big white sofas – swallows you up in blissful comfort. If you plan to stay here, make reservations well in advance.

Saturday, after your multicourse gourmet breakfast at the Black Walnut Inn, start the day with a visit to ❸ Domaine Serene, which is widely heralded for its Pinot Noir and is one of the Willamette Valley's best-known wineries. It's a modern place with a stunning wine cellar and lovely views over the rolling hills and vineyards that sweep across the valley. Along with Pinot Noir, the winery produces highly regarded Chardonnays and Syrah. You can go with the standard tasting-room-only wine tasting or tour the entire winery, including the cellar, as part of the VIP tour – that, however, will cost you extra.

After Serene, it's an easy hop over to ❹ Domaine Drouhin Oregon, which is famed as much for its history as it is for its Pinot Noir. The winery owes its existence in part to the 1979 Gault Millau "Wine Olympics," a blind tasting held in France. In the competition, Eyrie Vineyards, founded by David Lett, placed in the top 10, holding its own against France's most esteemed Pinots, including one from the respected Maison Joseph Drouhin. Drouhin's owner, Robert Drouhin, later repeated the tasting, and Eyrie's 1975 South Block Reserve placed second, right behind a Drouhin Pinot Noir. This stoked

Drouhin's already existing interest in the Willamette Valley (Drouhin first visited the valley in 1961), and he soon decided it was time to extend the family's operation. In 1988 he opened Domain Drouhin Oregon under the management of his daughter, winemaker Véronique Drouhin. She still makes the wine.

Although Danehower claims his ideal day is two wineries in the morning and two in the afternoon, three of his recommendations are close enough together to visit in a long morning. If you can comfortably squeeze it in before lunch, head to nearby ❺ **Vista Hills Vine-yard**, practically around the corner from Drouhin. Not only does Vista Hills offer wonderful views from the treetops – the Treehouse Tasting Room is literally up in the trees – but it also offers a unique approach to wine making: Vista Hills' wines lie in the hands of a changing cast of guest winemakers who all use Vista Hills grapes. The subtleties of vintages, in other words, are determined by more than just the weather (if you concentrate, you can taste the hardened cracks of the wine-maker's hands in one, and make out the broody nature of the next in another…sort of). The winery has another unique trait: 10% of its profits go to a foundation created by the owners to offer financial support to students pursuing higher education. It should come as no surprise that sustainability is one of the winery's core values.

MARK YOUR CALENDAR

Many Willamette Valley wineries offer visits by appointment only. If you're the type who cringes at the word "appointment" (especially when paired with "wine" and "weekend"), worry not. You have options. On Memorial Day and Thanksgiving Day weekends, nearly all of the valley's wineries open their doors to the public – no reservations required. These are widely publicized and very busy weekends. Cole Danehower offers an inside tip: most wineries also open their doors on the weekends prior to these…for those in the know.

With three of the Willamette Valley's top wineries under your belt, it's high time for lunch. Danehower recommends heading to the ❻ **Dundee Bistro**, which (for those of you who tend to ponder your social surroundings) happens to be a bit of a winemakers' hangout. This might be due to the food, which Danehower says is excellent, or the attached tasting room, which makes sampling boutique Willamette Valley wines a cinch.

After lunch, head west out of Dundee along SW 9th St (which turns into NE Worden Hill Rd) and swing right on NE Fairview Dr. Follow it north to ❼ **Lange Estate Winery & Vineyards**. The winery, founded by one of the valley's earlier families, has gorgeous views, good wines and (the marking of an authentic winery) "big old shaggy dogs." According to Danehower, "It's very much a family affair. They do a Pinot Noir that I like called Three Hills Cuvee. It's not the most expensive, but I'm very fond of it. It's a nice, solid, good-value wine."

From Lange, head back to Hwy 99W and follow it south to ⑧ **Stoller Vineyards**. "Fifty years ago," explains Danehower, "this was the largest turkey farm in Oregon." Bill Stoller, a successful entrepreneur, had been growing grapes for many years and a few years ago decided to build his own winery. The result? According to Danehower, it's one of the most ecologically sustainable wineries in the country, if not the world. Today, the winery building holds the US Green Building Council's gold-level certification for Leadership in Energy and Environmental Design. "Plus, the architecture is true to the site, not an imitation of a French or Italian villa," says Danehower. "And the wines are good and reasonably priced." What more could you ask for?

"…a stunning wine cellar and lovely views over the rolling hills and vineyards that sweep across the valley."

When it comes to sustainability, Stoller isn't alone. One of the Willamette Valley's distinguishing characteristics, Danehower explains, is the regional dedication to organic and sustainable production practices. "The question is not who is doing organic," he says. "It's who's *not* doing organic. The emphasis here is on quality over quantity, and on natural over mechanical or chemical practices." That means visiting organic or sustainable wineries is easy. And you don't have to skip the big ones. In fact, according to Danehower, some of the valley's most famous wineries use biodynamic and organic practices. "They just don't splash it across their labels or use it as a marketing strategy," he says.

After Stoller (and a late afternoon nap), have dinner at the ⑨ **Joel Palmer House**, in the wee town of Dayton. The chef, Jack Czarnecki, is a mushroom expert (some might say fanatic) and has created a menu based entirely around wild mushrooms gathered from the area. What ends up on your table? Dishes like wild mushroom soup, loin of elk with juniper cabbage and black chanterelles, and filet mignon with porcini sauce.

DETOUR

If you feel you just can't squeeze enough wineries into your trip, detour 9 miles southwest of McMinnville along Hwy 18 to the **Oregon Wine Tasting Room** (☎503-843-3787; 19690 SW Hwy 18). Located inside the Bellevue Market, the tasting room stocks nearly 150 wines from over 70 Oregon wineries. Although only seven or so wines are open for tasting at a given time, odds are they'll be wines you otherwise wouldn't have tasted. And the place can't be beat for stocking the wine rack back home!

Saturday night you can cozy up at the small, owner-operated ⑩ **Brookside Inn On Abbey Road**. The nine-room inn is nestled into the trees between Dundee and Carlton and it's divine luxury, from the breakfast to the beds. After a night here, you'll be well rested for Sunday's wine tasting.

With a leisurely Sunday morning start, head over to ⑪ **Scott Paul Wines**, which, according to Danehower, embodies the character of Oregon wine.

"It's another purely family affair, producing superb Pinot Noirs." In fact, the winery *only* produces Pinot Noirs. Plus, "they have a really pleasant and easy-going tasting room." That, of course, is a tough combination to beat.

From Scott Paul, it's a short trip over to **12** **Brick House Vineyards**, which lies within the Ribbon Ridge appellation and, Danehower insists, "is in many ways my prototype of the Oregon winery experience." Brick House's owner, Doug Tunnel, is a former CBS foreign correspondent and a native Oregonian. He's also one of Oregon's pioneers in organic farming. And the winery is great. "There's no pretension whatsoever," Danehower warmly explains. "You drive up and dogs come out to greet you. You stand in the barn and look out over the vines and the compost piles." The winery itself occupies a converted barn and the whole place appeals to Danehower as authentic and fun – and being there "somehow just makes you feel good."

Danny Palmerlee

TRIP INFORMATION

GETTING THERE
From Portland, take Hwy 5 south 8 miles to Hwy 99W (Exit 294). Follow 99W about 16 miles to Dundee.

DO
Brick House Vineyards
Longtime winery producing Pinot Noir, Chardonnay and Gamay Noir. ☎ 503-538-5136; www.brickhousewines.com; 18200 Lewis Rogers Lane, Newberg; tasting fee $10; ⊙ by appointment

Domaine Drouhin Oregon
Owned by renowned Burgundy producer Maison Joseph Drouhin. ☎ 503-864-2700; www.domainedrouhin.com; 6750 Breyman Orchards Rd, Dayton; tasting fee $10; ⊙ tasting room 11am-4pm Wed-Sun

Domaine Serene
Dundee Hills winery esteemed for Pinot Noir and Chardonnay. ☎ 503-864-4600; www.domaineserene.com; 6555 NE Hilltop Lane, Dayton; tasting fee $15; ⊙ tasting room 11am-4pm Wed-Mon

Lange Estate Winery & Vineyards
Top location, producing esteemed Pinot Noir and Pinot Gris. ☎ 503-538-6476; www.langewinery.com; 18380 NE Buena Vista Dr, Dundee; tasting free; ⊙ 11am-5pm

Scott Paul Wines
Small winery dedicated exclusively to Pinot Noir. ☎ 503-852-7300; www.scottpaul.com; 128 S Pine St, Carlton; tasting fee $5; ⊙ 11am-4pm Wed-Sun

Stoller Vineyards
Sustainable, family-operated winery that produces Pinot Noir and Chardonnay. ☎ 503-864-3404; www.stollervineyards.com; 16161 NE McDougall Rd, Dayton; tasting fee $10; ⊙ tasting room 11am-5pm Sat & Sun

Vista Hills Vineyard
Great wine and a tree-house tasting room. ☎ 503-864-3200; www.vistahillsvineyard.com; 6475 Hilltop Lane, Dayton; tasting fee $10; ⊙ noon-5pm Wed-Sun

EAT
Dundee Bistro
Well-appointed, great-value bistro focusing on local food and wine. ☎ 503-554-1650; www.dundeebistro.com; 100A SW 7th St, Dundee; mains $10-16; ⊙ 11:30am-9pm

Joel Palmer House
Fine dining; the chef, a fun guy, specializes in mushrooms. ☎ 503-864-2995; www.joelpalmerhouse.com; 600 Ferry St, Dayton; mains $29-37; ⊙ 5-9pm Tue-Sat

SLEEP
Black Walnut Inn & Vineyard
One of the Willamette Valley's most luxurious lodgings. ☎ 503-429-4114, 866-429-4114; www.blackwalnut-inn.com; 9600 NE Worden Hill Rd, Dundee; r $295-425

Brookside Inn On Abbey Road
Luxurious nine-room guesthouse in the heart of wine country; breakfast included. ☎ 503-852-4433; www.brooksideinn-oregon.com; 8243 NE Abbey Rd, Carlton; r $180-350

USEFUL WEBSITES
www.oregonwine.org
www.willamettewines.com

LINK YOUR TRIP
www.lonelyplanet.com/trip-planner

Dippin' Down the Cascades

WHY GO Because nothing beats a good soak. And when the tub in question sits beside a cold river, deep in the old-growth forests of the Cascade Range, and the water, rich in minerals, burbles from a hole in the forest floor, you're guaranteed one thing: bliss.

The Cascade Range lies on the Pacific Ring of Fire, that horseshoe-shaped chain of volcanic peaks that wraps the Pacific Ocean and coughs up most of the world's volcanic eruptions. For Oregon, that means there's a lot of geothermal activity beneath its tree-covered surface. The perk? Hot springs – *lots* of them.

Hidden within the Cascades' thick expanses of western hemlock and Douglas fir, edged with maidenhair ferns and often set beside a river, are some of the most paradisiacal hot springs imaginable. But they're no secret. Like it or not, most of the Cascades' hot springs are as much a social (if not cultural) phenomena as they are an excuse to spend some time in nature. At some, folks turn up with guitars and wads of burning sage, and joints get fired up when the atmosphere is right. At others, cans of beer outnumber Nalgene bottles, and bathing suits can outnumber bare buns. Often, it all depends on the day.

Of the dozens of hot springs spread around the state, we've chosen six that are accessible enough to make for a relaxing four-day trip, allowing you to soak yourself silly *at least* once a day. At all but one (Belknap), nudity is generally the norm, but no one should feel uncomfortable donning a bathing suit either. If anything, the vibe at all these places is *relaxed*. For exact directions to the hot springs, refer to Trip Information.

There's no better place to start a trip down the thermal trail than at ❶ **Breitenbush Hot Springs**. Set above the Breitenbush River on a

---

TIME
4 days

DISTANCE
240 miles

BEST TIME TO GO
Jun – Sep

START
Breitenbush Hot Springs

END
Umpqua Hot Springs

BEST TRIP

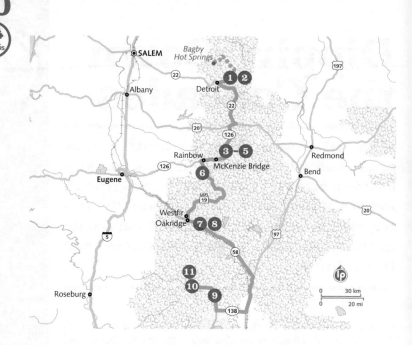

154-acre reserve inside Willamette National Forest, this place is as Oregon as it gets and, along with a fantastically relaxing soak, you'll get a solid dose of earthy Oregonian mellowness. Hot mineral water burbles out of several springs at a scorching 180°F to 200°F and is cooled to prime soaking temperatures with water from the river. There are seven pools in all. Three overlook a pretty meadow and one of these is a silent pool. Another four pools (the Spiral Tubs) are arranged in order of temperature, from 100°F to 107°F. Elsewhere, a sauna sits over an open spring and is entirely heated by steam from hot water below. You can stay in a cabin, a lodge room, a dorm room or in a tent (yours or one provided by Breitenbush). The rooms are geothermally heated and all electricity is generated by turbines on the river (once you're here, you're off the grid). Three organic vegetarian meals are included and served in a historic lodge. In all, it's one heck of a treat. You can also visit as a day guest and camp at nearby **2** **Humbug Campground**, only 3 miles below Breitenbush.

"...sitting in the deep pools and staring up at the trees remains an utterly sublime experience."

The following day (after an early morning soak, of course), make your way south along Hwy 22 to Hwy 126 East (south). About 9 miles south of Clear Lake, pull into **3** **Olallie Campground** and set up camp. There's heaps to do around here, including fishing on the McKenzie River, hiking on the nearby McKenzie River National Recreation Trail, and waterfall watching at Sahalie and Koosah Falls, only a stone's throw from the campground. By the end of the day you'll be well ready for a soak. Worry not, ❹ **Bigelow Hot Springs** is only a short distance away. This well-hidden, little-known hot spring sits on the banks of the McKenzie River, tucked into a sort of miniature grotto that drips into a perfectly heated pool (100°F to 104°F). It's shallow but a real treat, especially in the early morning, when you're likely to have it all to yourself. From the parking lot, cross to the downstream side of the bridge and take the first path down to the water. Follow the trail downstream 150 yards to the pool.

If you'd prefer to do your soaking in a bigger, clearer, sometimes hotter but always more crowded pool, stop at

> **DETOUR** For more great soaking, detour one hour (40 miles) northwest of Breitenbush Hot Springs to the eternal soakers' favorite, **Bagby Hot Springs**. From the former, continue on Forest Rd 46 (Breitenbush Rd) to Forest Rd 63. Turn left, then veer right on Forest Rd 70 and follow it 7 miles to the parking lot. Hike 1.5 miles on the well-marked trail to the free bathhouses with hollowed-log tubs. A $5 Northwest Forest Pass is required at the parking lot.

❺ **Belknap Hot Springs Resort,** only 4 miles south. Belknap is the sort of hot spring you can take your grandmother to and she won't feel out of place. But neither will you – and you'll both love the water. Two giant swimming pools filled with 103°F mineral water provide optimum soaking conditions in a family environment. The McKenzie River rushes by below, trees tower over everything and, as far as we could tell, everyone has a darn good time. The resort boasts an 18-room lodge, 14 private cabins and 15 tent sites, so it's affordable for nearly all budgets. It's also an excellent alternative to camping and, if you are camping, it's the perfect place to pop into on a day-use basis.

On day three, journey west of McKenzie Bridge and turn left on Hwy 19, better known as Aufderheide Memorial Drive (the turnoff is just past Rainbow). After almost 8 miles, you'll come to the well-signed ❻ **Terwilliger Hot Springs.** From the parking lot, a 0.25-mile trail leads through old-growth forest to one of the state's most stunning hot springs. From a fern-shrouded hole below the trees, thermal water spills out at a scorching 116°F and into a pool that maintains a steady minimum temperature of 108°F. Only hardcore soakers can handle it. From the upper pool, the water then cascades into three successive pools, each one cooler than the one above it. Over the years, Terwilliger became so popular and so party-prone that local caretakers and the US Forest Service were forced to institute a no-alcohol policy. Despite its continuing popularity, sitting in the deep pools and staring up at the trees remains an utterly sublime experience. After hiking back to the car, you can even jump into Cougar Reservoir from the rocky shore below the parking lot.

You could stretch this trip out by camping in one of several nearby campgrounds, but to stick with the four-day program continue south along glorious Hwy 19 to the sister towns of Westfir and Oakridge. From Oakridge, drive 8.7 miles east along Hwy 58 to **7** **Blue Pool Campground**, the only campground in the immediate area. It's on the banks of Salt Creek with several tent-only sites and enough trees to make most of the campsites feel secluded.

After pitching your tent and blowing up your sleeping pad, drive 0.5 miles east along Hwy 58 to **8** **McCredie Hot Springs**. Because McCredie lies just off the highway it's a very popular spot, for everyone from mountain bikers fresh off the trails near Oakridge to truckers plying Hwy 58. Despite this, it's worth a stop if only because it's the site of one of the largest – and hottest – thermal pools in Oregon. If you can hit it early in the morning – and we highly recommend you do – or late in the evening midweek, you could very well have the place to yourself. There are five pools in all: two upper pools that are often dangerously hot (as in don't-even-dip-your-foot-in hot), two warm riverside pools and one smaller, murkier but usually perfectly heated pool tucked back into the trees. Salt Creek, which rushes past only steps from the springs, is perfect for splashing down with icy water. Since you'll be camped only half a mile away, it's easy to visit before or after prime time.

From Blue Pool Campground, continue east on Hwy 58, to Hwy 97 S and swing west on Hwy 138 toward Crater Lake. About 22 miles from Hwy 97,

ADD A HIKE TO HOT WATER

Hiking and hot springs make a fabulous combination. Fortunately, outstanding trails can be found near almost every hot spring on this trip. Two major trails from Breitenbush lead eventually to the Pacific Crest Trail. The McKenzie River National Recreation Trail leads from Bigelow Hot Springs south to three major waterfalls. Before (and after) soaking in Umpqua Hot Springs, hike as much of the North Umpqua Trail as you can – it passes the trail to the springs.

you'll pass stunning Diamond Lake and **9** **Diamond Lake Resort**, the only hotel around. Shack up here if you don't plan to camp the final night. After passing several other lakes, a handful of campgrounds and some extremely high waterfalls that lie hidden in the forest, you'll come to **10** **Toketee Lake Campground**, just off Hwy 138 on the North Umpqua River. Although some of the other nearby campgrounds are arguably more scenic (though not by much),

Toketee Lake Campground is all about location. It offers excellent access to the spectacular 79-mile North Umpqua Trail, which you can hike in either direction along the along the federally designated "Wild and Scenic" section of the North Umpqua River. Best of all, it's the closest established campground to this trip's grand finale: **11** **Umpqua Hot Springs**.

Umpqua Hot Springs is the sort of place that sets you thinking, "Is this place real *and* free?" It's both. And although you have to work a little to get here, it is their remote setting that makes these springs so magical. Cascading down a precipitous ridge overlooking the North Umpqua River, seven warm pools range in temperatures from 110°F in the upper pools to about 99°F in the lower pool. Each is formed by colorful mineral deposits, and the lower pools are just big enough to accommodate two happy soakers. Sitting in the pools on a cold, misty morning, looking out over the river and the trees towering above the opposite side of the gorge must be one of Oregon's most memorable experiences.

To reach the springs from the parking lot, you need to cross the North Umpqua River. Winter storms destroyed the old footbridge, and it may be out for years. Until it's replaced, head downstream 100yd or so from the old bridge and walk across the wide log over the river. Once you're across, walk back upstream to the site of the old bridge and then hike uphill, away from the river, until you reach the main trail. Turn right and follow the trail about 0.25 miles up and over a ridge to the pools. Once you're there, slide into one of the natural tubs and enjoy the view – after all the hot tubbing you've done this week, you deserve every minute of it.

Danny Palmerlee

TRIP INFORMATION

GETTING THERE
To get to Breitenbush Hot Springs from Portland, drive 50 miles south on I-5 to Salem; head east for 49 miles on Hwy 22, then go 10 miles northeast on Breitenbush Rd.

DO

Bigelow Hot Springs
Traveling south on Hwy 126 from Clear Lake, turn right on the unsigned road between mileposts 14 and 15. Cross the McKenzie River and park on the right. **Admission free;** ☾ **24hr**

Breitenbush Hot Springs
Fees at this rustic resort include three meals, meditation rooms, soaking pools and saunas. ☎ **503-854-3320; Breitenbush Rd, Detroit; dm $47-58, tents $51-69, r $50-60, cabins $64-92**

McCredie Hot Springs
Extremely popular soaking pool 9.2 miles east of Oakridge on Hwy 58. Pools are directly below the parking lot. **Admission free;** ☾ **dawn-dusk**

Terwilliger Hot Springs
Closes for cleaning after around 10am on Thursdays in summer. (If you accidentally show up, you can help clean.) No alcohol, pets or glass bottles allowed. **Aufderheide Memorial Dr; admission $5;** ☾ **dawn-dusk**

Umpqua Hot Springs
From Hwy 138, turn onto Rd 34 at Toketee Lake. Drive 1 mile past Toketee Lake Campground; turn right on unsigned gravel road and continue 2 miles to the parking area on the left. **Admission free;** ☾ **24hr**

EAT & SLEEP

Belknap Hot Springs Resort
Family-oriented resort with two huge pools. Grill open in summer. ☎ **541-822-3512; www.belknaphotsprings.com; Hwy 126 near Hwy 242; campsites $30, r $100-185, cabins $60-400, day use only $7-12**

Blue Pool Campground
Wooded, 24-site campground near McCredie Springs. Water and pit toilets available. First-come, first-served. **Hwy 58; campsites $12;** ☾ **May-Sep**

Diamond Lake Resort
This widely loved family resort offers hotel rooms and cabins on the lakeshore. ☎ **541-793-3333, 800-733-7593; www.diamond lake.net; 350 Resort Dr, Diamond Lake; r $89-199, cabins $189-489;** ⚒

Humbug Campground
Lovely, 22-site campground on Breitenbush River with some very secluded sites. Water and pit toilets available. First-come, first-served. **Breitenbush Rd, Detroit; campsites $12;** ☾ **May-Sep;** ⚒

Olallie Campground
The closest campground to Bigelow Springs has a prime location on the McKenzie River. ☎ **877-444-6777; www.recreation.gov; Hwy 126; campsites $12;** ☾ **Apr-Sep**

Toketee Lake Campground
First-come, first-served campground with shady sites on the North Umpqua River; near Toketee Falls and Umpqua Hot Springs, 56 miles east of Roseburg. **Rd 34 at Hwy 138; campsites $7;** ⚒ 🐾

USEFUL WEBSITES
www.fs.fed.us/r6/willamette
www.oregonhotsprings.immunenet.com

LINK YOUR TRIP
www.lonelyplanet.com/trip-planner

Scenic Byways of the Central Cascades

WHY GO With lush forests and dry forests, thundering waterfalls on wild and scenic rivers, snowcapped peaks, high desert and lakes galore, Oregon's Central Cascades are a bonanza of natural wonder. This trip stitches together the finest segments of three national scenic byways. The result? One epic journey and loads of outdoor fun.

It's no wonder so many scenic byways meander their way around Oregon's Central Cascades. The region is, without a doubt, some of the most spectacular terrain in the entire state. Unless you're out for a day trip, however, one scenic byway just isn't enough. Here you have our version of a Cascades scenic byway, a route that will take you from dry, high mountain desert, into the lush Douglas fir forests of the western slopes, along the epic, lake-riddled Hwy 46 and, finally, back to the high desert and into the heart of a volcanic crater.

Kick off the trip in the mountain town of ❶ **Sisters**, 22 miles northwest of Bend. Straddling the Cascades and the high desert, Sisters began as a stagecoach stop, later evolved into a logging and ranch town and finally morphed into the outdoorsy, boutique-laden hotspot it is today. Since you may be eating camp food for the next four days, treat yourself to a meal at ❷ **Bronco Billy's Ranch Grill & Saloon** before setting off. It's an old-time family joint with a meat-heavy menu and lots of friendly chitchat.

With the snowcapped peaks of the Three Sisters watching over you, drive northwest from Sisters along Hwy 242. This is part of the McKenzie Pass-Santiam Pass Scenic Byway. About 17 miles outside of Sisters, you'll be cruising over 5325ft McKenzie Pass, surrounded on all sides by endless lava fields. Near the top, perched on a giant mound

TIME
4 days

DISTANCE
235 miles

BEST TIME TO GO
Jul – Sep

START
Sisters

END
Newberry Crater

ALSO GOOD FOR

OUTDOORS

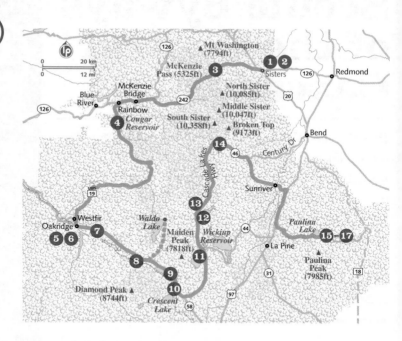

TRIP
31

OREGON SCENIC BYWAYS OF THE CENTRAL CASCADES

of lava rock, built entirely of lava rock, in the middle of a field of lava rock, stands the historic ❸ **Dee Wright Observatory**. The structure, built in 1935 by Franklin D Roosevelt's Civilian Conservation Corps, offers spectacular views in all directions. The observatory windows, called "lava tubes," were placed to highlight all the prominent Cascade peaks that can be seen from the summit, including Mt Washington, Mt Jefferson, North Sister, Middle Sister and a host of others. Supposedly, on a clear day, you can see as far north as Mt Hood. About 0.5 miles west of the observatory, the Pacific Crest Trail (PCT) crosses the road. For an interesting 5-mile round-trip hike follow the trail north of the road across the barren lava fields to Little Belknap Crater.

> "…trees hang so far over the road that the sky disappears altogether and all you see is green."

Beyond the PCT crossing, Hwy 242 passes several scenic viewpoints before winding down the dramatic Deadhorse Grade and pushing on to Hwy 126. When you reach Hwy 126, veer left (west). You're now on the West Cascades Scenic Byway. After 9.5 miles, near the "town" of Rainbow, turn left onto Aufderheide Memorial Drive (Hwy 19).

Snaking for 48 miles through dense deciduous and evergreen forest, Aufderheide Memorial Drive is one of the most beautiful forest roads in Oregon. Along some stretches, trees hang so far over the road that the sky disappears altogether and all you see is green. Eight miles south of Hwy 126, you'll pass ❹ **Terwilliger**

Hot Springs. Park your car in the dirt lot and hike the 0.25-mile trail through old-growth forest to four hot mineral pools set above a lagoon beside Cougar Reservoir. Camping options abound along Aufderheide Memorial Drive, but there are no hotels until you reach the sister towns of Westfir and Oakridge.

In Oakridge, a town of decidedly boring motels, your best bet is the **5** **Oakridge Motel**, if only for its inviting pseudo-log cabin ambience. Although it's not immediately apparent, Oakridge is one of Oregon's mountain biking meccas, thanks to the endless amount of trails around town. And with all the raven-ous mountain bikers rolling into town, it was only a matter of time before a place like the **6** **Trail Head Coffee House** popped up. Asian-inspired dishes, sandwiches, wraps and random concoctions such as tempeh stroganoff grace the menu, making this the best eating option around. If you've driven this far and want to camp, continue 8.5 miles east of Oakridge along Hwy 58 and pitch a tent at **7** **Blue Pool**

> **DETOUR**
>
> **Waldo Lake** lies on the very crest of the Cascades at an elevation of 5414ft. Not only is it Oregon's second-largest *and* second-deepest lake, it's also one of the purest bodies of water in the world. The lake's astounding clarity means ob-jects up to 100ft deep can be seen from above. A 22-mile trail circles the lake, campsites are plentiful and the wildlife viewing is superb. Make it a quick one-hour detour or stay a while. There's plenty to do!

Campground, a shady spot on the banks of Salt Creek. (Hint: you'll be closer than everyone else to McCredie Hot Springs, accessed via a parking lot 0.5 miles up the highway.)

On day three, head east out of Oakridge along Hwy 58, the only stretch of the trip that is not – surprisingly – a designated scenic byway. About 22 miles east of Oakridge, you'll pass **8** **Salt Creek Falls**, the second-highest waterfall in Oregon. After a good snowmelt, this aqueous behemoth really roars, making for one of the most spectacular sights on the trip. Pull off the highway at the signed parking lot and, within about 10 paces from the car, you'll reach the upper viewpoint. Be sure to hike the short trail downhill toward the bottom of the falls. It's lined with rhododendrons that put on a colorful show in springtime, and the views of the falls on the way down are stunning.

After Salt Creek Falls, Hwy 58 skirts the northern shore of beautiful **9** **Odell Lake**, which sits within a steep, forested glacial basin. At its eastern end, stop at **10** **Odell Lake Lodge** for an eggs-and-bacon breakfast. The lodge's mountain-style restaurant, with big windows overlooking the lake, makes the perfect spot to fill the stomach before continuing the drive. True to its name, the lodge offers cozy – albeit motel-like – rooms if you feel like breaking up the drive, and a cramped but gorgeously situated campground skirts the lake-shore nearby. Most of the campsites are literally two steps from the water's edge, and they're great if you have a kayak or canoe.

From Odell Lake, continue past the little hub of Crescent Lake (there's a store here if you need it) and swing left on Crescent Cutoff Rd toward Hwy 97. Instead of continuing to Hwy 97, however, turn left onto Hwy 46, the spectacular Cascade Lakes Scenic Byway. You'll wind through a ghost forest of burned lodgepole and ponderosa pines, and gorgeous ⑪ **Davis Lake** pops into view. The lake is shallow but huge and its wide soggy shoreline is edged with bright green grass and wildflowers. Presiding over the lake are Maiden Peak, Diamond Peak and, in the distance, Mt Bachelor. There are small campgrounds at either end of the lake that are popular with anglers.

After passing Davis Lake, the road winds past lake after beautiful lake – Wickiup Reservoir, Crane Prairie Reservoir, Cultus Lake, Lava Lake, Elk Lake – and they all deserve a stop. Most of them have at least one lakeside campground, making for outstanding camping, fun trout fishing, excellent boating and, if you can handle the cold water, invigorating swimming. Two of our favorite campgrounds are on ⑫ **Crane Prairie Reservoir**, whose shores offer sweeping views of the surrounding mountains; and a short way up the highway, Cultus Lake is home to the ⑬ **Cultus Lake Resort**, for those who prefer the comfort of a bed. It can be windier here, however, than by the lakes on the east side of the road – great if you're a windsurfer, not so great if you're looking to lounge on the shoreline or paddle a canoe around. Further north, on Sparks Lake, you'll find ⑭ **Sparks Lake Campground**, one the of most scenically situated campgrounds on the entire route. Although just off the highway, it's set beside Soda Creek, which winds through a giant meadow beneath Mt Bachelor.

BLAST FROM THE PAST

The Cascades are a region of immense volcanic importance. Lava fields can be seen from McKenzie Pass and along Hwy 46. Road cuts expose gray ash flows. Stratovolcanos like South Sister and Mt Bachelor and shield volcanoes like Mt Washington tower over the landscape. Although it's not instantly obvious when you drive to the center of Newberry Volcanic National Monument, you're actually inside the caldera of a 500-sq-mile volcano. What could be stranger than that? It's still active.

On day four, you'll leave the Cascade Lakes Scenic Byway. Seven miles beyond Sparks Lake, after skirting the north side of Mt Bachelor, turn right onto Hwy 45 (toward Sunriver). Follow this to Hwy 97 and turn right again. About 8 miles south of Sunriver, turn left on Paulina Lake Rd toward ⑮ **Newberry National Volcanic Monument**. This fascinating park showcases the giant Newberry Crater, which was formed by the eruption of what used to be one of the largest and most active volcanoes in North America. Like Crater Lake, the summit of the volcano collapsed during the eruption, creating the caldera you see today.

The monument is home to a massive solidified lava flow (the Big Obsidian Flow), a handful of choice trails and two stunning lakes. A 4-mile road leads to the top of 7985ft Paulina Peak and offers incredible views of the crater. While the volcanic landscape is the park's raison d'être, most people journey here for the icy blue waters of Paulina Lake and East Lake. And it's no wonder. You can camp beside them, float upon them, swim in them or lay in the hot, high desert sun beside them. No matter what you do, you'll be surrounded by stunning scenery. Of the campgrounds here, **16** **Cinder Hill Campground**, at the end of the road, is the quietest and our favorite. Many of the sites offer quick and easy access to a splendid beach on East Lake. Noncampers should book a room at the rustic **17** **East Lake Resort**, with fully equipped cabins, some of which are right on the lake. Wherever you sleep, one thing is certain: you're guaranteed a beautiful morning after.

Danny Palmerlee

TRIP
31

TRIP INFORMATION

GETTING THERE

From Portland, drive 50 miles south on I-5 to Salem; then drive east on Hwy 22 for 80 miles to Hwy 20; follow this 26 miles to Sisters.

DO

Newberry National Volcanic Monument

Spectacular volcanic region highlighted by the Newberry Crater; great swimming, fishing, camping, hiking and more. Located 35 miles southeast of Bend. ☎ 541-593-2421; day use $5; 🔧 🐾

Terwilliger Hot Springs

This popular spring closes for cleaning around 10am on Thursdays in summer. No alcohol, pets or glass bottles allowed. **Aufderheide Memorial Dr; admission $5;** 🕐 dawn-dusk

EATING

Bronco Billy's Ranch Grill & Saloon

Old-time family joint serving steaks, ribs, hot links, burgers, salads, sandwiches and a vegetable sauté. ☎ 541-549-7427; Hotel Sisters, 190 E Cascade Ave, Sisters; mains $11-20; 🕐 11:30am-9pm

Odell Lake Lodge

This classic mountain lodge on the east end of Odell Lake has a good family-style restaurant. ☎ 800-434-2540; www.odelllakeresort.com; Hwy 58; mains $6-11; 🕐 restaurant 8am-8pm, reduced hours in winter; 🔧

Trail Head Coffee House

Café and restaurant with a creative menu of vegetarian and meat dishes; pizza Thursday nights. ☎ 541-782-2223; 47434 Hwy 58, Oakridge; mains $6.50-11.95; 🕐 7am-2pm Tue & Wed, 7am-9pm Thu-Sun

SLEEPING

Blue Pool Campground

Wooded 24-site campground near McCredie Springs. Water and pit toilets available. First-come, first-served. **Hwy 58; campsites $12;** 🕐 **May-Sep;** 🔧 🐾

Cinder Hill Campground

First-come, first-served campground on East Lake. Easy access to swimming and other lake activities. Water and pit toilets only. **campsites $10;** 🕐 **May-Oct;** 🔧 🐾

Cultus Lake Resort

Offers 23 homey cabins with two-night minimum; week-only basis July 4 to September 1. Book well ahead. There's a restaurant, too. ☎ 541-389-3230, 800-616-3230; www .cultuslakeresort.com; Hwy 46; cabins per night $105-135; 🔧

East Lake Resort

Offers 12 rustic, comfortable cabins, most with kitchenettes and lake views. Four motel-type rooms with outside coin-op showers available. Reservations advised. ☎ 541-536-2230; www.eastlakeresort.com; r $75, cabins $110-185; 🕐 May-Oct; 🔧

Oakridge Motel

With a log exterior and wooden walls inside, this otherwise run-of-the-mill motel is slightly more interesting than some others. ☎ 541-782-2432; www.theoakridgemotel .com; 48197 Hwy 58, Oakridge; r $45

Sparks Lake Campground

Small, sunny campground near Soda Creek with views of Mt Bachelor and meadows. Pit toilets available; no water. **Hwy 46; campsites free;** 🕐 **Jun or Jul-Sep;** 🔧 🐾

USEFUL WEBSITES

www.byways.org/explore/states/OR
www.sisterschamber.com

LINK YOUR TRIP

www.lonelyplanet.com/trip-planner

The Way of the Waterfall

WHY GO Few things beat the sight and sound of water plunging off a cliff, especially when there's lots of it and the cliff is really, really high. With that in mind, we've crafted a trip to Oregon's highest, most powerful waterfalls outside the Columbia River Gorge.

When it comes to waterfalls, the Columbia River Gorge gets all the attention. Sure it's home to a bewildering number of falls, including Oregon's highest. But the state's second-highest waterfall is outside the gorge, so is its third highest, and so are plenty of others. In four leisurely days, you can easily see some of the state's most spectacular waterfalls. In fact, you'll find 10 breathtaking falls inside a single park. And no, we're not talking about the Columbia River Gorge – we're talking Silver Falls.

❶ **Silver Falls State Park,** Oregon's largest state park, lies just over an hour southeast of Portland. Within its 9000 acres stand cool forests of Douglas fir, western hemlock, big leaf maples and cedars. The leaves of vine maples glow bright green in the filtered sunlight, and sword ferns, maidenhair ferns, salal, Oregon grape and salmonberry cover the forest floor. Hidden amid all this lush greenery are 10 major waterfalls ranging in height from 27ft to 177ft. Best of all, you can see each and every one of them by hiking an 8-mile loop trail known as the ❷ **Trail of Ten Falls.**

The best place to start the hike is the South Falls parking lot, where you can kick off your hike with a bang by walking *behind* 177ft South Falls, the park's highest waterfall. From the top of South Falls, the trail winds downhill and into a dripping grotto behind the fall. Continue along the Canyon Trail to Lower South Falls (which you also are able to walk behind!) and on to Lower North Falls. Detour 0.1 miles up

TIME
4 days

DISTANCE
270 miles

BEST TIME TO GO
Jun – Aug

START
Silver Falls State Park

END
Umpqua Hot Springs

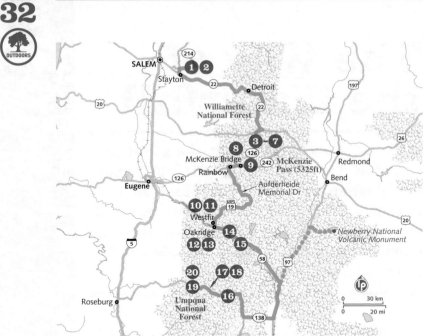

to Double Falls, then continue to Drake Falls and Middle North Falls. After Middle North Falls, you can either stay on the Canyon Trail to North Falls for the complete 8-mile loop or return to the parking lot along the Winter and Rim Trails for a more relaxing 6-mile loop. If you choose the latter, simply drive to North Falls later; you only end up missing Twin Falls. At the end of the day, spend the night at the park campground or in one of 14 fully equipped log cabins.

Day two takes you to the McKenzie River and two of Oregon's most impressive waterfalls: ❸ **Sahalie Falls** and ❹ **Koosah Falls**. In the old Chinook trading jargon, "Sahalie" means "heaven" and "Koosah" means "sky." Sahalie Falls measures 120ft and, after a good snowmelt, drenches everything around it in mist as it roars into the frothy pool below. Only 0.3 miles downstream, Koosah Falls measures 90ft and is wider and easier going than its upstream neighbor. The stretch of the McKenzie River between the falls is utterly spectacular, with roaring cascades that tumble over basalt boulders, through massive logjams and into deep, dark pools. Bright green moss clings to everything around the river, giving the whole area a moody, mystical feel.

To get to the Sahalie Falls area from Silver Falls State Park, head east (south) along Hwy 214 to Hwy 22 east. Follow this to Hwy 216, jog west along Hwy 20 and then south on Hwy 126 west to ❺ **Clear Lake**. Before chasing waterfalls, set up camp at one of two nearby campgrounds: **6 Cold Water Cove**, shaded by giant conifers on the east shore of Clear Lake, or **7 Ice Cap**, further south at the unimpressive but beautifully situated Carmen Reservoir. Cold Water is the prettier of the two, but Ice Cap is closer to the falls. From either campground you can hike part of the 26.5-mile McKenzie River National Recreation Trail to the waterfalls. Both falls are also immediately accessible by parking areas on Hwy 126. If you're driving to the falls, park at either of them and hike the 0.3 miles of narrow riverside trail that meanders through thick forest linking the two falls.

If you prefer the luxuries of bed, sink and shower, the nearest place to lay your head in a comfortable fashion is the town of McKenzie Bridge, about 19 miles southeast of Sahalie Falls. Here you'll find the excellent **8 Cedarwood Lodge**, which rents rustic, cozy cabins over the McKenzie River. Before getting to town, stop into the **9 McKenzie River Ranger Station**, about 2 miles east of McKenzie Bridge. The rangers are fountains of information, plus you'll find excellent maps and books and heaps of useful information on the McKenzie River National Recreation Trail.

On day three, make your way past McKenzie Bridge and hang a left on Aufderheide Memorial Dr (Hwy 19). This narrow, winding 48-mile national scenic byway is anything but your typical forest road. It's a study in green, with trees hanging so far over the highway, you feel as though you're tunneling through the forest.

A WATERFALL PRIMER

Take the plunge into waterfall geekiness by calling falls as you see them: Toketee is a tiered fall because it's composed of two distinct falls. Being wide and fairly flat, Koosah Falls is a sheet or block fall. Plunging off the rock into the air, South Falls (in Silver Falls State Park) is a classic plunge fall. Narrow, long Watson Falls is a typical ribbon fall. Paulina Falls, part curtain, part slide, part segmented and completely schizophrenic, is a combination fall.

At the end of the road, you'll hit the wee town of Westfir, where you can check into the plush, old-fashioned **10 Westfir Lodge**. Directly across the street from the restored **11 Westfir Bridge** (Oregon's longest covered bridge), this B&B is an elegant hodgepodge of antiques, old photographs and Victorian wallpaper. Despite its old, English feel, it's far from pretentious. And the breakfasts are huge.

If you'd prefer a good old standard motel room, head 3 miles east to the mountain-bike mecca of Oakridge and shack up at the perfectly adequate **12 Oakridge Motel**. On your way, you'll pass the **13 Trail Head Coffee House**, the best place to eat in the entire area (hence, the many ravenous mountain bikers devouring veggie wraps, Asian stir-fries, tempeh dishes, sandwiches, salads and everything else the tattooed staff carries out). Just over

8.5 miles east of Oakridge, you'll find the area's lone campground, ⑭ **Blue Pool Campground**, a relaxing spot in the trees on the banks of Salt Creek.

The following day, get an early start and head east on Hwy 58. About 22 miles out of Oakridge (or 12.5 miles east of Blue Pool), you'll come to the voluminous ⑮ **Salt Creek Falls**. At 286ft, this monster of a waterfall is Oregon's second highest and, except for the sign on the freeway, you'd never know it was here. But sure enough, walk from the parking lot to the viewpoint and there below, in a massive basalt amphitheater hidden by the towering trees, 50,000 gallons of water pour every minute over a cliff and into a giant, dark, tumultuous pool. From the upper viewpoint, a trail leads about 0.2 miles down through the trees nearly to the bottom of the falls, where you're guaranteed a drenching spray. Salt Creek Falls is also the starting point for some excellent short hikes, including a 1.5-mile jaunt to Diamond Creek Falls and a 4.75-mile hike to Vivian Lake.

"…50,000 gallons of water pour every minute over a cliff and into a giant, dark, tumultuous pool."

From Salt Creek Falls, continue east on Hwy 58, swing right (south) on Hwy 97 and right again (west) on Hwy 138. Now you're really in waterfall country. Once you pass Diamond Lake, Hwy 138 passes trailheads and parking lots that offer access to numerous gorgeous falls, including Clearwater Falls, Whitehorse Falls, Lemolo Falls, Toketee Falls, Fall Creek Falls and Susan Creek Falls. They're all worth seeing, but two in particular really stand out. The first is ⑯ **Watson Falls**, which, at 272ft, is Oregon's third-highest waterfall. It's a narrow, two-tiered fall, plunging gracefully over a dramatic basalt amphitheater topped by Douglas firs and western hemlocks that tower precariously over the cliff edge above. To reach the falls, hike the 0.3-mile trail from the parking lot 2.5 miles east of Toketee Lake. From the lot, the trail crosses Hwy 138, then winds along sprightly Watson Creek over a wooden bridge and ends at a misty, muddy viewing area above the base of the falls.

ASK A LOCAL

"If you're heading east, you have to stop at **Crescent Lake** to swim. And be sure to stop at **Waldo Lake** which, if I have my facts right, is the second-clearest lake in the world. It's absolutely gorgeous. And go to **Odell Lake Lodge** at the east end of Odell Lake. The restaurant here is excellent and big windows look out over the lake."
Kelly Botak, Westfir, OR

Then there's ⑰ **Toketee Falls**. At 120ft, this two-tier fall chalks in at less than half the height of Watson Falls, but its beauty makes up threefold for any lack in loftiness. The falls' first tier pours into a nearly hidden pool behind a cliff of columnar basalt and then over the rock columns themselves into yet another gorgeous pool below. Toketee Falls is reached by a 0.4-mile trail from a signed trailhead off Rd 34, immediately after turning off Hwy 138. It's clearly signed on Hwy 138, about 2.5 miles west of the Watson Falls parking lot.

Before you hike off to Toketee Falls, grab a campsite at ⑱ **Toketee Lake Campground**, which sits a stone's throw away on the banks of the Wild and Scenic North Umpqua River. There are no hotels in the immediate area, the closest being the tiny ⑲ **Steamboat Inn**, 17 miles west along Hwy 138. A favorite among fly-casters, the Steamboat sits on the shore of the North Umpqua River which can be seen (and heard) from many of the rooms' small balconies. From Toketee Lake Campground it's an easy walk to Toketee Falls. It's also an easy walk to the North Umpqua Trail, which runs for 79 miles up

DETOUR Add an extra day to your trip with a 72-mile (one-way) detour to **Newberry National Volcanic Monument**. Showcasing 50,000 years of volcanic activity, the park is also home to lovely Paulina Falls. Admittedly, they're somewhat less dramatic than the other falls on this trip, but they make for a superb excuse to see this marvelous area. Pick up a brochure and map at the park entrance. Access to the park is from Hwy 97, south of Bend.

and down the North Umpqua River, offering first-rate hiking in both directions. And here's another perk: it's only about 3.5 miles along the trail to ⑳ **Umpqua Hot Springs**. (To drive there, follow Rd 34 for 1 mile past the campground, turn right on an unsigned gravel road and continue 2 miles to the parking lot on your left.) Set on a mountainside overlooking the North Umpqua River, they're one of Oregon's most splendid hot springs, and the perfect place to put a close on your trip.

Danny Palmerlee

TRIP INFORMATION

GETTING THERE

From Portland, take I-5 28 miles south to Hwy 214. Follow Hwy 214 south 26 miles to Silver Falls State Park.

DO

McKenzie River Ranger Station

Stop here for trail maps, books and historical information on the McKenzie River area. ☎ 541-822-3381; 57600 McKenzie Hwy (Hwy 126), McKenzie Bridge; ☒ 8am-4:30pm, reduced hours in winter; ♿

Silver Falls State Park

Explore over 25 miles of trails, 10 waterfalls, swimming holes and picnic areas. Campgrounds and cabins, too. ☎ 503-873-8681, reservations 800-452-5687; day-use fee $3; tent/RV/cabin $16/20/35; ♿ ▦

EAT & SLEEP

Blue Pool Campground

Near McCredie Springs, this campground has water and pit toilets. The 24 sites available on a first-come, first-served basis. Hwy 58; campsites $12; ☒ May-Sep

Cedarwood Lodge

Ensconce yourself in one of eight rustic, comfortable, fully equipped cabins set above the McKenzie River. ☎ 541-822-3351; www.cedarwoodlodge.com; 56535 McKenzie Hwy (Hwy 126), McKenzie Bridge; cabins $95-175; ☒ Apr-Oct; ♿ ▦

Cold Water Cove

Small campground on the bushy, tree-lined shores of cold Clear Lake. Drinking water and pit toilets available, and it's 18 miles northeast of McKenzie Bridge. ☎ 877-444-6777; www.recreation.gov; Hwy 126; campsites $14; ☒ May-Oct; ♿ ▦

Ice Cap

Near Koosah Falls, this 22-site campground offers easy access to the McKenzie River and nearby waterfalls. ☎ 877-444-6777; www.recreation.gov; Hwy 126; campsites $14; ☒ May-Oct; ♿ ▦

Oakridge Motel

Standard motel accommodations is somewhat enhanced by a log-cabin theme both inside and out. ☎ 541-782-2432; www.theoakridgemotel.com; 48197 Hwy 58, Oakridge; r $45

Steamboat Inn

Pamper yourself at this deluxe anglers' favorite overlooking the river, or simply stop for a great meal. ☎ 541-496-3495; www.thesteamboatinn.com; 42705 N Umpqua Hwy, Steamboat; r $170-295, lunch $6-12, dinner $50

Toketee Lake Campground

First-come, first-served campground with shady sites on the North Umpqua River; near Toketee Falls and Umpqua Hot Springs, 56 miles east of Roseburg. Rd 34 at Hwy 138; campsites $7; ♿ ▦

Trail Head Coffee House

Café and restaurant with a creative menu of vegetarian and meat dishes; pizza Thursday nights. ☎ 541-782-2223; 47434 Hwy 58, Oakridge; mains $6.50-11.95; ☒ 7am-2pm Tue & Wed, 7am-9pm Thu-Sun

Westfir Lodge

Lovely B&B chock-full of antiques. Baths are private but most are outside the room. Full English breakfast included. Cheesecake served most evenings. ☎ 541-782-3103; www.westfirlodge.com; 47365 1st St, Westfir; r $60-90

USEFUL WEBSITES

www.fs.fed.us/r6/umpqua
www.fs.fed.us/r6/willamette

www.lonelyplanet.com/trip-planner

LINK YOUR TRIP
TRIP

Secret Seafood Spots

WHY GO One word: seafood. But not just any seafood. This tour of Oregon's northern coast will set you in the seats and stand you at the counters of chef Bob Neroni's favorite seafood haunts. And Neroni, co-owner of Cannon Beach's popular EVOO Cannon Beach Cooking School, certainly knows seafood.

The Oregon coast can be notoriously overcast. Expect a sunny vacation and odds are you'll be disappointed. But arrive with an appetite for seafood and you're guaranteed fulfillment – especially if you know where to eat. For guidance, we've turned to Bob Neroni, who not only recommended his favorite seafood purlieus, but threw in some activities to boot. From his favorites (and a few of ours), we've tailored this three-day trip to fill your stomach with some of the best seafood you'll have eaten – *anywhere*.

First, make your way to ❶ **Astoria**, an artist colony turned resort town set on the mouth of the Columbia River. Check into the genteel ❷ **Rosebriar Inn B&B** and head directly to the ❸ **Ship Inn** for a fish-and-chips lunch. According to Neroni this is *the* place for true British-style fish and chips. After filling up, head over to the ❹ **Columbia River Maritime Museum**. This $6 million, 44,000-sq-ft museum features state-of-the-art exhibits on everything from local lighthouses to the salmon fishing industry. And the life-size replica of a Coast Guard boat, frozen in motion as it crests a massive wave on the Columbia River Bar, is unforgettable.

For dinner, head to the ❺ **Bridgewater Bistro**. "This is where you go for upscale food," Neroni says. "It's in an old cannery and, once you're inside, you really feel you're someplace you want to spend some time." Accompanying the unbeatable atmosphere are delicacies including

TIME
4 days

DISTANCE
25 miles

BEST TIME TO GO
Sep – Oct

START
Astoria

END
Cannon Beach

ALSO GOOD FOR

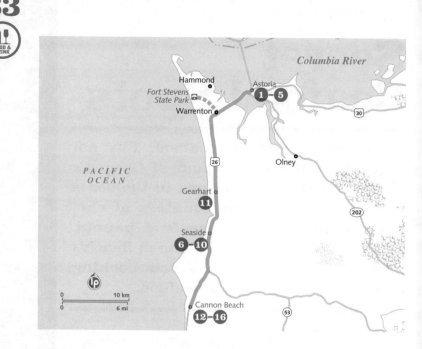

chili-lime prawns, Nova Scotia steamed blue mussels, New Orleans–style baked king salmon and pan-fried Willapa Bay oysters.

The following day, drive 17 miles south to ⑥ **Seaside**, where you can check into the ⑦ **Hillcrest Inn**, a Cape Cod–style home with six modest but comfy rooms. Although the coast's largest resort town is undoubtedly crowded, it has its charms. The 2-mile boardwalk, known as "the Prom," is a kaleidoscope of kitsch, with surrey rentals, video arcades, fudge, elephant ears, caramel apples, saltwater taffy and more. It's also where you'll find the ⑧ **Seaside Aquarium**. Opened since 1937, the privately owned aquarium "takes all of about five minutes to go through," Neroni says, "and the owner is a great guy to talk to." It's hardly world class, but, with a sense of humor, it's undeniably fun.

> **DETOUR** If you have time to kill, head 10 miles west of Astoria to **Fort Stevens State Park**, which Bob Neroni recommends for lake kayaking, horseback riding and cycling. You can even check out the century-old remains of the *Peter Iredale* shipwreck down on the beach. The park also has a campground if you'd rather skip the luxury of a roof.

After exploring the Prom, head to ⑨ **Bell Buoy**, a fish market and restaurant on the south end of town. The restaurant serves classics such as clam chowder, fish-and-chips and razor clams, but Neroni really talks up the Buoy's salmon jerky and smoked fish. The obvious solution: eat in, and take the jerky to go.

Neroni's other Seaside favorite is ❿ **Lil' Bayou.** "It's sort of tamed down Cajun cooking, so it's not as spicy," he says. "They do whole crawfish, gumbo, jambalaya – it's all fantastic." Lil' Bayou features live music on weekends and does a darn good job creating that Creole atmosphere. And yes, hurricanes are on the cocktail list.

After two days of restaurants, it's high time for some DIY. Check out of the Hillcrest, check your tide table and head to the beach at ⓫ **Gearhart**, imme-diately north of Seaside and famous for its razor clamming. All you need are boots, a shovel or a clam gun, a cut-resistant glove, a license (avail-able in Gearhart) and a bucket for your catch. When you're hunting, avoid digging up undersized clams by passing up "shows" (the siphon holes created by the clams) smaller than a dime. And watch your fingers – the name razor clam is well earned. Boiling up a batch at the campsite or in the cottage kitchen will likely result in the most memorable meal

COOKING YOUR CLAM CATCH

"The trick," explains Neroni, "is to bring a pot of water to boil and drop in the clams for about 10 seconds. This shocks them and loosens the shell, and then you can pull out the clam. Rinse them immediately and put them in a pool of cream. They're not alive at this point, but their filters are still working so they absorb the cream. Then roll them in cracker crumbs and cook them in olive oil and butter. Don't overcook them – just until they're tender, about two to three minutes per side."

of your trip. For heaps of information on where to clam, how to clam, when (and when not) to clam, red tide and domoic acid blooms, visit the Oregon Department of Fish & Wildlife website – it's a maze of a site, so just Google "ODFW clamming."

Of course, digging your own clams means you need a place to cook them. Drive 11 miles south to ⓬ **Cannon Beach** and check into the ⓭ **Waves Motel,** which offers rooms with kitchens. Then chef up your clam lunch and swallow it down with a glass of Oregon wine. If you're still in a cooking mood, take a class from Neroni himself at ⓮ **EVOO Cannon Beach Cook-ing School.** In the evening, wander down to the beach at ⓯ **Haystack Rock,** the third-tallest sea stack in the world. "I love our beach at Haystack Rock," Neroni says. "It might sound trite, but we get puffins and oystercatchers and even eagles from time to time." And the tide pools are excellent.

Whatever you do in Cannon Beach, don't miss ⓰ **The Wayfarer,** Neroni's choice for clam chowder. For without clam chowder, a visit to the coast is hardly complete.

Danny Palmerlee

FOOD & DRINK

TRIP INFORMATION

GETTING THERE
From Portland, drive north on I-5 for 50 miles to Longview; take Exit 36, follow the signs to Hwy 30 and continue 50 miles west to Astoria.

DO

Columbia River Maritime Museum
Exhibits highlight the salmon-packing industry and local lighthouses. Don't miss the excellent 12-minute film on the Columbia River Bar. ☎ 503-325-2323; www.crmm.org; 1792 Marine Dr, Seaside; adult/child 6-17yr/senior $8/4/7; 🕙 9:30am-5pm; ♿

EVOO Cannon Beach Cooking School
Fun, recreational cooking school with classes that end with the dinner you cook. Also a specialty food and kitchen items store. ☎ 503-436-8555; www.evoo.biz; 188 S Hemlock, Cannon Beach; classes $45-125

Seaside Aquarium
Old-time, unembellished aquarium with touch pool and seal tank. Don't expect state-of-the-art and you'll enjoy yourself. ☎ 503-738-6211; 200 N Promenade, Seaside; adult/child 6-13yr/senior $7/3.50/6; 🕙 9am-7pm; ♿

EAT

Bell Buoy
Family-style seafood restaurant within a fish market. ☎ store 503-738-2722, restaurant 503-738-6348; www.bellbuoyofseaside.com; 1800 S Roosevelt Dr, Seaside; mains $8-18; 🕙 store 9:30am-6pm, restaurant 11:30am-7:30pm, closed Tue & Wed winter; ♿

Bridgewater Bistro
Upscale bistro serving lunch, dinner and, from 3pm to 5pm, a small-bites menu. Sunday brunches, too. ☎ 503-325-6777; www.bridgewaterbistro.com; 20 Basin St, Astoria; mains $8-27; 🕙 11:30am-9pm Mon-Sat, 10am-9pm Sun

Lil' Bayou
Cajun cooking is the specialty here: gumbo, blackened chicken, hush puppies, crawfish, jambalaya, blackened catfish, étouffée and more. ☎ 503-717-0624; www.lilbayou.net; 20 N Holladay, Seaside; mains $16-24; 🕙 dinner Wed-Mon

Ship Inn
Neroni's favorite for fish-and-chips; choose cod or halibut and enjoy them on the patio facing the water. ☎ 503-325-0033; 1 2nd St, Astoria; fish & chips plates $9.25-25; 🕙 11:30am-9:30pm

Wayfarer
Oceanfront restaurant with a wide array of seafood choices, including Dungeness crab dishes, fish and its Wayfarer clam chowder. ☎ 503-436-1108; www.wayfarer-restaurant.com; 1190 Pacific Dr, Cannon Beach; mains $9-18; 🕙 8am-10pm

SLEEP

Hillcrest Inn
Cape Cod–style inn with a wide variety of simple, comfortable rooms and suites. ☎ 503-738-6273, 800-270-7659; www.seasidehillcrest.com; 118 N Columbia, Seaside; r $80-149; ♿

Rosebriar Inn B&B
Elegant 12-room inn with small but comfy rooms. Also a spacious "carriage house" and a "captain's suite" with kitchenette and awesome views. ☎ 800-487-0224; www.rosebriar.net; 636 14th St, Astoria; r $90-192

Waves Motel
Furnishings are elegant and rooms are comfortable and bright; some have kitchens, two bedrooms and decks over the beach. ☎ 800-822-2468; www.thewavesmotel.com; 188 W 2nd St, Cannon Beach; r $118-415; ♿

USEFUL WEBSITES
www.evoo.biz
www.visittheoregoncoast.com
www.lonelyplanet.com/trip-planner

LINK YOUR TRIP

Life Aquatic: The Nature of the Coast

WHY GO With everything from tide pools to marine geysers to fog-shrouded forests, Oregon's coast is one exceptionally wild place. For a professional's take on how best to see it, we tracked down Bill Hanshumaker, Marine Education Specialist at the Hatfield Marine Science Center. Then we asked, "Where would you take your friends?"

The town of ❶ **Newport** sits on the mouth of the Yaquina River and is home to two of the most important coastal exhibits in Oregon: the ❷ **Oregon Coast Aquarium** and the ❸ **Hatfield Marine Science Center**. Combined, they offer the best possible introduction to the coast's extraordinary geography, from the critters that hide in its tide pools to the forests that tower over its windswept capes.

But once you leave Newport, where should you go? We figured the best person to answer that question was Bill Hanshumaker, the science center's Marine Education Specialist. After he explained the Houdini-like abilities of the giant pacific octopus, Hanshumaker told us where he'd take his friends if they wandered out to his piece of the coast.

The first place Hanshumaker recommends (after the science center, of course) is ❹ **Yaquina Head Outstanding Natural Area**. "What attracted me to Newport originally," Hanshumaker says, "was Yaquina Head, which has some of the best touch pools in the world." The grassy, narrow headland juts defiantly out to sea immediately north of Newport. Along with an excellent interpretive center, it's home to the coast's tallest still-functioning lighthouse.

Another great spot for tide pooling is ❺ **Devil's Punchbowl State Park**, about 5 miles north of Yaquina Head, and adjacent to the

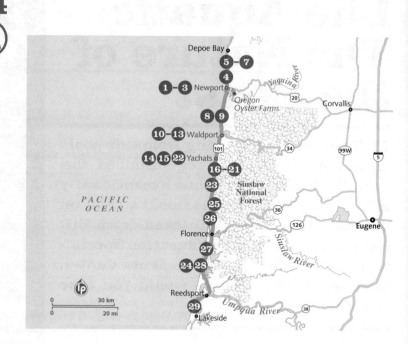

seaside community of Otter Rock. From the parking lot, stairs descend to a series of tide pools that burble beneath wave-sculpted cliffs and stupendous rock bridges. After Devil's Punchbowl, head back to the car and follow Otter Crest Loop Rd north to the fittingly named **6** **Cape Foulweather**, where you'll find a doozy of a lookout perched 500ft over the sea. Cape Foulweather was "discovered" by English explorer Captain James Cook (a name you'll hear more than once along this stretch of the Pacific coast) in 1778. The day he named it, the weather was apparently pretty bad, although not unusually so – winds of 100mph are not uncommon on the cape.

"Dense forests of Sitka spruce, Douglas fir and western hemlock tower over the storm-pounded headland..."

From Cape Foulweather, return to Highway 101, and head south. Shortly after passing Otter Rock, you'll hit **7** **Beverly Beach State Park**, the perfect place to spend the night. The campgrounds, which lie on the inland side of Highway 101, are sheltered by trees and lie a short walk from expansive Beverly Beach. Those lacking the gear (or inclination) to camp can shack up in one of the park's heated yurts.

From Beverly Beach, drive south along Highway 101 to **8** **Seal Rock State Recreation Site**, another prime tide-pooling site. This small day-use park protects a spectacular beach hemmed in by a row of jagged rocks that protrude dramatically from the waves. If it's anywhere near lunchtime when you finish exploring, head directly across the highway to the **9** **Seal Rock Store**, where you can dig into a paper plateful of self-serve tamales.

About 2 miles south of Seal Rock, you'll hit the town of **10** **Waldport** on **11** **Alsea Bay**. As you roll into town, you'll cross the **12** **Alsea Bay Bridge**, which most people admire from inside their car before driving on to Waldport. But, when the tide is right, this bridge offers a very worthwhile view: at low tide more than 800 harbor seals lounge on the sand below. See for yourself.

In Waldport, head down to the old bayfront and check out its salt-crusted strip of businesses, including **13** **Salty Dawg Bar & Grill**. This cavernous local haunt serves stick-to-your-ribs Mexican food, but it's really about the cold beer and dive-bar atmosphere.

Leaving Waldport, head south to the quiet town of **14** **Yachats**, and check into **15** **Shamrock Lodgettes**, a collection of unfathomably cozy seaside cabins with wonderful sea views. If you'd rather camp, continue 3 miles south to **16** **Cape Perpetua Campground**, one of the prettiest campgrounds on the coast. Both Yachats and the campground make the ideal base for exploring the old-growth forests, tide pools and rocky shoreline of **17** **Cape Perpetua Scenic Area**.

> **DETOUR** Good oysters should never be passed up. This 12-mile round-trip detour up the Yaquina River to **Oregon Oyster Farms** (☎541-265-5078), at 6878 Yaquina Bay Rd, is well worth the leisurely hour or so it takes you to poke along beautiful Yaquina Bay Rd, stop at the farm, fill your cooler with fresh oysters and head back to Highway 101. You could also shuck and eat them on the picnic tables out back. It's been here since 1907.

Cape Perpetua is undoubtedly a coastal highlight. Dense forests of Sitka spruce, Douglas fir and western hemlock tower over the storm-pounded headland, famous for its basalt rock formations, sea churns and marine geysers. From **18** **Cape Perpetua Visitor Center**, walk the paved **19** **Captain Cook Trail** down to a group of tide pools which, according to Hanshumaker, require a good low tide to really be accessible. At high tide, stop at the **20** **Spouting Horn**, a sea geyser that heaves frothy seawater high into the air; it's especially spectacular during winter storms. At sunset, the best place to be is **21** **Cape Perpetua Viewpoint**, which, at 803ft, is the highest car-accessible point on the Oregon coast. The viewpoint is capped by an old rock shelter, built in 1934 by the Civilian Conservation Corps.

Of course, all this running around requires fuel for your body. If you haven't packed your lunch, head back to Yachats for a meal at **22** **Grand Occasions Deli**, where you can devour delicious homemade soups and pies, or order sandwiches and fresh cheeses to go.

About the only sea treat Cape Perpetua lacks is a sandy beach. But this can be found immediately south at **㉓ Neptune State Beach**. Here, Cummins Creek winds out of the trees, passes under one of the coast's many arched bridges and flows across the sand, through piles of driftwood into the ocean. North of the creek, giant black rocks create a labyrinth in the sand.

Last on the list is **㉔ Oregon Dunes National Recreation Area**. Stretching for 50 miles from Florence to Coos Bay, the Oregon Dunes form the largest expanse of oceanfront dunes in the US. Some reach a height of 500ft and undulate inland as far as 3 miles. In their midst lie numerous lakes and creeks, patches of unique coastal forest and rich bird life. Although the most visible and accessible dunes have been taken over by off-road vehicles, there are plenty of areas where nothing can be heard but the birds.

As you're heading south from Cape Perpetua, and before entering the recreation area itself, two off-the-beaten-path spots offer a good look at dune ecology. The first is **㉕ Alder Dune Day Use Area**, accessible via Alder Dune Campground. From the campground, a short hike leads around Alder Lake over a hill and into an interesting area of coastal forest and dunes. For a completely different dunescape, stop at **㉖ Sutton Beach**, about 3 miles south. The dunes here are low, but tiny lakes and a meandering creek make for an excellent place to shake out a blanket for a picnic.

About 7 miles south of Florence you'll come to the Siltcoos Recreation Area. Pull in here and grab a campsite at **㉗ Lagoon Campground**. After the tent's pitched, continue 5 miles south to **㉘ Oregon Dunes Overlook**, the easiest place to get a close-up look at some big dunes. Here, follow the 1-mile loop trail over the dunes to the beach and back. If you have the energy, hop back in the car and continue south, past Reedsport, to the **㉙ John Dellenback Trailhead**. You can hike into the Umpqua Dunes area, where you'll find some of the highest dunes in the park. Once you're good and sandy, head back to Florence. From there it's a straight shot east via Hwy 126 to Eugene and Hwy 5.

Danny Palmerlee

TRIP INFORMATION

GETTING THERE
From Portland, take I-5 south 65 miles to Hwy 20; follow Hwy 20 west for 67 miles to reach Newport.

DO

Alder Dune Day Use Area
Unmaintained trails through large dunes and coastal forest. Accessed via parking area inside Alder Dune Campground, 6 miles north of Florence. **Admission $5;** ☐ ☐

Cape Foulweather
Scenic viewpoint; technically Otter Crest State Scenic Viewpoint, about 9.5 miles north of Newport on Otter Crest Loop Rd. **Admission free;** ☐ ☐

Cape Perpetua Scenic Area
Rich tide pool life, rock formations, trails, old-growth forest and views, 3 miles south of Yachats on Hwy 101. **Day-use sites $5;** ☐

Cape Perpetua Visitor Center
Information on Cape Perpetua, with trail maps. Turnoff immediately south of Cape Perpetua Campground. ☎ **541-547-3289; 2400 Hwy 101;** ☐ **10am-4pm Sep-May, 9am-5:30pm Jun-Aug;** ☐

Devil's Punchbowl State Park
Great tide pooling and rock formations. Signed access from Hwy 101 via Otter Rock, about 8 miles north of Newport. ☎ **1-800-551-6949; admission free;** ☐

Hatfield Marine Science Center
More education-oriented, less bustling alternative (or complement) to the aquarium. ☎ **541-867-0271; www.hmsc.orst.edu/visitor; 2030 S Marine Science Dr, Newport; admission free;** ☐ **10am-5pm daily, 10am-4pm Thu-Mon only in winter;** ☐

John Dellenback Trailhead
Six-mile round-trip trail through dunes; beach access. Located about 10.5 miles south of Reedsport and 0.2 miles south of Eel Creek Campground. **Hwy 101; day use $5;** ☐ ☐

Neptune State Beach
Wide beach, best at low tide. Located 1.1 miles south of turnoff to Cape Perpetua Visitor Center. **Hwy 101; admission free;** ☐ **dawn-dusk;** ☐ ☐

Oregon Coast Aquarium
Exceptional aquarium with seals, sea otters, deep-sea exhibit, jellyfish room and more. ☎ **541-867-3474; www.aquarium.org; 2820 SE Ferry Slip Rd, Newport; adult/child 3-13yr/senior $13/8/11;** ☐ **9am-6pm;** ☐

Oregon Dunes National Recreation Area
Largest expanse of oceanfront sand dunes in USA. For information, contact Reedsport Chamber of Commerce. ☎ **541-271-3495; www.fs.fed/us/r6/siuslaw; 855 Highway Ave, Reedsport;** ☐

Oregon Dunes Overlook
Wheelchair-accessible dunes overlook with short trails. About 10.5 miles north of Reedsport (signed "Oregon Dunes Day Use Area"). **Hwy 101, milepost 201; day use $5;** ☐ ☐

Seal Rock State Recreation Site
Excellent beach, tide pools and views, 10 miles south of Newport. Day-use only. **Hwy 101; admission free;** ☐ ☐

Sutton Beach
Great spot for a picnic on Sutton Creek. Turnoff 3 miles south of Alder Dune Day Use Area. **Hwy 101; parking free;** ☐ **dawn-dusk;** ☐ ☐

Yaquina Head Outstanding Natural Area
Tide pools, views and visitors center, plus the coast's tallest functioning lighthouse. ☎ **541-574-3100; 750 Lighthouse Dr; admission $5;** ☐ **dawn-dusk;** ☐ ☐

EAT

Grand Occasions Deli
Greek pita wraps, oyster po'boys, hummus plates, baked Brie, sublime pies. ☎ **541-547-4409; 84 Beach St, Yachats; mains $7-12;** ☐ **10am-6pm Sun-Thu, to 8pm Fri & Sat;** ☐

Salty Dawg Bar & Grill
Mexican food, burgers, fish-and-chips, chicken, booze and more. ☎ 541-563-2555; **1260 E Port St, Waldport;** ◷ **breakfast, lunch & dinner**

Seal Rock Store
General store with tamales, hot dogs and biscuits and gravy. Directly across from the Seal Rock Site. **Hwy 101;** ◷ **7am-9pm;** ♿

SLEEP

Beverly Beach State Park
Large campground a short walk from Beverly Beach, 7 miles north of Newport. ☎ **877-444-6777; www.recreation.gov; Hwy 101; tents $17-21, yurts $30;** ◷ **year-round;** ♿ ⛺

Cape Perpetua Campground
Lovely, forested 38-site campground; no showers. ☎ **877-444-6777; www.recreation**

.gov; Hwy 101, Cape Perpetua Scenic Area; campsites $20; ◷ **mid-May–Sep;** ♿ ⛺

Lagoon Campground
The best of several campgrounds in the Siltcoos Recreation Area, but no showers. Located 7 miles south of Florence. ☎ **877-444-6777; www.recreation.gov; Siltcoos Beach Access Rd; campsites $20;** ◷ **year-round;** ♿ ⛺

Shamrock Lodgettes
Modest yet supremely cozy log cabins, "spa" cabins and hotel-style rooms with ocean views. ☎ **877-547-3312; www.shamrock lodgettes.com; 105 Hwy 101, Yachats; r $69-129, cabins $99-189;** ♿

USEFUL WEBSITES
http://hmsc.oregonstate.edu/visitor
www.fs.fed.us/r6/siuslaw

LINK YOUR TRIP

www.lonelyplanet.com/trip-planner

Oddball Oregon

WHY GO From a museum of velvet paintings in Portland, to a strange vortex near the California border, Oregon has plenty of oddities. Link the strangest of them and you have the perfect route for a road trip. Let the Twilight Zone theme song begin.

To get the energy you need for this oddball outing start at ❶ **Voodoo Donuts** in downtown Portland. It's a punk rock doughnut shop serving over-frosted, sickly sweet doughnuts with names such as "Cock-n-Balls", "Butter Fingering" and "Dirty Snowball". You'll even get a few surprises: like the fact you can take Swahili classes from the fry guy or get married inside the shop – legally. Time it right and you might even get an eyeful at their annual (male only) doughnut-stacking contest. (Ask about it while you're there.)

There's nothing like black velvet paintings when you're high on sugar. At ❷ **Velveteria**, probably the world's only museum of velvet paintings, 300 works of fuzzy, funky art grace the walls, including masterpieces such as *God Bless our Truckers* (depicting Jesus blessing a semi); a brilliant purple-haloed Isaac Hayes; and a frightening version of the tabloid freak Bat Boy. The paintings are not for sale but you take home copies of the best in the owners' book, *Black Velvet Masterpieces: Highlights from the Collection of the Velveteria Museum.*

Portland's brimming with great accommodations, but to keep things offbeat, stay at ❸ **Inn at Northrup Station**. With its Jetsons-meets-Tim-Burton atmosphere and a color scheme that conjures images of a box of crayons exploding, it's definitely not your everyday hotel. It's also convenient for exploring downtown and the Pearl District, Portland's most prominent upscale arts precinct.

TIME
3 days

DISTANCE
475 miles

BEST TIME TO GO
Jun – Sep

START
Portland

END
Cave Junction

235

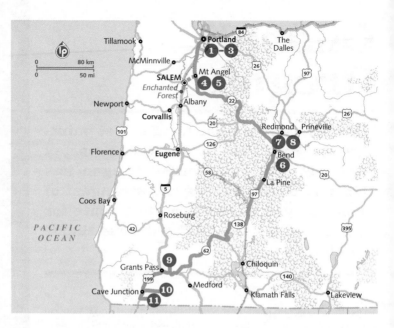

There's no reason to limit your ogling of the odd to Portland. In fact, there's enough strange stuff lurking out in the Oregonian forests to keep you busy for days. Hop in your car and head south via I-5 and Hwy 214 to the town of Mt Angel, where you'll find the ④ **Mount Angel Abbey and Seminary**. Like any abbey, it's a quiet, relaxing, peaceful place. Nothing out of the ordinary here. And then, inside the small museum, you suddenly find yourself face to face with … the ⑤ **world's largest hairball!** Pulled from the slimy insides of a slaughtered pig, this massive 2.5lb hairball is one holy sight to see. Why it ended up in the abbey museum is anyone's guess.

"On day three, things really get freaky."

After marveling at what you'd only hack up in your worst possible nightmares, make your way south to Bend. Once there, check into ⑥ **McMenamins Old St Francis School**, housed in a remodeled schoolhouse. Former classrooms are now guest rooms (complete with chalkboards) and bars now occupy the former Detention Room and Honors Room. There's even a wee movie house and a soaking pool on sight. Once you've dropped your bags, take Hwy 97 6 miles north of town to the ⑦ **Fun Farm** (aka the "Funny Farm"). Among the odd creations spread haphazardly about the property, you'll find the cow that jumped over the moon, an agitator wall (think washing machine parts), a bowling ball garden, a life-size holy cow, an electric kaleidoscope, a bowling ball tree, Dorothy's house and, last but not least, the Love Pond, complete with giant Cupid arrows stuck into the shoreline. It's all the work of Gene Carsey, an active member of the Wizard of Oz Club and a man who will quickly impress upon you the basic truth that life, indeed, can be fun.

If you think Carsey's place is odd, wait until you see the work of Rasmus Petersen, about 5 miles north, in Redmond. Petersen, a Danish immigrant who died in 1952, spent the last two decades of his life building what are today known as the **⑧ Petersen Rock Gardens**. After retiring from farming, Petersen covered 4 acres of his property with rock sculptures that would make any 21st-century trailer park landscaper fall to his knees in dumfounded awe. The result, cooking in the high desert sun, is a decaying display of giant rock castles, ponds, bridges, houses, pathways and more. Despite the fact that the place has fallen into mild disrepair since Petersen passed away (the underground rock shop positively wreaks of cigarettes and cats), it's still an impressive sight.

On day three, things really get freaky. About four hours (178 miles) south of Bend, just outside the town of Gold Hill, lies the **⑨ Oregon Vortex**. Whether the laws of physics are truly disturbed in this neck of the Oregon woods, or it's all an optical illusion created by skewed buildings on steep hillsides is up to you. However you see it, the place is definitely bizarre: objects roll uphill, a person's height changes depending on where they stand, and brooms stand up on their own…so it seems.

DETOUR If all the oddities in this trip still aren't enough to make you wide-eyed, detour 25 miles (30 minutes) southwest of Mt Angel to the **Enchanted Forest** (www.enchantedforest.com). This mildly psychedelic theme park is the place to drag your car-crazed children and turn them loose on attractions like Storybook Lane, the haunted house and what's allegedly the longest log ride in the Pacific Northwest. For the complete experience, add a half-day to your trip. The park is 9 miles south of Salem.

About 55 miles southwest of the Oregon Vortex, channel your inner caveman at **⑩ Oregon Caves National Monument**. Drag your partner out of the sunlight (club him over the head if you must) and into this dripping 3-mile labyrinth of cave popcorn, moonmilk, cave pearls, pipe organs and those good ol' cave classics, stalactites.

After the 90-minute walking tour, you'll be ready to sleep up above – in a tree house. About 27 miles away, just south of Cave Junction, **⑪ Out 'n' About Treesort** offers comfortable rooms literally up in the trees. The strange thing is, after all these curiosities, sleeping in a tree house might not seem so abnormal at all.

Danny Palmerlee

TRIP INFORMATION

GETTING THERE
To get to Portland from Seattle, drive 175 miles south on I-5. From Vancouver, drive 315 miles south on Hwy 99 and I-5.

DO

Fun Farm
Eclectic antique store and outdoor museum (of sorts). Also known as the Funny Farm. ☎ 541-389-6391; www.funfarm.com; 64990 Deschutes Market Rd, Bend; admission free; ⏱ from 11:02am Fri-Mon; 🏛

Mount Angel Abbey and Seminary
Benedictine monastery with museum on a hilltop 18 miles northeast of Salem. ☎ 503-845-3345; www.mtangel.edu; off College St, Mt Angel; admission free; ⏱ 10-11:30am & 1-5pm Mon-Sat, 1-5pm Sun; 🏛

Oregon Caves National Monument
This vast limestone cave is visited by guided tour only. ☎ 541-592-2100; www.nps.gov /orca; Hwy 46; adult/child 16yr & under $8.50/6; ⏱ 10am-4pm Apr, May, Oct & Nov, 9am-5pm Jun-Sep, closed Dec-Mar; 🏛

Oregon Vortex
Supposed paranormal locus near Gold Hill. ☎ 541-855-1543; www.oregonvortex.com; 4303 Sardine Creek L Fork Rd, Gold Hill; adult/child 6-11yr $9/7; ⏱ 9am-4pm Mar-May, Sep & Oct, 9am-5pm Jun-Aug; 🏛

Petersen Rock Gardens
Rock garden and museum outside Redmond, about 13 miles north of Bend. ☎ 541-382-5574; 7930 SW 77th St, Redmond; ⏱ 9am-5:30pm, to 4:30pm in winter; 🏛

Velveteria
Works are not for sale at this museum of velvet paintings, but the book *Black Velvet Masterpieces* is. ☎ 503-233-5100; www.vel veteria.com; 2448 E Burnside St, Portland; admission $5; ⏱ noon-5pm Thu-Sun

EAT & SLEEP

Inn at Northrup Station
Huge, modern, wildly decorated rooms all include kitchens; great location in northwest Portland. ☎ 503-224-0543, 800-224-1180; www.northrupstation.com; 2025 NW Northrup St, Portland; r $146-196; 🏛

McMenamins Old St Francis School
Old schoolhouse remodeled into a classy 19-room hotel. Guests sleep in former classrooms. ☎ 541-382-5174; www.mc menamins.com; 700 NW Bond St, Bend; r $145-175, cottages $190-330; 🏛

Out 'n' About Treesort
Rents a dozen rustic tree houses, from small rooms 35ft up to suites with kitchens. ☎ 541-592-2208; www.treehouses.com; 300 Page Creek Rd, Cave Junction; r from $106; 🏛

Voodoo Donuts
This standing-room-only, downtown doughnut shop takes doughnuts far beyond the normal hole-in-the-dough standard. Swahili offered 9am Mondays. ☎ 503-241-4704; www.voodoodonut.com; 22 SW 3rd Ave, Portland; ⏱ 24hr

USEFUL WEBSITES
www.roadsideamerica.com
www.traveloregon.com

LINK YOUR TRIP
www.lonelyplanet.com/trip-planner

Cheesemonger's Cheese Trip

WHY GO Ride shotgun with cheese-monger Steve Jones, owner of Steve's Cheese of Portland, on this whirlwind trip around Oregon. En route, you'll visit Jones' favorite artisanal cheese producers and – since Jones feels no cheese trip is complete without a cold beer and a good hike – his favorite nearby breweries and walks, too.

TIME
4 days

DISTANCE
565 miles

BEST TIME TO GO
Jun – Sep

START
Portland

END
Ashland

Oregon is one of the best cheese states in the country. More than 15 artisan cheesemakers can be found within the state's borders, and several new producers were set to open as this book went to press. When it comes to cheese, says Portland cheesemonger Steve Jones, "we're having a sort of rebirth." And that makes tripping around Oregon in search of the perfect *fromage* one very rewarding trip.

Although you won't find commercial cheesemakers in ❶ Portland proper, the city's cheese shops and restaurants make it the perfect starting point. Talking to the cheesemongers and sampling the locally produced cheeses will prime your palate for the road ahead. Specialty shops such as ❷ Pastaworks, ❸ Foster & Dobbs and, of course, ❹ Steve's Cheese, offer cut-to-order cheeses and allow you to taste before you buy. That's a key component in any good cheese shop. "Basically, if they won't give you a taste of cheese," says Jones, "forget it."

Once you've stockpiled enough cheese, throw it in a daypack and hit the Wildwood Trail in Portland's ❺ Forest Park, the largest urban park in the US. After putting some miles on your hiking shoes, you'll be ready for dinner at ❻ Wildwood. "It's the quintessential Portland dining experience," says Jones, "with local, sustainable ingredients." Four cheeses grace the dessert menu, and although they might not always be Oregonian, they're almost always from the Pacific North-

BEST TRIP

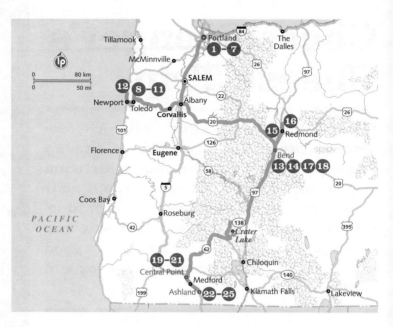

Tillamook •
Portland
The Dalles

McMinnville •

1 – 7

SALEM

12 **8 – 11**

Newport • •
Toledo
Albany

Corvallis

Florence •
Eugene

15 **16**
Redmond

Bend

13 14 17 18

Coos Bay •
Roseburg

PACIFIC
OCEAN

Crater
Lake

19 – 21
Central Point •
Chiloquin

Medford

Ashland • **22 – 25** • Klamath Falls
Lakeview

0 ____ 80 km
0 ____ 50 mi

west or neighboring California. At the end of the night lay your head at
7 Bluebird Guesthouse, a lovingly converted Arts and Crafts era home with
a guest kitchen and superbly comfortable communal rooms.

On day two, it's time to head for the coast. From Portland, drive southwest to
the wee town of **8 Logsden** (via I-5 and Hwy 20), where you'll visit **9 Three
Rings Farm at River's Edge Chèvre**. Owned and operated by Pat Morford,
River's Edge Chèvre produces award-winning goat cheeses using milk from
Morford's Three Rings Farm goat herd. Her "Up in Smoke" and "Sunset Bay"
cheeses both took seconds in Wisconsin's 2008 World Championship Cheese
Contest – no mean feat. In other words, you'll be eating some seriously good
cheese. Be sure to call first, as the farm only accepts visits by appointment.

From Logsden head to the nearby and equally petite town of **10 Siletz** and
quaff a pint and eat a late lunch at **11 Siletz Roadhouse,** run by the Siletz
Brewing Co, whose brewery is next door. After lunch, head west to oceanside
12 Beverly Beach State Park, where you can pitch a tent or, if you prefer a bit
more comfort, sleep in a cozy yurt. But before you lay down that cheese-filled
head, go for a sunset walk on beautiful Beverly Beach, just across Highway
101 from the campground.

Day three is a long one. From Beverly Beach, take Hwy 20 over the Coast
Range, across the Willamette Valley and through the Cascades to the city of

13 Bend, which has excellent snow skiing, rock climbing, rafting, kayaking, hiking and fly fishing all within 30 miles of its handsome downtown. The 190-mile trip to Bend takes about 4½ hours, so you'll need an early start. Check in at **14** **McMenamins Old St Francis School** (this former school now houses a restaurant, soaking pool, hotel rooms and bars) and grab a bite and a pint at the on-site restaurant. Once you're rested, drive out to the cheese shop at **15** **Juniper Grove Farm**, a farmstead goat cheese producer located just west of the town of Redmond. Juniper Grove's cheese is all made from milk that is produced by the farm's alfalfa-fed goat herd.

Next, head 9 miles northwest to **16** **Smith Rock State Park** for a sunset hike (remember, cheese plus hike plus beer equals perfect day) along the Crooked River. The jagged, rust-

FARMERS MARKETS

When it comes to sampling and purchasing local cheeses, few things beat a good farmers market. At the **Portland Farmers Market** (www.portlandfarmersmarket.org) Jones says, "You can see anywhere from five to seven local cheesemakers on any Saturday." On Wednesdays, at the **Bend Farmers Market** (www.bendfarmersmarket.us), you'll find cheese from Juniper Grove Farm, plus a host of other products from local vendors. Rogue Creamery has a booth at Ashland's **Rogue Valley Growers & Crafters Market** (www.rvgrowersmarket.com), held on Tuesdays.

colored cliffs that tower 800ft over the river turn to blazing ochre and red as the sun disappears behind the Cascades. It's quite an experience. If you can't muster the energy for the trip to Smith Rock (heaven forbid), end the day instead with dinner at **17** **Merenda** in Bend. "It has a great feel and they do local foods well," Jones says. "And it's comfortable." If you did the Smith Rock hike, there's no better way to seal the day than a pint of ale from **18** **Bend Brewing Co**. Then, drag your tired body back to McMenamins and soothe it in the gorgeous soaking pool before hitting the sack.

The following day, pull yourself out of bed at an early hour for the four-hour, 197-mile drive south to the town of **19** **Central Point**. In the center of town, you'll find one of Oregon's longest-running cheese operations: **20** **Rogue Creamery**. "For The Middle of Nowhere, Oregon, this place is really something else," Jones says. It's true. No cheese trip is complete without a stop at this 70-year-old creamery, which not only produces internationally known, award-winning blue and cheddar cheeses, but does so organically and sustainably. The creamery was founded by Tom Vella, who is best known for Vella dry jack, which he created at Vella Cheese, his Sonoma, California operation. Vella died in 1988 (at the age of 100) and passed the business to his son, Ig Vella, who later sold it to its current owners. At the creamery store (where you can taste and purchase all the cheese you want), you can chat with the cheesemonger and see into the make-room.

"Juniper Grove's cheese is all made from milk that is produced by the farm's alfalfa-fed goat herd."

Whenever Jones makes the journey to Rogue, he stops at Central Point's **㉑ Walkabout Brewing Co**. Owned by an Australian, Walkabout produces ales with fitting names like Jabberwocky Old Ale, Wallaby Wheat, Outback Stout and Point the Bone IPA. And, as with all Oregon breweries open to the public, there's plenty of pub grub to satisfy your hungry belly (provided you didn't already fill it with cheese).

Central Point is hardly a travelers' town, so drive 17 miles south to **㉒ Ashland** to close the evening and spend the night. Just north of the California border and famed for its annual Oregon Shakespeare Festival, Ashland is bursting at the seams with special places to sleep and eat. When it comes to value and setting, our choice for sleeps is the **㉓ Country Willows**, a nine-room B&B on the south end of town. After checking in, head downtown for an afternoon treat at **㉔ Mix Sweet Shop**, a European-style bakery and coffee shop that Jones swears is worth two stops. "It's probably my favorite bakery in the entire state," Jones says. "I like to grab a coffee and a pastry and then hike up the trail. And then I'll stop in again when I get back."

DETOUR Although it has nothing to do with cheese – unless you make the stretch from craters to Swiss Emmental – **Crater Lake** (www.nps.gov/crla) is well worth the 25-mile detour from Hwy 97. If you have three or four hours to spare, swing west on Hwy 138, then left on N Entrance Rd and drive all or part of the 33-mile Rim Drive loop road. If you only drive half of it, you can return to Hwy 97 via S Entrance Rd and Hwy 62, avoiding the need to backtrack.

The trail Jones refers to is the Creek to Crest Trail, which you can reach from nearby **㉕ Lithia Park**, a gorgeous 93-acre green space bisected by the burbling Ashland Creek. You can walk into the park from the plaza, follow the creek south and eventually pick up the Creek to Crest Trail, which you can hike as far as you'd like. And when you return, do as Jones does; treat yourself to another pastry. You deserve it after all that cheese.

Danny Palmerlee

TRIP INFORMATION

GETTING THERE
Via I-5, Portland lies 175 miles south of Seattle and 315 miles south of Vancouver.

DO

Forest Park
The park's 30-mile Wildwood Trail starts at Hoyt Arboretum (4000 SW Fairview Dr). www.portlandonline.com; park at NW 29th Ave & Upshur St to Newberry Rd; admission free; ⏰ 6am-10pm; ♿ ☺

Foster & Dobbs
Features locally produced and imported cheeses, cured meats, beverages and more. Truly a mouthwatering experience. ☎ 503-284-1157; www.fosteranddobbs.com; 2518 NE 15th Ave, Portland; ⏰ 11am-7pm Mon-Sat, noon-6pm Sun

Juniper Grove Farm
Produces farmstead goat milk cheeses in numerous varieties and has an on-site cheese store. ☎ 541-923-8353; www.junipergrovefarm.com; 2024 SW 58th St, Redmond; ⏰ cheese shop 8:30am-6pm, Mon-Sat; ♿

Pastaworks
European-style specialty foods market with a mouthwatering cheese selection, plus wine, fresh pasta and deli meats. ☎ 503-232-1010; 3735 SE Hawthorne Blvd, Portland; ⏰ 9:30am-7pm Mon-Sat, 10am-7pm Sun

Rogue Creamery
Oregon's original artisan cheese producer famed especially for its blue cheese; has on-site cheese shop. ☎ 541-664-1537; www.roguecreamery.com; 311 N Front St, Central Point; ⏰ 9am-5pm Mon-Fri, 9am-6pm Sat, 11am-5pm Sun; ♿

Smith Rock State Park
Protects a series of glorious rock spires and is best known for rock climbing; also has several miles of fine hiking trails. ☎ 541-548-7501; www.oregonstateparks.org; day use $3, walk-in campground $4; ♿ ☺

Steve's Cheese
Specialty retail cheese counter inside Square Deal Wine Shop; stocks loads of Pacific Northwest cheese. ☎ 503-222-6014; www.stevescheese.biz; 2321 NW Thurman St, Portland; ⏰ 11am-7pm Tue-Sat, noon-6pm Sun & Mon

Three Rings Farm at River's Edge Chèvre
Friendly operation producing award-winning farmstead goat milk cheeses in all shapes and sizes. ☎ 541-444-1362; www.threeringfarm.com; 6315 Logsden Rd, Logsden; ⏰ by appointment; ♿

DRINK

Bend Brewing Co
The smaller of two breweries in Bend; delicious, award-winning beer and good pub food. ☎ 541-383-1599; www.bendbrewingco.com; 1019 NW Brooks St, Bend; mains $8-15; ⏰ 11:30am-late

Siletz Roadhouse
The public house of the Siletz Brewing Co serves food and microbrewed ales. ☎ 541-444-2335; www.siletzbrewing.com; 214 N Gaither St, Siletz

Walkabout Brewing Co
Central Point's only brewery is one of the best reasons to visit. It's toward the north end of town. ☎ 541-664-7763; 5204 Dobrot Way, Central Point

EAT

Merenda
Elegant, brick-walled restaurant with over 100 wines by the glass; cuisine includes Kumamoto oysters, handmade gnocchi, roasted halibut and braised lamb. ☎ 541-330-2304; 900 NW Wall St, Bend; mains $15-26; ⏰ 11:30am-midnight

Mix Sweet Shop
Bakery-cum-coffee house serving homemade croissants, tarts, cupcakes, bread and sweets. ☎ 541-488-9885; 57 N Main St, Ashland; pastries $2-4; ⏰ 7am-10pm

Wildwood
A classic Portland restaurant focusing on local and sustainable ingredients; great cheese plates. ☎ 503-248-9663; www.wildwoodrestaurant.com; 1221 NW 21st Ave, Portland; mains $18-35; ☽ lunch & dinner Mon-Sat

SLEEP
Beverly Beach State Park
This large state campground 7 miles north of Newport is just a short walk from Beverly Beach. ☎ 877-444-6777; www.recreation.gov; Hwy 101; tents $17-21, yurts $30; ☽ year-round; ☒ ☒
Bluebird Guesthouse
Seven modest but immaculate, comfy rooms in a restored Arts and Crafts home. ☎ 503-238-4333, 866-717-4333; www.bluebirdguesthouse.com; 3517 SE Division, Portland; r $50-90

Country Willows
Luxurious B&B with country setting, complete with a few farm animals. ☎ 541-488-1590, 800-945-5697; www.countrywillowsinn.com; 1313 Clay St, Ashland; r $125-244

McMenamins Old St Francis School
Old schoolhouse remodeled into a classy 19-room hotel; includes saltwater Turkish bath, restaurant-pub, three bars and a movie theater. ☎ 541-382-5174; www.mcmenamins.com; 700 NW Bond St, Bend; r $145-175, cottages $190-330; ☒

USEFUL WEBSITES
www.oregoncheeseguild.org

LINK YOUR TRIP
www.lonelyplanet.com/trip-planner

TRIP
29 Willamette Valley Wine Tour p201
35 Oddball Oregon p235

Prehistoric Oregon Trip

WHY GO If fossils of three-toed horses, short-faced dogs and saber-toothed felines aren't enticing enough, consider this: Wild West rock formations, multicolored Painted Hills and mountains of eroded pinnacles are what really make this lesson in paleontology well worth the drive.

Fair enough, fossils make you yawn. And the thought of driving to the middle of nowhere to read about the grazing habits of Cenozoic mammals on sun-bleached signs without a lick of shade sight pretty much spells "three-day nightmare." Worry not: appreciating the scenery of John Day country doesn't require a petrified ant larvae's worth of interest in paleontology. Even without the fossils, the place is spectacular.

John Day Fossil Beds National Monument comprises three separate units: Clarno, Sheep Rock and Painted Hills. First, visit **①** **Clarno Unit**, home to the region's oldest, most remote fossil beds. The fossils here reveal leaves, trees and animals from a tropical forest that was washed over by volcanic mud flows some 40 million years ago. Wander the 0.5-mile Geologic Time Trail to the Trail of Fossils, and you'll see boulder-sized fossils of logs, seeds and other remains from the ancient forest. The 0.25-mile Arch Trail leads to a natural arch in the striking Palisade Cliffs.

From the Clarno Unit, head 18 miles northeast to the town of **②** **Fossil**, whose whopping population of 370 makes it the second-biggest town on the trip. Check into **③** **Bridge Creek Flora Inn**, a casually but lovingly maintained B&B with modest, country-style rooms, a giant front porch and massive home-cooked breakfasts. Then wander over to **④** **Big Timber Family Restaurant** for a hearty diner-style meal.

The following day, hit the road early and drive south on Hwy 19 through **⑤** **Service Creek**, an old stagecoach stop with a current

TIME
3 days

DISTANCE
190 miles

BEST TIME TO GO
Jun – Sep

START
Clarno

END
Mitchell

ALSO GOOD FOR

OUTDOORS

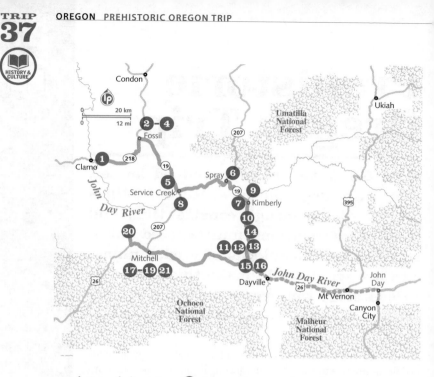

population of about two; ⑥ **Spray**, whose residents figure its population of 140 makes it big enough to divide the town into North Spray and South Spray; and ⑦ **Kimberly**, another former stagecoach stop which today consists of a store.

If you're skipping the luxury of a bed, Service Creek is the nearest place to Fossil to (legally) pitch a tent. When you "enter" Service Creek, swing right over the bridge (toward Mitchell) and you'll see ⑧ **Donnelly Service Creek River Access Park** on your left. It's a small, cramped and rather barren campground (there's hardly a tree in sight), but its location on the banks of the John Day River, with hills all around, makes it a welcoming spot. ⑨ **Lone Pine** campground, 3 miles east of Kimberly (heading toward Monument), is more secluded.

ASK A LOCAL
"When we were kids we used to go out to the Painted Hills and run around on them. They're really soft, so soft I just kept moving to keep from sinking. Of course, today you can't do that. They'd be flat if everyone went out and ran around on them."
Skeeter Reed, Mitchell, OR

South of Kimberly, Hwy 19 winds through orchards into ranch land nestled between the narrowing slopes of the John Day River canyon. About 8 miles south of Kimberly, you'll reach the ⑩ **Foree Picnic Area** of the Sheep Rock Unit. It's a small site but well worth a stop for the rock formations and burnt-red cliffs. From the Foree Area, continue 7 miles south to the ⑪ **Thomas**

Condon Paleontology Center, set in the heart of the ⑫ Sheep Rock Unit. This is where everything comes together. With giant murals and exhibits of fossilized skulls, skeletons, leaves, nuts and branches, the center brings to life the region's history. Standing outside the visitors center, you can see successive layers of volcanic mud and ash flows in the deeply eroded mountainsides: the Clarno strata (preserving remnants of tropical forest), the John Day strata (deciduous forest), the Mascall strata (savannah) and, at the very top of Sheep Rock itself, the distinctive Rattlesnake strata (semi-arid grasslands).

After filling your head with paleontology, drive across the highway to the historic ⑬ Cant Ranch House and spread a picnic lunch out on the wooden tables overlooking the John Day River. Then backtrack 3 miles (north) to the ⑭ Blue Basin Area parking lot. Here you have two hiking options: the 0.6-mile Island in Time Trail and the 3-mile Blue Basin Overlook Trail. The former passes replicas of large mammal fossils and ends in a massive amphitheater of towering pinnacles. The latter leads around and above the amphitheater.

Leaving the Sheep Rock Unit, drive east on Hwy 26 through ⑮ Picture Gorge, a narrow canyon hemmed in by tightly bunched clusters of hexagonal stone pillars known as Picture Gorge Basalts. Continue east about 2 miles to the ⑯ Mascall Formation Overlook, where you'll get a spectacular view of the John Day River Valley, the Strawberry Mountains, Picture Gorge and the Mascall and Rattlesnake formations.

If you backtrack through Picture Gorge and swing left (west) on Hwy 26, after 45 minutes you'll reach the Old West town of ⑰ Mitchell. Pull off the highway and check into the historic ⑱ Oregon Hotel, a two story building with cozy themed rooms, a downstairs reading area and a big front porch. De-

> **DETOUR**
>
> If you have the time, detour 38 miles east along Hwy 26 to the town of John Day, and the highly regarded **Kam Wah Chung State Heritage Site** (www.oregonstateparks.org/park_8.php). Described by one local as "the best thing in eastern Oregon," the building, which served as an apothecary for the noted Chinese herbalist and doctor, Ing Hay, offers a fascinating look at the history of the region's 19th-century Chinese immigrants. Allow three to four hours for the detour.

pending on the time, either eat dinner at ⑲ Little Pine Cafe, a diner next door with all the mom-and-pop nostalgia you could hope for, or skip supper altogether and drive 12-miles west to the ⑳ Painted Hills Unit. The goal is to see the low-slung, colorfully banded Painted Hills at sunset, when the evening light emphasizes the ochres, blacks, beiges and yellows of the eroded hillsides.

The following morning, devour a big home-cooked breakfast at Mitchell's ㉑ Bridge Creek Cafe. Drive north on Hwy 207 to complete the loop and return to Hwy 84 via Hwys 19 and 206.

Danny Palmerlee

TRIP INFORMATION

GETTING THERE
Clarno Unit of the John Day Fossil Beds is 180 miles from Portland: take Hwy 84 100 miles east to Hwy 97; drive south 55 miles to Hwy 218 via Shaniko then east through Antelope.

DO

Cant Ranch House
Peek into this 1917 ranch house for exhibits on the region's human history. **Hwy 19, Sheep Rock Unit; admission free; 9am-5:30pm, reduced hours in winter;**

John Day Fossil Beds National Monument
Twenty-two sq miles of fossils and fantastic scenery. **www.nps.gov/joda; Clarno Unit, Hwy 218; Sheep Rock Unit, Hwy 19; Painted Hills Unit, Hwy 26; admission free; all units daylight hours year-round;**

Thomas Condon Paleontology Center
The monument's only visitors center is outstanding; also a research center. **541-987-2333; 32651 Hwy 19, Sheep Rock Unit; admission free; 9am-5:30pm, reduced hours in winter;**

EAT

Big Timber Family Restaurant
Down-home restaurant with big breakfasts, burgers and country-style dinners. **541-763-4328; 540 1st St, Fossil; mains $4.50-19.95; 7am-7pm Sun-Thu, 7am-8pm Fri & Sat;**

Bridge Creek Cafe
Petite diner with homemade pie and the usual country cooking. **541-462-3434; 208 Hwy 26, Mitchell; mains $4.50-7.50; 6am-3pm Sun-Fri;**

Little Pine Cafe
Fabulous country diner with burgers, sandwiches, soups and ice-cream pancakes. **541-462-3532; www.littlepinecafe.com; 100 E Main St, Mitchell; mains $8-13; 7am-9pm Tue-Sun;**

SLEEP

Bridge Creek Flora Inn
This wonderfully friendly B&B is split between two adjacent historic houses; rates include a superb breakfast. **541-763-2355; www.fossilinn.com; 828 Main St, Fossil; r $75-95;**

Donnelly Service Creek River Access Park
Bare-bones riverside campground popular with rafters. Pit toilets, no water. **Hwy 207 near Hwy 19, Service Creek; sites $5;**

Lone Pine
This pleasant campground, 2 miles east of Kimberly, has pit toilets but no running water. **Hwy 402; sites $5;**

Oregon Hotel
Historic 13-room hotel with kitschy, comfy rooms, each with its own theme; dorm room available. **541-462-3027; 104 E Main St, Mitchell; dm $15, r $29-89;**

USEFUL WEBSITES
www.nps.gov/joda

LINK YOUR TRIP

Journey Through Time Scenic Byway

WHY GO During this epic drive across windswept plains, desolate badlands and forested mountain passes, you'll dig deep into Oregon's history. Along the way you'll visit everything from ghost towns to fossil beds, from gold-mining sites to small-town museums. The one thing you won't see much of? Crowds.

TIME
4 days

DISTANCE
301 miles

BEST TIME TO GO
Jun – Sep

START
Maryhill

END
Baker City

ALSO GOOD FOR

Unless you count the futuristic-looking windmills around the town of Wasco, a more precise name for this state scenic byway would be Journey *Back* in Time Scenic Byway. From the moment you leave Hwy 84 it's truly a time warp: ghost towns lie off the roadside, fossils expose millions of years of history, and even the restaurants and hotels make you feel you've driven into decades past.

Although it's not part of the official byway, the perfect place to kick off your time travel is at the full-scale replica of ❶ Stonehenge, on the Washington side of the Columbia River, just east of Hwy 97. Built by eccentric businessman Sam Hill, the site is a complete version of the Salisbury Plain monument, although its detractors argue that the keystone is incorrectly aligned with the stars.

After Stonehenge, stop at nearby ❷ Maryhill Museum of Art, just west of the Hwy 97 junction on Hwy 14. This spectacular mansion, set on a bluff above the Columbia River, was another Sam Hill project. Among its eclectic exhibits is a noteworthy collection of Native American baskets and other artifacts, including a seal intestine parka and carved walrus tusks.

Traveling south on Hwy 97, you begin the *official* scenic byway as soon as you cross the Columbia River. South of the river, the two-lane road winds over rolling, grain-covered hills, past the town of Wasco

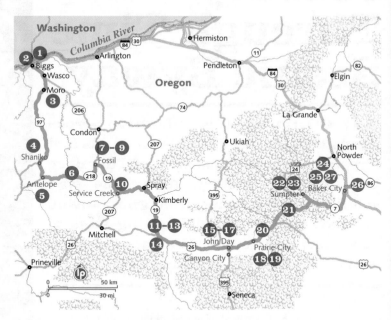

to Moro, where you'll find **3 Sherman County Historical Museum**. For a small-town museum it has some surprisingly interesting exhibits, including those on the history of wheat production, Native Americans and rural living in the days of old. Back on Hwy 97, you'll be treated to views of several volcanoes in the distance as you head south, including Oregon's Mt Hood and Mt Jefferson and Washington's Mt Adams.

"After the road behind, entering the one-stoplight town of John Day is like rolling into the big city."

Then you hit **4 Shaniko** (population 26). This wee ghost town, contrary to everything it now seems, was once the wool shipping center of the US. Its decrepit old buildings make for exceptional photo ops, and its architectural *grand dame,* the Shaniko Hotel, is one of the finer historic buildings in eastern Oregon. (It was closed and up for sale at the time of publication.)

From Shaniko, continue south on Hwy 218 and you'll soon hit the town of **5 Antelope** (population 59), founded in the 1870s and named for the pronghorn antelope that roamed the surrounding hills. After the boom days of the wool trade were over, Antelope floundered. It then (miraculously?) sprang back to life in the mid-1980s when "Rajneeshees," followers of Indian guru Bhagwan Shree Rajneesh, settled here after the mystic founded the nearby religious community of Rajneeshpuram.

About 16 miles west of Antelope, the dramatically eroded Palisade Cliffs come into view and mark your arrival at the **6** **John Day Fossil Beds Clarno Unit**. The short trails and fossil remains here plunge you into a far more distant past, to a time more than 40 million years ago, when the region was subtropical forest. The astounding collection of fossils found in the area are exactly what gave the town of **7** **Fossil** (population 370), 18 miles northeast, its name.

In Fossil, check into the homey **8** **Bridge Creek Flora Inn**, which – we coincidentally discovered – is owned by Lyn Craig, the creator of the official Journey Through Time Scenic Byway. Needless to say, Craig is a wealth of information. She's also an inspired cook and serves a whopping all-natural breakfast to her overnight guests. To-night though, grab dinner at **9** **Big Timber Family Restaurant**, where good grub and small-town hospitality both come in big doses.

On day two, take Hwy 19 south to **10** **Service Creek** (population 2), another old stagecoach stop which today consists of an inn (where you'll find the town's two residents) and a rafting-put-in-cum-campground on the John Day River (just south of the

> **ASK A LOCAL**
>
> "If you're heading east through Picture Gorge [on Hwy 26], at the far end you'll see a sign on the left and a gravel parking area big enough for about two cars. There's a little footpath from the pullout. Walk down the footpath and then hang onto the rock wall on your left and lean around and you'll see some red pictographs. It's really cool. And you can't hurt them because you can't reach them."
>
> *Lyn Craig, Fossil, OR*

junction). Follow Hwy 19 east from Service Creek through the town of Spray (which, with a population of 140, actually *is* a town) and on to Kimberly, where you'll find a store with snacks and cold drinks. From Kimberly south, the road follows the swift and increasingly scenic John Day River. The rust-colored walls of the river canyon narrow and then open up again before reaching the spectacular **11** **John Day Fossil Beds Sheep Rock Unit**. For a fascinating paleontology lesson stop at the **12** **Thomas Condon Paleontology Center**, which doubles as the visitors center for the surrounding John Day Fossil Beds National Monument. The museum, packed with fossilized skulls, leaves, skeletons and superb murals, will help you understand exactly what you're seeing in the mountains around you.

Just south of the paleontology center, Hwy 19 becomes Hwy 26E, and you follow the John Day River east through a narrow basalt-walled canyon known as **13** **Picture Gorge**. Upon leaving here, watch for the turnoff about 2 miles east of the gorge on your right that leads up to the **14** **Mascall Formation Overlook**, where you can take in astounding 360-degree views of the surrounding mountains.

Back on Hwy 26, about 38 miles from the paleontology center, is ⑮ **John Day** (population 1821). After the road behind, entering the one-stoplight town of John Day is like rolling into the big city. Watch out for all those cars and make your way to the outstanding ⑯ **Kam Wah Chung State Heritage Site**, which served as an apothecary, community center, temple and general store for Chinese gold miners and settlers from the late 19th century until the 1940s. Today it's a widely acclaimed museum featuring the history of the building and the region's Chinese past. John Day is the logical place to spend the night and, although the town is hardly acclaimed for its sleeping options, the kitschy ⑰ **Dreamers Lodge** (actually a motel) does the trick.

Get an early start to day three and eat breakfast 12 miles east in ⑱ **Prairie City**, at ⑲ **Chuck's Little Diner**. This snug family diner serves the nothing but the classics: bacon-and-egg breakfasts with butter-laden toast, hot pancakes and – in true diner fashion – mediocre coffee. With Strawberry Mountain towering over the town, Prairie City has a stunning setting. The town is also home to the DeWitt Depot Museum (currently closed), which is worth a quick peek just to see the depot building itself. Prairie City was the terminus of the narrow-gauge Sumpter Valley Railroad that ran between here and Baker City.

From Prairie City, leave the barren scenery of the John Day River Valley behind and make your way east into the lush, conifer-clad Blue Mountains. As you head up the first grade, pull off at the ⑳ **Strawberry Mountain Overlook** (on the left), which affords stunning views of the John Day River Valley below and the Strawberry Mountains in the distance. Continue northeast over Dixie Pass (elevation 5280ft), swing left onto Hwy 7, cross Tipton Summit (elevation 5124 ft) and you'll eventually drop into a lovely valley hemmed in by trees before hitting ㉑ **Whitney**. This isolated prairie settlement, a ghost town in the best sense of the word, was once a busy logging town and the primary stop on the Sumpter Valley Railroad. Its sagging wooden buildings, which lie on either side of a dirt road that branches south (right) from Hwy 26, are certainly worth a stop.

DETOUR

Two miles south of John Day lies the tiny town of Canyon City, home of the **Grant County Historical Museum** (open May to September only). Depending on your perspective, it's either (a) just another Podunk museum or (b) a fascinating glimpse into the region's human history. Just don't lose yourself among the relics: wood clamps, antique clothing, house wares, pianos and other musical instruments, a Native American exhibit and loads of interesting old photographs. You can easily see the museum in an hour.

About 9 miles east of Whitney, turn left on Sumpter Valley Hwy to visit the former gold-mining camp of ㉒ **Sumpter**. Once home to 3500 people, the town today is a sleepy cluster of Old West buildings huddled along a dusty main drag – reason alone to visit. The official attraction, however, is the **23 Sumpter Valley Dredge**, a massive relic of gold-mining engineering sitting beside the river. The dredge's 72-bucket "digging ladder" cost $300,000 to build and, during its operational lifespan, extracted some 9 tons of gold.

Return to Hwy 7 and make your way 26 miles east to the bustling eastern Oregon hub of **24 Baker City**. In the gold rush days, Baker City was the largest metropolis between Salt Lake City and Portland, and a heady mix of miners, cowboys, shopkeepers and loggers kept the city's many saloons, brothels and gaming halls boisterously alive. Today, the city's wide downtown streets and historical architecture recall its rich bygone days. Before you live it up (now that you're in civilization once again), check into the landmark **25 Geiser Grand Hotel**. This masterpiece of Italian Renaissance revival architecture will keep you firmly planted in the past, *and* you'll sleep in style.

"...miners, cowboys, shopkeepers and loggers kept the city's many saloons, brothels and gaming halls boisterously alive."

If you're not too beat from the drive, head to the evocative **26 National Historic Oregon Trail Interpretive Center**, the nation's foremost memorial to the pioneers who migrated west along the Oregon Trail. Lying atop a hill 7 miles east of town, the center contains interactive displays, artifacts and films that brilliantly illustrate the day-to-day realities of the pioneers. Outside you can stroll on the 4-mile interpretive path and spot the actual Oregon Trail.

Return to Baker City and make your way to **27 Barley Brown's Brewpub**, with pressed-tin ceilings, big wooden booths and a good-old pub-style menu. Most importantly, it serves some seriously good award-winning beer, that's brewed in small batches just like it was in the days back when...

Danny Palmerlee

TRIP INFORMATION

GETTING THERE
From Portland, follow Hwy 84 east to Hwy 97, go north to Hwy 14 and then follow the signs east to Stonehenge (100 miles in total).

DO

Kam Wah Chung State Heritage Site
This must-see museum features the history of Chinese settlement and culture in eastern Oregon. ☎ 541-575-2800; 250 NW Canton St, John Day; admission free; ☉ 9am-5pm; ♿

Maryhill Museum of Art
Eclectic museum in a stunning location and building to match. ☎ 509-773-3733; www .maryhillmuseum.org; 35 Maryhill Museum Dr, Goldendale, WA; adult/child/senior $7/2/6; ☉ 9am-5pm Mar 15-Nov 15; ♿

National Historic Oregon Trail Interpretive Center
This brilliant memorial to Oregon Trail pioneers is not to be missed. ☎ 541-523-1843; www.oregontrail.blm.gov; 22267 Hwy 86, Baker City; adult/senior $5/3.50; ☉ 9am-6pm Apr-Oct, 9am-4pm Nov-Mar; ♿

Sherman County Historical Museum
Thousands of artifacts bring Oregon's Native American and early US history to life. ☎ 541-565-3232; www.shermanmuseum.org; 200 Dewey St, Moro; adult/student $3/1; ☉ 10am-5pm May 1-Oct 31; ♿

Stonehenge
America's first Stonehenge replica dates back to 1918. Just south of OR-14 on Stonehenge Dr, Maryhill; admission free; ☉ dawn-dusk

Thomas Condon Paleontology Center
Visit John Day Fossil Beds National Monument's visitors center for its extraordinary fossils and knowledgeable staff. ☎ 541-987-2333; 32651 Hwy 19, Sheep Rock Unit; admission free; ☉ 9am-5:30pm, reduced hours in winter; ♿

LINK YOUR TRIP

TRIP

37 Prehistoric Oregon Trip p245

39 From Heaven to Hells Canyon p255

EAT

Barley Brown's Brewpub
Baker City's brewpub serves everything from clam linguini to teriyaki salmon and BBQ ribs – and eight delicious microbrews. ☎ 541-523-4266; 2190 Main St, Baker City; mains $12-18; ☉ 4-10pm Mon-Thu, to 11pm Fri & Sat

Big Timber Family Restaurant
Family restaurant with big breakfasts, burgers and country-style dinners. ☎ 541-763-4328; 540 1st St, Fossil; mains $4.50-19.95; ☉ 7am-7pm Sun-Thu, 7am-8pm Fri & Sat; ♿

Chuck's Little Diner
With its Formica-top bar, tarnished chrome bar stools, friendly staff and greasy classics, this is a diner par excellence. ☎ 541-820-4353; 142 Front St, Prairie City; mains $6-9; ☉ 6am-2pm Wed-Sun

SLEEP

Bridge Creek Flora Inn
Occupying two adjacent, historic homes, this country-style B&B minimizes frilliness and maximizes friendliness; superb breakfasts. ☎ 541-763-2355; www.fossilinn.com; 828 Main St, Fossil; r $75-95; ♿

Dreamers Lodge
Friendly, immaculately kept 1960s-era motel with spacious rooms, coffee makers, mini-fridges and a decor that's brilliantly outdated. ☎ 541-575-0526, 800-654-2849; 144 N Canyon Blvd, John Day; r $71

Geiser Grand Hotel
Baker City's downtown landmark and fanciest lodgings. Elegant rooms are spacious and decorated with old-style furniture. Don't miss the saloon. ☎ 541-523-1889, 888-434-7374; www.geisergrand.com; 1996 Main St, Baker City; r $105-165

USEFUL WEBSITES
www.eova.com

www.lonelyplanet.com/trip-planner

From Heaven to Hells Canyon

WHY GO Don't let the name fool you. North America's deepest river gorge is more than just scorching temperatures and desolate landscapes. You'll find both, true enough, but you'll also find forested ridge tops, peaceful river valleys and hamletlike towns on this jaunt around one of Oregon's wildest parks.

In the remote northeast corner of Oregon, at the foot of Idaho's rugged Seven Devils Mountains, lies one of the Pacific Northwest's most spectacular sights: Hells Canyon. Measuring 8043ft deep from the top of He Devil Peak to the Snake River, it is the deepest river gorge in North America. Except for a handful of dirt roads and a paved road up the Snake River, along the park's eastern boundary, the canyon is largely inaccessible to all but the most intrepid hikers and off-roaders. However, the roads that do access Hells Canyon offer spectacular vistas: from Hat Point on the gorge's west rim; from the road alongside Hells Canyon Reservoir; and from the Hells Canyon Lookout, reached from Wallowa Mountain Loop Rd. But first, you have to get out here.

Oregon's gateways to Hells Canyon are the neighboring cities of Enterprise and Joseph, two Old West towns at the foot of the Wallowa Mountains. Traveling from Portland, just before you roll into Enterprise, you'll pass the excellent ❶ **Wallowa Mountains Visitor Center**, a great place to stock up on information about Hells Canyon and surrounding areas. Books, free brochures and short films cover everything from backcountry trails to wildlife and geology. The center is also worth a stop for the views across the Wallowa Valley to Ruby Peak, Chief Joseph Mountain and the other snowcapped peaks of the Wallowa Mountains.

From the visitors center, it's just over half a mile to ❷ **Enterprise**, which like its sister town of Joseph 6 miles away, is home to a handful

Sidebar

TIME
3 days

DISTANCE
170 miles

BEST TIME TO GO
Jun – Sep

START
Enterprise

END
Hells Canyon Dam

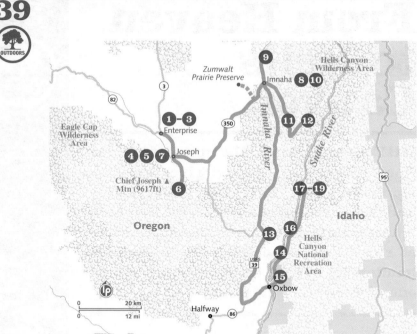

of artists and urban refugees who found the town's idyllic setting the perfect place to set up shop and put down roots. Unlike Joseph (which has arguably become *too* cute), Enterprise still maintains its good-old small-town atmosphere. In fact, its downtown, which consists of two blocks of handsome buildings, is downright lonesome at times. It's well worth a wander, but the best reason to stop is to drop into ❸ **Terminal Gravity Brewing**. Here you can pay tribute to one of Oregon's best breweries by downing a delicious IPA at a creekside picnic bench beneath the cottonwoods out front. Complement it with an outrageously delicious buffalo burger and you're in paradise.

CHIEF JOSEPH

Chief Joseph was a Nez Perce chief known to his people as Hin-mah-too-yah-lat-kekt, or "Thunder Rolling Down the Mountain." He was best known for his courageous but ultimately unsuccessful resistance to the US government, which forcibly relocated the Wallowa Valley Nez Perce to a distant reservation. After the removal, Chief Joseph continued to speak out for the rights of his people, demanding equality for all Native Americans. It is said he died of a broken heart.

After lunch, drive south to ❹ **Joseph** and check into the ❺ **Bronze Antler B&B**, a handsomely restored Craftsman bungalow on the south end of town. With a large, cozy living room and only four guest rooms, it's an intimate and divinely comfy place. If you'd rather camp (or you're up for a little exploring), drive 6 miles south of town to the southern end of Wallowa Lake. Here you'll find the somewhat cramped but beautifully situated campgrounds of ❻ **Wallowa Lake State Park**. Over 5 miles long, Wallowa Lake is a glacially formed lake at the foot of the Wallowa Mountains, dominated at its southern end by 9617ft Chief Joseph Mountain. Giant old-growth conifers tower over a grassy beach area here, and families lounge in the sun, fish and otherwise frolic away the summer afternoons. A good hike leaves the park's south-unit parking lot and climbs into the Eagle Cap Wilderness Area.

For dinner, head to Joseph's **7** **Embers Brewhouse**, a groovy brewery and restaurant with a fabulous outdoor patio. Beneath the trees you can quaff pints of microbrewed beer, eat pizza, sandwiches or salads and take in the views of the Wallowa Mountains. Even if you're camping at Wallowa Lake, it's only about 10 minutes away by car.

On day two, it's time to leave civilization behind. Get an early start for the 30-mile drive to **8** **Imnaha**, one of the most isolated towns in the US. After leaving Joseph, the road passes a highway sign that tellingly reads "Open Range Next 23 Miles," then meets up with Little

> **DETOUR** If you have a high clearance vehicle and three to five hours to spare, detour up to **Zumwalt Prairie Preserve**. Owned by the Nature Conservancy, this 51-sq-mile preserve is the largest remaining grassland of its kind in the US. Several trails meander through the prairie, which is home to a vast number of hawks and eagles. To get there, take the dirt Camp Creek Rd, which departs Little Sheep Creek Hwy about 1 mile south of Imnaha.

Sheep Creek, which it follows all the way to Imnaha. Once you're in Imnaha, you can either drive 6 miles north of "town" to the deluxe **9** **Imnaha River Inn** or pitch at tent at the RV park (more like a grassy parking lot) operated by the **10** **Imnaha Store & Tavern**. The former is a log-cabin-style lodge with a stunning great room and seven comfortable rooms with big windows. The owners will take care of all your meals while you're here (lunch and dinner cost extra), offer transportation to hikers and are a wealth of information. At the RV park, you're on your own, but you can eat breakfast, lunch and dinner inside the tavern. Whether you're staying there or not, the tavern is worth popping into, if only to walk across the creaky, crooked floor and sit at the old fashioned bar. It's also the best place to inquire about road conditions up to Hat Point.

Hat Point (elevation 6982ft) offers the best drive-to viewpoint over Hells Canyon. But to get here you have to brave a 16% to 18% grade and 24 miles of gravel road. The good news: only the first 5 or 6 miles are steep. After that the road follows a spectacular forested ridge offering view after stunning view along the way. Be sure to stop at the **11** **Granny View Vista** pullout. By the time you get to Hat Point you'll wonder if the views could actually get any better. They do. Atop Hat Point stands the 82ft **12** **Hat Point lookout tower**, a fire lookout offering dizzying 360-degree views of the Seven Devils, the Wallowas and Hells Canyon itself. And, yes, you can climb to the top. Without a doubt this is one of the grandest views in the entire Pacific Northwest. In summer, the road is usually passable for all passenger cars.

After a night in Imnaha, follow the gravel Upper Imnaha Rd south along the Imnaha River to USFS Rd 39 (also known as Wallowa Mountain Loop Rd). This is a dusty but scenic drive, from the Imnaha River Valley's deep northern end through bucolic golden pastureland into the pine forests. Although the southern end of the road is heavily potholed, it's fine for passenger vehicles. If you wish to avoid the dust, backtrack along Little Sheep Creek Hwy as far as USFS Rd 39 and swing left. Whichever route you take, after joining USFS Rd 39, continue southeast until the turnoff for the ⑬ **Hells Canyon Overlook**. This is the *only* overlook into Hells Canyon that's accessible by paved road, so take advantage of it. Although you don't get the same 360-degree views as from Hat Point, it's a marvelous vista nonetheless.

From Hells Canyon Overlook, continue down USFS Rd 39 to the junction of Hwy 86 and turn left toward Copperfield and Oxbow. At Copperfield, you'll reach the Snake River and officially be at the bottom of Hells Canyon. Down here, it's hot, and the canyon has no problem living up to its name. Cross the Snake River into Idaho and turn onto Idaho's Forest Rd 454 (also called Hells Canyon Dam Rd), which eventu-

> **ASK A LOCAL**
>
> "We love to go up to Hat Point because it's your best view of the canyon – of the deepest part of the canyon. Another of our favorite spots to go is Ollokot Campground, not that we camp there, but because it's so beautiful in there with the river and the trees. It's just off the Wallowa Mountain Loop Rd [USFS Rd 39], about an hour or so from Imnaha."
>
> *Sandy Vidan, Imnaha, OR*

ally dead ends at Hells Canyon Dam. Before heading for the dam, however, decide where you want to spend the night. There are plenty of primitive camping options to choose from along the reservoir's edge, but none of them have water. For water and showers, head to ⑭ **Hells Canyon Park**, a short way up the Idaho side of the river. Although it's primarily an RV park for water-skiers, it has some grassy tent sites that are surprisingly peaceful. For something with a roof and four walls, check into ⑮ **Hells Canyon B&B** near Oxbow. Though far from fancy, it's immaculate and extremely welcoming.

Once you're situated, head north along FR 454 for 22 miles of nonstop rust-colored Hells Canyon scenery. If there's time for a hike, tackle the 4.5-mile (out and back) ⑯ **Allison Creek Trail**, which you'll pass about 12 miles north of Oxbow (10 miles before the dam). With a total elevation gain of about 1200ft, this is a gorgeous hike from the trailhead on FR 454, up Allison Creek Canyon, past some fantastic limestone rock formations to a saddle at about 3000ft. It can be brutally hot in summer, however, and the poison ivy is abundant. And watch out for rattlesnakes. If you want to do any hiking in Hells Canyon, you're best off driving all the way to the Hells Canyon Dam and popping into ⑰ **Hells Canyon Visitor Center** for trail information.

North of Hells Canyon Dam and the visitors center, the Snake River returns to its natural flowing self, descending through epic scenery and roaring rapids. You can float those rapids by signing on with ⑱ **Hells Canyon Adventures**, which offers rafting and jet-boat trips into an otherwise inaccessible area. Afoot, you can get a taste of the Snake in its natural, roadless, undammed form by hiking the 1-mile ⑲ **Stud Creek Trail** downstream from the dam. The trail begins immediately below the visitors center and passes some great spots to relax above the river and ponder the immensity of your surroundings – and the fact that yesterday, you were looking down on near where you are now from thousands of feet above.

"Afoot, you can get a taste of the Snake in its natural, roadless, undammed form..."

From Hells Canyon, return by way of Hwy 86 through Halfway to Baker City. From there, you can pick up Hwy 84 west to Portland.
Danny Palmerlee

TRIP INFORMATION

GETTING THERE
From Portland, take Hwy 84 east 260 miles to La Grande, then follow Hwy 82 for 65 miles to Enterprise.

DO

Hells Canyon Adventures
Hells Canyon's main adventure outfitter runs raft and boat trips May through September. Reservations required. ☎ 541-785-3352, 800-422-3568; www.hellscanyonadventures .com; 4200 Hells Canyon Dam Rd, Oxbow

Hells Canyon Visitor Center
Get trail information, maps and books. Find out exactly what poison ivy looks like. ☎ 541-785-3395; Hells Canyon Dam, FR 454; 8am-4pm summer only;

Wallowa Lake State Park
The center of activities at Wallowa Lake's south end. Swimming beach, boat launch, boat rentals, 200 campsites and yurts. ☎ 541-432-4185, reservations 800-452-5687; www.oregonstateparks.org/park _27.php; 72214 Marina Lane, Joseph;

Wallowa Mountains Visitor Center
Excellent information on natural history, outdoor recreation and camping in Hells Canyon and the Wallowa Mountains. ☎ 541-426-5546; www.fs.fed.us/r6/w-w; 88401 Hwy 82, Enterprise; 8am-6pm Mon-Sat;

EAT & DRINK

Embers Brewhouse
Joseph's lone brewery serves pizza, sandwiches, salads and microbrews. Fabulous front deck. ☎ 541-432-2739; 206 N Main St, Joseph; mains $8-15; 7am-9pm Sun-Thu, to 10pm Fri & Sat;

Imnaha Store & Tavern
This store, restaurant and tavern stocks minimal supplies but has a reliable bar menu and offers tent sites. ☎ 541-577-3111; 71300 Lower Imnaha Rd, Imnaha; mains $6-17.50, tent sites $5; 9am-9pm

Terminal Gravity Brewing
One of Oregon's best breweries with outdoor tables and pastas, salads, burgers and sandwiches. ☎ 541-426-0158; 803 School St, Enterprise; mains $7-11; 11am-10pm Wed-Sat, 4-9pm Sun & Mon

SLEEP

Bronze Antler B&B
This lovingly restored Craftsman bungalow offers four elegant rooms, each with its own bathroom. ☎ 541-432-0230, 866-520-9769; www.bronzeantler.com; 309 S Main St, Joseph; r $85-259

Hells Canyon B&B
Friendly B&B with modest rooms and a deck overlooking Hells Canyon Reservoir. The owners are veritable fountains of local information. ☎ 541-785-3373; www.hells-canyon-bed-and-breakfast.com; 49922 Homestead Rd, Oxbow; r $60

Hells Canyon Park
Geared toward the water-skiing crowd, but still an extremely pleasant lakeside spot for tent campers. ☎ 800-422-3143; www .idahopower.com; FR 454, Hells Canyon Reservoir, ID; campsites/RV sites $10/16;

Imnaha River Inn
Gorgeous log-sided B&B with comfy, themed rooms and a common area reminiscent of a mountain lodge. ☎ 541-577-6002, 866-601-9214; www.imnahariverinn.com; Lower Imnaha Rd, Imnaha; r $120-130

USEFUL WEBSITES
www.eova.com
www.fs.fed.us/hellscanyon

LINK YOUR TRIP
www.lonelyplanet.com/trip-planner

Day Trips Around Portland

DAY TRIPS

One of Portland's finest features is its proximity to so much outdoor fun: take your coffee to go and, before you finish it, you'll be hiking the Columbia River Gorge, stepping into skis on Mt Hood or wine tasting in the Willamette Valley.

SAUVIE ISLAND

It's hard to believe that only twenty minutes from downtown Portland there exists a place like this. An agricultural oasis of gently rolling hillside farms, Sauvie Island is *the* classic summertime Portland getaway. Head out here and pick all the strawberries, blueberries, raspberries and peaches you can drag back to Portland. Or head out to Walton Beach, a fine stretch of sand on the island's eastern side. Better yet, do both. Every Thursday evening in July and August Kruger's Farm (www.krugersfarmmarket.com) hosts its fabulous Thursday's at the Farm, with live music, berry picking, food and family fun. It's not to be missed. Sauvie Island is also a popular cycling destination, thanks to the 12-mile loop road around the island. The island is also home to 12,000-acre Sauvie Island Wildlife Area, a wetland sanctuary for thousands of migratory ducks, geese, tundra swans, bald eagles and sandhill cranes. Permanent residents include peregrine falcons, great blue herons, foxes and beavers. The refuge is open mid-April to October. Return traffic can be bad on summer weekends. **From Portland, take US-30 west toward St Helens. This becomes NW St Helens Rd. About 3.5 miles after passing the St Johns Bridge, turn right on NW Sauvie Island Rd; after crossing the Sauvie Island Bridge, you'll be on Sauvie Island.**

See also **TRIP 26**

EAGLE CREEK TRAIL

The crown jewel of trails in the Columbia River Gorge is the 13.2-mile Eagle Creek Trail. The historic path, an impressive feat of trail engineering, was built around 1915 to coincide with the opening of the Columbia Gorge Hwy. It passes 11 waterfalls as it meanders up wooded slopes and sheer rock walls through a narrow basalt canyon. Parts of the trail traverse ledges blasted into the rock walls and are perilously high. Although these ledges have metal aid ropes, they lack guard rails, making them dangerous for children and dogs, but utterly thrilling for everyone else. Although you could hike the entire trail in one long day, most people simply bite off shorter chunks of it for a more pleasantly paced day hike. From the trailhead across Hwy 84 from the Bonneville Dam, it's a 4.2-mile round-trip hike to Punchbowl Falls and a 6.5-mile round-trip hike to High Bridge. For an exciting 12-miler (round-trip), hike all the way to 130ft Tunnel Falls. The trail passes a swimmable pool at the foot of a cliff and crosses a dizzying bridge over a 150ft chasm before reaching a 35ft tunnel, just above the falls. **To Reach the Eagle Creek Falls trailhead, drive 39 miles east of Portland on Hwy 84/US-30 and get off at exit 41 toward Eagle Creek Recreation Area. Turn right at the end of this road and follow the forest road about 0.5 miles to the parking lot.**

See also **TRIPS 27 & 28**

HOOD RIVER

Hood River is one of the world's premier windsurfing and kiteboarding destinations, but there's more to this dynamic little town than big winds. It's also the perfect base for driving the so-called Fruit Loop, a 35-mile trip through Hood River's orchard country. In spring, the trees put on a spectacular flower display, and in summer U-pick farms open their gates for all the fruit-picking fun you can handle. Roadside fruit stands peddle apples, pears, cherries, berries and vegetables. Premier wineries have also put down roots in the region, so wine-tasting opportunities are blooming, too. In the town of Parkdale, about halfway around the loop, be sure to stop at the Elliot Glacier Public House for a handcrafted brew and a snack. Of course, you could always entertain yourself shopping, eating and drinking the day away in the cute shops and excellent restaurants of Hood River itself. To watch windsurfers and kiteboarders rip up the Columbia River (or learn how to do it yourself), make your way down to the marina and over to the waterfront area known as The Hook. **Follow Hwy 84/US 30 east for about 62 miles to Hood River. Take Exit 64 toward Hwy 35/Government Camp. Hwy 35 begins the Fruit Loop; Mt Hood Country Store (on Hwy 35) offers free Fruit Loop maps or you can download one at www.hoodriverfruitloop.com.**

See also **TRIPS 27 & 28**

MT HOOD

On a clear day, the state's highest peak, Mt Hood (11,240ft), pops into view all over northern Oregon, exerting its magnetic tug on skiers, hikers and sightseers. In summer wildflowers bloom on the mountainsides and hidden ponds shimmer in blue, making for some unforgettable hikes. In winter, Portlanders flock to one of five ski parks for outstanding downhill skiing and snowboarding. And the cross-country skiing and sledding opportunities are endless. Drive a scant 60 miles from downtown Portland, and you too can be hiking, mountain biking, skiing or sightseeing on Mt Hood's big, forested sometimes snow-covered shoulders. Mount Hood Meadows (www.skihood .com) is the mountain's largest ski area. If you're heading up in summer, the best place for information is the Mt Hood Information Center (www.mthood .info) in Mt Hood Village Resort. For hikers, Ramona Falls, Mirror Lake and the gentle Salmon River Trail all make easy day trips from Portland. **From Portland take Hwy 84/US-30 east from Portland for about 13 miles. Take Exit 16 to NE 238th Dr (go right), which becomes NE 242nd Ave. Turn left after about 3 miles on NE Burnside Rd, which becomes Hwy 26 to Mt Hood.**

See also **TRIPS 27 & 28**

SILVER FALLS STATE PARK

Positively gushing with waterfalls, Oregon's largest state park (day-use fee $3) is an easy day trip from Portland. Silver Falls offers camping, swimming, picnicking and horseback riding and – best of all – hiking. The park's most famous hike is the marvelous Trail of Ten Falls Loop, a relatively easy 8-mile loop that winds up a basalt canyon through thick forests of Douglas firs, western hemlocks, ferns, moss and wildflowers. It also passes – you guessed it – 10 waterfalls! Some of the falls plunge far enough out from the cliffs that you even walk behind them. Because it's so close to Portland *and* so beautiful you'll have plenty of company on the trail, but the beauty of the walk far outshines the occasional annoyance of too many people. The park is open year-round, and the falls are at their raging best in springtime. A few roadside trailheads access this hike, but the best place to start is the South Falls day-use area parking lot, near the park's main entrance. **From Portland, take I-5 28 miles south to Hwy 214 toward Woodburn/Silverton. Follow Hwy 214 another 26 miles, through Silverton, to the park. Drive through the park and stop at the South Falls day-use parking lot. Total distance is 60 miles.**

See also **TRIP 32**

DUNDEE & CARLTON

Once the heart of hazelnut country, the Willamette Valley town of Dundee, 27 miles southwest of Portland, is now the heart of wine country. The surrounding Dundee Hills produce some of the state's finest Pinot Noir, Pinot Gris, Riesling, Gewürztraminer and Pinot Blanc. It is your responsibility to sample as much of it as you possibly can. Within minutes of downtown Dundee you can drive to several of Oregon's best and oldest wineries, including Argyle Winery, Erath Winery, Lange Estate Winery & Vineyards, Archery Summit and Domaine Drouhin Oregon. And there are loads of others. Although the town of Dundee is nothing to go gaga over, it has developed a bit of a culinary scene and makes a good base for exploring the surrounding wine country. To the west, Carlton, at the heart of the Yamhill-Carlton District subappellation, makes for another good base. You could extend your jaunt through wine country (and miss the return traffic on 99W) by winding your way south to the town of Wheatland (via Amity or otherwise) and then crossing the

Willamette River on the Wheatland Ferry and returning to Portland on I-5. **To get to Dundee from Portland, take I-5 6 miles south to Hwy 99W (Exit 294), which you'll follow about 16 miles to Dundee.**

See also **TRIPS 29 & 36**

VANCOUVER, WA

You can't really talk about Portland without talking about Vancouver, WA, directly across the Columbia River from its larger, more cosmopolitan neighbor. So many people live in Vancouver and work and play in Portland, however, it's practically just another suburb of Portland. While Vancouver can't compete in cultural terms with Portland, the city does boast a refurbished central park, a thriving farmers market, and some of the state's earliest and most important pioneering history. Fort Vancouver is one of the oldest military installations in the Pacific Northwest and a key piece of Washington's historical jigsaw. Elsewhere the city offers a county museum, a handful of ethnic restaurants and plenty of interesting Lewis and Clark memorabilia. If you have time to spare in Portland, it's worth a quick day trip, if only to see the rest of Portland. Taking the train there also gives you the perfect excuse to check out Portland's historic Union Station and Vancouver's unique location within a "wye" rail formation (it's a big deal for railroad nuts). **You can drive to Vancouver from Portland on I-5 in about 15 minutes, but a far more interesting way to get there is by train from Union Station. Six trains make the 15-minute journey to Vancouver daily ($7-12 one way).**

See also **TRIP 26**

BRITISH COLUMBIA TRIPS

Even BC locals are often guilty of not straying much further into their own backyard than Vancouver's Stanley Park. The rest of the province – peeking at you from the dark crags on the horizon or the tree-lined islands shimmering offshore – sometimes seems almost too much to take in. But lifting the lid on evocative pioneer towns such as Lillooet, tapping into charming coastal communities on the Sunshine Coast or supping on a few lip-smacking wineries in the Okanagan are reason enough to take a deep breath, jump in the car and hit the road for a BC odyssey.

Culinary fans will enjoy the Fraser Valley's produce-packed farmlands and Victoria's surprisingly diverse tearooms, while off-the-beaten-path explorers should delve into the Queen Charlotte Islands or take a nature-hugging northern BC train trek. And if you're looking for something different, the Quirky BC route weaves you around the region's most surprising attractions. Toast your road-trip finds back in Vancouver: our local expert offers some insider tips for creating your own pick-and-mix pub crawl in the glass-towered metropolis.

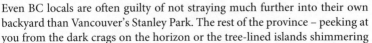

PLAYLIST ♫♪ Set the scene with these BC artist driving tunes or tap 99.3 FM The Fox, Vancouver's station for new rock music.

- "Letter from an Occupant," The New Pornographers
- "Everything is Automatic," Matthew Good Band
- "I Love Myself Today," Bif Naked
- "Vox," Sarah McLachlan
- "In My Fingertips," The Buttless Chaps
- "Rockstar," Nickelback
- "Smash the State," DOA
- "Summer of '69," Bryan Adams

★ BRITISH COLUMBIA'S BEST TRIPS

0   200 km
0   120 mi

BRITISH COLUMBIA TRIPS

48 Hours in Vancouver

WHY GO Serial winner of those international "most livable city" contests, Vancouver's biggest asset is its famously alluring ocean, forest and mountain setting. But if you can tear yourself away from the mesmerizing scenery, it's well worth wandering the city's neighborhoods to uncover what really makes this West Coast metropolis tick.

TIME
2 days

BEST TIME TO GO
Jul – Sep

START
Stanley Park

END
Granville St

ALSO GOOD FOR

FOOD &
DRINK

Abandoning your car and hoofing the streets of downtown Vancouver is the best way to explore here and your first stroll should take you straight to the ocean-fringed woodlands of ❶ **Stanley Park**. If you're looking for the visual equivalent of a spa treatment, bring a picnic and plonk yourself down on a grassy bank overlooking the shimmering Burrard Inlet. If you're feeling more active, join the joggers and cyclists on the 9km (5.5 mile) seawall, stopping for photos at the handsome totem poles, squat Brockton Point lighthouse and log-strewn Third Beach: Consider dipping in the water here or dropping by in the evening for the best sunset in town.

The park's kid-friendly ❷ **Vancouver Aquarium** and fascinating ❸ **Lost Lagoon Nature House** are also highlights. At the aquarium you can see illuminated jellyfish and take a behind-the-scenes tour with a trainer to see a pair of highly playful otters. Ask at the Nature House about the 2006 storm that wiped out hundreds of trees here. If you make it all the way around the seawall (in summer there's a free shuttle bus to help you), you'll arrive at palm tree–fringed ❹ **English Bay** on the edge of the West End. The patio at ❺ **Raincity Grill** has sea views, and you can tuck into a menu of delectable, regionally sourced dishes.

Originally an area of summer homes for rich settlers, the West End still contains some of Vancouver's best-preserved heritage houses. Drop by

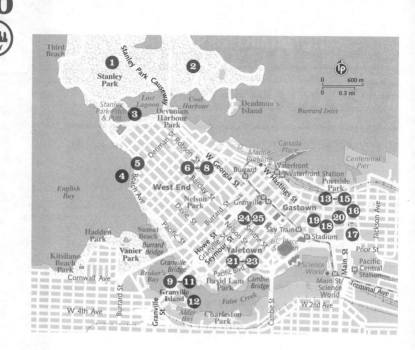

6 Barclay Heritage Square, an enclave of pretty Victorian clapboard structures, and make a beeline for **7** Roedde House Museum, a mothballed, antique-lined mansion that colorfully evokes the area's rich history. The garden is lovely, too, and you can take afternoon tea here on summer Sundays. If you're hooked on history, consider staying at the nearby old-school **8** West End Guest House. It was built in 1906 as a home for the Edwards family,

VANCOUVER'S ART-DECO TOWER

Dominating the corner of Burrard and Hastings Sts in the downtown financial district, the **Marine Building** is Vancouver's favorite heritage skyscraper. The tallest building in the British Empire when it was completed in 1930, the 321ft tower has been dwarfed by the area's glass office blocks in recent years, but it still stands tall as a design icon. Check out the exterior friezes of seafaring explorers, legendary vessels and aquatic flora and fauna, then nip inside to view the sumptuous gold-flecked interior.

owners of Vancouver's first photography shop – check out some of their photos on the 2nd floor. The West End isn't just about the past, though: Davie St is the heart of one of North America's most vibrant gay districts. It's lined with gay-friendly bars, clubs and stores, along with striking pink-painted bus shelters.

Looking over False Creek, you'll see the bright-painted restaurants and sharply gabled roofs of bustling **9** Granville Island; a miniferry from the West End's Sunset Beach will take you across. It's the best place in town to spend a languid afternoon, and it's easy to wile away a few hours

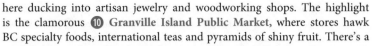

here ducking into artisan jewelry and woodworking shops. The highlight is the clamorous ❿ **Granville Island Public Market,** where stores hawk BC specialty foods, international teas and pyramids of shiny fruit. There's a good food court here, but, it you fancy something more substantial, head to ⓫ **Bridges** for fish-and-chips and views of the North Shore mountains framed by the art-deco Burrard Bridge. The boutique ⓬ **Granville Island Hotel** is a five-minute stroll away: you can catch up on local gossip on its lively brewpub patio, then roll into bed a few hours later.

> **DETOUR** ▸ Stroll the seawall for 15 minutes from Granville Island to **Vanier Park**, a green space in seafront Kitsilano that's ideal for picnicking among the kite flyers. The summertime home of the annual Shakespeare festival **Bard on the Beach** (www .bardonthebeach.org), it's also the permanent residence of three small but popular museums. The **Vancouver Museum** (www.vanmuseum .bc.ca) and **HR MacMillan Space Centre** (www .hrmacmillanspacecentre.com) occupy the same building and it's just a short walk to the friendly **Vancouver Maritime Museum** (www .vancouvermaritimemuseum.com).

Back on the downtown trail the next day, join the international shopping throngs shuffling along Robson St, where buskers of the robotic-statue and fortune-telling variety are also de rigueur, then amble over to Gastown, the atmospheric cobblestoned 'hood where Vancouver began. It's still lined with older buildings, many now housing galleries, chichi stores and some of the city's best bars; make sure you stop to pay homage at the jaunty statue of Gassy Jack Deighton in ⓭ **Maple Square.** His makeshift 1860s pub kick-started the region's first big settlement of loggers and fur trappers, culminating in the official creation of the city a few years later. Toast his legacy with a mini bar crawl here: ⓮ **Irish Heather,** the city's favorite gastropub, and ⓯ **Chill Winston,** with its sprawling patio, are recommended.

Traditionally Vancouver's no-go skid-row area, the Downtown Eastside has undergone surging gentrification in recent years. You'll still see homeless and destitute residents here but also a growing clutch of new condominium projects plus a plethora of heritage buildings, old-school painted advertising hoardings and several magnificent old neon signs: check the twinkling Only Seafoods, Ovaltine Cafe and Save-on-Meats examples. For more on the area's historic vice and crime issues, drop by the excellent ⓰ **Vancouver Police Centennial Museum** and consider its summertime Sins of the City walking tour.

You're on the edge of North America's third-largest Chinatown here, so head for dim sum at ⓱ **Hon's Wun-Tun House** then wander the pagoda-roofed streets of Asian grocery stores, fragrant apothecaries and bustling tea emporiums. Save time to explore the tranquil ⓲ **Dr Sun Yat-Sen Classical Chinese Garden.** The guided tour here explores the yin and yang of traditional landscaping, and there's also a free-entry garden next door. Back on the streets, stand well back to snap some pics of the brightly painted ⑲ **Chinatown Millennium Gate**, with its handsome lion sentries. You're also not far from ⑳ **Wanted – Lost Found Canadian**, an unusual artsy store with a cool recycling bent – check out the cushions made from old blankets.

If you've been on your feet all day, it's probably time to wind down for the evening in Yaletown. Formerly a district of brick warehouses, the atmospheric old sheds here have been transformed into chic apartments, boutique clothing stores and some of Vancouver's best restaurants. If you feel like some casual patio dining and a beer, head to ㉑ **Yaletown Brewing Company** for a local Red Truck Ale and a thin-crust Italian sausage pizza. For something more dressy, ㉒ **Blue Water Café** has a superswanky sushi bar and a brick-and-beam dining room that combines high-end dining with a warm and friendly approach to service.

BIKING THE CITY

Looking for a great Vancouver bike ride? Consider a jaunt along the 24km (15 mile) seawall route. From Canada Place, head northwest and around Stanley Park toward English Bay, then peddle southeast along Sunset Beach and the north side of False Creek. At Science World, turn and weave along the south side of False Creek toward Granville Island, Kitsilano and, eventually, the verdant University of British Columbia campus. Strap your wheels in a transit-bus bike rack for the journey back to town.

If you want to end your night in style, you're not far from ㉓ **Opus Hotel**, the city's best contemporary boutique property, complete with mod-furnished rooms and feng-shui bed placements. But before you hit the sack, check out the sometimes-raucous nightlife options on the nearby Granville St strip. There are dozens of bars and clubs here and it's the destination of choice for regulars from the suburbs who want to party it up in town. Check what's on at the ㉔ **Commodore Ballroom**, the city's best live music venue and home to an ultrabouncy dancefloor. Alternatively, end your stay in Western Canada's favorite city by shaking your thang at the two-level ㉕ **Caprice** nightclub across the street: it's dominated by party-hard 20-somethings at weekends.

John Lee

TRIP INFORMATION

GETTING THERE
From Portland (505km; 315 miles) or Seattle (225km; 140 miles) head northbound on I-5 and take Hwy 99 from the Blaine border crossing to Vancouver.

DO
Dr Sun Yat-Sen Classical Chinese Garden
An oasis of calm from the city streets – look for the turtles in the pond. ☎ 604-662-3207; www.vancouverchinesegarden.com; 578 Carrall St; adult/child C$10/8; 9:30am-7pm mid-Jun–Aug, with seasonal variations

Granville Island Public Market
Popular with locals and visitors alike and teeming with deli produce and arts and crafts stalls. ☎ 604-666-6477; www.granvilleisland.com; Johnson St, near cnr of Duranleau St; 9am-7pm

Lost Lagoon Nature House
Exhibits and educational talks on Stanley Park's history, wildlife and diverse ecosystem. ☎ 604-257-6908; www.stanleyparkecology.ca; Stanley Park; admission free; 10am-7pm Tue-Sun May-Sep, with seasonal variations Oct-Apr;

Roedde House Museum
This antique-packed 1893 mansion offers colorful insights into early Vancouver life. ☎ 604-684-7040; www.roeddehouse.org; 1415 Barclay St; admission C$5; 1-5pm Tue-Sat, 2-5pm Sun, with seasonal variations May-Sep

Vancouver Aquarium
Styling itself a conservation center, highlights here are the playful otters and glowing jellyfish, plus behind-the-scenes trainer tours. ☎ 604-659-3474; www.vanaqua.org; Stanley Park; adult/child/youth C$25/17/20; 9:30am-5pm Sep-Jun, to 7pm Jul & Aug;

Vancouver Police Centennial Museum
This small, quirky museum illuminates the murky history of crime and vice on the city's gritty streets. ☎ 604-665-3346; www.vancouverpolicemuseum.ca; 240 E Cordova St; adult/child C$7/5; 9am-5pm Mon-Sat

Wanted – Lost Found Canadian
Eccentric little shop dedicated to recycling found objects and materials into artworks and accessories. ☎ 604-633-0178; www.wantedshop.ca; 486 Columbia St; noon-5pm Tue-Sun

EAT
Blue Water Café
Swish Yaletown eatery serves a magnificent menu with dishes of wild and sustainable-harvest fish; there's also a sushi bar. ☎ 604-688-8078; www.bluewatercafe.net; 1095 Hamilton St; mains C$22-44; 5pm-midnight

Bridges
Dazzling-yellow restaurant on Granville Island has fab waterfront views and a hearty menu of pizzas, quesadillas and fish-and-chips. ☎ 604-687-4400; www.bridgesrestaurant.com; 1696 Duranleau St; mains C$12-20; 11:30am-10pm

Hon's Wun-Tun House
Good-value restaurant in the heart of Chinatown that's often stuffed with chatty locals; try the signature dim sum. ☎ 604-688-0871; www.hons.ca; 268 E Keefer St; mains C$6-16; 11:30am-10pm

Raincity Grill
Hit the patio for delectable West Coast dishes or try the popular weekend brunch. ☎ 604-685-7337; www.raincitygrill.com; 1193 Denman St, mains C$20-30; 5-11pm daily & 10:30am-2:30pm Sat & Sun

DRINK
Caprice
Mainstream, bilevel nightclub that's popular with a dressed-to-the-nines younger crowd.

Queues are the norm on weekends, so arrive early. ☎ 604-685-3288; www.capricenight club.com; 967 Granville St; ☟ 9pm-2am Mon-Wed, to 3am Thu-Sat

Chill Winston
Enjoy a martini on the giant patio and peruse the menu of fusion West Coast cuisine.
☎ 604-288-9575; www.chillwinston.com; 3 Alexander St; mains C$10-24; ☟ 11am-1am Mon-Sat, to midnight Sun

Commodore Ballroom
Vancouver's favorite live music venue, with art-deco ballroom flourishes and hoppy dancefloor. Also hosts club nights and all-ages shows. ☎ 604-739-4550; www.live nation.com; 868 Granville St

Irish Heather
With floorboards made from old Guinness barrels and an excellent gastropub menu, the narrow, dual-bar Heather is a locals' favorite. ☎ 604-688-9779; www.irish heather.com; 210 Carrall St; mains C$10-22; ☟ noon-midnight Sun-Wed, to 1am Thu-Sat

Yaletown Brewing Company
Popular pub-style bar and restaurant with a large patio; serves its own brews and hearty grub. ☎ 604-681-2739; www.markjames group.com; 1111 Mainland St; mains C$8-16;

☟ 11:30am-midnight Sun-Wed, to 1am Thu, to 2am Sat & Sun

SLEEP

Granville Island Hotel
This post-and-beam boutique property at the quiet end of the island also has a good onsite brewpub. ☎ 604-683-7373; www.gran villeisland.com; 1253 Johnston St; r C$125-250; 🐾

Opus Hotel
Contemporary boutique accommodation much favored by visiting celebrities; the sleek rooms here are lounge-cool without being austere. Popular see-and-be-seen lobby bar.
☎ 604-642-6787; www.opushotel.com; 322 Davie St; r C$250-550; 🐾

West End Guest House
Heritage, antique-laden B&B with eight rooms, a sun-dappled communal deck and loaner bikes available for touring nearby Stanley Park. ☎ 604-681-2889; www .westendguesthouse.com; 1362 Haro St; r C$130-265

USEFUL WEBSITES
www.discovervancouver.com
www.tourismvancouver.com

LINK YOUR TRIP

www.lonelyplanet.com/trip-planner

FOOD &
DRINK

Pub Crawl Vancouver

WHY GO Expat Brit Nigel Springthorpe knows a thing or two about great beer – hence the 19 distinctive microbrews on tap at his Alibi Room bar in Gastown. But, given the chance, Springthorpe likes to pull up a stool at several other favored drinking holes around his adopted city.

Thirsty Vancouverites with a penchant for BC craft beer have been rolling up at the long tables of the ❶ **Alibi Room** since northern England native Nigel Springthorpe took over the bar a couple of years ago. The edge-of-Gastown boozer serves up the city's largest selection of on-tap regional tipples, including lip-smacking regulars like Old Yale Pale Ale from Chilliwack and organic Back Hand of God Stout from Sorrento. It's like taste-tripping around the province without leaving the city. "I've built some great relationships with the smaller BC brewers because I'm genuinely interested in what they're doing," says Springthorpe, who encourages curious drinkers to experiment with a few sample glasses.

His taste-tripping approach extends to his recommendations for Vancouver's bar scene. Not far from the Alibi – and suitably situated near a statue of pioneer Gassy Jack perched on a whisky barrel – ❷ **Six Acres** symbolizes how far the once-grungy Gastown district has transformed as a nighttime hangout. The exposed-brick bar is warm and animated with chatter and has plenty of eccentric flourishes. Check out the menus bound with old book covers, the bathrooms playing German-language tapes and the selection of three-dozen bottled beers, offered with shareable plates of hearty nosh. "I love their attention to detail and they really influenced me when I was starting out," says Springthorpe.

At the other end of Gastown is the landmark ❸ **Steamworks Brewing Co**, another of Springthorpe's favorites. This two-level bar has a menu of pub classics (pizzas recommended) and makes several brews on site,

TIME
2 days

BEST TIME TO GO
Year-round

START
Gastown

END
South Main St

ALSO GOOD FOR

CITY

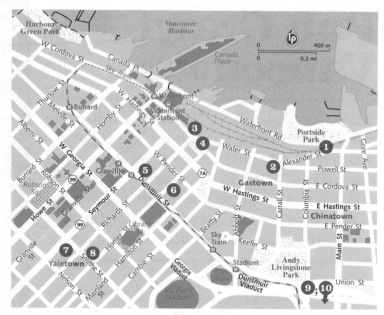

including Oatmeal Stout and Lions Gate Lager. With its mix of tired office workers and younger beer connoisseurs, the cozy, wood-lined downstairs bar is the place to find a perch. "It never feels dark or basementy down there, and it's an ideal place to work through some good beer," says Springthorpe.

GREEN MIXER

If you fancy nattering about all things ecological and making friends with some of Vancouver's most environmentally aware locals, drop by the monthly **Green Drinks** event at Steamworks Brewing Co. Attracting upwards of 100 regulars, the lively, free-entry evening involves sipping a few beers and rubbing shoulders with a diverse crowd of ex-hippies, urban professionals and just about everyone in between. For more information on the event – and events in other cities around the world – visit www.greendrinks.org.

Consider nipping across the street and hitting **4** Shine nightclub for an hour or two. Its compact dancefloor is a local favorite and its intimate back room is ideal for getting to know your new-found dance buddies. Otherwise, it's a short uphill weave from here to what is arguably Vancouver's best traditional bar. With a convenience store dominating the corner, it's easy to miss the unassuming entrance to the upstairs **5** Railway Club. Starting life as a bar for railroad workers more than 70 years ago, it now stages an eclectic roster of nightly live music. If you're lucky, the model train will be trundling around the knickknack-lined ceiling when you visit. Despite the grubby carpets and dinged wooden tables, the Rail, as it is known, has a healthy approach to great microbrews, with taps from BC's Tree Brewing,

Phillips Brewing and Central City Brewing jostling for bar space. "They just do their thing, but they're not complacent about it. It's a very welcoming and convivial place for a drink," comments Springthorpe. It's also not far from the antique-lined heritage ❻ **Victorian Hotel** if you need a place to rest your hangover for the night. Alternatively, try the more contemporary ❼ **Moda Hotel** further south. It's close to Granville St's nightclubs and its rooms have a loungey, mod-cool appeal.

Next up is ❽ **Subeez Café**, a cavernous downtown favorite that comes alive after nightfall. Check out the giant dripping candles theatrically placed around the interior or hit the outside benches on a summer evening. There's a comfortingly large food menu here – Cajun yam fries are recommended – or you can stand around the circular bar supping beers and martinis from the extensive selection. "This place is a Vancouver institution," says Springthorpe. "It has a great Montreal café feel and some decent beers on tap."

Turning his back on downtown, the Alibi boss suggests more adventurous visitors should head up Main St to a clutch of hipster hangouts. A good place to start, 1km south of Union St, is the ❾ **Whip**, where a traditional English-pub exterior is subverted by a laid-back interior lined with local artworks. "They support the same BC breweries I do, so we often draw the same crowds," says Springthorpe, adding the best time to visit is Sunday afternoon, when the Whip cracks open a guest barrel from a distinctive local beermaker.

It's not far from here to one of Vancouver's best-kept bar secrets. The windowless ❿ **Narrow Lounge** – the red light outside tells you it's open – is dark and brooding with high ceilings, filigree chandeliers and wall-mounted antler horns. But if you can find a seat among the artsy regulars (the room seats about 25 people), you'll likely stay all evening, stroking your chin in the half-light. Tuck into a charcuterie

BC BREWERIES & THEIR BEST TIPPLES

- Phillips Brewing (Victoria): Double Chocolate Porter
- Red Truck Beer (North Vancouver): Red Truck Lager
- Howe Sound Brewing (Squamish): Devil's Elbow IPA
- Lighthouse Brewing (Victoria): Beacon IPA
- Central City Brewing (Surrey): Steelhead Oatmeal Stout
- Russell Brewing (Langley): Russell Cream Ale
- Tree Brewing (Kelowna): Hop Head IPA
- R&B Brewing (Vancouver): Red Devil Ale
- Storm Brewing (Vancouver): Highland Scottish Ale
- Crannóg Ales (Sorrento): Back Hand of God Stout

platter and work your way through some creamy ales from R&B Brewing. "This is an excellent little spot and there's always a couple of surprises on the beer menu," says Springthorpe, who adds that he's already planning his next self-directed pub crawl to uncover another round of great Vancouver bars.

John Lee

TRIP INFORMATION

GETTING THERE
From Portland (505km; 315 miles) or Seattle (225km; 140 miles) head northbound on I-5 and then take Hwy 99 from the Blaine border crossing to Vancouver.

DRINK & EAT
Alibi Room
Vancouver's best selection of BC beers served in a convivial, communal-bench setting near the Gastown railway tracks. ☎ 604-623-3383; www.alibi.ca; 157 Alexander St; sample glasses C$3; ☽ 5pm-midnight Tue-Fri, 10am-1am Sat, 10am-3pm Sun

Narrow Lounge
Tiny, mood-lit Main St bar favored by local hipsters; arrive early and tuck into sharing plates, eclectic ales and martinis. ☎ 778-737-5206; www.narrowlounge.com; 1898 Main St; ☽ 5am-midnight

Railway Club
Old-school, English-style pub setting with regional microbrews and live music nightly. ☎ 604-681-1625; www.therailwayclub.com; 579 Dunsmuir St; ☽ noon-2am Mon-Thu, noon-3am Fri, 2pm-3am Sat, 4pm-midnight Sun

Shine
Sexy subterranean nightclub attracts a younger crowd as intent on dancing as they are on drinking. ☎ 604-408-4321; www.shinenightclub.com; 364 Water St; ☽ 10pm-2am Sun, Mon & Wed, to 4am Fri & Sat

Six Acres
Quirky watering hole with a giant bottled-beer selection, tasty sharing plates and a small patio. ☎ 604-488-0110; www.sixacres.ca; 203 Carrall St; ☽ noon-midnight Tue-Thu, noon-1am Fri, 5pm-1am Sat

Steamworks Brewing Co
This handsome bar is arguably Vancouver's best brewpub and also serves a good array of pub grub – head downstairs for cozy quaffing. ☎ 604-689-2739; www.steamworks.com; 375 Water St; ☽ 11:30am-midnight

Subeez Café
Atmospheric nighttime hangout with good grub, outdoor seating and a cave-cozy, candlelit interior. ☎ 604-687-6107; www.subeez.com; 891 Homer St; ☽ 10am-1am Mon-Sat, to midnight Sun

Whip
Art-lined bar popular with the Main St set; drop by on Cask Sunday for regional guest kegs. ☎ 604-874-4687; www.thewhiprestaurant.com; 209 E 6th Ave; ☽ 11:30am-1am Mon-Fri, 10am-1am Sat, 10am-midnight Sun

SLEEP
Moda Hotel
Modish white-painted rooms with a lounge flavor have revitalized this once-grungy hotel property into a far swankier option. Close to the Granville St entertainment strip. ☎ 604-683-4251; www.modahotel.ca; 900 Seymour St; r C$89-199; ☷

Victorian Hotel
Well-located and immaculately maintained downtown heritage property with creaky floors, antique-lined rooms and a welcoming ambience. Staggering distance from several nearby bars. ☎ 604-681-6369; www.victorianhotel.ca; 514 Homer St; r C$99-189

USEFUL WEBSITES
www.bcbeer.ca
www.tourismvancouver.com

LINK YOUR TRIP
www.lonelyplanet.com/trip-planner

FOOD &
DRINK

Teatime in Victoria

WHY GO BC's waterfront capital was built upon crusty olde English traditions, but afternoon tea in today's Victoria is not just about cucumber sandwiches and clotted cream. Trawl the city for a good cuppa and you'll come across some surprisingly cosmopolitan enclaves, plus side dishes of colorful history and culture.

TIME
2 days

BEST TIME TO GO
Jun – Sep

START
Inner Harbour

END
Esquimalt

ALSO GOOD FOR

HISTORY &
CULTURE

Historic Victoria is dripping with tea-flavored traditions fueled by generations of robust seniors who view Assam as a life-giving force. But behind the colonial facade, the picturesque old city has quietly evolved in recent years and even afternoon tea has changed with the times. Visitors can still don their monocles and sip like an ancient Brit, but they can also dunk their shortbread in some unexpected experiences.

Traditional tea drinkers quaff at the ivy-clad ❶ **Fairmont Empress Hotel Tea Lobby**, overlooking the Inner Harbour like a grand but slightly dotty Miss Haversham. With a tinkling piano accompaniment in a high-ceilinged dining room lined with Edwardian furnishings, silver-service tea is proffered by waistcoated staffers. Ask for recommendations, but consider the hotel's Centennial Blend, a cocktail of black teas from five regions. It's served with strawberries and cream, followed by tiered plates of dainty sandwiches, fruit scones, rich cakes and an indulgent chocolate cup.

Strolling to the nearby ❷ **Royal BC Museum** will help walk off your indulgence. The province's best museum, it houses atmospheric First Nations galleries and an evocative re-creation of the sights and sounds of a pioneer-era street. Save time for the museum's exterior, where a mini-forest of bright totem poles and a clutch of preserved old buildings jostle for camera time. Across the street, the turreted ❸ **Parliament Buildings** offers an illuminating free walking tour –

BEST TRIP

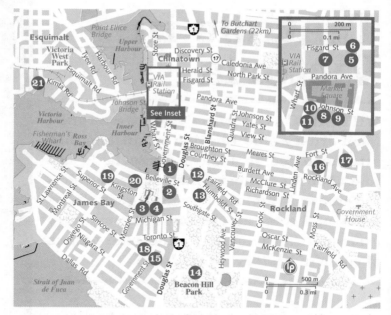

check out the golden statue of Captain George Vancouver peering down from the central dome before you head inside. The subterranean ④ **Legislative Dining Room** here serves great-value meals and is a well-kept local secret.

Wandering north on Government St, you'll soon come to the edge of Canada's oldest Chinatown and arguably Victoria's most exciting tea experience. Founded by Daniela Cubelic, ⑤ **Silk Road** takes a winery approach, with tastings of the leafy tipple. One side of her shop offers a kaleidoscopic array of quality tea-making paraphernalia – "We can't sell a teapot that drips," says Cubelic reassuringly – while the other has a long tasting bar enlivened by percolating jazz music. The tastings frequently cause surprises, with quaffers discovering a thirst for flavors they would never try on their own. For drivers, Cubelic recommends jasmine green tea for its combination of caffeine and calming effects.

ASK A LOCAL

"Victoria's English settlers used to buy their tea in Chinatown, so there's been an Asian tea tradition here at least as long as the English one. In fact, of all the places in Canada, Victoria has always had the best tea."

Daniela Cubelic, Silk Road tea shop, Vancouver, BC

It's a short hop from here to the brightly decorated ⑥ **Chinatown Gate**. Settled in 1858, Victoria's Chinatown is now just a short stretch of grocery emporiums and twinkling neon restaurant signs, but there's still a permanent presence of old Asian residents keeping things authentic. The area's highlight is **7** **Fan Tan Alley**, a narrow brick-lined passageway now colonized by a tarot store, vintage-record outlet and a barbershop that looks like it hasn't changed since the 1940s.

Nearby Johnson St offers a more contemporary take on shopping. Once a dilapidated strip of crumbling colonial buildings, the edifices here have been brightly repainted and now house independent boutiques and stores selling wacky artworks and T-shirts. Now designated as LoJo (Lower Johnson), the best shop here is **8** **Smoking Lily**, a tiny storefront hawking locally designed skirts and tops with intriguing insect and seahorse prints. Alternatively, **9** **Fiber Options** offers environmentally sound clothing, soaps and just about everything else.

"…think organic chai Darjeeling and Japanese popcorn tea – served in transparent teapots."

If you're grinding to a halt, break your tea habit with a late-afternoon java at nearby **10** **Willie's Bakery & Café**. Often filled with chatty patrons, this brick-lined nook serves bulging homebaked pastries – you won't regret cramming in a cinnamon bun – and is also a popular breakfast spot. Above the café, **11** **Isabella's Guest Suites** are a pair of contemporary self-contained suites for travelers who like the idea of staying in a home away from home.

Back on the Darjeeling trail, Victoria's newest tearoom is in a developing area of downtown that's oddly called Humboldt Valley. Rather than rolling hills and dense forest, it's actually a street of swanky new apartment blocks in a former no-man's-land of parking lots. With new residents come new businesses and one of these is **12** **Mela's Tearoom**. Chefing-up an elegant, contemporary version of afternoon tea, its menu of organic croissants, freshly baked quiches and exquisite cakes changes daily and keeps the regulars happy. Watch out for the dangerously addictive chocolate orange brownie, especially if you've left your pants with the elasticized waist at home.

It's not far from here to **13** **St Ann's Academy**, a magnificent Victorian school building surrounded by attractive gardens dripping with heritage fruit trees. There are usually a few volunteers around in summer to tell you all about the site's interesting provenance. Continue on from here and you'll soon come to Victoria's finest natural jewel. **14** **Beacon Hill Park** is an ideal combination of planted garden areas and wild and woody sections where it's just you and the wind-whipped clifftop trees. Look out for the marker denoting Mile 0 of Hwy 1, the western tip of the Trans-Canada Hwy.

Back along Government St, you'll encounter the legacy of Emily Carr (1871–1945), BC's most famous artist and a woman who appreciated West Coast nature perhaps more than anyone. With its yellow-painted clapboard exterior, the ⑮ **Emily Carr House** is one of Victoria's most handsome heritage homes. Many of its rooms have been re-created to recall Carr's life here, and some of her swirling forest and First Nations canvases dot the walls. If you have time, consider a 10-minute bus ride (No 14) from town to the ⑯ **Art Gallery of Greater Victoria**, which has an even bigger Carr collection. Near the gallery, the magnificent ⑰ **Craigdarroch Castle** is also worth a visit. A fanciful confection of turrets and towers, it's lined with antiques and features re-created period rooms from the Victorian era.

It's worth spending some time wandering the streets of old houses around James Bay – you'll likely pass the ⑱ **James Bay Inn**, a well-preserved old hotel with not-quite-antique furnishings and a wide array of comfortable, well-priced rooms. Head further northwest and you'll come across the swanky ⑲ **Oswego Hotel**, the kind of swish, contemporary accommodation that would be equally at home in trendy Vancouver. Just around the corner from here, the ⑳ **Hotel Grand Pacific's Pacific Restaurant** also offers one Victoria's best alternative afternoon teas.

DETOUR Extend your Vancouver Island leaf odyssey for half a day with afternoon tea at the **Butchart Gardens** (www.butchartgardens.com). The Dining Room Restaurant is an idyllic Edwardian setting for salmon sandwiches and quiche savories, followed by Grand Marnier truffles and some marzipan Napoleons (you'll just have to visit if you want to find out what they are). Your tea is served in a proper "brown betty" teapot that looks hewn from solid rock. The gardens are a 30-minute drive north of Victoria via Hwy 17. Take exit 18 and follow the signs.

Snag a window seat in the otherwise nondescript room and you'll be treated to a surprisingly diverse Asia Pacific fusion tea service. There's an excellent selection of exotic leaf teas – think organic chai Darjeeling and Japanese popcorn tea – served in transparent teapots. The accompanying triple tier of treats includes candy smoked salmon bannock, cucumber wasabi cream cheese sandwiches and dainty desserts such as chai brûlée, cashew shortbreads and delectable Thomas Haas chocolates and soft candied fruits.

If you still have room in your belly, make the long walk or short cab ride to ㉑ **Spinnakers Gastro Brewpub** to toast the end of your Victoria odyssey. Canada's first brewpub, it's an ideal place to kick back and watch the sun set over the water. The Blue Bridge Double IPA is enough to make anyone graduate from a tea-only diet.

John Lee

TRIP INFORMATION

GETTING THERE
Drive south from Vancouver 30km (18 miles) to Tsawwassen for BC Ferries services to Swartz Bay (1½ hours), then take Hwy 17 for 30km (18 miles) into downtown Victoria.

DO

Art Gallery of Greater Victoria
Comprehensive Emily Carr collection, plus regular temporary exhibitions and lively events roster. ☎ 250-384-4101; www.aggv .bc.ca; 1040 Moss St; adult/child C$12/2; ☼ 10am-5pm Fri-Wed, to 9pm Thu

Craigdarroch Castle
An elegant wood-lined Victorian mansion built by an industrialist who died before its completion. ☎ 250-592-5323; www.the castle.ca; 1050 Joan Cres; adult/child C$11.75/3.75; ☼ 10am-4:30pm Sep– mid-Jun, 10am-7pm mid-Jun–Aug

Emily Carr House
Historic, antique-lined residence of BC's most famous artist. ☎ 250-383-5843; www.emi lycarr.com; 207 Government St; adult/child C$6/4; ☼ 11am-4pm Tue-Sat May-Sep, reduced hours Oct-Apr

Fairmont Empress Hotel Tea Lobby
Grand old lady of the Inner Harbour offers Victoria's most famous afternoon tea. ☎ 250-389-2727; www.fairmont.com/e mpress; 721 Government St; afternoon tea per person C$49-55; ☼ noon-5pm

Fiber Options
Ecofriendly store offering cool green options on all your clothing and beyond purchases. ☎ 250-386-4367; www.ecoeverything.com; 577 Johnson St; ☼ 10am-5:30pm Mon-Sat, noon-5pm Sun

Hotel Grand Pacific: Pacific Restaurant
Asian-fusion afternoon tea with plenty of exotic brews and spicy baked treats. ☎ 250-380-4458; www.hotelgrandpacific.com; 463 Belleville St; afternoon tea per person C$36; ☼ 2-4:30pm Jul & Aug, 2-4:30pm Thu-Sat Sep-Jun

Mela's Tearoom
Adjoining the Winchester Gallery, this elegant tea nook offers exquisites tipples and great fresh baking. ☎ 250-382-8528; 792 Humboldt St; afternoon tea for two C$39.95; ☼ 10am-5:30pm

Parliament Buildings
A magnificent turreted edifice that's still the seat of BC government; offers free tours. ☎ 250-387-1400; www.leg.bc.ca; 501 Belleville St; ☼ 8:30am-5pm May-Sep, 8:30am-5pm Mon-Fri Oct-Apr

Royal BC Museum
Victoria's leading attraction covers the province from prehistoric to postcolonial times. ☎ 250-356-7226; www.royalbcmuseum .bc.ca; 675 Belleville St; adult/child C$14/9.50 ☼ 9am-5pm, to 10pm Fri & Sat mid-Jun–Sep; ♿

St Ann's Academy
Preserved Victorian boarding school set in elegant landscaped grounds. ☎ 250-935-8829; www.stannsacademy.com; 835 Humboldt St; adult/child C$5/2; ☼ 10am-4pm mid-May–Oct, by appointment Nov–mid-May

Silk Road
Contemporary tea shop with must-have accessories and winery-style tasting sessions; check the website for extra events. ☎ 250-704-2688; www.silkroadtea.com; 1624 Government St; ☼ 10am-6pm Mon-Sat, 11am-5pm Sun

Smoking Lily
Victoria's coolest (and possibly smallest) shop, selling artsy designer clothing for pale and interesting hipsters. ☎ 250-382-5459; www .smokinglily.com; 569 Johnson St; ☼ 11am-5:30pm Thu-Sat, noon-5pm Sun & Mon

EAT & DRINK

Legislative Dining Room
Subterranean Parliament Buildings restaurant serves regional dishes to MPs and in-the-know

visitors. ☎ 250-387-3959; Room 606, Parliament Buildings, 501 Belleville St; mains C$6-16; ⏱ 9am-3pm Mon-Thu, to 2pm Fri

Spinnakers Gastro Brewpub
Victoria's best pub serves its own great brews and finger-licking bistro meals and has smashing sunset views. ☎ 250-386-2739; www.spinnakers.com; 308 Catherine St; mains C$11-20; ⏱ 11am-11pm

Willie's Bakery & Café
A laid-back brick-lined hangout that's good for coffee and baked treats; the heaping breakfasts are also a local fave. ☎ 250-381-8414; 537 Johnson St; mains C$8-12; ⏱ 8am-5pm, with seasonal variations

SLEEP

Isabella's Guest Suites
Two immaculate, self-contained suites in the heart of downtown, close to all the action. ☎ 250-595-3815; www.isabellasbb.com; 537 Johnson St; r C$150-225

James Bay Inn
This charming hotel has plenty of character, a plethora of comfy room configurations – no two seem alike – and a friendly downstairs bar. ☎ 250-384-7151; www.jamesbayinn.bc.ca; 270 Government St; r C$130-225

Oswego Hotel
Sophisticated boutique property oozing West Coast style – the upper floors have panoramic waterfront views. ☎ 250-294-7500; www.oswegovictoria.com; 500 Oswego St; r from C$250; 🐾

USEFUL WEBSITES
www.bcferries.com
www.tourismvictoria.com

LINK YOUR TRIP
www.lonelyplanet.com/trip-planner

TRIP
40 48 Hours in Vancouver p267
43 Southern Vancouver Island Tour p283
48 Vancouver Coastal Loop p305

Southern Vancouver Island Tour

WHY GO Shaped by the Pacific and striped with ancient, fern-lined forests, Vancouver Island is an ideal rustic retreat for those who like to explore off the beaten path. Heading west from Victoria, you can uncover wild, wave-battered coastlines before looping inland to historic communities flavored with tasty farms and wineries.

Depart north from Victoria on Hwy 1 then weave west on Hwy 14 and it won't be long before the tidy city streets are replaced with the fenced farmsteads and overgrown woodlands of ❶ **Sooke**. Surprisingly close to the comparatively bustling provincial capital, the southern tip of Vancouver Island is all about the locals. You'll drive by several neighborhood restaurants and a clutch of homey B&Bs; ideal if you feel like sticking around and tapping the quiet community vibe. Alternatively, just drop into ❷ **Mom's Café**, a throwback old-school diner with vinyl banquettes and a predilection for heaping fruit pies.

For an introduction to the area, stop in at ❸ **Sooke Region Museum**, which has intriguing exhibits on the district's tough pioneer past, including a tiny preserved cottage that's one of the island's oldest structures. If the outdoors is more your thing, bring a picnic and consider stopping for the afternoon at ❹ **Sooke Potholes Provincial Park**. A signposted drive 5km (3 miles) from Hwy 14 just after Sooke, it's a popular swimming and rock-pool-hopping spot – every local kid hangs out here in summer – and ideal for an hour of languid sun worshipping.

Dry off and continue past Jordan River into the dramatic coastal wilderness of ❺ **Juan de Fuca Provincial Park** – Hwy 14 takes you right through it. There are several good stop-off points along this rugged stretch, each with memorable views of the rocky, ocean-carved

TIME
3 days

DISTANCE
**257km
(160 miles)**

BEST TIME TO GO
Jul – Sep

START
Sooke

END
Victoria

ALSO GOOD FOR

FOOD &
DRINK

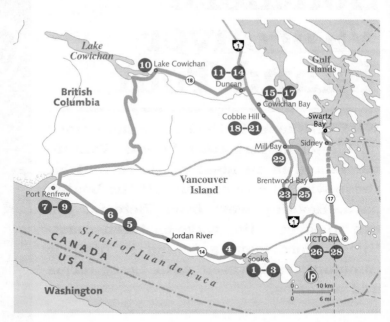

seafront where trees cling for dear life and whales slide past just off the coast. **6** **China Beach** is recommended and it also has campsites. If you're a hardy hiker, the 47km (29 mile) Juan de Fuca Marine Trail (www.juandefuca marinetrail.com) winds along a spine of little beaches here. Due to the slippery rocks and dense forest, it takes a few days to complete the trek.

If you prefer viewing the wilderness without stretching your legs, continue your rustic drive to the little town of **7** **Port Renfrew**, about 64km (40 miles) from Sooke. This is a good base for hitting the area's woodland and waterfront trails (not all of which are challenging), and Renfrew's **8** **Lighthouse Pub & Restaurant** (its red roof is a hard-to-miss landmark) is an ideal pit stop for hearty pub grub and a chat with the locals. If you plan to stick around in the region, book ahead in summer for a night at the **9** **Trailhead Resort**, where accommodation includes private wooden cabins and a handsome, rustic-chic lodge.

Wave a tearful goodbye to the coast the next day and curve inland toward the town of **10** **Lake Cowichan**. This is another 64km (40 mile) stretch (without services) through the heart of the island and some parts of the route comprise loose-gravel logging roads, although it is slowly being upgraded. You'll encounter cathedral-calm old-growth woodland here where towering spruce and Douglas firs, many more than five centuries old, dominate the landscape. Once you emerge from the forest and reach the lake (the island's second largest), you'll be cruising east along Hwy 18 with the glassy-calm waters of Lake Cowichan on your left. Fishing, hiking and kayaking are popular here and several campgrounds punctuate the route.

"…towering spruce and Douglas firs, many more than five centuries old, dominate the landscape."

It's 32km (20 miles) from here to ⑪ Duncan, one of the region's biggest towns. If you're hungry, hold on until you reach ⑫ Duncan Garage, a landmark locals' hangout that's been transformed into a café, bookstore and organic grocery market. Grab a bulging omelette brunch and enjoy the view overlooking the heritage train station – which also houses the lovely little ⑬ Cowichan Valley Museum – then wander the town, counting the dozens of totem poles dotting the area. You can meet their makers at the excellent ⑭ Quw'utsun' Cultural Centre, a re-created Cowichan First Nations village with artisan demonstrations.

Leaving Duncan behind, hit Hwy 1 south and you'll soon come to one of Vancouver Island's most attractive waterfront communities. On a mountain- and forest-lined sea inlet, ⑮ Cowichan Bay – called Cow Bay by the locals – is a string of brightly painted clapboard structures, many built on piles over the water. It was originally a fishing and boat-building settlement, and the heritage buildings have been colonized by artisan studios, ice-cream shacks and cheesemakers. This is a good place to gather a picnic, so start your food shopping at ⑯ True Grain Bread, where hot baking aromas envelop you the moment you push through the bead-curtain entrance. You'll soon be eagerly clutching a warm bag of ginger cookies and French chocolate buns.

If you're looking for a more substantial dinner, drop by the bay's smashing ⑰ Masthead Restaurant, occupying an old white-painted 1863 hotel building. Snag a patio seat and tuck into local foraged morels, sweet spot prawns and tipples from 10 regional wineries. Keep in mind that parking can be severely limited here on balmy summer evenings, so arrive early if you want a spot near the restaurant. Check into your accommodations for the night – the tranquil, forest-surrounded ⑱ Ambraden Pond B&B is a 15-minute drive away in ⑲ Cobble Hill. The B&B's contemporary-furnished suites overlooking the lake are popular with couples, but there's also a self-contained apartment if you'd prefer a kitchen-equipped home away from home.

The next day can be spent winding around the Cobble Hill area following your taste buds. A labyrinth of gently rolling farmlands, wineries and pioneer-flavored communities, here the Cowichan Valley is all about getting lost. En route to the following highlights, duck off the beaten path whenever you see signs offering lip-smacking honey, preserves, fruit wine or just about anything that takes your fancy. Make sure you visit **20 Merridale Estate Cidery**, with its rustic-chic buildings, alfresco dining (try an oven-baked pizza) and free tastings: the smooth fortified cider is a surprisingly good sweet dessert wine. Alternatively, try some delectable local organic chocolate at **21 Organic Fair Farm & Garden** – the blueberry and hazelnut Westcoaster bar is best.

If you can fit behind your steering wheel after all that scoffing, continue south along Hwy 1 to **22 Mill Bay** where you can drive onto a BC Ferries boat service for a sigh-inducing 25-minute crossing to **23 Brentwood Bay**. And if you're still hungry, drop in for a local seafood feast at **24 SeaGrille**, the restaurant at the luxurious waterfront Brentwood Bay Lodge. If the halibut with truffle Dijon is available, snap it up. You can walk off your increasing excess at the nearby **25 Butchart Gardens**, BC's most famous botanical attraction. The century-old landscaped gardens, which originated from an attempt to beautify an old cement factory site, have been cleverly planned to ensure there's always something in bloom, no matter what the season. Escape the summertime crowds here in the peaceful Japanese garden.

DETOUR Instead of heading to Victoria from Brentwood Bay, consider side-tripping 20 minutes north to **Sidney**, signposted from Hwy 17. This sunny seaside community proclaims itself "Canada's only booktown." Almost every other business is a bookstore, some specializing in crime or travel tomes, others offering more dog-eared, used volumes. There are also plenty of restaurants to keep you otherwise engaged – head to the end of the little pier for fish and chips with a view. Information at www.sidneybooktown.ca.

You're now just 20 minutes, via Hwy 17, from downtown **26 Victoria**. Follow the signs south for the big smoke and end your Vancouver Island odyssey with a bracing cliff-top walk in **27 Beacon Hill Park**. There's a plethora of hotel options in the city and also several regionally focused restaurants that are well worth an extra day's stay. Consider **28 Camille's**: an intimate downtown joint combining adventurous takes on seasonal ingredients; it's a fitting end to your foodie-flavored wilderness trek.

John Lee

TRIP INFORMATION

GETTING THERE

From Vancouver, head south for Tsawwassen BC Ferries services to Swartz Bay (1½ hours), then drive 30 km (18 miles) on Hwy 17 to Victoria.

DO

Butchart Gardens

BC's favorite landscaped garden attraction, with year-round blooming policy. ☎ 250-652-5256; www.butchartgardens.com; 800 Benvenuto Ave, Brentwood Bay; adult/child/youth C$26.50/3/13.25, with seasonal reductions; ☼ daily from 9am with seasonal variations in closing time, 9am-10pm Jun-Aug

Cowichan Valley Museum

Knickknack filled museum in Duncan's red, gable-roofed train station – ask about its guided downtown walking tours. ☎ 250-746-6612; www.cowichanvalleymuseum.bc.ca; 130 Duncan Ave, Duncan; adult/child C$2/free; ☼ 10am-4pm Mon-Sat Jun-Sep, with seasonal variations

Juan de Fuca Provincial Park

Rugged stretch of forests, cliffs and sandy little beaches with hiking trails and stop-offs where you can pull over and inhale the coastal vistas. ☎ 250-474-1336; www.bcparks.ca

Merridale Estate Cidery

Free tastings, orchard walks (including a fairy trawl for kids) and a restaurant that makes an ideal lunch stop. ☎ 250-743-4296; www.merridalecider.com; 1230 Merridale Rd, Cobble Hill; ☼ 10:30am-5pm; ⅊

Organic Fair Farm & Garden

Landscaped gardens and a small farmstead producing organic chocolate including Canadiana, Little Monkey and Westcoaster. ☎ 250-733-2035; www.organicfair.com; 1935 Doran Rd, Cobble Hill; ☼ 10am-5pm, with seasonal variations; ⅊

Quw'utsun' Cultural Centre

A longhouse and artisan studio introduction to the Cowichan First Nations, with summertime dance performances. ☎ 250-746-8119; www.quwutsun.ca; 200 Cowichan Way, Duncan; adult/child/youth C$10/2/8; ☼ 10am-4pm Jul & Aug, with seasonal variations; ⅊

Sooke Potholes Provincial Park

Rock pools, swimming, sunbathing and rustic picnicking are popular at this locals' favorite park. ☎ 250-474-1336; www.bcparks.ca; Sooke River Rd, Sooke; ⅊

Sooke Region Museum

Illuminating the area's hardy pioneer days with preserved buildings and jagged-toothed logging machinery. ☎ 250-642-6351; www.sookeregionmuseum.com; 2070 Phillips Rd, Sooke; admission free; ☼ 9am-5pm, closed Mon in winter

EAT

Camille's

Try the adventurous C$50 tasting menu at this cozy, candlelit nook – char, caribou and wild boar are often available. ☎ 250-381-3433; 45 Bastion Sq, Victoria; mains C$18-28; ☼ 5:30-10pm Tue-Sat

Duncan Garage

The center of all the Duncan action, this refurbished heritage building houses an organic coffee shop with treats, brunches and light lunches (including vegetarian options). ☎ 250-748-6223; 330 Duncan St, Duncan; mains C$4-8; ☼ 7:30am-5pm

Lighthouse Pub & Restaurant

This large pub and family restaurant combo is the area's main meeting place and a good spot for rocking fish and chips. ☎ 250-647-5505; Parkinson Rd, Port Renfrew; mains C$8-14; ☼ 11am-10pm

Masthead Restaurant

A wood-built waterfront setting complements a menu of regional Cowichan Valley ingredients, from duck to seafood, and wine. ☎ 250-748-3714; www.themastheadrestaurant.com;

1705 Cowichan Bay Rd, Cowichan Bay; mains C$20-30; ☎ 5-10pm

Mom's Café
Authentic old-school diner with home-cooked comfort foods, giant fruit pies and a real jukebox. ☎ 250-642-3314; 2036 Shields Rd, Sooke; mains C$5-13; ☎ 8am-10pm; ☎

SeaGrille
Tuck into seasonal meat and seafood, plus a glass or two of BC wine. Luxury accommodations is also available. ☎ 250-544-5100; www.brentwoodbaylodge.com; 849 Verdier Ave, Brentwood Bay; mains C$18-30; ☎ 5:30-11pm

True Grain Bread
Exemplary bakery offers mouthwatering loaves and sweet baked treats fresh from the oven. ☎ 250-746-7664; Cowichan Bay Rd, Cowichan Bay; ☎ 8am-6pm Wed-Sat, 8am-5pm Sun

SLEEP

Ambraden Pond B&B
Secluded woodland B&B with an idyllic pondside setting; accommodations include two rooms with contemporary furnishings rooms and a self-contained suite with a kitchen. ☎ 250-743-2562; www.ambradenpond.com; 971 Aros Rd, Cobble Hill; r from C$150

China Beach Campground
Popular with summer trail hikers. The basic facilities include pit toilets and cold taps. ☎ 604-689-9025; www.discovercamping.ca; Juan de Fuca Provincial Park; tent sites C$16; ☎

Trailhead Resort
Fishing charter guests take precedence at peak times, but there are usually enough rooms and cabins for nonfishing visitors. ☎ 250-647-5468; www.trailhead-resort.com; 17268 Parkinson Rd, Port Renfrew; r C$125-250

USEFUL WEBSITES
www.cowichan.bc.ca
www.vancouverisland.travel

LINK YOUR TRIP
www.lonelyplanet.com/trip-planner

Whistler Adrenaline Rush

WHY GO Canada's favorite alpine resort, gable-roofed Whistler combines a plethora of wintertime snow activities with a surprisingly diverse array of summer action for adrenaline junkies. Drop by in either season for a pulse-popping good time, and rub shoulders with ski bunnies and bike barons at choice bars and restaurants.

TIME
2 days

BEST TIME TO GO
**Dec – Feb;
Jul – Aug**

START
**Whistler
Village**

END
**Whistler
Village**

Your legs will feel like limp spaghetti when you're teetering on a tiny platform 150ft up a fir tree between Whistler and Blackcomb Mountains. Luckily, you'll be in full harness and after a few seconds you'll be soaring over the forest, screaming like a banshee and ruing the fact that it's over way too quickly. Happily there are several more ziplines on which to practice your yelling at ❶ **Ziptrek Ecotours**, BC's favorite breakfast-agitating activity.

The famed twin peaks of Whistler and Blackcomb may be the mountain venue for the 2010 Olympic and Paralympic Winter Games, but summer is when the real thrill seekers come out to play. Just check out the bruise-inducing selection of mountain-, forest- and river-based activities at the one-stop ❷ **Whistler Activity Centre**.

On the melted ski slopes, ❸ **Whistler Mountain Bike Park** creates most of those bruises. Accessed via lifts at the village's southern end, the barreling downhill runs are an orgy of jumps, beams and bridges winding along 250km (155 miles) of forested trails. You don't have to be a bike courier to stand the pace: routes range from green (easy) to black (advanced).

"Riders choose their level as they ride," says Bernie Duval owner of ❹ **Fanatyk Co**, a popular bike-rental shop. "The bottom part is accessible to everyone – that's where most people stay – while the top part

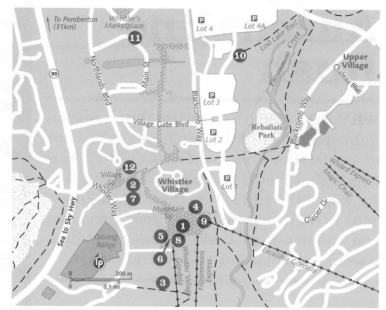

is steeper, greasier and ruder," he says, adding that Crank it Up is his favorite trail. He also suggests exploring regional routes like Comfortably Numb and the ever-popular Valley Trail, an easy 15km (9 mile) Whistler 101 loop lined with lake, meadow and mountain-chateau vistas. Free trail maps are available at the Activity Centre.

DETOUR Escape the slopes with a side trip to Pemberton, 20 minutes north of Whistler on Hwy 99. Here you'll find the **Pemberton Soaring Centre** (www.pembertonsoaring.com), where you'll be strapped into the front of a glider (the pilot sits behind you), towed into the sky and let loose like a bird. Surfing the currents, you'll pass over glacial crags and verdant valley scenes – tell the pilot you're a thrill fan and he'll treat you to some extra banks and rolls.

If you prefer to work your arm muscles, ⑤ **Whistler River Adventures** offers the kind of activity where it's OK to wet your pants. The wildest of its three tours is a day-long rollercoaster along the Elaho and Squamish Rivers. You'll be kitted up with a wetsuit and arranged with an oar around the edges of the eight-person boat – the guide stands in the middle and keeps order with a giant paddle. It's one of the best ways to see outback BC: Keep your water-whipped eyes open for tumbling waterfalls, looming glaciers and the occasional bear. You can also partake of some optional cliff jumping along the way.

After all that activity, rub your muscles at the village's ⑥ **Garibaldi Lift Company**, where you can absorb a Kootenay Mountain Ale and a bulging, house-specialty burger while the bikers (or skiers) clatter downhill outside. It's a five-minute stroll from here to ❼ **Adara Hotel**, Whistler's coolest boutique option. Rooms have an artsy, minimalist élan; the lobby looks like a ski lodge from a '70s James Bond movie. Hang out in your tuxedo for maximum impact.

Winter brings its own selection of white-knuckle Whistler experiences, especially since there are more than 8100 acres of accessible terrain stretched across a one-vertical-mile drop studded with chutes, bowls and long cruisers. Savvy powder hogs can beat the crowds with an early-morning Fast Tracks ticket at the ❽ **Whistler Village Gondola**. It's a slightly different story on next door's Blackcomb Mountain, accessed via the adjacent ❾ **Excalibur Gondola**. Blackcomb is more about terrain parks where obstacles are laid out for your skiing and snowboarding pleasure.

Since thrills don't have to be scary (just drinking in the icicle-covered Christmas-card views here can be breathtaking), ❿ **Lost Lake** on the edge of the village is an ideal spot to wind down after all that pulse-crunching exertion. This tranquil, heavily forested wilderness is a magical locale for dead-of-winter snowshoeing and cross-country skiing – some trails are floodlit for atmospheric nighttime trawls. It's also popular for summer hikes, where black bear appearances are not uncommon (stay calm and back away slowly).

Whatever the season, Whistler's best comfort-food hangout is the

ROSS REBLIATI'S WHISTLER

Recommendations from the 1998 Olympic snowboarding gold medalist

"Whistler and Blackcomb are two of the biggest mountains most people will ever have the chance to ski or ride on. My favorite runs on a powder day are Cat Skinner, Upper and Lower Gear Jammer, Ross' Gold and Ross' Gold Trees as well as the Chimney and CBC North. These are all found on Blackcomb. There are plenty more runs or lines hidden in the trees, out of sight from the average visitor. Whistler Mountain has lots of amazing runs that are easily accessible to the experienced rider, but for the typical visitor runs under the Red Chair, Christmas Trees and the vast selection of lines found on the Harmony Chair offer deep powder turns that never give you the feeling of being lost. I should mention that I have barely scratched the surface of possibilities. My main recommendation for visitors is get on the hill early and, unless you are an amazing athlete, be prepared to make around three or four quality runs before lunch. Then take it easy for the rest of the day: beer and sun or beer and hot tub or beer and physiotherapy. See you there!"

⓫ **Beet Root Café** where porridge-thick soups and hearty wraps are a specialty. But if you want to reward yourself for not breaking too many limbs during your weekend of derring-do, head to ⓬ **Araxi**, the village's fine-dining superstar. It's the kind of place you can swap war stories at the swanky bar before tucking into seasonal BC specialties such as Vancouver Island octopus, Fraser Valley duck and Queen Charlotte halibut – a menu for thrill seekers of the culinary variety.

John Lee

TRIP INFORMATION

GETTING THERE

From Vancouver, head north on Hwy 99 via Squamish: Whistler Village is 127km (79 miles) from the big city.

DO

Excalibur Gondola

Blackcomb Mountain's main lift (one of 37 lifts servicing the twin peaks) is right next door to the Village Gondola. ☎ 604-932-3434; Whistler Village; 2-day lift tickets adult/child/youth C$148/77/126, reduced off-season; 👤

Fanatyk Co

Wide selection of rental bikes – book ahead in summer – and winter ski rentals. ☎ 604-938-9455; www.fanatykco.com; Whistler Mountain base, Whistler Village; 🕑 10am-5pm mid-May–mid-Oct, with seasonal variations

Whistler Activity Centre

A one-stop shop for booking your wild winter- or summer-season activities throughout the mountain region, run by the Tourism Whistler folks. ☎ 604-938-2769; 4010 Whistler Way, Whistler Village; 🕑 9am-5pm

Whistler Mountain Bike Park

An obstacle-driven downhill tangle of trails with something for all skill levels. ☎ 604-932-3434; www.whistlerbike.com; Whistler Mountain base, Whistler Village; 1-day ticket adult/child/youth C$49/27/43; 🕑 10am-5pm mid-May–mid-Oct, to 8pm mid-Jun–Aug; 👤

Whistler River Adventures

From family-friendly runs to eyeball-popping rapids, there's a paddle for every skill and energy level here. ☎ 604-932-3532; www.whistlerriver.com; Village Gondola, Whistler Village; adult/child from C$75/54; 🕑 mid-May–Aug; 👤

Whistler Village Gondola

Whistler Mountain's main lift – consider an advance-purchase Fresh Tracks tickets for an early morning (7am) crowd-beating ski. ☎ 604-932-3434; Whistler Village; 2-day lift tickets adult/child/youth C$148/77/126, reduced price in summer; 👤

Ziptrek Ecotours

Choose from two five-cable zipline courses that, after initial training, will have you screaming with gut-quivering pleasure. ☎ 604-935-0001; www.ziptrek.com; Carleton Lodge, Whistler Village; adult/child C$119/99; 🕑 year-round; 👤

EAT & SLEEP

Adara Hotel

An immaculate, service-savvy contemporary hotel with an ironic eye for artsy details – hence the stylized antler horns in the lobby. ☎ 604-905-4665; www.adarahotel.com; 4122 Village Green, Whistler Village; r C$250-450; 🐾

Araxi

Arguably Whistler's best dine-out splurge, this swanky but snob-free village-center joint focuses on regional cuisine. ☎ 604-932-4540; 4222 Village Sq, Whistler Village; mains C$30-45; 🕑 11am-3pm & 5pm-midnight

Beet Root Café

Surround yourself with a nest of cushions and cuddle up to a menu of soups, sandwiches and home-baked treats. ☎ 604-932-1163; 4340 Lorimer Pl, Whistler Village; mains C$6-12; 🕑 8am-5:30pm; 👤

Garibaldi Lift Company

Overlooking the slopes, the GLC is an ideal after-piste bar with a hearty beer selection and good pub grub. ☎ 604-905-2220; Village Gondola, Whistler Village; mains C$10-13; 🕑 11am-11pm

USEFUL WEBSITES

www.tourismwhistler.com
www.whistlerblackcomb.com
www.lonelyplanet.com/trip-planner

LINK YOUR TRIP

Okanagan Wine Tour

WHY GO Western Canada's hilly lakeside wine region is never going to be mistaken for Napa, but with around 100 wineries the Okanagan is BC's must-see destination for tipple fans. Winding around the area (with a designated driver, of course) delivers a tasty flight of producers in an idyllic, laid-back setting.

TIME
2 days

DISTANCE
**35km
(22 miles)**

BEST TIME TO GO
Jul – Sep

START
Westbank

END
South Kelowna

ALSO GOOD FOR

The Okanagan Valley, originally a regional enclave of busy little fruit farms, started sprouting wineries in the 1980s when striping the region's hillsides with vines became de rigueur – though you can still giddily gorge on summertime peaches and cherries here. Cool winters and long summers makes whites a staple of the valley's northern region, while further south reds rise to prominence. Icewine, a dessert quaff made from grapes frozen on the vine, is also a favorite take-home tipple.

If you're traveling in from Vancouver, you can start your leisurely taste-tripping trawl on the western shore of the 100km (62 mile) long Okanagan Lake, the region's centerpiece. It's not hard to travel for hours between the winery areas in this region, but this easy route gives you more time for quaffing and less time spent driving. Follow Boucherie Rd, between the lake and Hwy 97. Your first stop will be Westbank's **1 Mission Hill Family Estate**, complete with its fortified, Fort Knox–like entrance. A modernist reinterpretation of a mission building, the hilltop complex's black and dark-wood interiors are like a palatial bachelor pad for the mega rich. Several tours and tastings are available – try to snag some Oculus, a complex Bordeaux-inspired blend – but you can also wander the grounds on your own. Look out for the amazing Chagall tapestry in one of the meeting rooms.

If you like the look of the water winking at you in the valley below, the **2 Lake House on Green Bay** is a classy waterside guesthouse

FOOD &
DRINK

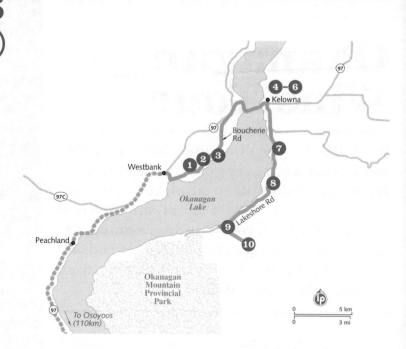

with West Coast wood and stone accents and a homey feel. Drop your bags and continue north and you'll soon come to ③ **Quail's Gate Estate Winery**. Attractive stone and beam architecture prevails at this warm and welcoming spot, where visitors can chill at vine-side picnic benches with a bottle. Inside, a three-tipple tasting is free – the rhubarby Chenin Blanc and pleasantly peppery reserve Pinot Noir are recommended – while the on-site restaurant is a foodie favorite. Its menu showcases seasonal BC ingredients and is committed to sourcing sustainable seafood.

DETOUR Add a day to your visit and sample one of the region's most distinctive wineries at **Nk'Mip Cellars** (www.nkmipcellars.com), North America's only First Nations–owned winery when it opened in 2003. Rather than being a novelty producer, it has since created some celebrated tipples from its pueblo-style, desert-fringed site in the town of Osoyoos. Knock back some Pinot Blanc then check out the rattlesnake enclosure at the adjoining **Nk'Mip Desert Cultural Centre** (www.nkmipdesert.com). The winery is about 112km (70 miles) south of Westbank along Hwy 97.

Cross the lake at the new William R Bennett Bridge and head for the "east coast" town of Kelowna, the Okanagan capital. It's a good base for exploring the region, with lots of accommodations options, such as picturesque ④ **Hotel Eldorado**, which features both antique-lined and modern South Beach–style rooms. If you want to continue your wine education, make for the town's ⑤ **BC Wine Museum**, where you can also pick up surprisingly well-priced wines from producers throughout the valley. Ask at the counter and they'll point you toward some rarities. Nearby ❻ **Calona Vineyards** was the Okanagan's first winery when it kicked off production in 1932. It's melon-note Pinot Blanc is ever-popular and its port-style dessert wine makes an ideal cheese partner.

Instruct your driver to head south from the city at this point. In the hills along the lake's eastern shore, you'll soon come to one of the Okanagan's most colorful wineries. ❼ **Summerhill Pyramid Winery** combines a traditional tasting room with a huge concrete pyramid where every Summerhill wine ages in barrels. "The pyramid has become a landmark and it's part of all our wines now," says twinkle-eyed founder Stephen Cipes. "The conditions are great here for making sparkling wine and we're also organic – the absence of toxins really make it a health drink." It's hard to argue when you quaff some of his delightful Peace Chardonnay Icewine.

Consider stopping at Summerhill for lunch or continue along Lakeshore Rd to ❽ **St Hubertus Estate Winery**. Another twist on the winery approach, this one is like stepping onto the grounds of a traditional northern European vineyard, complete with Bavarian architectural flourishes. "It's like Switzerland on steroids here," says a jocular Andy Gebert, who owns the winery with his brother. "We produce lots of Germanic varieties, including Riesling, which is not exactly the Pamela Anderson of wines. Actually, it's more like Mother Teresa." But St Hubertus is anything but conservative: try its floral, somewhat spicy Casselas and the rich Marechal Foch, for example.

WINE FESTIVALS

The Okanagan now stages four seasonal wine festivals (www.thewinefestivals.com) throughout the year. Time your visit right and dip into one of these:

- **Icewine Festival**, mid-January, five days
- **Spring Wine Festival**, early May, four days
- **Summer Wine Festival**, August, three days
- **Fall Wine Festival**, early October, 10 days

If you're thinking of treating your designated driver to something they can sample, too, head for the hills and ❾ **Carmelis Goat Cheese Artisan**. Offered samples from the 16 or so cheeses available, many favor the mild yogurt varieties – an ideal starter for those who think goat cheese will be too intense. More practiced palates prefer the mushroomy Picollo or the nutty, Camembert-style Blue Velvet. It's the rich and earthy Goatgonzola that really packs a punch, though. And it's not far from here to the fragrant ❿ **Okanagan Lavender Farm**, where you can end your trek with some lavender lemonade to cleanse your wine-soaked palate.

John Lee

TRIP INFORMATION

GETTING THERE
Head eastbound from Vancouver on Hwy 1, then follow Kelowna signs via Hwys 5, 97C and 97. The total distance is 380km (235 miles).

DO
BC Wine Museum
Check out the Okanagan's fruity wine heritage, plus one of its best regional wine stores. ☎ 250-868-0441; www.kelownamuseum.ca; 1304 Ellis St, Kelowna; admission free; ⊙ 10am-6pm Mon-Sat, 11am-5pm Sun

Calona Vineyards
BC's oldest winery has its visitors center in downtown Kelowna and offers four samples for C$4. ☎ 250-762-9144; www.calonavineyards.ca; 1125 Richter St, Kelowna; ⊙ 9am-6pm Jun-Sep, with seasonal variations

Carmelis Goat Cheese Artisan
The Kelowna region's best foodie destination. A tour plus sampling of cheeses costs C$4. ☎ 250-870-3117; www.carmelisgoatcheese.com; 170 Timberline Rd, near Kelowna; ⊙ 10am-6pm May–mid-Oct, reduced hours off-season; ♿

Mission Hill Family Estate
Three tour and tasting options, ranging from C$5 to C$42. Plus restaurant. ☎ 250-768-6448; www.missionhillwinery.com; 1730 Mission Hill Rd, Westbank; ⊙ 10am-9pm Jul & Aug, with seasonal variations

Okanagan Lavender Farm
Offering a free self-guided tour and a shop full of fragrant bath and culinary products. ☎ 250-764-7795; www.okanaganlavender.com; 4380 Takla Rd, near Kelowna; ⊙ 9:30am-5pm Jul & Aug, with seasonal variations; ♿

Quail's Gate Estate Winery
Handsome vineyard setting for a lovely, laid-back winery where tastings are three for free. Plus restaurant. ☎ 250-769-4451; www.quailsgate.com; 3303 Boucherie Rd, Westbank; ⊙ 9am-7pm Jun-Sep, with seasonal variations

St Hubertus Estate Winery
One of the region's friendliest, family-owned operations. Tastings are free here – try the Germanic whites. ☎ 250-764-7888; www.st-hubertus.bc.ca; 5205 Lakeshore Rd, near Kelowna; ⊙ 10am-5:30pm May-Oct, with seasonal variations

Summerhill Pyramid Winery
Organic wines, uniquely aged in a pyramid, where the C$5 public tour includes several tastings. Plus restaurant. ☎ 250-764-8000; www.summerhill.bc.ca; 4870 Chute Lake Rd, near Kelowna; ⊙ 9am-9pm, with seasonal variations

SLEEP
Hotel Eldorado
Smashing character hotel combining both antique-lined and contemporary-themed rooms, many overlooking the sparkling lake. Great on-site restaurant, too. ☎ 250-763-7550; www.eldoradokelowna.com; 500 Cook Rd, Kelowna; r C$150-400

Lake House on Green Bay
Sophisticated waterfront guesthouse with a comfortable, adult-oriented appeal. Rates include tour passes to Mission Hill. ☎ 250-768-8886; www.lakehouseongreenbay.com; 1454 Green Bay Rd, Westbank; r C$205

USEFUL WEBSITES
www.okanaganwines.ca
www.tourismkelowna.com

LINK YOUR TRIP
www.lonelyplanet.com/trip-planner

OUTDOORS

Fraser Valley Farmlands

WHY GO With gently rolling farmlands, friendly artisan producers and small communities dripping with history, BC's mountain-fringed Fraser Valley is a taste-tripping revelation. Trekkers on a short hop from Vancouver can follow this route and lick their lips at the farms, dairies and wineries of Langley, Abbotsford, Mission and beyond.

TIME
2 days

DISTANCE
97km (60 miles)

BEST TIME TO GO
Jul – Sep

START
Langley

END
Agassiz

ALSO GOOD FOR

FOOD & DRINK

Generations of Vancouverites have enjoyed the fresh fruit and veggies of the Fraser Valley without ever registering the existence of the verdant farmlands that stock their larders. But with neighborhood produce and 100-mile diets recently gaining kudos, locals and visitors are finally driving out to meet their food makers, sampling a deep dish of flavors and communities into the bargain. If 100 miles seems too far to go, nearby Langley and Abbotsford offer a "30-mile diet" alternative. And if you want to explore a little further, follow your taste buds into the heart of the mountain-lined valley region.

Head via Hwy 1A to ❶ Langley and the charming ❷ Vista D'oro. At this family farmstead with an exemplary approach to great nosh, you'll be welcomed by Lee and Patrick Murphy, ever-happy to explain their current crops to visitors. Fresh pears, plums, apples and stripy heirloom tomatoes are available in season, but there's also a smorgasbord of exotic potted treats in the little farm shop. Sample preserves such as piquant mango lime salsa and sweet rhubarb and vanilla jam and you'll soon be loading up the car. But save room for some surprisingly good port-style walnut wine made from nuts grown just outside the shop.

With winey taste buds primed (and designated driver decided), it's not far from here to the vine-covered grounds of ❸ Domaine de Chaberton. This French-influenced 55-acre vineyard, the Fraser Valley's

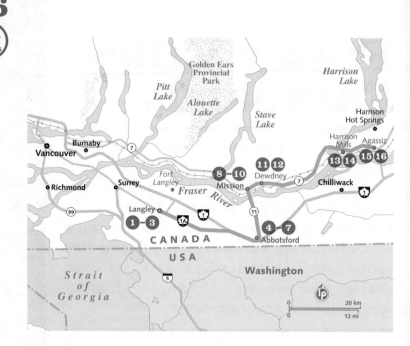

oldest winery operation, has been here since 1981 and specializes in cool-climate whites: its subtle, Riesling-style Bacchus is dangerously easy to drink too much of on a languid sunny afternoon, but there's also a handy bistro here if you need to soak up your overindulgence with a hearty meal.

Continue on to ④ Abbotsford and ⑤ Goat's Pride Dairy for a taste of idyllic farm life. Visitors can wander the tree-shaded acreage here and chat to owner Jo-Ann Dykstra about her organic approach to farming.

> "…its subtle, Riesling-style Bacchus is dangerously easy to drink too much of on a languid sunny afternoon."

Check out the bleating baby goats – with names like Socks, Cyclone and Baby Doll – and ask for recommendations from a selection that includes sun-dried tomato feta and the farm's signature Roquefort-style blue capri, each crafted by Dykstra's friendly son Jason. If your trunk isn't already full, also drop by ⑥ Rossdown Farm Market. In summer, Okanagan cherries, peaches and apricots fill the outside fruit buckets, while Chilliwack corn on the cob and local blueberries often jostle for attention. Abbotsford is also the home of loungey ⑦ Restaurant 62, one of the region's best eateries, with plenty of locally sourced ingredients to tempt your palate. Ask the waiter for recommendations or boldly assert your preference for local Fraser Valley chicken, duck or pork.

Drive on north via Hwy 11 after dinner and make it to ⑧ Mission for a sleepover at ⑨ Mission City Lodge, where the large pool is perfect for cooling off after your drive. Up early the next morning, you'll find several wineries and visitor-friendly farms in the area, so keep your eyes open for signs as you meander through. If you're ready to eat, drop by **⑩ Mission Springs Brewing Company**, a brewpub-style operation with a hearty pub grub menu and a patio overlooking the river. Also consider heading a few miles east of town on Hwy 7 to rustic **⑪ Dewdney** village where you'll find **⑫ Kermode Wild Berry Wines**. This family-run business uses local foragers to pick the 40 or so edible berries that grow wild in BC, transforming them into exotic and often-celebrated tipples. The blackberry and blueberry wines are particularly recommended.

> **ASK A LOCAL**
>
> "We only grow for taste and we don't ship anything off the farm, unless it's in a jar. You can get a real taste of the Fraser Valley here but if you're just passing through, we're a good place to stop and create a picnic – our shop has just about everything you might need."
>
> *Patrick Murphy, owner of Vista D'oro farm, Langley, BC*

Continue your farmlands exploration east from here on Hwy 7 and head to **⑬ Harrison Mills**, where you can step back in time at **⑭ Kilby Historic Site**, an atmospheric reminder of the thriving pioneer farms that kick-started the area. Costumed interpreters bring the place to life as you wander through the working heritage farm, complete with replicated heritage buildings and attention-hungry goats angling for a head scratch or two. The centerpiece is the evocative General Store Museum, lined with essential products from decades past, and if you're here in late summer or early fall you can sample apples from the old orchard (they also make great cider).

There's a restaurant on-site or continue along Hwy 7 to **⑮ Agassiz** and lovely **⑯ Limbert Mountain Farm**, dominated by its traditional wooden barn and smashing gable-roofed yellow farmhouse. Here you

FARM COMMUNITIES ONE BY ONE

If you want to explore the Fraser Valley's farm settlements in more detail, try a self-guided **Circle Farm Tour**. With recommended farm-themed pit stops in communities including Langley, Abbotsford, Chilliwack, Mission, Agassiz, Harrison Mills, Maple Ridge and Pitt Meadows, the tours can be accessed using free downloadable maps available at www.circlefarmtour.ca.

can commune with nature in the herb- and flower-strewn hillside garden – the fragrant lavender will slap your nostrils as soon as you approach – then nip into the shop to pick up whatever might be in season, including products from other regional producers. The chestnuts and salad blends are recommended if you're hunting for picnic fixings, but there's also a weekend tearoom here if you fancy dining indoors.

John Lee

TRIP INFORMATION

GETTING THERE
From Vancouver, head eastbound on Hwy 1 and follow the signposted exits for Langley. The drive is 47km (29 miles).

DO

Domaine de Chaberton
Free tours and tastings at the region's oldest winery, where there's also a popular French bistro. ☎ 604-530-1736; www.domaine dechaberton.com; 1064 216 St, Langley; ⏱ 10am-6pm Mon-Sat, 11am-6pm Sun

Goat's Pride Dairy
An idyllic farmstead home of cute goats and organic piquant artisan cheeses with a warm, family-run feel. ☎ 604-854-6261; www .goatspride.com; 30854 Olund Rd, Abbots-ford; ⏱ 8:30am-6pm; ♿

Kermode Wild Berry Wines
Drop into the tasting room for some surprising berry wines, ports and liqueurs, all made from locally foraged fruit. ☎ 604-814-3222; www .kermodewildberry.com; 8457 River Rd S, Dewdney; ⏱ noon-6pm

Kilby Historic Site
Costumed interpreters and re-created herit-age buildings bring to life this busy century-old farmstead. ☎ 604-796-9576; www.kilby .ca; 215 Kilby Rd, Harrison Mills; adult/child C$9/7; ⏱ 11am-5pm May-Aug, with sea-sonal variations; ♿

Limbert Mountain Farm
Hillside farmstead site with verdant gardens, local produce shop and a weekend tearoom. ☎ 604-796-2619; www.limbertmoun tainfarm.com; 5493 Limbert Rd, Agassiz; ⏱ 10am-5pm Mon-Sat, noon-5pm Sun

Rossdown Farm Market
Offers fresh poultry cuts and a wide array of fruit, vegetable and artisan foodie treats from the Fraser Valley and beyond. ☎ 604-856-5578; www.rossdown.com; 29709 Downes Rd, Abbotsford; ⏱ 10am-5pm Mon-Sat

Vista D'oro
A boutique farmstead with a shop full of preserves, walnut wine and seasonal fruit and vegetables. ☎ 604-514-3539; www .vistadoro.com; 20856 4th Ave, Langley; ⏱ Thu-Sat mid-Mar–mid-Dec

EAT & SLEEP

Mission City Lodge
Large, gable-roofed motel – request a Fraser River view – with typical business-traveler facilities plus pool and spa extras. ☎ 604-820-5500; www.bestwestern.com; 32281 Hwy 7, Mission; r C$80-140; 🐾

Mission Springs Brewing Company
Car memorabilia decorates the bar and restaurant at this popular brewpub. ☎ 604-820-1009; www.missionspringsbrewingcom pany.com; 7160 Oliver St, Mission; mains C$8-16; ⏱ 11am-11pm Sun-Thu, to 1am Fri & Sat

Restaurant 62
Abbotsford's coolest eatery features an appealing menu with an emphasis on local ingredients. ☎ 604-855-3545; www.restau rant62.ca; 2001 McCallum Rd, Abbotsford; mains C$20-27; ⏱ 11:30am-9pm Mon-Thu, 11:30am-10pm Fri, 10am-2pm & 5-10pm Sat & Sun

USEFUL WEBSITES
www.bcfarmfresh.com
www.vcmbc.com

LINK YOUR TRIP

www.lonelyplanet.com/trip-planner

Northern BC Train Trek

WHY GO Railroads were the key catalyst for development in BC's pioneer years. But although air and road travel eventually rose to prominence, today's trains remain the best way to penetrate the province's sprawling wilderness. Nowhere is an epic outback trundle more appealing than on the charming Skeena service through northern BC.

Consider easing into your train trek with a leisurely overnight stay in ❶ **Jasper National Park**. The mountain-shaded town ❷ **Jasper** is a friendly and eminently walkable visitor hub where you'll find bookstores, galleries and plenty of family-style eateries. Sup on a glass of 6060 Stout at ❸ **Jasper Brewing Company**, a busy brewpub with a stone-walled interior, and sleep in style just outside town at ❹ **Fairmont Jasper Park Lodge**, a classy, old-school resort nestled in lakeside woodlands.

Inching from the gable-roofed station on VIA Rail's *Skeena* train the next day, you'll be forgiven for thinking that time has suddenly slowed. With the snowcapped Rockies dozing on the horizon, absent-minded deer feeding off spilled grain and a warm blanket of sun-dappled scenery wrapping itself around you, your city-stressed neck muscles will soon be unknotting as you slide past birch forests that roll from the train and up local foothills in undulating waves.

Don't spend all your time staring at the scenery, though. Wander to the lounge car, where passengers – some tourists and some locals – congregate for a chat, a few beers and light lunches from the galley kitchen (bringing your own nosh is recommended, as onboard dining is limited). There's a glass-roofed dome area above the galley offering immersive, panoramic views of the wilderness. Some passengers sit here for hours in a hypnotic trance, watching the uninterrupted natural world slip by.

TIME
2 days

DISTANCE
**1167km
(725 miles)**

BEST TIME TO GO
Jun – Sep

START
Jasper

END
Prince Rupert

ALSO GOOD FOR

ROUTE

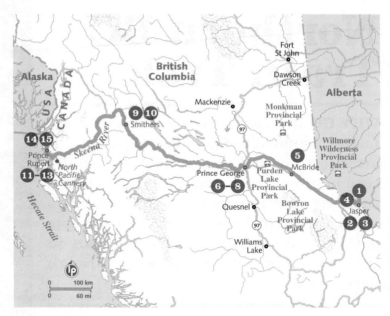

When the train pulls into the tiny old stucco station at ⑤ **McBride**, you'll have a few minutes' break to pick up a piping-hot latte and a snack from the café's smiling staff. Try to stay awake in the afternoon sun, though. The north is heavily populated with wildlife, and alert passengers often spot elk, coyotes or wolves. There are also black bears, usually crashing away from the tracks at top speed or, if they're cubs, hanging in the trees while mom forages for supper.

BC BY TRAIN

While many BC railroad lines have been closed to passengers in recent decades, some VIA Rail services remain, often as vital links between remote communities. These include the *Skeena*, the BC leg of the cross-Canada *Canadian* between Vancouver and Jasper and the charming Vancouver Island *Malahat* service between Victoria and Courtenay. For more information, visit www.viarail.ca. For more luxurious BC rail excursions – think cruise ships on wheels – check out the packages offered by Rocky Mountaineer Vacations (www.rockymountaineer.com).

By early evening, as the sun casts a golden glow, you'll likely be as relaxed as you've ever been in your life when the train pulls into ⑥ **Prince George**, northern BC's hard-working capital. It's edged by rusting forest machinery but there are plenty of facilities for those just passing through. The *Skeena* service stops here overnight (you can't sleep on the train) so make sure you book a hotel room before leaving Jasper. Try ⑦ **Coast Inn of the North**, a tower-block hotel with business-traveler rooms in the heart of the city. And if you're hungry, drop by the ⑧ **White Goose Bistro**, an elegant restaurant with a serious menu of French-influenced classics: try the elk tournedos.

Up early the next day, wend your way back to the station for an 8am departure. While day one was characterized by forests and crags, today there are dozens of babbling little streams, tree-covered fjords stretching along wide rivers and a smattering of farms and disused pulp mills – a reminder of the region's once-thriving forest sector. By mid-afternoon, you'll stop at **9** **Smithers** where the station's **10** **Iron Horse Café** chef dishes up soups, sandwiches and ice creams to the train-bound masses.

As the light wanes during late afternoon, keep an eye out for eagles swooping around the area. You'll also encounter the trip's most spectacular terrain. There are several tunnels and a couple of jaw-dropping trestle bridges here but it's the sharp peaks of the close-by Coast Mountains that dominate. It's a fitting final taste of the province's immense

"There are also black bears, usually crashing away from the tracks at top speed..."

wilderness as the sun languidly sinks over the wide Skeena River. Around 8pm, you'll hit the end of the road in **11** **Prince Rupert** on BC's west coast.

Rupert is well worth a stopover before you leave the region. The **12** **Crest Hotel**, fronted by a glassy-calm seafront, is a good place to drop your bags, (try for a waterside view). Then amble down to the patio bar where everyone in town seems to be congregating for a beer. If your hangover is manageable and you're exploring on foot the next day, check out the clapboard homes and pockets of handsome architecture (the town was once considered a possible BC capital), then make for the excellent **13** **Museum of Northern BC** for an introduction to the area's First Nations and pioneer-era past.

Head from here for a lazy wander around edge-of-town Cow Bay, a brightly painted elbow of heritage buildings now housing coffee shops, fish-and-chip emporiums and the kaleidoscopic **14** **Artists' Co-op Gallery**, stuffed with paintings, photography and crafts created by talented locals. For an early dinner, make for **15** **Cow**

 Extend your Prince Rupert stay with a 16km (10 mile) drive or bus trek to **North Pacific Cannery**. Evocatively documenting the rise and fall of BC's once-dominant fishing sector, the mothballed, gracefully paint-peeled buildings – some built on piles across the water – include the re-created residences of workers and managers (spot the difference) plus the noisy production line where blister-fingered canners toiled all day to meet their challenging quotas. For information, visit www.cannery.ca.

Bay Café. Arguably Rupert's best eatery, its seasonal menu often features delectable dishes like halibut chowder and BC lamb. Snag an alfresco waterfront table and a glass of wine while you reflect on your epic northern rail odyssey.
John Lee

TRIP INFORMATION

GETTING THERE
From Vancouver, take the train, or drive northeast via Hwys 1, 5 and 16 to Jasper, a journey of 796km (495 miles).

DO
Artists' Co-op Gallery
Showcasing the distinctive, sometimes quirky works of more than 100 local artists and artisans. ☎ 250-624-4546; 215 Cow Bay Rd, Prince Rupert; ☻ 10am-5:30pm May-Sep, with seasonal variations

Jasper National Park
This wild Rocky Mountains expanse, one of Canada's largest parks, is studded with glacier-cut crags, rumbling rivers and hungry wildlife. The town of Jasper is a handy hub. ☻ 780-852-6176; www.jaspernationalpark.com

Museum of Northern BC
A longhouse-style building packed with colorful regional history. ☎ 250-624-3207; www.museumofnorthernbc.com; 100 1st Ave W, Prince Rupert; adult/child/youth C$5/1/2; ☻ 9am-5pm Mon-Sat Sep-May, 9am-8pm Mon-Sat, to 5pm Sun Jun-Aug; ☻

EAT
Cow Bay Café
Cozy and chatty waterfront nook with seasonal regional mains (seafood is recommended) and some truly delectable desserts. ☎ 250-627-1212; 205 Cow Bay Rd, Prince Rupert; mains C$10-22; ☻ 11:30am-9pm

Iron Horse Café
Hearty bakery fare and sandwiches for passengers, or burgers and chili if you're sticking around. ☎ 250-877-7870; 8815 Railway Ave, Smithers; mains C$4-12; ☻ 9am-4pm Mon & Sun, to 9pm Tue-Sat

Jasper Brewing Company
West Coast–style brewpub with wood and stone interior, six own-brand brewskies and a menu of quality pub classics. ☎ 780-852-4111; www.jasperbrewingco.ca; 402 Connaught Dr, Jasper; mains C$9-22; ☻ 11am-11pm

White Goose Bistro
Surprisingly elegant white tablecloth restaurant with a French-influenced approach to hearty regional dinner ingredients and a lighter lunch menu. ☎ 250-561-1002; 1205 3rd Ave, Prince George; mains C$8-22; ☻ 11:30am-10pm

SLEEP
Coast Inn of the North
A large tower-block hotel not far from the train station with business-traveler-friendly rooms and wi-fi. ☎ 250-563-0121; www.coasthotels.com; 770 Brunswick St, Prince George; r C$125-195; ☻

Crest Hotel
Waterfront rooms are best at this visitors' favorite where facilities include business-hotel-style rooms and a good restaurant/bar combo. ☎ 250-624-6771; www.cresthotel.bc.ca; 222 1st Ave W, Prince Rupert; r C$125-225; ☻

Fairmont Jasper Park Lodge
Magnificent lake and woodland setting for this classic nature-bound resort, complete with activities like boating and horseback riding. ☎ 780-852-3301; www.fairmont.com/jasper; Old Lodge Rd, Jasper; r C$250-650; ☻

USEFUL WEBSITES
www.hellobc.com

www.nbctourism.com

LINK YOUR TRIP

www.lonelyplanet.com/trip-planner

Vancouver Coastal Loop

WHY GO Depending on how you measure it, BC's craggy, multi-fjorded coastline stretches for around 15,000 miles. But you don't have to drive that far for a taste of the region's salty, character-packed waterfront communities. Take this leisurely tour for a slice of life on both the mainland and Vancouver Island.

Depart west from Vancouver on Hwy 1A and weave through verdant Stanley Park to the BC Ferries terminal at ❶ **Horseshoe Bay**, where you'll drive on board the Langdale ferry to the Sunshine Coast. It's just a 20-minute traversal but you'll be surprised how few Vancouverites actually make this trip – ask the big-city locals where Powell River is and you'll hear some wildly divergent replies. Once the vessel inches away from the dock, nip out of your car and catch some of the stunning views of glassy Howe Sound, the looming Coast Mountains, and the tree-lined Southern Gulf Islands shimmering in the distance.

Drive off the ferry (wait until they bring the ramp down) and follow Highway 101 northwest. It's the main artery for the Sunshine Coast – an area that claims to receive more rays than Hawaii – and it passes through all the communities you'll be visiting on this mainland portion of your trek. This region certainly has a different feel to the Lower Mainland and is characterized by the insular, island-like mentality of its communities and colorful local characters. Drive on toward ❷ **Gibsons** for an initial taste of this local flavor. The town's crenulated waterfront area – known as Gibsons Landing – is where you'll spend most of your time here.

Many bright-painted clapboard buildings back on to the water's edge and there are several intriguing artisan stores to keep your credit card sweating. Head along the town's main wooden jetty – check out

TIME
3 – 4 days

DISTANCE
483km (300 miles)

BEST TIME TO GO
Jul – Sep

START
Horseshoe Bay

END
Vancouver

ALSO GOOD FOR

OUTDOORS

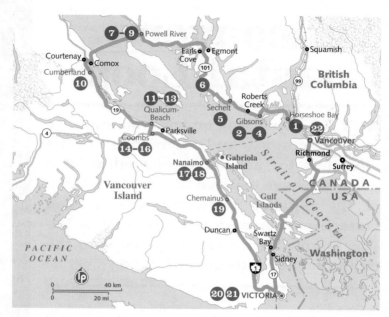

some of the houseboats and floating garden plots along the way – and you'll come to the sun-dappled, gently bobbing gallery of ❸ **Sa Boothroyd**. The artist is often on hand to illuminate her browse-worthy and often humorous works. Although her bigger canvases are suitably pricey, there are lots of original fridge magnets and tea cozies to temp your shopping muscles. Back on terra firma, you can peruse your purchases at the legendary ❹ **Molly's Reach**, a locals' hangout that chefs-up comfort food specials (brunch is recommended) along with mesmerizing views of the marina bristled with boats.

Fully fortified, continue along the winding, tree-lined Hwy 101 – expect to glimpse sandy coves winking at you through the forests on your left – until you reach ❺ **Sechelt**. One of the Sunshine Coast's largest settlements, it has a smattering of restaurants and accommodation options, handy if you haven't booked anything else in the region. There are also some popular woodland cycling routes here, so consider packing your bike. Drop in at the local visitor centre on Teredo St: it has a handy flyer on local bike routes. The best place to stay in the area, though, is a 15-minute drive past town at ❻ **Rockwater Secret Cove Resort**. Book ahead to snag one of the luxury tent suites clinging to the cliffs among the arbutus trees. There's also an excellent on-site restaurant here that specializes in regional cuisine: ideal if you're looking for somewhere to dine en route that also has romantic bayside views.

Back on the road the next day, it won't be long before you reach **7** **Powell River**, the Sunshine Coast's most vibrant community. There's an active and artsy vibe to this waterfront town of 14,000 people that was originally built to service the pulp mill at the head of the river. In fact, many of the town's oldest streets are named after trees and some are still lined with the heritage workers' cottages that kick-started the settlement. The steam-plumed mill is still here, too – although it's shrinking every year and its former grounds are slowly being transformed into parkland. Dip into this local history at **8** **Powell River Museum**, which covers the area's First Nations heritage and its tough pioneer days: check out the black-and-white photos of early settlers here. If you're hungry, drop by the edge-of-town **9** **Shinglemill Pub & Bistro** for a chatty afternoon of beer and barbecued ribs.

Wave goodbye to the mainland and take a 15-minute BC Ferries boat from Powell River to Comox on central Vancouver Island, where you can head south on Hwy 19. Like many Vancouver Island communities, the Comox Valley region was founded on the logging trade but, with its verdant waterfront location and mountain proximity, it's moved increasing to tourism in recent years. Uncover a taste of the old pioneer days at small-town **10** **Cumberland**, where the main street is lined with wood-built stores now occupied by cool cafés and a great old-school pub where live music rocks the floorboards on weekends. One of Vancouver Island's most intriguing little communities, it has a surprisingly youthful population.

SUMMER FESTIVALS

Time your visit right and you can dip into a plethora of local festivals staged annually at communities along your route. Check these out before you hit the road:

- **Gibsons Landing Jazz Festival** (mid-June; www.coastaljazz.com)
- **Sechelt Arts Festival** (August; www.sechel tartsfestival.com)
- **Powell River Sunshine Music Festival** (late August; www.sunshinemusicfest.com)
- **Comox Valley Shellfish Festival** (mid-June; www.comoxvalleyshellfishfestival.ca)
- **Cumberland's Big Time Out** (mid-August; www.thebigtimeout.com)
- **Nanaimo Marine Festival** (late July; www .bathtubbing.com)

Continue south and you'll soon arrive at **11** **Qualicum Beach**, the area's most popular destination for family vacations. A small community of minigolf attractions, classic seafront motels and a giant beachcomber-friendly bay, the highlight nosh spot here is **12** **Fish Tales Café**. If it's a balmy summer evening, snag a table in the cottage garden – as the sun sets, the fairy lights come on – and tuck into golden battered salmon and butter-soft chips plus a bottle of English pale ale. Then spend a night in one of BC's most unusual accommodations: **13** **Free Spirit Spheres** is a pair of cozy round tree houses where you'll feel at one with the surrounding forest, especially in the morning when the dawn chorus reverberates through the surrounding woodlands like a rolling symphony.

You'll find even louder birdlife the next day in nearby ⓮ **Coombs**, home of the impressive ⓯ **World Parrot Refuge**. Dedicated to saving pet parrots from a life of depressing captivity – highly sociable animals, they are not meant to be kept alone in cages – there are more than 750 rescued birds here, all of them apparently intent on screeching at the top of their lungs, which explains the ear plugs handed out at the front desk. As your stroll through the clamorous menagerie, expect some of the multicolored specimens to call a cheery "hello" as you pass, while others, under supervision, will climb on your shoulders for a closer visit. Restore your jangled nerves with a giant ice cream along the street at ⓰ **Coombs Old Country Market**. A destination in itself, here you can easily spend an hour or two weaving among the handicraft stores, deli hall and patio eatery, where goats on the grass-topped roof will eye you inquisitively.

PULP NONFICTION

Powell River was founded in the early 1900s when three Minnesota businessmen dammed the river to create a massive hydroelectric power plant. Not long after, a pulp mill was built to take advantage of the surrounding forests and handy deep-water harbor, with the first sheets of paper trundling off its steamy production line in 1912. Within a few years, the mill – still there today, but much reduced in size – had become the world's largest producer of paper newsprint, churning out 275 tons daily.

Continuing south via beachfront Parksville, you'll arrive within an hour or so at ⓱ **Nanaimo**, Vancouver Island's second city. Much smaller than Victoria, this harborside community has plenty of worthwhile restaurants lining its downtown core, plus a Spanish tapas joint and a fish-and-chip emporium floating in the harbor. But Nanaimo isn't just a food stop: spend some time wandering the streets here and you'll find good bookstore and independent boutiques worthy of your attention. If you don't have the time to get lost, head uphill from the harbor to the Old City Quarter around Selby, Wesley and Fitzwilliam Sts. Lined with brightly painted heritage buildings that have been reinvented as new businesses, there are some eclectic record, clothing and gallery stores here, and a smattering of good eateries.

"…expect some of the multicolored specimens to call a cheery "hello" as you pass…"

And if it feels like time to stretch your muscles after all that driving, head to the edge-of-town ⓲ **Wild Play Element Parks**. This woodland adventure facility has several sweat-triggering obstacle courses winding through the trees: You'll be hanging, jumping and swinging yourself via ropes, ladders and ziplines. If you're feeling really adventurous, book a heart-stopping leap from the bungee-jump bridge that hangs over the river here. Don't be surprised if you're a few inches taller when you finally ease yourself back into the car, though.

Continue south on Hwy 1 to ⓳ **Chemainus**. This former resource town almost died a few years ago, but in the 1980s the residents of this tree-ringed settlement began commissioning murals for the walls. Recalling the good old days, the paintings – there are now more than three dozen dotted around the town – soon became visitor attractions, triggering the town's rebirth. Among the best are the 54ft-long pioneer-town painting of Chemainus circa 1891 on Mill St; the 50ft-long depiction of First Nations faces and totems on Chemainus Rd; and the evocative mural showing the waterfront community as it was in 1948, on Maple St. The town is an ideal place to stop for an hour or two and there are several restaurants and coffee shops plus lots of boutique galleries to keep you and your wallet occupied. The town's surprisingly large theater is also popular – consider checking ahead to see what's on before you arrive.

DETOUR If you're tempted by those mysterious little islands peeking at you off the coast of Vancouver Island, take the 20-minute BC Ferries service from Nanaimo's Inner Harbour to **Gabriola Island** (www.gabriolaisland.org). Home to dozens of artists plus a healthy smattering of old hippies and 1960s US-draft dodgers, there's a tangible air of quietude to this rustic realm. Pack a picnic and spend the afternoon communing with the natural world in a setting rewardingly divorced from big-city life.

With the end of the island stretch of your journey in sight, continue south to **20 Victoria**. BC's capital city is dripping with old-school colonial architecture and has enough museums, attractions, hotels and restaurants – many showcasing lip-smacking regional ingredients – to keep most visitors happy for an extra night or two. If all you want to do is toast your grand tour, though, make for the patio of **21 Canoe Brewpub** and sup on a Red Canoe Lager. Extend your stay for as many days as you can, then follow the signs north from the city on Hwy 17 to the BC Ferries terminal at Swartz Bay and your boat back to mainland **22 Vancouver**.

John Lee

TRIP INFORMATION

GETTING THERE
From Vancouver, head through Stanley Park on Hwy 1A and follow the signs for Horseshoe Bay ferry terminal, a distance of 21km (13 miles).

DO

Coombs Old Country Market
Dozens of art, boutique and trinket stores clustered around a central deli, grocery, restaurant and market. ☎ 250-248-6472; www.oldcountrymarket.com; 2326 Alberni Hwy, Coombs; ☺ 9am-6pm, extended hours in summer; &

Powell River Museum
Colorful introduction to pioneer and logging history – plus an intriguing exploration of First Nations heritage. ☎ 604-485-2222; www.powellrivermuseum.ca; 4798 Marine Ave, Powell River; adult/child C$2/1 ☺ 9am-4:30pm Jun-Aug, 9am-4:30pm Mon-Fri Sep-May

Sa Boothroyd
This sun-soaked waterfront art studio on the wharf is lined with the quirky, smile-triggering works of this popular Sunshine Coast artist. ☎ 604-886-7072; www.saboothroyd.com; Government Wharf, Gibsons; ☺ 10am-5pm

Wild Play Element Parks
Woodland adventure facility with canopy obstacle courses and a daredevil bungee-jump zone. ☎ 250-716-7874; www.wildplayparks.com; 35 Nanaimo River Rd, Nanaimo; courses priced C$20-40; ☺ 10am-5:30pm Jun-Aug, with seasonal variations Sep-May; &

World Parrot Refuge
An important rescue center for former pet parrots with a strong educational (antipet) bent. ☎ 250-248-5194; www.worldparrotrefuge.org; 2116 Alberni Hwy, Coombs; adult/child/youth C$12/8/10; ☺ 10am-4pm; &

EAT & DRINK

Canoe Brewpub
Brick-lined bar with waterfront patio, own-brew beers and a menu of superior pub nosh. ☎ 250-361-1940; 450 Swift St, Victoria; mains C$9-18; ☺ 11:30am-midnight Sun-Thu, 1to 1am Fri & Sat

Fish Tales Café
Perfect fish-and-chips plus more sophisticated seafood treats served at a café with a knickknack-lined interior and idyllic garden. ☎ 250-752-6053; www.fishtalescafe.com; 3336 Island Hwy W, Qualicum Beach; mains C$8-22; ☺ 4-10pm; &

Molly's Reach
Locals' nook with waterfront seating and a menu of home-style breakfast, lunch and dinner classics. ☎ 604-886-9710; 647 School Rd, Gibsons; mains C$8-12; ☺ 7am-9pm

Shinglemill Pub & Bistro
Atmospheric lakeside bar-and-restaurant combo seves pub grub as well as more gourmet fare. ☎ 604-483-3545; 6233 Powell Pl, Powell River; mains C$8-22; ☺ 11am-10pm

SLEEP

Free Spirit Spheres
Twin wood-built spherical tree houses where you'll be at one with the surrounding forest. ☎ 250-757-9445; www.freespiritspheres.com; 420 Horne Lake Rd, Qualicum Beach; r C$125-175

Rockwater Secret Cove Resort
Combines cliff-top tent suites and swish lodge accommodation; there's also a great water-view restaurant. ☎ 604-885-7038; www.rockwatersecretcoveresort.com; 5356 Ole's Cove Resort Rd, Halfmoon Bay; r C$140-300; ❀

USEFUL WEBSITES
www.vancouverisland.travel
www.vcmbc.com
www.lonelyplanet.com/trip-planner

LINK YOUR TRIP

OFFBEAT

Quirky BC

WHY GO BC is a hotbed of unlikely road-side kitsch and strange attractions, with communities proudly displaying mammoth figures of bygone loggers or angry-looking bighorn sheep as their main welcome signs for visitors. For an alternative take on the province, try this off-the-beaten-path trawl through BC's small-town treasures.

TIME
3 days

DISTANCE
**362 km
(225 miles)**

BEST TIME TO GO
Jul – Sep

START
Vancouver

END
Hope

ALSO GOOD FOR

If you haven't yet spotted the world's largest cuckoo clock, its biggest hockey stick or even its burliest burl – a warty tree outgrowth improbably corralled in a parking lot in Port McNeil – you may be feeling there's something missing from your visit to BC. Luckily, you can make up for this lack of kitsch-tastic sustenance by weaving east from the bright lights of ❶ Vancouver. But before you jump into your Oscar Meyer Weiner truck with your polka-dot cowboy hat and purple-flowered leotard (or whatever you like to wear for your oddball road trips), get in the mood with a couple of eccentric experiences in the big city.

Stay overnight in Fairview's ❷ Shaughnessy Village tower-block hotel, a wacky sleepover that looks and feels like an eyeball-popping 1950s Vegas resort, complete with miniature golf garden, petrified rock display and pink-carpeted corridors. It's immaculately maintained, right down to the porthole windows in the doors. Similarly, if you're craving the perfect traditional experience, head via Hwy 99 across the Lions Gate Bridge to North Vancouver and the stone-and-log-built ❸ Tomahawk Restaurant, complete with exterior totem poles and a gabled roof marked with colorful First Nations carvings. Inside, the cozy diner is crammed with oddball knickknacks collected over the eatery's 80-year history, including painted spears, carved paddles and grimacing masks hanging from the ceiling like overripe fruit.

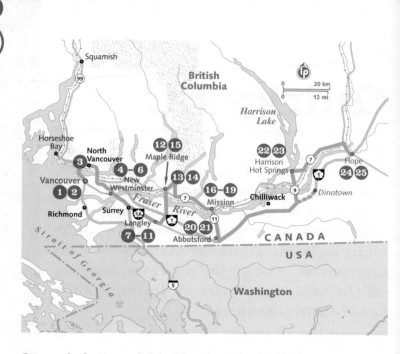

Once you've burst your belt buckle with a heaping breakfast (the mountain-sized Yukon-style bacon and eggs is recommended), it's time to hit the road. Head back south across the Burrard Inlet via Hwy 1 and the Second Narrows Bridge and you'll soon reach ④ **New Westminster**, a 23km (14 mile) drive away. The first capital city of the colony of British Columbia, this paint-peeled town is somewhat past its glory days but it still has a few surprises for curious visitors. Movie trivia buffs might know, for example, that the Will Smith sci-fi epic *I Robot* was filmed under the concrete arches near the waterfront here, with the area improbably doubling for a run-down future Chicago.

BC'S ROYAL CITY

Originally known as Queensborough, the freshly named New Westminster (a nomenclature reputedly chosen by Queen Victoria) was selected as the first capital of the new colony of British Columbia in 1859, a year after the region was originally proclaimed at Fort Langley. Soon nicknamed the Royal City, its golden age was not to last long: Victoria on Vancouver Island became the new and current capital in 1871 when BC joined the Canadian Confederation.

In fact, this stretch is the heart of the action in New West and it's where you'll find one of the Lower Mainland's best-known follies: the ⑤ **World's Largest Toy Soldier**. This red-jacketed, 32ft-tall steel-built fella spends most of his time smiling indulgently at the tourists huddled around his feet. He was built by a Burnaby steel fabricator to showcase its skills – although it's not known how many additional effigy orders flocked in after the soldier appeared. After you've taken the required photos, drop into nearby **6** **Westminster Quay Public Market** for a coffee and cake pit stop. Inside, you'll find a large, evocative painting of what the city looked like in its more elegant days.

Primed for more kitsch, cross the expansive Fraser River on the Pattullo Bridge and head southeast using Hwy 1A to **7** **Langley**, an old farm town that's increasingly become a suburban commuter enclave for Vancouver workers who can't afford to live in the city anymore. If you're here in summer, drop by the fruit stands that dot the roadside every few hundred yards – cherries and peaches are a must-scoff – then sniff out the towering, black-painted **8** **Chair** at the northeast corner of Hwys 7 and 10. Weighing around 2 tons and standing 24ft tall, it's made from solid Douglas fir and advertises a nearby furniture store, presumably for giants. Not far away, on Glover Rd, there's also a **9** **Giant Spider's Web** stretched across a pitchfork-shaped frame and occupied by a large black metal spider.

"It looks ready to pounce without notice on any passing car that takes its fancy…"

You can calm your shattered arachnophobic nerves at Langley's **10** **Fort Wine Company**. Fans of the unusual will enjoy the salon bar look to the tasting room, where own-brand fruit wines are the specialty. The on-site bistro also serves as a handy lunch stop. Next up, drop by the town's little airport to check out one of BC's best-kept-secret attractions. At the unexpected home of the **11** **Canadian Museum of Flight**, you can feast your eyes on vintage jets such as the fang-toothed DH100 Vampire parked outside, then nip inside the two crammed hangars for quirky aviation memorabilia. Peruse the scratchy-looking 1970s airline uniforms, an ultralight helicopter that resembles a flying armchair and a lacquered wooden glider that looks more like an airborne chocolate egg.

Continue your trek northward from here for 40km (25 miles), via the free Albion car ferry, to **12** **Maple Ridge**, where you can observe the hulking **13** **Mountain Goat** carving at the entrance to **14** **Golden Ears Provincial Park**. It looks ready to pounce without notice on any passing car that takes its fancy, but it's worth the risk to spend an hour or two in the park, one of BC's largest. It's riddled with tree-lined hiking trails and has a popular lake that's ideal for swimming, fishing and kayaking (rentals available). Deer and black bears are resident here and the park is also one of the region's most popular camping sites.

If it's summer, consider an alternative stop at nearby **15** **Meadows Maze** in Pitt Meadows, a dual circuit 15-acre corn labyrinth that also features a bee observatory, a corn-bale construction site and a firing range where you can hit targets using a corn cannon. The place is teeming with wild, crazy-eyed kids, especially on weekends, but apparently you're not allowed to aim the corn cannons at them. Corn mazes are a common oddball feature of BC's farmland interior in the summer months, and some of these farms also transform into Halloween pumpkin "theme parks" in the fall, complete with scary ghost displays and battalions of freaky scarecrows guaranteed to give you nightmares.

Continuing east, via Hwy 7, into the farmlands of the Fraser Valley, it won't be long (about 32 km; 19 miles) before you hit **16 Mission**, nestled into an elbow of the seemingly ever-present Fraser River. Fans of the bizarre should make straight for London Ave and Save-on-Foods supermarket, where a **17 set of giant kitchen utensils** presumably acts to remind passers-by they'll need to prepare a meal or two sometime today. In fact, this is an unusual public art waterfall, with water tumbling from the tipped saucepan into a large plate. A pole-mounted knife and fork stand nearby to complete the Brobdingnagian domestic scene and the rest of the building's facade has been built to resemble a mammoth cupboard.

DETOUR ➤ If giant toy soldiers don't cut it with your kids, consider an afternoon detour to **Dinotown** (www.dinotown.com), 30 minutes east of Abbotsford. They'll likely go nuts for the cartoonish caveman community, complete with dino-driven trains, a junglelike adventure playground and live shows with oversized plush T-Rexs. Kids definitely know how to live and breathe kitsch. Drive south from Mission on Hwy 11, turn east on Hwy 1 at Abbotsford, take Exit 135 and follow the signs for Bridal Falls.

Consider a change of pace at the area's unusual **18 Power House at Stave Falls**, an industrial museum housed in a 1912 BC Hydro power plant. There are lots of push-button displays and kid-friendly features here but the old Generator Hall – like a cathedral of power – impresses most, with its enormous shiny turbine and generator units primed and ready for action. Also save time to check out the vivid movie presentation showing what it was like to live and work here in the early 20th century. If you want to call it a day and you're looking for somewhere to stay, downtown Mission's good-value **19 Diamond Head Motor Inn** is a typical old-school motel with a touch of kitsch-tastic class: some rooms have waterbeds and kitchenettes and there's even a honeymoon suite if you really want to get married in the area.

Up early the next day, nip south via Hwy 11 and roll into **20 Abbotsford**. At the town's **21 Tanglebank Country Gardens**, an artful garden center that's also home to a series of immaculately coiffured, free-entry public gardens, you can stretch out on a sunny day. Wander the dainty Japanese garden, fragrant rhododendron walk and a water-wise section populated with hardy Mediterranean plants. Expect to be joined by Sir Frederick, a permanently purring cat always looking for tummy rubs. Follow Hwy 1 east from here and head through Chilliwack – there are plenty of eateries here if you're starving –

eventually winding back north across the river via Hwy 9 toward lakefront ㉒ **Harrison Hot Springs**.

Here, you can wave hello to ㉓ **Woodie**, a giant spear-wielding local carved from cedar, before continuing on to ㉔ **Hope**, where you'll hit the mother lode of chainsaw wood sculptures. The city has more than two dozen dotted around the town and more are added every year. While some have First Nations themes or represent historic pioneer figures, most depict the area's multitudinous wildlife. You can pick up a route map of all the carvings at the town's visitors centre. On your town-based safari, you can expect to come across lifelike carvings of cougars, salmon, wolves and a bear with her cheeky cubs, plus a grinning prospector and mule combo outside the district council offices. Anticipate some fitful dreams as you lay your head for the night at the immaculate, family-friendly ㉕ **Holiday Motel and RV Resort** before making your way back to Vancouver.

John Lee

WORLD'S CARVING CAPITAL

When many old trees in Hope's Memorial Park were hit with devastating root rot in the early 1990s, local artist Pete Ryan suggested transforming them into giant public sculptures. Hope's wealth of chainsaw artworks was born, resulting nearly 20 years later in the city's World Class Chainsaw Carving Competition, held every September, where visitors can watch as artists from around the world transform giant blocks into artworks. If you have room in your luggage, drop by **Ryan's Gallery of Wood Carvings** (www.pete-ryan.ca).

TRIP INFORMATION

GETTING THERE
From Portland (505km; 315 miles) or Seattle (225km;140 miles) head northbound on I-5 and then take Hwy 99 from the Blaine border crossing to Vancouver.

DO

Canadian Museum of Flight
Smashing aviation museum with 25 moth-balled planes and thousands of quirky flight-themed artifacts. ☎ 604-532-0035; www.canadianflight.org; 5333 216th St, Langley; adult/child C$7.55/5; ☉ 10am-4pm; ♿

Fort Wine Company
Specializing in fruit and dessert wines. There's also a good bistro here if you need to fuel up. ☎ 604-857-1101; www.thefortwineco.com; 26151 84th Ave, Langley; ☉ 10am-6pm, with seasonal variations

Golden Ears Provincial Park
One of the province's largest parks. Hiking, horseback riding, windsurfing and boating are encouraged here and camping is also available. ☎ 604-795-6169; www.env.gov.bc.ca/bcparks; Maple Ridge; ♿

Meadows Maze
Farmland fun with mazes, animal petting and corn cannons. ☎ 604-460-0603; www.meadowsmaze.com; 13672 Reichenbach Rd, Pitt Meadows; adult/child C$11/8; ☉ 11am-6pm Sun-Thu, to 10pm Fri & Sat mid-Jul—early Sep; ♿

Power House at Stave Falls
Unusual power station museum with hands-on displays and a magnificent turbine hall. ☎ 604-462-1222; www.bchydro.com/stavefalls; 31338 Dewdney Trunk Rd, Mission; adult/child C$6/5; ☉ 10am-5pm mid-Mar—mid-Oct, 11am-4pm Wed-Sun Nov—mid-Mar; ♿

LINK YOUR TRIP

Tanglebank Country Gardens
Peaceful cottage garden center with several free-entry themed display gardens and a roving cat. ☎ 604-856-9339; www.tanglebank.com; 29985 Downes Rd, Abbotsford; ☉ 9:30am-5pm Mon-Sat Feb-Mar

Westminster Quay Public Market
Large waterfront indoor market with a food court, coffee shop and boutique stores. ☎ 604-520-3881; www.westminsterquay.com; 810 Quayside Dr, New Westminster; ☉ 9:30am-6:30pm May-Sep, with seasonal variations

EAT & SLEEP

Diamond Head Motor Inn
Good-value motel sleepover with air con, Mt Baker views and proximity to downtown Mission eateries. ☎ 604-826-8144; www.diamondheadmotorinn.com; 32550 Logan Ave, Mission; r C$60-75

Holiday Motel and RV Resort
Excellent family-friendly hideaway with pool, playground and flower-decked lodge and cabin accommodations. ☎ 604-689-5352; www.holiday-motel.com; 63950 Old Yale Rd, Hope; r C$65-135; ♿ 🐾 🛏

Shaughnessy Village
Vancouver's best oddball overnighter, this immaculate tower-block hotel has a pool, gym and small, wood-lined rooms. ☎ 604-736-5511; www.shaughnessyvillage.com; 1125 W 12th Ave, Vancouver; r C$65-110

Tomahawk Restaurant
Dripping with First Nations artifacts and kitsch-cool memorabilia, the huge breakfasts here are a local legend. ☎ 604-988-2612; www.tomahawkrestaurant.com; 1550 Philip Ave, North Vancouver; mains C$6-14; ☉ 8am-9pm Sun-Thu, to 10pm Fri & Sat; ♿

USEFUL WEBSITES
www.roadsideattractions.ca.bc/htm
www.vcmbc.com

www.lonelyplanet.com/trip-planner

BC's Pioneer Past

WHY GO Modern-day British Columbia was forged by pioneers who pushed into the region's intimidating forests, mountains and rivers itching to discover what was out there. On this leisurely driving tour, you'll come face-to-face with the natural obstacles they encountered and some of the historic legacies they left in their wake.

For a taste of just how inhospitable BC would have been to the wide-eyed pioneers who began arriving here in the 1800s, start your provincial history lesson in the town of ❶ **Lillooet** in the heart of the Fraser Canyon. The jagged-toothed mountain landscape here (this semi-arid region records some of Canada's highest summertime temperatures) was prospector country for many years, with dusty-faced characters frequently rolling into town with lumps of gold they'd panned or dug from the treacherous Cariboo outback.

While the gold rush swelled Lillooet's 1860 population to more than 15,000 – it was said to be one of North America's largest cities – today's town has a more modest 2500 inhabitants. Spend time wandering around the sites that echo these pioneer days: on the town's Golden Mile, you'll find clapboard houses and stores straight out of the cowboy era, including the Camel Barn where a 19th-century entrepreneur stabled 23 humped beasts he hired to prospectors to transport their goods. Not the brightest idea – the camels ate anything they could find and escaped whenever they could. Unearth more quirky gold rush stories at the excellent ❷ **Lillooet Museum**.

If the heat is getting to you, it's time to head south on Hwy 12 to ❸ **Lytton**, a tiny pioneer town nestled among the pine forests at the crossroads of the Fraser and Thompson Rivers. These mighty

TIME
3 days

DISTANCE
400km (249 miles)

BEST TIME TO GO
Jun – Sep

START
Lillooet

END
Squamish

waterways were the first roads for early explorers, who were only able to penetrate deep into the region on dangerous white-water rapids – not surprisingly, some of these stretches have names like Witch's Cauldron and Devil's Gorge. If you're feeling brave, consider a watery roller-coaster ride with ④ **Kumsheen Raft Adventures**: it's a reminder of what early explorers like Simon Fraser would have encountered when they first tumbled through the region.

CHINESE ROCKS

On the banks of the Fraser River throughout the Lillooet region keep your eyes open for stacks of rocks that look a little too organized to be natural. These formations, known as Chinese Rocks, are reminders of the time when Chinese prospectors searching for elusive gold residues washed the sand and gravel here and piled the rocks in neat stacks as high as 10ft. There are some clustered near the town's suspension bridge on the Fraser's eastern shore.

You'll be hooking up with Hwy 1 on your southern exit from Lytton. During the 108km (67 mile) drive to Hope check out the magnificent mountainside views along the route. Age-old nature rules the roost in this part of the world and pioneer settlements must have seemed like fragile tumbleweeds rolling through. Shadowed by looming peaks, ⑤ **Hope** is the biggest town in the region and has plenty of eateries and sleeping options. Consider the ⑥ **Blue Moose Café** for a hearty meal with the locals, then flop down for a night in the trees at ⑦ **Kw'o:kw'e:hala Eco Retreat**, a forest cabin resort dedicated to sustainable practices and organic food.

Up early the next day and continuing west along Hwy 1, you'll be entering the verdant Fraser Valley, BC's main farmland region. Many of the families here, including pockets of Dutch and German residents, are direct descendants of the early European settlers. Save time to drop in at the dairies and berry farms signposted along the route, where you'll find many owners happy to tell you an evocative story or two about their grandparents' pioneer origins.

Arriving in ⑧ **Abbotsford**, head to the heritage ⑨ **Clayburn Village** area where a string of historic workers' homes faces a grassy meadow that once housed the largest brick-making operation in the province when it opened in 1905. The plant's dedicated village, made from the first bricks manufactured here, also includes a preserved old church and schoolhouse. Drop by ⑩ **Clayburn**

ASK A LOCAL

"There was a hierarchy of houses along this strip – as you can see, they get bigger as you go along. The manager's house has three floors and is all fancy bricks and it has a balcony overlooking the works so he could check on the workers. The middle managers' houses were made from rejected bricks but they were still luxurious compared to the workers' cottages around the back. These were usually made from wood and were shared."

Cyril Holbrow, 86-year-old lifelong resident of Clayburn Village, BC

Comforts Soap & Body Works, where the handmade shampoo bar – shaped like the bricks that used to be made across the street – is an ideal traveler's buy. If you're hungry, go into downtown Abbotsford from here and drop by the ⑪ **Little Farmhouse in the City**. The back dining room at this popular restaurant has a bulging menu of chunky soups, huge sandwiches and piled-high salads.

West on Hwy 1 you'll get your next history fix at the excellent ⑫ **Fort Langley National Historic Site**. This is where, in 1858, James Douglas read out the proclamation that created the new province, giving the site a strong claim to being the birthplace of British Columbia. But the fort isn't just a mothballed museum piece. Within its fortified timber perimeter, you'll find costumed interpreters and working smithies, plus stores and inhabited old homes that bring the pioneer era to life. Save time to take in the movie presentation about the fort's past and, when you see anyone in a costume, ask as many questions as you can about settler life. First Nations and fur-trading questions are particularly hot topics. The historic site is a great place for kids – they spend most of their time feverishly panning for gold in a little trough – and it's also worth strolling the pretty village outside the walls for an ice cream or three.

If this reenactment approach floats your historic boat, continue along Hwy 1 for another 32 km (20 miles) to ⑬ **Burnaby Village Museum**, which brings BC's bustling 1920s period to life. The collection of preserved and replica homes and businesses in this evocative 10-acre site includes farmsteads and a garage with carefully restored cars and motorcycles. There's also a meticulously restored electric tram that recalls the time when these old bone-shakers rattled around towns throughout the region. The village's highlight, though, is the magnificent century-old working fairground carousel: take a whirl, close your eyes and you'll experience the good old days as if you were actually there.

DETOUR ➤ Drop into **Playland** (www .pne.ca/playland) on the Burnaby side of Vancouver's eastern boundary, 10 minutes along E Hastings St from the intersection with Hwy 1, and home to Canada's most celebrated heritage roller coaster. The creaky wooden ride was constructed by Norwegian boat builders from Douglas fir planks in 1958. You'll slide around all over the place, gripping the rickety rail as you fly down the first hill, swearing that you can hear nuts and bolts popping out all around you.

Skirting the eastern edge of Vancouver, continue north along Hwy 1 and across the ⑭ **Second Narrows Bridge**. Though not as famous as the more attractive Lions Gate Bridge that arches out of Stanley Park, the Second Narrows has a tragic history. The first bridge to link Vancouver and the North Shore was built here in 1925, but in 1957 work began on a new span to replace the old one, which was redesignated as a railway crossing. The steel-built construction was a complicated project and during a critical phase, the part-finished span collapsed and dozens of workers plunged more than 100ft into the water below. Nineteen (including one rescue diver) were killed in what was later attributed to an engineering miscalculation. The bridge was officially renamed the Ironworkers Memorial Second Narrows Crossing in 1994.

Continue west on Hwy 1 from here – you can stop off for the night at North Vancouver's ⑮ **Grouse Inn**, with its 1980s decor and handy swimming pool – then take Hwy 99 north. Hwy 99 is also known as the Sea-to-Sky Hwy and you'll see why as you hit the craggy coastline after West Vancouver. Try not to take your eyes off the road too much as you enjoy the spectacular island-studded vistas of Howe Sound on your left. Before you get sucked in by nature, though, there are still a couple of colorful historic sites to check out.

Within an hour or so, you'll spot a mammoth yellow dump truck shadowing your view on the right-hand side. Turn in just behind and you'll come across a reminder of how the pioneers treated the natural abundance they discovered in the region. The wonderful ⑯ **BC Museum of Mining** at Britannia Beach was once a dangerous but highly lucrative copper mining operation that leached poison for decades into the nearby inlet. The clean-up operation was long and complex but the resulting museum, now a National Historic Site, is one of the best industrial heritage destinations in the province. You can wander the restored workshops and giant sheds housing unfathomable heavy machinery but make sure you also save time for an underground tour on one of the little trains that used to transport the workers and copper ore. It's pitch-black in there and after the nervous laughter subsides, it's quite creepy.

You can recover your senses by continuing along Hwy 99 to ⑰ **Squamish**, a former logging settlement that's developed into a satellite commuter town for nearby Whistler. There are many forest and mountain-bike trails in this area (ask for maps at the local visitors centre), but if all you need is food, there are plenty of options in and around the town.

On the other side of Squamish, follow the signs to the giant ⑱ **West Coast Railway Heritage Park**, the conclusion of your history-themed odyssey. The railroad was the spine that linked BC to the rest of Canada when it arrived in the province in 1885, creating new towns along its winding route. Almost 100 railcars from these early days to the later golden age of BC trains line the evocative, mostly outdoor site and it's fun to spend an afternoon here clambering onboard or perusing the restored station buildings and meticulous displays. Save time to hang out with the *grand dame,* though. The region's most famous steam train, the *Royal Hudson,* has been recently restored to her former glory and is a fitting reminder of BC's colorful past.

John Lee

TRIP INFORMATION

GETTING THERE
From Vancouver, drive 260 km (162 miles) eastbound on Hwy 1 to Lytton then take Hwy 12 63km (40 miles) north to Lillooet.

DO

BC Museum of Mining
Atmospheric industrial museum exploring a giant copper mining operation, including the tunnels. ☎ 604-896-2233; www.bcmuseum ofmining.org; Britannia Beach; adult/child/youth C$17/12/14; ☽ 9am–4:30pm May–mid-Oct, with seasonal variations; ♿

Burnaby Village Museum
Bringing 1920s BC to life with interpreters, replica homes and businesses, and shiny restored vehicles. ☎ 604-293-6501; www.burnabyvillagemuseum.ca; 6501 Deer Lake Ave, Burnaby; adult/child/youth C$12/6/9; ☽ 11am–4:30pm May-Aug, with seasonal variations; ♿

Clayburn Comforts Soap & Body Works
Friendly little handmade soapery, with all-natural soaps, balms and creams. ☎ 604-855-0420; www.clayburncomforts.com; 34866 Clayburn Rd, Abbotsford; ☽ noon–5pm Tue-Fri, to 4pm Sat, with seasonal variations

Fort Langley National Historic Site
Re-created pioneer community with costumed interpreters. ☎ 604-513-4777; www.pac.gc.ca.fortlangley; Mavis Ave, Fort Langley; adult/child C$7.80/3.90; ☽ 9am-8pm Jul & Aug, 10am-5pm Sep-Jun; ♿

Kumsheen Raft Adventures
With paddle frenzies or powered boat trips through the rapids, it also offers tepee and tent cabin accommodations. ☎ 250-455-2296; www.kumsheen.com; 1345 Hwy 1, Lytton; adult/youth from C$115/89; ♿

LINK YOUR TRIP
TRIP

Lillooet Museum
In a former church, this is a artifact-packed introduction to BC pioneer life. ☎ 250-256-4308; 790 Main St, Lillooet; admission free; ☽ 9am-7pm Jul & Aug, with seasonal variations

West Coast Railway Heritage Park
Pilgrimage site for BC railroad fans with dozens of trains and exhibits about the province's pioneering rail system. ☎ 604-898-9336; www.wcra.org; 39645 Government Rd, Squamish; adult/child C$10/8.50; ☽ 10am-5pm; ♿

EAT

Blue Moose Café
Convivial, artsy and with great coffee, soups and sandwiches, this is the definition of a perfect local café. ☎ 604-869-0729; www.bluemoosecafe.com; 322 Wallace St, Hope; mains C$7-12; ☽ 7:30am-10pm

Little Farmhouse in the City
Well-prepared comfort food and tea served in candle-warmed teapots. ☎ 604-854-2382; www.littlefarmhouse.com; 2552 Montrose Ave, Abbotsford; mains C$6-12; ☽ 8:30am-2:30pm Sun & Mon, to 8:30pm Tue-Sat

SLEEP

Grouse Inn
A bright, well-equipped classic motel with a pool if you want to cool off after your drive. ☎ 604-988-1701; www.grouseinn.com; 1633 Capilano Rd, North Vancouver; r C$99-289; ❀

Kw'o:kw'e:hala Eco Retreat
Hidden in the trees outside Hope, this green lodge resort offers organic meals, saunas and yoga activities for tranquility seekers. ☎ 604-869-3799; www.eco-retreat.com; 674000 Tunnels Rd, Hope; r C$169-269

USEFUL WEBSITES
www.hellobc.com

www.vcmbc.com

www.lonelyplanet.com/trip-planner

Queen Charlotte Islands

WHY GO Howling winter tempests are part of everyday life on the rugged Queen Charlotte Islands, also known as Haida Gwaii. But for summertime visitors, a trek to this remote northwestern archipelago offers rich First Nations culture, mouthwatering fresh seafood and a smattering of quirky communities populated by colorful locals.

TIME
2 days

DISTANCE
137km
(85 miles)

BEST TIME TO GO
Jul – Aug

START
Skidegate

END
North Beach

ALSO GOOD FOR

HISTORY &
CULTURE

Arrange a hire car far in advance of your BC Ferries arrival in Skidegate on Graham Island, then spend some time perusing the clapboard houses or fueling up at the home-style pub or coffee shop near the dock. Save an hour or two for the area's highlight: the ❶ **Haida Heritage Centre** is a striking crescent of totem-fronted cedar longhouses that's arguably BC's best First Nations attraction. Check out ancient carvings and artifacts recalling 10,000 years of Haida history and look for the exquisite artworks of the legendary Bill Reid – his glorious painted canoe bobs in the adjoining bay.

Hitting Hwy 16, head north to explore the distinctive settlements that make the latter-day Charlottes tick. You'll wind along stretches of rustic waterfront and through shadowy woodland areas while a permanent detachment of beady-eyed eagles follows your progress. Make note of the location of ❷ **Keenawi's Kitchen** for a unique dinner later in your stay. Roberta Olson will welcome you to her waterfront home with a traditional Haida song before serving a memorable feast of crunchy dried seaweed, chunky shrimp chowder and dishes of butter-soft halibut and spring salmon.

Try not to drool too much as you continue north and pull over, just before Tlell, at the charming ❸ **Bottle & Jug Works**. Exemplifying the region's pioneer spirit, friendly potters John and Jennifer Davies

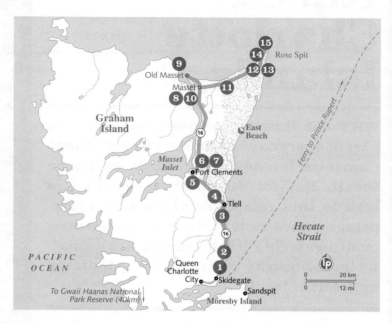

will happily chat to you about life on the island as you peruse their selection of fat-bellied mugs and handsome rustic teapots. If you're inspired to have a cuppa, head on to Tlell's ❹ **Rising Tide Bakery**, the locals' favorite coffee-shop hangout.

A little further along Hwy 16, you'll come to one of the most tragic sites in recent island history. An easy 3.2km (2 mile) trail through the forest will bring you to the banks of the Yakoun River and a felled tree hanging haplessly over the water. Cut down in 1997 by a misguided logging protester, the ❺ **Golden Spruce** – a 150ft, 300-year-old genetic aberration with luminous yellow needles – was revered by local Haida as the transformed spirit of a little boy. The tree's death was highly traumatic for residents and several cuttings, some in secret locations, are being grown to hopefully replace it.

RETURN OF THE HAIDA

The Haida are one of Canada's First Nations peoples, the locals who lived here for thousands of years before 18th-century Europeans turned up. Centered on the Charlottes, these fearsome warriors had no immunity to diseases like smallpox and tuberculosis brought from the outside and their population was quickly decimated. By the early 20th century, they had been almost wiped out. Since the 1970s the Haida population – and its cultural pride – have grown anew.

Also consider nipping into nearby ❻ **Port Clements Museum**, where the main exhibits focus on logging, hence the forest of rusty clear-cutting machinery outside. Inside, you'll find a stuffed albino raven, another genetic aberration that was also revered until it electrocuted itself on local power lines. Not far from here, **7** Golden Spruce Motel is a little spartan, but it's still more than comfortable and is a popular sleeping option.

If you're not ready to call it a night, continue north to the settlements of **8** Masset and **9** Old Masset. The former primarily occupies the stark institutional buildings of a disused military base and the adjoining latter is a First Nations' village where wood-fired homes are fronted by broad, brooding totem poles. There are several stores here where visitors can buy Haida carvings in argillite, a glasslike slate only found in this part of the world. End your day at Masset's **10** Copper Beach House, a book-lined B&B run by

"...the Golden Spruce was revered by local Haida as the transformed spirit of a little boy."

inveterate foodie David Phillips: breakfast is often a stomach-stuffing buffet of berry-packed muffins and home-cooked wild salmon that threatens to topple over the table. Phillips is a force of nature, and knows more than anyone about the challenges and attractions of island life.

Hop back in your car the next day and head for the region's wild northern tip. Via a well-marked logging road that juts east off the highway, you'll come to **11** Naikoon Provincial Park. The rustic, wind-whipped **12** Agate Beach Campground is here if you want to commune with nature for the night or you can drop by **13** Moon Over Naikoon, a coffee shop that seems entirely constructed from driftwood and bleached whale bones, for its next batch of oven-warm cinnamon buns.

Continue on the tree-lined dirt road until you reach **14** Tow Hill, a steep, dense and mercifully short forest walk. Look out for trees where strips of bark have been carefully removed for Haida basket making over the decades, then catch your breath at the summit while you gaze over the impenetrable coastal forest stretching into the mist. Finally, head for the

> **DETOUR** Famed for its mystical élan, **Gwaii Haanas National Park Reserve** (www.pc.gc.ca/gwaiihaanas) covers much of the Queen Charlottes' southern section, a rugged region only accessible by boat or plane. The reserve is the ancient site of Haida homes, burial caves and the derelict village of Ninstints with its gracefully eroding seafront totem poles (now a Unesco World Heritage Site). Visitors often remark on the area's magical and spiritual qualities, so consider an extended visit if you have the time.

park's extreme coastal tip and you'll come to **15** North Beach. Leave the car here and tramp along the wave-smacked sandy expanse, where locals walk along in the surf plucking Dungeness crabs for dinner. With the wind watering your eyes, you'll feel closer to nature than you've ever felt before.

John Lee

TRIP INFORMATION

GETTING THERE
From mainland Prince Rupert in northern BC, take the BC Ferries service to Skidegate on Graham Island. The crossing usually takes seven to eight hours.

DO
Bottle & Jug Works
Homestead stoneware pottery studio with chunky, Hobbit-friendly mugs, cups and teapots, plus a pair of warm and chatty hosts. ☎ 250-559-4756; 858 Hwy 16, near Tlell

Haida Heritage Centre
Showcasing Haida culture, with hundreds of ancient and contemporary artifacts. ☎ 250-559-7885; www.haidaheritagecentre.com; Second Beach Rd, Skidegate; adult/child/ youth C$12/5/9; ☉ 10am-5pm Tue-Sat mid-Sep–Apr, 10am-6pm Mon-Sat May–mid-Sep, plus 10am-6pm Sun mid-Jun–mid-Sep; ♿

Naikoon Provincial Park
A dense, treed park with more than 60 miles of expansive white-sand beach. This northern feature is the area's most popular destination for summertime nature fans. ☎ 250-557-4390; www.env.gov.bc.ca/bcparks

Port Clements Museum
Menagerie of logging machinery outside and a clutch of local history artifacts inside. ☎ 250-557-4285; www.portclementsmuseum.org; 45 Bayview Rd, Port Clements; admission C$2; ☉ 11am-4pm Mon-Fri Jun-Sep, 2-4pm Sat & Sun Oct-May

EAT
Keenawi's Kitchen
Delectable Haida seafood dishes (and songs) prepared and served by the family in Roberta Olson's waterfront home. ☎ 250-559-8347; 237 Hwy 16, Skidegate; dinner feast C$60; ☉ by appointment

Moon Over Naikoon
Rustic art- and artifact-lined coffee stop in the forest, featuring organic oven-fresh baked treats and ever-changing pizza and pasta specials. ☎ 250-626-5064; Tow Hill Rd, Naikoon Provincial Park; mains C$4-8; ☉ 8am-5pm Jun-Aug

Rising Tide Bakery
Bright and sunny bakery where the locals chat over home-baked goodies; look for the daily lunch specials. ☎ 250-557-4677; 37580 Hwy 16, Tlell; mains C$4-9; ☉ 8am-5pm

SLEEP
Agate Beach Campground
Basic back-to-nature 43-site waterfront campground with fees and services (cold faucets and pit toilets) from mid-May to mid-September only. ☎ 250-557-4390; www.env.gov.bc.ca/bcparks; Naikoon Provincial Park; campsites C$16

Copper Beach House
The Charlottes' best B&B with a chatty ambience, three cozy rooms and plenty of foodie treats. ☎ 250-626-5441; www.copperbeachhouse.com; 1590 Delkatla Rd, Masset; r C$75-150

Golden Spruce Motel
Clean and comfortable B&B with a warm welcome, good breakfast café and some kitchenettes. ☎ 250-557-4325; www.qcislands.net/golden; 2 Grouse St, Port Clements; r C$55-65; 🐾

USEFUL WEBSITES
www.haidagwaiitourism.ca
www.qcinfo.ca

LINK YOUR TRIP
www.lonelyplanet.com/trip-planner

Up the Inside Passage

WHY GO Alaska is thousands of rugged miles from the Lower 48 – so remote and wild that it's almost a mythical land. But there's a link between dream and reality: every Friday the Alaska Ferry sets sail from Bellingham, Washington, tracing the Canadian coastline before slipping into the foggy emerald maze of Alaska's Inside Passage.

Of the 27 All-American Roads, the Alaska Marine Highway is the only one that floats. Churning 3500 nautical miles from Bellingham and out to the far tendril of the Aleutian Chain, some of the highway's most dramatic scenes are pressed into the steep fjords and waterlogged fishing towns of the Inside Passage. A three-day trip on the ❶ **Alaska State Ferry** ends in Skagway, traveling through the US's largest national forest, the Tongass, and stopping in several ports along the way. If you have more time, your options for detours are unlimited. A through-ticket will give you a small sample of time in each port, while point-to-point tickets let you decide how long to stay in each town.

In ❷ **Bellingham**, you can walk, bike or drive onto the vessel, which departs from brick-paved, historic ❸ **Fairhaven District**. Make sure to give yourself at least an afternoon to explore this city neighborhood, stamped onto several blocks and crammed charmingly with flower shops, cafés and bookstores. Arrive the night before and sack out at the vintage-style ❹ **Fairhaven Village Inn**. An excellent district-center option, the Inn is across the way from the Village Green Park's farmer's market and outdoor evening movies. Be sure to fill up with housemade desserts at the nearby ❺ **Colophon Café & Deli**, and choose your reading material for your trip at the stacked Village Books, which mingles with the café.

TIME
4 days

DISTANCE
1800km
(1119 miles)

BEST TIME TO GO
Jun – Sep

START
Bellingham, WA

END
Skagway, AK

ALSO GOOD FOR

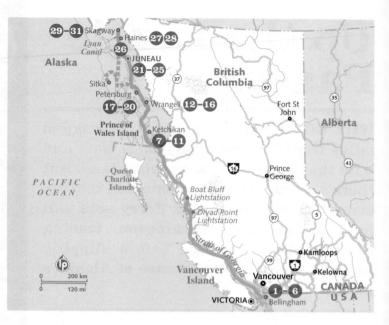

As the ferry slides out in to ⑥ **Bellingham Bay**, you'll be treated to views of Mt Baker, sienna-colored brick buildings, and Victorian homes peering from the town's hillside. Not long after leaving port, the ferry squeezes between Canada's Vancouver Island and the mainland through the Strait of Georgia. This is the time to mix with the locals and travelers who share the ferry with you. This isn't a cruise ship, but that makes the experience all the more authentic. The solarium will be filled with the sleeping bags of adventurers hunkered down under heat lamps, while brightly colored tents flap in the wind on deck. The snack-bar fare is what you'd expect of public transportation, but warming up with a cup of coffee in a booth is a comfortable way to watch the coast pass by.

Thirty-six hours after departing Bellingham, the ferry makes its first stop in ⑦ **Ketchikan**. Here you'll skim along the town's thin band of colorful buildings – with equally colorful histories – before docking north of the town center. The ferry stays in port long enough for you to explore the historic, albeit touristy, ⑧ **Creek Street**. Though this boardwalk is now safe for families, in Ketchikan's early boom-town years the street was a clatter of brothels and bars. Pop into ⑨ **Dolly's House Museum**, where you can get an insider's view of what was a working parlor. Namesake Dolly Arthur operated the brothel until prostitution was outlawed in the 1950s, and lived here until her death in the '70s.

A quality introduction to the Southeast region (simply called 'Southeast' by locals) is at the ⑩ **Southeast Alaska Discovery Center**. Exhibits on Southeast's ecosystems and Native Alaskan traditions are showcased upstairs, while a re-created rain forest looms downstairs. It's a good place to help you identify what you're seeing from the windows of the ferry.

For some spiced-up local flavor head to ⑪ **That One Place**, on the ground floor of the New York Hotel. This seafood-stuffed tapas restaurant is an inexpensive place to fill up on local fare before heading back to the boat.

After departing Ketchikan, the ferry hums through Clarence Strait before arriving at tiny, false-fronted ⑫ **Wrangell** several hours later. You'll be greeted by the town's children, who set up folding tables (often in the rain) to sell their wares – deep-purple garnets that they've mined from the nearby Stikine River.

Wrangell practically spills over with historic, cultural and natural sights, including compelling ⑬ **Petroglyph Beach**. Less than a mile from the ferry terminal, the beach is dotted with boulders depicting faces and figures that were carved thousands of years ago. Lifelike whales and owls peer up at you, while some spirals eerily resemble crop circles. If you're just popping off the ferry during its quick stop, you can lace up your running shoes and jog there and back for a speedy examination of the stones. More recent Tlingit culture is showcased on the other side of town at ⑭ **Chief Shakes Island & Tribal House**, an oddly peaceful site in the middle of the humming boat harbor. Here, six totem poles tower among pines, and

BC'S STAFFED LIGHTHOUSES

The misty stretch of Canada between Washington and Alaska is home to 40 lighthouses, more than half of which require keepers. The ferry glides by picturesque **Dryad Point Lightstation**, which features an old-school style lighthouse perched on the northeastern tip of Campbell Island. Further north, **Boat Bluff Lightstation** is a simple aluminum skeleton, but the red-roofed outbuildings cling pleasantly to a small hillside and the keepers often emerge to wave to ferry passengers.

eagles often congregate in the trees' branches. The island is always open to walking, though the tribal house usually only opens for cruise-ship groups.

For an overnight stay – and Wrangell is certainly worth it – check out the ⑮ **Alaskan Sourdough Lodge**. This family-owned lodge features a sauna, steam room and 16 spotless rooms, and it's a nice place to thaw out if you've been exploring in the rain.

Just after leaving Wrangell, the ferry enters the 22-mile long ⑯ **Wrangell Narrows**. Too skinny and shallow for most large vessels, the Narrows (dubbed "Pinball Alley") requires nearly 50 course corrections as boats thread between more than 70 green and red channel markers. The ferry M/V *Columbia* is the largest boat to navigate the Narrows, as water depth can get as shallow as 24ft at low tide.

At the end of the Narrows sits **⑰ Petersburg**, a fishing village with blond roots. Petersburg's thick Norwegian history is evident not just in the phonebook full of Scandinavian names, but also in the flowery rosemaling, a decorative Norwegian art form found on buildings throughout town. But to really get into the heart of Petersburg, walk the docks of its **⑱ North Boat Harbor**. Here fisherfolk unload the day's catch from small purse seiners, distinguishable by the large nets piled in the stern. To sample locally caught seafood, plant yourself at a window seat at **⑲ Rooney's Northern Lights Restaurant**, where you can watch fisherman in the harbor unload your potential dinner.

MOUNTAIN BIKING POW ISLAND

The third-largest island in the US, mountainous Prince of Wales Island isn't a well-known mountain-biking destination, but that's due more to its remote location than its lack of spectacular terrain. Veined with over 1300 miles of mostly unpaved road and spotted with tiny villages, POW also has 21 public-use cabins scattered along its inlets and alpine lakes. There are dispiriting clear-cuts, but they're the reason for all those roads.

The Inter-Island Ferry (www.interislandferry .com) has service from Ketchikan, Wrangell and Petersburg.

Complement a layover in Petersburg with a kayak tour to **⑳ LeConte Glacier**, at the head of serpentine LeConte Bay. Constantly calving, the glacier is somewhat infamous for icebergs that release under water and then shoot to the surface like icy torpedoes. If you're lucky you'll see one – from afar.

After brushing through quiet fishing towns, arriving to hustle of **㉑ Juneau** can be somewhat surprising. This is the only US capital with no road access, yet it still bustles with the importance of a government center. It's also postcard perfect, with massive green cliffs rising importantly above the city center. Be sure to stroll past the **㉒ Governor's Mansion**, its assertive columns and articulately landscaped shrubs a sharp contrast to the usual rain forest–rotted cabins of Southeast. If the political climate gets to be too much, head back toward the ferry terminal to the laid-back **㉓ Alaskan Brewing Company** for a tour and samples of beers that rival the Pacific Northwest's. The brewery is in the same neighborhood as the massive **㉔ Mendenhall Glacier**, which tumbles down from the Juneau Icefield and is one of the few glaciers in Southeast you can drive up to. The sleek visitors center offers a movie with the glacier as its star, as well as hiking trails and a salmon-viewing platform.

If your trip calls for a night in town, cozy up at the **㉕ Silverbow Inn**, where the smell of baking bread from the bakery downstairs wakes you in the morning. One of the amenities of this historic hotel is a bottomless cookie jar – at least it's easy to work them off on one of Juneau's many downtown hiking trails.

From Juneau, the ferry travels up the **㉖ Lynn Canal**, which is North America's longest (90 miles) and deepest (2000ft) fjord. The Canal is equally endowed with glaciers and waterfalls, and it's hard not to stare at the scenery. Seventy-five miles from Juneau lies **㉗ Haines**, where most passengers with cars disembark as the town is the main link to the Alaska Hwy. Free from cruise-ship crowds, Haines has a laid-back vibe with almost extravagant scenery. Don't miss the **㉘ Hammer Museum**, which displays 1500 hammers and chronicles the history of man through them.

The ferry continues to **㉙ Skagway**, a gold-rush era town that revels in all its gaudy glory. The ferry deposits you about 100yd from the action of **㉚ Broadway Street**, where you'll find women dressed in feathered hats and bright satiny dresses vying for the attention of the many tourists wandering off cruise ships. Since Skagway is likely your last ferry stop, you'll have time to take the **㉛ White Pass & Yukon Railroad**, a narrated sightseeing tour aboard vintage parlor cars. This dramatic ride rumbles along a narrow-gauge line, through

DETOUR

Sitka is off the main route, but if you have some extra days or want to end your journey there, this town of 8800 people is well worth the extra time. The only city in Southeast that fronts the Pacific Ocean, Sitka looks out to the cone of Mt Edgecumbe as well as a clutter of small, treed islands. A hikers' and kayakers' delight, Sitka is a full day's journey from Juneau or Petersburg.

Glacier Gorge and over White Pass (a 2885ft climb), and also connects to the Yukon Territory. It's a refreshing change from the ferry, and, if you fly home, you'll be able to say you traveled by boat, rail and air.

Whether you end your trip in Skagway or another port, you'll need to backtrack on the ferry, or fly south, to get home. There are few commercial flights from smaller towns, and to catch a major airline flight to Seattle you'll first need to fly to Juneau, Ketchikan or Sitka on a smaller carrier.

Catherine Bodry

TRIP INFORMATION

GETTING THERE
From Vancouver, drive south on Hwy 99 and I-5 53 miles to Exit 250 in Bellingham. From Seattle, take I-5 north 89 miles to Exit 250. Follow the signs to the Alaska Ferry Terminal.

DO
Alaska State Ferry
Ride from point to point, or one-way from Bellingham to Skagway ($363). Accommodation includes camping on deck (no extra charge) or basic cabins (r from $337). ☎ 907-465-3941, 800-642-0066; www.alaska.gov/ferry; terminal at end of Harris Ave, Bellingham, WA; ⊛

Alaskan Brewing Company
The largest brewery in Alaska offers complimentary tours (and beer samples!). ☎ 907-780-5866; www.alaskanbeer.com; 5429 Shuane Dr, Juneau, AK; ⊗ 11am-6pm

Dolly's House Museum
This was the home of Ketchikan's most famous madam. ☎ 907-225-6329; 24 Creek St, Ketchikan, AK; adult/child $5/free; ⊗ 8am-5pm

Hammer Museum
See 1500 hammers on display, from Roman relics to Tlingit artifacts. ☎ 907-766-2374; 108 Main St, Haines, AK; adult/child $3/free; ⊗ 10am-5pm Mon-Fri

Southeast Alaska Discovery Center
A great introduction to the great outdoors; in addition to cultural and natural exhibits, has spotting scopes for wildlife viewing. ☎ 907-228-6220; 50 Main St, Ketchikan, AK; adult/child $5/free; ⊗ 8am-5pm Mon-Fri, to 4pm Sat & Sun; ⊛

White Pass & Yukon Railroad
Several tours available; note that some cross into Canada so you'll need your passport. ☎ 907-983-2217, 800-343-7373; www .whitepassrailroad.com; depot on 2nd Ave, Skagway, AK; Yukon Adventure adult/child $165/82.50, White Pass Summit Excursion adult/child $103/51.50

EAT
Colophon Café & Deli
Renowned for its African peanut soup and chocolate brandy cream pies, the café has an outside wine garden and is popular with local literati. ☎ 360-647-0092; 1208 11th St, Bellingham, WA; mains $7-10; ⊗ 9am-10pm Mon-Sat

Rooney's Northern Lights Restaurant
Overlooks the bustling harbor; all the crab, halibut and shrimp on its seafood platter is locally caught. ☎ 907-772-2900; 203 Sing Lee Alley, Petersburg, AK; breakfast $5-10, dinner $16-30; ⊗ 6am-9pm

SLEEP
Fairhaven Village Inn
A vintage hotel in the Fairhaven District that is a class above standard motel fare. ☎ 360-733-1311, 877-733-1100; www.fairhavenvillageinn.com; 1200 10th St, Bellingham, WA; r $180-220

Alaskan Sourdough Lodge
Offers free shuttle from the ferry, and home-cooked meals are served family-style. ☎ 907-874-3613, 800-874-3613; www.akgateway.com; 1104 Peninsula St, Wrangell, AK; s/d $105-115

Silverbow Inn
This artsy, six-room hotel has a rooftop hot tub and serves a full breakfast. ☎ 907-586-4146, 800-586-4146; www.silverbowinn .com; 120 2nd St, Juneau, AK; r $170-210

USEFUL WEBSITES
www.fs.fed.us/r10/tongass/
www.wingsofalaska.com

www.lonelyplanet.com/trip-planner

LINK YOUR TRIP

Day Trips Around Vancouver

Hit the road and explore BC's diverse Lower Mainland region with these short excursions to mountainside North Vancouver, historic Fort Langley, nature-hugging Buntzen Lake and beyond. You'll be surprised at just how different the rest of the province is to Vancouver's glass-towered cityscape.

RICHMOND

If you flew into Vancouver International Airport, you've already been to Richmond – although the sprawling seafront airstrip is not representative of North America's most vibrant contemporary Asian community. While Vancouver's downtown Chinatown is home to all the oldsters living among pagoda-roofed heritage buildings, the region's young Koreans, Vietnamese and Hong Kong Chinese prefer to live here. You'll find buzzing Asian shopping malls, cheap and cheerful bubble tea and sushi emporiums, as well as authentic higher-end restaurants offering every dish imaginable. But the best place to lift the lid on modern expat Asia is at the summertime weekend Night Market. It's a cacophony of shiny trinket stalls and live music performances supplemented by a steaming, ever-crowded food section where adventurous culinary explorers spend the night. Tuck into fresh-fried squid, fish balls and Shanghai noodles and save room for the delectable pork buns. **Head south from Vancouver on Hwy 99, via the Granville St Bridge. Follow Granville St and cross the Arthur Laing Bridge, taking the first exit onto Russ Baker Way. Take the next right and cross the Moray Channel Bridge into central Richmond.**

STEVESTON

On the southern edge of Richmond but really a destination in itself, historic Steveston is a preserved reminder of BC's pioneer fish industry. Wander the pretty waterfront boardwalks here, making sure you stop for fish-and-chips at one of the many aromatic restaurants, then duck into the Gulf of Georgia Cannery National Historic Site. One of BC's best museums, this preserved old clapboard processing plant is where fish (primarily salmon) were processed and canned for export around the world. Only closed in 1979 – there were still fish guts in some of the machinery when the later restoration began – the atmospheric site is brought to life by recorded stories and life-size images of the hardy workers who toiled here. **Head south from Vancouver on Hwy 99, via the Granville St Bridge. Follow Granville St and cross the Arthur Laing Bridge, taking the first exit onto Russ Baker Way. Continue over the Dinsmore Bridge and take Number Two Rd into Steveston.**

BUNTZEN LAKE

You won't find many tourists at this off-the-beaten-path natural gem, but that doesn't mean you'll be on your own. Locals have been flocking to this breathtaking mountain-lake-and-forest retreat on the fringes of Coquitlam for decades. They come for the sigh-triggering scenery, gently sloping sandy beach and the chance to picnic in the wilderness without traveling too far from home. There are lots of marked trails through the woods here if you want to get active and you can rent kayaks at the park entrance if you fancy a paddle – be careful, though, the lake is bigger than it looks. Originally named Lake Beautiful – can you guess why? – this is an ideal place to bring the kids: you can keep an eye on them splashing in the water while you sit back on the grass in the shade of the trees. **Drive east from Vancouver on Hwy 7A through Burnaby and into Coquitlam, where it becomes Barnet Hwy. Take the loco Rd exit and follow loco to the left. Turn right on 1st Ave, continue to Sunnyside Rd, then turn right again to the Buntzen Lake entrance.**

See also **TRIP 49**

BOWEN ISLAND

A favorite day-trip (or weekend) destination for generations of sanctuary-seeking Vancouverites, it's a 20-minute ferry ride from West Vancouver's Horseshoe Bay to Howe Sound's lovely Bowen Island. Once here, you can rub shoulders with the Bowenians in Snug Cove, the community's waterfront heart and home to clapboard pubs, restaurants and galleries, or hit the island's diverse natural treasures. The 20-sq-mile landmass is lined with fir, hemlock and arbutus-filled woodlands and its comb-friendly beaches are slippery with rock pools and furtive birdlife. If the call of the water proves too strong, you can also rent a kayak and explore the craggy coastline from a whale's-eye perspective. **From Vancouver, drive north across the Lions Gate Bridge on Hwy 99, then head west on the same road to Horseshoe Bay. Ferries leave from here every hour.**

See also **TRIP 48**

UNIVERSITY OF BRITISH COLUMBIA

With around 50,000 full-time students, the province's biggest university – located on the tree-lined tip of Point Grey – is really a city in itself. And it also has enough attractions to warrant an off-the-beaten-path Lower Mainland day out. The highlights here include the magnificent Museum of Anthropology, occupying a stunning waterfront setting, and lined with Canada's best array of northwest coast First Nations artifacts; the UBC Botanical Garden, divided into eight sections ranging from a medieval apothecary garden to a giant rhododendron garden; and Pacific Spirit Regional Park, a mystical, trail-lined woodland striped with giant fir and cedar trees. Music recitals are open to the public at the Chan Centre here and the beaches include Spanish Banks (complete with its idyllic sunset views) and Wreck Beach, the city's only nudist enclave, with its own distinctive hippy-flavored subculture. **Head south from Vancouver, crossing Granville St Bridge, then turn west onto 4th Ave. This runs straight to the campus, where it merges into Chancellor Blvd.**

See also **TRIP 40**

CLOVERDALE FLEA MARKET

Between the suburban Lower Mainland and the farm-lined Fraser Valley, Cloverdale comes from cowboy stock, which explains why the Cloverdale Exhibition Grounds is home to BC's biggest annual rodeo. The rest of the year, the venue hosts a more modest, but equally popular, tradition. Cloverdale Flea Market is a Sunday habit for many regional residents, transforming the parking lots and exhibition sheds into a clamorous smorgasbord of professional hawkers, amateur regular sellers and first-timers who just want to clear their spare room. The biggest garage sale you'll ever come across, it's like entering a physical version of eBay. Among the hundreds of vendors, you can expect to find rare and collectible antiques, dog-eared novels and comic books, 1970s kitsch for that cool apartment look and ultracheap souvenir T-shirts: you can cover everyone back home with a "5 for C$10" deal. **From Vancouver, head east on Hwy 1 over the Port Mann Bridge, exit right onto 176th St (Hwy 15) and continue south until you see the signs for the market.**

See also **TRIP 46**

NORTH VANCOUVER

With almost as much history as Vancouver, "North Van" is the city you can see from downtown just across the Burrard Inlet. Backing increasingly up the nearby mountain slopes ("bear issues" are not uncommon here), this short hop from downtown delivers enough of its own attractions to justify at least an afternoon trip. The main reasons to come here are the Capilano Suspension Bridge, a steel-cable walkway swaying over a dramatic river and forest landscape; and Grouse Mountain, the closest snow hill to Vancouver and home to restaurants, ski and snowboard activities and a full roster of summertime hiking trails and outdoor activities. Also, if you fancy a budget version of Capilano, the Lynn Canyon Suspension Bridge is free and less crowded, while additional hiking and skiing areas are located in Mount Seymour Provincial Park. **From downtown Vancouver, take Hwy 99 north via the Lions Gate Bridge and follow the signs for North Vancouver. Capilano Suspension Bridge and Grouse Mountain are accessed via Capilano Rd.**

See also **TRIP 50**

DEEP COVE

When you're battling the downtown crowds on Robson St, it's easy to forget that Vancouver is blessed with an amazing natural setting. If it's time to chill out and you have a spare afternoon, head across the Burrard Inlet and make for the little community of Deep Cove. Standing on the waterfront here, with the waves gently lapping your feet and the tree-furred mountains standing sentinel around you, you'll find yourself sighing involuntarily as the cares of the world evaporate. With time cranking down a notch, you'll feel like you're having a mental cleanse. Spend time wandering the streets here (expect the locals to smile and say hello) and grab lunch in one of the cafés before weaving back to the water and Deep Cove Canoe and Kayak Centre. This friendly outfit will teach you how to kayak if you're a newbie or they'll lead you into the glassy calm waters of Indian Arm on a chatty guided tour. **From downtown Vancouver, head east on Hastings St, then head north across the Second Narrows Bridge on Hwy 1. Turn east again on the Dollarton Hwy, which runs to Deep Cove.**

WEST VANCOUVER

The other major settlement just across Burrard Inlet, "West Van" is one of the richest communities in Canada – which explains all those multi-million-dollar houses clinging to the cliffs overlooking Howe Sound. For visitors, the highlights here include the nature and waterfront trails in Lighthouse Park and the bustling community of Horseshoe Bay, where you can hop on a Zodiac with Sewell's Sea Safari, the closet whale-watching operator to downtown Vancouver. West Van is also home to the third ski mountain area within easy driving distance of the city. Cypress Provincial Park is a popular hiking destination for summer visitors, while in winter its family-friendly Cypress Mountain area – snowboarding and freestyle skiing venue for the 2010 Olympic and Paralympic Winter Games – attracts locals intent on skiing, tubing, snowboarding and snowshoeing. **From downtown Vancouver, take Hwy 99 via the Lions Gate Bridge into the heart of West Vancouver.**

See also **TRIPS 48 & 50**

Behind the Scenes

THIS BOOK

This guidebook was commissioned in Lonely Planet's Oakland office, and produced by the following:
Product Development Manager & Commissioning Editor Heather Dickson
Coordinating Editor David Carroll
Coordinating Cartographer Corey Hutchison
Coordinating Layout Designer Jacqueline McLeod
Managing Editor Brigitte Ellemor
Managing Cartographer Alison Lyall
Managing Layout Designer Laura Jane
Assisting Editors Anne Mulvaney, Charlotte Orr, Donna Wheeler
Assisting Cartographers Alissa Baker, Karen Grant, Carol Jackson, Carlos Solarte
Series Designer James Hardy
Cover Designers Gerilyn Attebery, Jennifer Mullins
Project Manager Glenn van der Knijff

Thanks to Imogen Bannister, Yvonne Bischofberger, David Burnett, Dora Chai, Jay Cooke, Catherine Craddock, Hunor Csutoros, Melanie Dankel, Owen Eszeki, Jennye Garibaldi, Suki Gear, Mark Germanchis, Chris Girdler, Michelle Glynn, Brice Gosnell, Liz Heynes, Geoff Howard, Lauren Hunt, Naomi Jennings, David Kemp, John Mazzocchi, Darren O'Connell, Paul Piaia, Julie Sheridan, Cara Smith, Geoff Stringer & Tamsin Wilson

THANKS
Danny Palmerlee Huge thanks to Steve Jones, Cole Danehower, Bill Hanshumaker, and Bob Neroni for meeting with me and sharing their knowledge. Not only were their suggestions superb, they were a joy to talk with. Thanks heaps to my editor Heather Dickson for sending me to Oregon's most beautiful corners. And Cheers! to Lonely Planet coauthors.

Catherine Bodry Many thanks to Heather Dickson for commissioning me for this project, sending me on the ferry, and answering heaps of questions. Thanks to Jim Dufresne, whose work in *Alaska 8* was an inspiration and resource for this trip. And to my fam: thanks for hosting, driving, encouraging and supporting.

Mariella Krause Hats off to Tim Bauer for driving me all over the Pacific Northwest. Thanks to Kathryn Brethold and Pete and Kay Bauer for helping me sample the Seattle cuisine (including that enormous fried fish). Big smooches to my editor Heather Dickson and coordinating author Danny Palmerlee. And thanks to Tim and Jeff Fowler for the moral support, patience, and proofreading.

John Lee Thanks to all the folks I ran into on the road in BC as well as all the mostly useful tips from friends, family et al on the best places to sample. Kudos also to the experts at Tourism BC. Finally, thanks to the Lonely Planet team for this, my 13th book project in five years.

Bradley Mayhew A veritable tsunami of enthusiasm greeted me once word got out that I was writing a piece on Lewis and Clark. Thanks to Aaron Webster at the Cape Disappointment Interpretive Center, as well as Steve Wang, Barb Kubik and Jon Schmidt. Thanks also to Chris Drysdale in Nelson and Emily White and Ben Schifrin at Wilderness Press. Back at Lonely Planet, Heather Dickson went above and beyond answering all my myriad questions and Danny was a very cool coordinating author. Cheers to Sacha, Paul, Emma and Holly for looking after me in Vancouver and Kelli for joining me out in Washington.

ACKNOWLEDGMENTS

Many thanks to the following for the use of their content.

Internal photographs: p5 Digital Vision/Alamy; p12 Greg Vaughn/Alamy; p13 Ron Niebrugge/Alamy; p15 Craig Lovell/Eagle Visions Photography/Alamy; p24 (top) Danita Delimont/Alamy; p22 (bottom) David L Moore – Oregon/Alamy; p16 (bottom), p19 (bottom), p21 (top) Danny Palmerlee; p20 Adrian Burden/Flickr; p16 (top) Jay Schlegel/Getty; p15 (middle) Liz Devine/McMenamins.

All other photographs by Lonely Planet Images: p6 (top) Judy Bellah; p6 (bottom) Glenn van der Knijff; p7, p19 (top) Richard Cummins; p8 (top) Ruth & Max Eastham & Paoli; p8 (bottom) Lee Foster; p9 Ann Cecil; p10 Mark Newman; p11 (top) James Marshall; p11(bottom), p14, p17, p21 (top), p23 John Elk III; p18 Lawrence Worcester; p22 (top) Ross Barnett; p24 (bottom) Emily Riddell.

All images are the copyright of the photographers unless otherwise indicated. Many of the images in this guide are available for licensing from Lonely Planet Images: www.lonelyplanetimages.com.

SEND US YOUR FEEDBACK

Got feedback? We'd love to hear your corrections, suggestions, compliments or complaints, so feel free to use our feedback form: **lonelyplanet.com/contact**.

Note: We may edit, reproduce and incorporate your feedback comments in Lonely Planet products such as guidebooks, websites and digital products. If you send it in, then that counts as permission for us to use it. If you don't want your name acknowledged, please let us know.

To read our privacy policy, visit **lonelyplanet.com/privacy**.

Index

000 map pages
000 photograph pages

000 map pages
000 photograph pages

O

P

000 map pages
000 photograph pages

000 map pages
000 photograph pages